Financial Planning

For The Older Client

3rd Edition

by

Dana Shilling, J.D.

NATIONAL
UNDERWRITER®

The National Underwriter Co. / 505 Gest Street / Cincinnati, OH 45203-1716

This publication is designed to provide accurate and authoritative information in regard to the subject matter covered. It is sold with the understanding that the publisher is not engaged in rendering legal, accounting or other professional service. If legal advice or other expert assistance is required, the services of a competent professional should be sought. — **From a Declaration of Principles jointly adopted by a Committee of the American Bar Association and a Committee of Publishers and Associations.**

ISBN: 0-87218-193-6

Copyright © 1992, 1994, 1997
The National Underwriter Company
505 Gest Street, Cincinnati, Ohio 45203

3rd Edition

Printed in U. S. A.

ABOUT THE AUTHOR

Dana Shilling, a member of the Harvard Law School class of 1975, has spent more than a decade researching and writing about issues of personal finance and law. Recently, she has concentrated on the study of elder law, and is co-author of a major legal treatise on this subject (and is co-author of almost two dozen other books on legal and financial planning topics). She has also produced a two-videocassette series on basic elder law concepts for professionals.

PREFACE TO THE THIRD EDITION

ELDERPLANNING AS A SEPARATE SUBJECT

As financial planners you, the reader, are already accustomed to making portfolio recommendations, giving tax advice, and generally assuring clients that they will be able to provide for their needs, comply with tax and other requirements, and generate wealth for themselves and their heirs.

Such needs do not vanish when the planning client is 75 rather than 45. However, a different perspective, and some different skills, are required. For the senior citizen client, the topic is less likely to be career planning than retirement planning or making good use of the proceeds of a retirement plan that is already in pay status. It is crucially necessary to make a plan for what might happen if the client's mental capacity diminishes — or has already diminished. There is a related, but not identical, need to make sure that quality health care will be available — including both acute medical care and custodial care of the physically and/or mentally impaired elder.

For the younger client, health care planning revolves around the employer's group health plan. Some senior citizens continue to work full-time or part-time, so the employer plan remains relevant. For retirees, however, the factors are different. Some of them will be entitled to retiree health benefits from their ex-employers. Nearly all of them will use Medicare benefits. However, the Medicare program concentrates on acute health care, and does little to cope with the common need for custodial care of the elderly.

TRENDS OF 1995-1996

Originally, this book was published in 1992. The Second Edition of this book was published in 1994; the Third Edition appears in mid-1997. In the interim, some trends continued (demographic shifts toward an older population, with a particular predominance of the very old) and others established themselves.

As our society ages, we must be prepared to meet the needs of millions of people over 90 (and no small number of centenarians). That means that retirement planning must take into account the real possibility that income must last for 25 or 30 years, not just 10 or 15. That means that retirement savings must be greater, and investment returns must at least equal inflation, or the sum might be depleted during the elderly person's lifetime. Furthermore, those who choose a single-life annuity, or an annuity for a term of years (in order to increase the size of each payment) face two potentially disagreeable choices. Either they accept a longer stream of smaller payments (and thus risk having an income inadequate for their preferred standard of living) or they take the larger payments and risk outliving the income.

Longevity also has significant implications for the insurance industry. Technically, a conventional whole life policy annuitizes at age 100. Nowadays, there are plenty of centenarians — and they may prefer life insurance to annuity payments! An insured with a lifetime policy may be entitled to ten years or more of long-term care insurance benefits — and, perhaps, benefit eligibility began only a short time after the policy was purchased.

In 1995 and 1996, there was a surge of stock market activity and unprecedented price levels for the Dow-Jones Industrial Index. Other indexes were also high. Thus, interest in variable and index-linked products (such as investment annuities and life insurance) grew. There was a corresponding degree of anxiety: will the market collapse dramatically, and what will happen to vulnerable older investors such as retirees after a collapse? Clearly, the prudent planner will not assume that today's over-heated market will continue forever, and he or she must not base the entire plan on a single market-dependent index fund or indexed annuity.

Congress provided incentives for the elderly to remain in the labor force longer — although not many older workers took the hint! There is a brief period (lasting until the year 2000) when unlimited sums can be taken as lump-sum qualified plan payouts without the excise tax penalty that was formerly imposed. In fact, the excise tax penalty on excessive accumulation within the estate remains — so there is, if anything, an incentive for those with very large pension accounts to reduce the size of the pension account during lifetime. The taxation of pensions paid in annuity forms has been simplified.

The Health Insurance Portability and Accountability Act of 1996 clarifies many disputed questions about long-term care insurance, with the clear objective of making LTC insurance a more attractive purchase. LTC insurance is now more or less equal to accident and health (A&H) insurance for tax purposes. Most benefits can be received tax-free, and some insurance purchasers will receive a tax deduction for their premiums.

An annuity payable for 10 years certain may leave its 75 year-old purchaser short of income if he or she survives significantly past 85: yet a lifetime annuity may provide benefits that are smaller than the annuitants' everyday needs.

The funds accumulated by an investor before retirement, plus benefits from the employer (and any benefits actually paid by the Social Security system) must satisfy not only normal expenses of everyday living, but also the cost of medical and nursing care that is not covered by insurance or government programs. These costs can be very substantial, and they are hard to predict.

It's hard enough to predict how the economy will fare in the next quarter, and which stocks and bonds will prosper. The task of scoping out economic trends three decades ahead is almost impossibly daunting. Furthermore, ten, twenty, or thirty years from now, the client who is now intellectually vigorous and eager to make investment decisions may be cognitively impaired and unable to perform even the simplest tasks...so the portfolio must either be frozen or transferred to professional management while the client is still capable of making decisions.

The ban on Medicaid transfers, read against a political background in which both parties seek to cut back on Medicare and Medicaid in order to balance the budget, shows a clear trend. Congress wants to encourage private-sector planning (as the new incentives for LTC insurance show) and also wants to discourage reliance on government programs. Therefore, the planner should focus more on long-term care insurance (if necessary, replacing inferior early-generation products with newer and better ones) and should give more consideration to annuity investing, especially for higher-bracket middle-aged and older persons who are close to or over age 59 1/2, and who find tax-deferred investing attractive.

COMPUTERS AND THE WEB

Since the last edition of this book, there's been a quantum leap in the use of computers, and especially on-line technologies, in elderplanning. There are many ways in which information stored on your own computer, clients' computers, the home office computer, or downloaded from the Internet affects your job.

For one thing, laptop computers have gotten much more sophisticated. Although they're still expensive, the price may be well justified if you can carry a computer that permits you to go anywhere (including the client's home or office) and do a full-scale, multi-media presentation for a client — including sophisticated calculations based on a variety of scenarios. Once, it would have taken a professional actuary hours or days to perform those calculations. Today, you can do them in minutes, with a few keystrokes. The ability to personalize the analysis has an obvious appeal to prospects.

Interest in the Internet, and especially the World Wide Web (the graphical part of the Internet) has also mushroomed. Most insurance companies have Web sites that permit agents to communicate with the home office, and that distribute detailed information about products. It's much easier to maintain an attractive, well-designed Web site that always has the latest information about products than to try to keep track of which print brochure has been mailed to which prospective customer. You can easily use this information to answer questions about products, service existing accounts, and show prospects how particular products would fit into their financial plans.

Financial services companies also have a major presence on-line. Sites maintained by banks, brokerage houses, and financial publishers give you easy (and, usually, free) access to worthwhile planning tools. There are many sites that feature tools for analyzing stocks before investing, tailoring a portfolio to meet specific objectives, and retirement planning.

If your company does not have specific retirement planning tools on its own Web site, or has not distributed retirement planning software, you can still customize these tools to feature the products you sell (if your practice is product-based) or the products you find most attractive and cost-effective (if your practice is fee-only).

PRACTICE TIP: There are many ways to get and use electronic information. It often makes a lot more sense to download information and planning tools to the hard disk of your own computer, and turn the information into a business presentation (using a program such as Persuasion or Powerpoint) instead of trying to do it "live" from the Internet.

Why? There can be a lot of snags in connecting to the Internet, especially at popular times during the workday and in the evenings when recreation "surfing" often occurs. Of course, those are the times you see your clients. You appear much more professional, and much less flustered, if you can proceed with your well-tailored presentation than if you have to spend half an hour or more to get an Internet connection...or if the computer crashes during your presentation.

Web sites aren't just for major corporations, either. Your Internet Service Provider (ISP) probably offers you the chance to maintain your own Web page free, or for a small monthly service charge. There is probably also simple software available from the service that will help you design and manage your page. (If not, you can easily download it from other Internet sites, or buy it from a software store or through the mail.) There are also plenty of computer-savvy freelancers who can handle the design tasks inexpensively.

The benefit of having your own Web page is that you can handle inquiries from prospects; answer service questions about your customers; and distribute information easily and inexpensively. If you add your URL (Internet address of the Web site) to your business card, brochures, and other marketing materials, the recipients will know that you are comfortable using electronic tools. That can make them feel you're on the same wavelength (if they have a lot of computer sophistication themselves) or can be a good guide to the confusing cyber-world (if they don't).

The strategic consulting group Datamonitor found that it costs only about $2,000 to set up and maintain a simple Web site for a year. In this minimal scenario, you might even design your own Web page (using special software that you buy, or even simple templates furnished by your ISP), or hire a freelancer to help with design and programming.

However, this minimal approach would not allow you to control your own computer server, provide very sophisticated graphics, music, or video, or have a lot of interactive features on your site. A company can expect to spend about $125,000 for a year of designing and maintaining a more elaborate site that provides extensive interaction between the site and its users (such as personalized searches for suitable policies or price quotations). If a company wants to do actual transactions on-line (not just provide access to product information and price lists), and if it wants a professionally-designed site with the latest in multimedia, the cost could be as much as $500,000 a year.

SUMMARY

For various reasons, planning in the last few years of the twentieth century is likely to revolve more and more around the private sector, including investments and insurance. Furthermore, retirement planning is shifting away from the traditional defined-benefit pension and toward more market-oriented, employee-controlled mechanisms such as the defined contribution pension and the 401(k) savings plan. The planner must still understand public benefit programs and help clients use them effectively — but more and more clients will want advice about integrating investments and purchasing insurance, especially long-term care insurance.

TABLE OF CONTENTS

INTRODUCTION

Today, as the number of aging and aged Americans increases, individuals and our nation face a social and financial crisis. One of the factors creating this crisis is that we have done *too* good a job. Medicine has been too effective in increasing life expectancy (but has not always been successful in keeping people healthy). Therefore, many elderly people need a great deal of medical care and social assistance. This help is usually very expensive, and people must make sophisticated financial plans and understand a number of confusing government programs to get the assistance they need.

The insurance industry has also done its job well enough to run into problems. If the only product to be sold was whole-life insurance, the agent's job would be a simple (if less gratifying) one. However, insurance professionals and financial planners have done an excellent job of educating people to combine a variety of products to make long-term plans for retirement and estate plans to provide for their families' welfare. The ironic result is that many families find their careful plans disrupted by a nursing home stay or the need to hire home health care workers. The estate plan was well-drawn, but there is no estate left once health care costs are paid!

The insurance industry has responded with many new or altered products (Medigap insurance; long-term care insurance; second-to-die insurance; living benefits in life insurance policies). The right combination of these products will be very helpful to an individual or family making plans for the predictable (and unpredictable) financial problems of the aging process. The challenge for the insurance or planning professional is to learn what products exist (and to keep up to date with product changes).

Brokers must know about the products of many companies in order to market them effectively. Fee-only planners must be able to offer informed, objective advice to clients about the products of competing companies. Agents must be aware of the competition, so that they can inform potential clients of the valid reasons for selecting their companies' products.

Successful financial planning for the older client is difficult because the planner has to make people confront their deepest fears: not just the fear of dying and the fear of leaving a family unprotected, but the fear of being old and alone; the fear of being abandoned by children when one's needs are greatest; the fear of being physically feeble; the fear of losing mental alertness. The fear of seeing a lifetime of savings and investments wiped out by a few years of nursing home care is a realistic one.

A comprehensive plan involves a whole family, not just an individual or a married couple. Frequently, the adult "children" of the older client are very concerned about their parents' fate, and are willing to provide financial and practical assistance with their problems. The planner — and the planning team — can be especially helpful when the children and parents live far apart. The planning team takes over part of the burden traditionally assumed by family members. (There is a price for this — the planning team often ends up in the middle of long-simmering conflicts and sibling rivalries.)

Planning for the older client is difficult for many other reasons. If people wait until an emergency strikes — such as the death or serious illness of a spouse — the alternatives open to them will be drastically limited. Yet if they are sensible and plan ahead, they may find that future events make their plans meaningless. For instance, a long-term care insurance (LTC) policy that pays an indemnity of $50 a day may seem like an excellent choice if it is purchased today — yet, ten years in the future when the insured person collects benefits, the cost of nursing home care may be $200 a day, leaving the family with a difficult financial challenge even after insurance benefits are paid.

The usual assumption is that the husband in a married couple will be older than his wife, and will become ill and die first; that he will own most of the couple's assets in his own name; and that most of the couple's post-retirement income will come from his pension and Social Security benefits. While these assumptions remain true for many couples, the wise planner will not make an inflexible plan that depends on them coming true. For instance, a woman who is several years younger than her husband may still need home care or nursing care before he does, because of an accident, stroke, cancer, or Alzheimer's disease. Her assets, income, or pension may be larger than his.

The high incidence of divorce and remarriage means that there may be several sets of children and step-children to be taken into account, and an individual making an estate plan may want to benefit his or her children rather than the second or third spouse. In this situation, the financial planner may want to arrange options (such as QTIP trust) that provide lifetime income for the spouse, but ensure that the capital passes to the children of the person for whom the plan is created.

It certainly is not true that every person over 65 is retired, physically weak, or "senile." It is not even true that these conditions are an inevitable part of the aging process that afflict everyone sooner or later. Nevertheless, there is a real risk that *every* senior citizen will suffer some degree of physical and/or mental incapacity. The well-made, comprehensive plan must take this into account. It is certainly a good idea for a man to maintain adequate life insurance coverage — but it is not too helpful for a mentally incapacitated widow to receive a large lump sum insurance benefit that she cannot administer herself and that will keep her from qualifying for Medicaid for the nursing home care she needs. In this circumstance, use of settlement options or an insurance trust to provide income, with professional management, might be a better choice. It might also be worthwhile to name the man's children as his beneficiaries so that the widow will be more likely to qualify for Medicaid.

The possibility of incapacity creates a need to pay for nursing home care or alternatives to institutionalization (such as home care and "nursing home without walls" programs). This can be done by accumulating a lot of assets (with the accent on "a lot"; private payment of nursing home care nearly always runs more than $30,000 a year, often costs more than $50,000 a year, and an elderly person can need more than a decade of care — not to mention the fact that both spouses may need such care); by using government benefits such as Medicare, Medicaid, and the elder care programs provided by the various states; by using insurance to supplement the deficiencies of the Medicare program or to pay for long-term care; by enlisting the practical and financial help of the entire family; or by combining all the approaches.

In other words, the financial planner or insurance professional who wants to give the best possible service to older clients has to keep current in many areas (the changing availability and terms of government programs; new and improved insurance and investment products; laws affecting taxes and estate planning; what employers are doing about pensions and retiree health benefits). As the next chapter will show, the successful elder-care planner works best as part of a team, where each team member contributes a different assortment of skills and expertise.

Before the 1990s, the toughest task for the elder care financial planner was protecting clients (who often lived on fixed incomes) against inflation. Today, the inflation monster has been tamed, but the cost of health care looms huge in the planning process. Furthermore, clients may have less income than anticipated. Many elderly financial planning clients are net creditors: that is, they have few or any debts, but receive much of their funds from income-oriented investments like bonds. When interest rates drop, their income decreases, and they do not benefit because they have little or no debt to repay.

In the 1980s, there was a trend away from defined-benefit pension plans toward defined-contribution plans, including 401(k) plans. Some fortunate people got higher pensions than they would otherwise have received; but any market-linked system will also harm some people who collect their pensions when the market is down, or when poor investment choices have been made. (There was also a trend toward greater employee control over investment of their own pension accounts, so often the employees themselves made the poor choices.) What this means in the 1990s is that some retirees will find their pensions smaller than anticipated.

The Revenue Reconciliation Act of 1993 increased income tax rates — and also increased the potentially taxable portion of the Social Security benefit to 85%. What this means is that some high-income retirees will be paying higher income taxes on their retirement income, and much of their Social Security benefit will also constitute taxable income. The bottom line is that many financial planning clients will have less money after taxes than they anticipated before retirement — yet may face health care expenses far higher than anticipated.

A NOTE ON METHODS: It is easier to learn about insurance policy design by comparing the features of various policies available in the market. However, there is significant lead time between researching a book and the date the book appears in print — and a good deal more time may elapse before the reader buys a book, or before he or she consults the book for reference.

Therefore, I have avoided describing specific policies and identifying them by name and issuer. By the time you read a description of a particular policy, it may have been discontinued, or its terms modified (often very much in the best interests of consumers). Furthermore, describing one company's products may create an inference that they are superior to other company's products which are, in fact, at least as good.

To combat these tendencies, I have included summary descriptions of various products, purely as a tool so the reader can think about policy design issues, and identified them only as "Policy A" or "Rider B." (No inference is intended that a policy described as "A" is better than "B" through "G", or whatever.)

Chapter 1

THE PLANNING APPROACH

Planning for the aging process is not simple. The finished plan must include information and input from several professions.

(1)　The finished plan has *legal* implications, and an attorney will be required to draft documents such as wills, trusts, durable powers of attorney (documents that allow a competent person to name an agent to act for him or her in case of later incapacity). Lawyers often handle tax planning and tax compliance. They administer trusts and handle the probate of wills and the administration of the estates of deceased or incompetent persons. The best lawyer for the planning team is one who is well-informed about current developments in elder law, especially the regulations of the local Medicaid agency and federal and state regulation of nursing homes, and one who is up-to-date in tax and estate planning issues.

(2)　Accountants keep track of financial transactions. Their expertise is especially useful when a person's assets have to be valued when a business is sold, during a divorce, or as part of the settlement of an estate. Accountants also have a major responsibility in connection with income and estate tax.

(3)　Geriatric care managers (GCMs) are members of a new profession that has developed in response to the needs of the elderly and their families. GCMs are usually trained as social workers, psychologists, or members of other helping professions. The GCM handles the practical side of elder care: hiring home care workers; keeping track of bed availability and quality in local nursing homes; informing the elderly and their families about programs such as Meals-on-Wheels and adult day care; and handling the never-ending paperwork.

Most important, the GCM works with the other team members to develop a plan for day-to-day care — and then manages and monitors the plan to see that it is carried out properly, and that a different package of services is assembled as the needs of the elderly person change. For instance, an elderly couple initially might need only a little assistance with heavy housekeeping chores and a visit from a trained nurse every few months. If one spouse falls and breaks a hip, the GCM can supervise hospitalization, a short stay in a skilled nursing home for recuperation, and provision of a home health aide to help the other spouse care for the recovering spouse.

Later, as both spouses get frailer, the GCM can make sure that they get home-delivered meals, more extensive chore service, and more frequent nursing visits. If one or both spouses need to be institutionalized, the GCM can advise the family on the best available nursing facilities, and superintend the difficult process of "assessment" (a state-required examination to make sure the person really needs nursing home care and the chosen facility is suitable) and make sure all the paperwork is completed properly. If a Medicaid application will be made, the GCM helps with the application.

The GCM stays in contact with other members of the family to reassure them that the elderly parent or relative is receiving appropriate care. This reassurance can be literally priceless if Mom is in Denver and the kids are in Detroit, Trenton, and Amarillo and can't be on the scene personally to provide or supervise care, yet are vitally concerned that adequate care be provided.

(4)   Appraisers are specialists in valuation of property. They will not be needed in every elder care plan; however, their services are critical if the elderly person's assets include a major asset of uncertain value, such as a block of stock in a closely-held corporation or an art collection.

(5)   As you know, the financial planner has broad perspective and analyzes a person's or family's income, assets, and expenses and creates a plan of saving, investments, and insurance protection to make sure that the family can meet its needs, create wealth, and pass along the wealth to future generations.

However, not all financial planners understand the special needs of older persons. As our population ages, it will become ever more important to understand Medicaid planning and other forms of planning for potential incapacity and for the cost of chronic care. A special need that financial planners can fill is providing advice to relatives and friends who serve as "fiduciaries" for impaired older people; those who are trustees of trusts for older persons; or who are agents under durable powers of attorney. Frequently, the fiduciaries are people of good will but without financial sophistication, and they need help in choosing appropriate, safe investments for the impaired person's funds and help in the routine tasks of trust management (such as paperwork and filing tax returns).

(6)   Some financial planners are licensed to sell insurance and/or securities; others are not. If the financial planner does not have these licenses, or feels uncomfortable about offering advice and selling products at the same time, the team must include a knowledgeable securities broker (to handle the necessary purchases and sales of stocks, bonds, and mutual funds) and an insurance agent or broker (because the typical elder-care plan requires an insurance portfolio custom-tailored to family needs). The team members must be sophisticated about elder law and elder care needs, and must be very sensitive to potential ethical problems. The elderly can be very vulnerable, and it is unfortunate that some people in the financial industry have taken advantage of this vulnerability by steering their older clients into unsuitably risky investments, or "churning" their portfolios merely to earn higher commissions.

ELEMENTS AND FUNCTIONS OF A PLAN

The complete elder-care plan unites lifetime planning with estate planning. The first task is to make sure that the older person or couple will have a comfortable life during retirement, with income adequate for their needs, suitable housing (whether in a rented apartment, a private home, special housing for the elderly, a retirement community, life-care community, or nursing home), and with adequate resources to cope with emergencies. The right combination of public benefits, retiree health benefits from the former employer, private health insurance, Medigap insurance and LTC insurance must be selected so that health care needs can be anticipated and met. Investments must be monitored for suitability and performance. Many lifetime plans include trusts, so that the trustee can manage assets and distribute income and perhaps principal based on the needs of elderly beneficiaries who do not want to, or cannot, manage assets personally. Reasonable tax-planning steps must be taken to cut down the yearly tax burden.

The best scenario occurs when clients approach the team even before retirement. That way, their choice of retirement payouts, and their use of pension, IRA, and Keogh funds can be based on sound professional advice about taxes, Medicaid impact, and market trends. However, no matter how late a person or couple waits before getting planning help, professional advice can still do a great deal to avoid mistakes and keep the harshest of regulations from applying.

Based on a sound forecast of lifetime needs, the planning team can then go on to make a practical estate plan. If it seems likely that one or both spouses will have a taxable estate, steps can be taken to cut down or eliminate the tax. (It is important for planners to keep a sense of perspective, and not do such aggressive estate planning that the people whose estates are being planned are left without adequate resources for their own lifetime!)

For instance, interspousal gifts can be used for "estate splitting" so each spouse will have an approximately equal estate on which little or no estate tax is due. Gifts to children, grandchildren, other relatives and friends, and charities can remove assets from the estate. A gift of up to $10,000 each year can be made to each recipient without gift tax; if both spouses join in the gift, each recipient can get $20,000 a year without gift tax. As you can see, a "giving program" that continues for several years can do a great deal to reduce the estate.

Irrevocable trusts can also be used to get assets out of the estate, especially under circumstances when an outright gift is undesirable (for instance, if minors or someone the trust grantor does not think is capable of handling large sums of money are the recipients). Trusts can be created either during a person's lifetime ("inter vivos" trusts) or as part of the terms of his or her will (testamentary trusts). Revocable trusts, whose assets are not part of the person's probate estate, can be used as will substitutes, to avoid the delays, expense, and loss of privacy inherent in the probate process. However, it costs something to set up and manage a trust, and revocable trusts do not provide any significant tax advantages, so the disadvantages of probate must be balanced against these costs.

Revocable trusts are sometimes called "will substitutes" because the assets in the trust are disposed of according to the trust, not according to the will. There are other important will substitutes which form a part of many plans. When property is owned jointly (also called "in joint tenancy") and one of the joint owners dies, the property passes automatically to the other joint tenant(s). This contrasts with property owned by "tenants in common", each of whom can transfer his or her interest in the property by will. Joint bank accounts work similarly. There are also "Totten trust" or "P.O.D." (Payable on Death) bank accounts under which a person designates who will receive the balance of the account when the depositor dies. Will substitutes are very convenient — unless the owner of the property covered by the will substitute drafts a will and wants to do something else with the property! Will substitutes should not be used without legal advice about their tax and Medicaid consequences.

In short, the task of the planning team is to advise about budgeting and investing to create wealth; how to use the assets that have already been accumulated; how to minimize the tax burden; how to cope with health-care needs; how to use insurance to protect family wealth; and how to transmit the wealth to future generations using wills, trusts, powers of attorney, and other mechanisms, again at the lowest permissible tax cost.

WHY A TEAM?

As you see from this brief sketch, unifying lifetime and estate planning is a subtle and complex task, and many kinds of skills are needed to do the best possible job. Yet, too often, people who seek professional advice see only one professional, or get advice on a piecemeal basis that never integrates into a coherent multi-disciplinary plan. As mentioned above, short-sighted attorneys often draft an estate plan that becomes worthless because the cost of medical care (especially nursing home or long-term home care) depletes the estate. Insurance professionals may recommend the purchase of a large policy that compromises the beneficiary's Medicaid eligibility. Brokers can put together a portfolio that requires intensive attention from a client who is now competent, but whose physical or mental condition may deteriorate in the future. Even lawyers who are sensitive to elder law issues, and who draft good plans, may be ignorant about investment or insurance matters, or about the practical, hands-on tasks handled by the GCM.

To give the clients the kind of service they need and deserve, *all* of the relevant professional skills must be marshalled, and the client must be contacted regularly to see if he or she wants a review or update of the plan. There are two ways to do this. When you sell insurance or perform financial planning for an older client, you can alert them to the need for legal, accounting, brokerage, and/or GCM services, and inform them where to find a competent professional. In addition to the practitioners you meet in your own practice, specialty organizations (such as the National Association of Elder Law Attorneys and the Association of Private Geriatric Care Managers) maintain referral listings. Local professional groups such as bar associations also make referrals.

The other way is to operate as a team. The first professional to be contacted by a potential client can advise the client of the desirability of a joint team effort, and suggest that the client meet with the entire team so that the team can assess the client's needs and prepare a joint plan that covers all the bases.

Especially if the client's mobility is limited, it is easier to have a single interview to gather all of the necessary information than to start from the beginning with three, four, or five professional advisors. After the initial interview, the team can make up the plan, get it approved or modified by the client, then carry out all necessary steps (such as drafting legal documents, hiring home care workers, processing insurance applications, changing beneficiary designations, or making the purchases or sales of securities to fit the plan).

FORMING THE TEAM

The team approach is very far from the traditional method of separate professional practices. Therefore, you will have to alert other professionals to the advantages of this way of practicing. One way to do this is to write up a short pamphlet (perhaps one that will fit on a single sheet of paper, folded three ways and divided into six panels; or two or three sheets folded in half in a heavy paper cover) or a few display pieces that will fit into a 9" x 12" folder. Indicate your own credentials and knowledge of elder law and elder care issues and stress the advantage that the attorney, accountant, or broker will have over the competition if he or she is able to offer complete, "one-stop" service by fielding a planning team. Send the brochure or folder to local professionals in the fields you want to target.

Use networking to meet and work with other professionals. For instance, bar associations frequently give lectures and instructional programs on estate planning and elder law issues; most of these programs are open to the public. At first, the lectures and questions afterwards may be Greek to you — but soon, you will absorb the vocabulary and learn a great deal about both basic legal issues and recent developments. Furthermore, you will meet the local practitioners, and form an opinion about who is the most knowledgeable and sophisticated. During coffee breaks, or after the meeting, you will have an excellent opportunity to exchange business cards!

Volunteer work can prove very rewarding in business terms as well as in the satisfaction of helping others. Joining a local organization that helps the aging will allow you to use your skills and impress potential clients. If you are a good speaker, why not make up a short presentation on a topic such as the use of second-to-die insurance in estate planning, insurance settlement options, or proper investments for fiduciaries. You can present the talk at a bar association meeting or a meeting of CPAs or GCMs. (If you are not a good speaker, this is a great way to hone your skills.) Professionals are always hungry for up-to-date information that they can use to benefit their clients and improve their skills. Organizations are always hungry for new programs instead of the same old stuff! It is a great way to meet top professionals under circumstances that establish that you are knowledgeable, competent, and authoritative.

Helping others can help you. If you refer clients who need legal or accounting services to lawyers and CPAs, you are likely to get referrals in turn when their clients need insurance. Besides, many lawyers are severely underinsured and lack a financial plan — matters with which you can help them once they get to know you as a person to trust. Many law or accounting firms are excellent prospects for group-term life insurance, key-person insurance for partnerships, or health plans.

As an insurance professional or financial planner, you must be skillful in meeting objections. What if a lawyer, CPA, GCM, or broker asks why he or she should include you in a team instead of doing everything personally (and collecting the entire fee)? Point out that your work involves not only a lot of study and expertise, but certain licenses (e.g., for sale of insurance or securities). Does the objector have the time to learn new information and techniques, get the necessary licenses, and keep abreast of a new body of information? Will the extra fees justify the time and effort — or does it make more sense to delegate these tasks to someone who is already up to speed?

Furthermore, lawyers and CPAs are usually at the tip of the pyramid in terms of income and hourly fees. Will clients be willing to pay the lawyer's or accountant's usual fee for the larger number of hours needed for the inexperienced professional to handle the tasks, instead of a smaller fee or commission to someone who has the experience to handle the task quicker and more efficiently? Even if the answer is "yes", a good argument can be made that there is an ethical duty to advise the client of the availability of related services at a lower price from someone else. If the answer is "no", the lawyer or accountant must either accept a reduced fee or lose a client. The client gets the best service, with the greatest degree of cost-effectiveness, when each task in the plan is performed by the person who knows the most about it, can do it most efficiently, and charges the lowest fee. The client loses out twice if the highest-priced professional does the task, and takes extra time because of lack of experience.

ETHICAL AND COMPETENCY ISSUES

In order to be legally valid, an action (such as selling property or signing a will or trust) must be taken by a person who is competent: one who understands the action and its implications, and whose judgment is not too impaired to make the decision an invalid one. Once an action is undertaken, those who are unhappy about it (for instance, people who would have inherited property if it had not been sold, transferred, or left to someone else) may be able to challenge the action by claiming that it was motivated by fraud, or that the person who took the action was under duress or was subjected to undue influence.

Clearly, all of these dangers can affect and afflict the elderly. Not everybody becomes "senile", losing capacity to understand financial matters and self-care. However, it is true that, for a variety of reasons, some older people are forgetful, confused, or downright incapable of making financial decisions or understanding decisions made on their behalf.

It is clear that a person who has been named a "ward" by a court, and for whom a guardian has been appointed, is either legally incapable of financial dealings, or is only permitted those dealings permitted by the court that heard the guardianship case. If a conservator has been appointed for a person who a court deems incapable of handling financial affairs, then the conservatee's future actions will be limited, depending on the scope of the court order and what state law says about the rights of conservatees. Usually, the guardian or conservator, and not the ward or conservatee, will carry out transactions such as investing and selling property.

Guardianship and conservatorship cases are brought for only a small percentage of the elderly. These cases are expensive, take time, and can create enormous hostility within the family. If a son or daughter brings the proceeding, the parent is likely to be very hurt and resentful; and one sibling can be furious at other siblings who either support or oppose the petition. In some cases, no one really wants to serve as guardian or conservator; in other cases, whoever is chosen, there will be two or three other family members or friends who feel they are better qualified and resent someone else's appointment. These proceedings can be brought by someone who honestly believes that the elderly person is mentally impaired (and this belief can be either correct or incorrect) or by someone who wants to exploitively gain control of the older person's assets.

Where there is no guardian or conservator, the team must make its own decisions about the capacity of the elderly person. The first step is to discard prejudices. Senility is not an inevitable part of aging. Many older people have mobility problems or perceptual problems (deteriorating sight or hearing) but are fully capable of thinking, analyzing, and understanding. Make an adequate effort to enunciate and speak loudly and clearly (without shouting); use large, dark type in written communications (a copier that enlarges can be invaluable in this respect); and take plenty of time to explain things.

Make your older clients feel comfortable about asking questions; do not give them the feeling that you look down on them, or that you resent the extra time involved. Use clues such as "Is that all right?" "Do you understand?" and "What do you think will happen if..." to test your clients' understanding. If your clients' hearing is better than their vision, rely on face-to face and telephone conversations rather than written material. Try making a tape cassette with explanations that they can take home and play as often as they need to become fully familiar with your plan. If their vision is better, rely more on charts and large-type pamphlets.

There are many other ethical problems that confront planners. There is a lot of debate about whether it is proper, fair, or ethical to transfer assets so that people who are not really poor can qualify for Medicaid. There are also practical problems with aggressive Medicaid planning: old people can be left without the resources they need for everyday living, or the plan can be badly done and backfire. The plan can succeed in the sense that the older person qualifies for and receives Medicaid nursing home benefits — but fails in the sense that the only Medicaid facility with available beds does not provide quality care.

Congress and the state legislatures frequently change Medicaid laws — sometimes expanding the scope of Medicaid benefits, but usually in the direction of reducing Medicaid eligibility. Major changes were imposed in 1993 and 1996. As discussed in Chapter 7, the Medicaid treatment of trusts was changed; and states were given explicit permission to impose transfer penalties and estate recovery in cases of Medicaid home care (not just nursing home care).

In 1993, the look-back period before a Medicaid application, during which transfers will affect eligibility, was extended from 30 months to 36 months (and to 60 months for some transactions involving irrevocable trusts). The penalty period was extended from a maximum of 30 months to an indefinite period that can be of any length. State power to recover against a Medicaid recipient's estate was extended from the homestead to the Medicaid recipient's entire probate and non-probate estate in real and personal property. Planners were given virtually no time to change clients' plans to escape the harshness of the new rules.

In 1996, criminal penalties became a possibility.

That raises the question of what the planner's ethical obligations are to society as a whole. Usually, the ethical obligations run only to the client. But it is not always easy to decide who the client is. You may be contacted by an older married person, whose spouse may or may not participate actively in the planning process. Then you will have to decide if it is ethical to take steps that benefit one spouse but not the other.

You may also be hired by someone who is worried about the personal and financial well-being of his or her parents. There are also potential ethical problems in this model. Presumably the person who hired you is interested in inheriting from the parents. What if your plan calls for the parents to spend much of their money themselves, for instance by hiring a private home health agency to provide care, or entering a life-care community, leaving little or nothing to be inherited? What if the plan calls for leaving the homestead vulnerable to Medicaid recoupment, again making inheritance unlikely? What if the parents are willing to make transfers as part of a Medicaid plan, but they want to make the transfers to their own siblings, or to a child other than the one who hired you?

There are few legal guidelines for these very tough questions; about all that can be done is to raise the question, and remind the planner to be careful and watch out for complaints and lawsuits from parties who think themselves deprived of what they deserve.

A third ethical question is whether the planner is a kind of "hired gun" who will undertake any action that the client wants, as long as it does not violate any laws or ethical duties. Or should the planner do whatever is best for the client, even if the client finds it distasteful? This one is a little easier. It is probably your duty to grit your teeth and carry out the client's wishes. Once you have explained the pro and cons of the situation thoroughly, and are sure that your client understands and is competent to make the decision (remember, not everyone who agrees with you is competent, and not everyone who disagrees with you is incompetent!), then resign yourself to the fact that clients — whether they are 22 or 82 — have the right to make their own mistakes.

Also remember that the professional perspective can be very different from the client's perspective. The professional is proud to create an elaborate plan that copes with every contingency and saves every last penny of tax. The client may well prefer something simpler, easier to understand, and less cumbersome to carry out. Clients may also be willing to accept higher income tax or estate tax liability in order to make sure that assets are disposed of as they prefer.

THE TOUGHEST QUESTIONS

Once you have gotten those questions under your belt, you can deal with something *really* difficult: discussing living wills and proxy designations with your clients. Understandably, it is hard for you even to mention these frightening issues, and it can be hard for your clients to express their real feelings. They may not want life support, yet may express a wish for maximum medical intervention because they think this is what their children want. The children may believe that a quick death is more merciful, yet insist on resuscitation or life support because they feel guilty about not having done enough for their parents, or because they are afraid that other relatives will criticize them. The elderly may also prefer maximum medical treatment, yet claim that they *do not* want this, because they are afraid of being "in the way" or because they do not want to deprive their children of an inheritance.

The "right to die" issue is a very complex and emotional one. The fundamental legal analysis centers on "informed consent": explaining the risks and benefits of treatment to the potential patient, who then chooses to accept or reject the treatment — even if the treatment is life-saving, and refusal is likely to mean death. This is a terrifying responsibility for any patient, and the problems multiply if the patient is old and comatose, or demented, or confused. States have evolved many different solutions to the problem of the incompetent person who needs medical treatment. Sometimes it is necessary to get court approval of treatment, or of refusal of treatment. A court-appointed guardian, however, does not always have the power to order with-drawal or refusal of life support. Sometimes a competent person can designate another person as decision-maker in case the first person ever becomes unconscious or incompetent, and incapable of making decisions personally. The 1990 Supreme Court case of *Cruzan v. Missouri Department of Health* allows a state to require "clear and convincing proof" of a non-incompetent person's wishes, expressed while he or she was competent, before allowing a representative to order termination of life support (in this case, tube feeding).

A living will or other document often serves as proof of a person's intentions. Nearly all of the states have some kind of "living will" law. Living wills, which are often misunderstood, are documents that express a preference with regard to life support (such as respirators). Living wills become effective only if the person making the will is a "qualified patient", which basically means that he or she is terminally ill, and will die shortly whether or not life support is applied. (During the 1990s, there has been a trend for state legislatures to adopt new definitions, under which a person who is comatose or in a Persistent Vegetative State will also be considered a "qualified patient.") Living wills do *not* become effective merely because a person is seriously ill but has a fairly long life expectancy, or merely because a person's illness or condition is so severe that life has become burdensome.

The "health care proxy" (sometimes referred to as a "Durable Power of Attorney") is another important health care document. The signer of a proxy designates someone else to make health care decisions (including, but not limited to, decisions about life support) if the signer ever requires medical care but is unconscious, mentally incapacitated, or otherwise unable to give informed consent personally. Health care providers consult the proxy when consent must be given to medical procedures.

Another legislative trend is the adoption of "surrogate decision-maker" statutes. These laws set out a statutory hierarchy (typically, spouse, parent, adult child sibling, other relative) of people who will be legally empowered to make medical decisions for an incapacitated person who has not left written instructions or designated a proxy. These laws solve some difficult medical-legal problems, but it is always preferable for the client to have a living will and/or proxy, expressing his or her own wishes; the surrogate decision-maker does not always make the choices that the sick person would have preferred.

One of the most controversial areas is the treatment of people who are able to breathe without machinery, but cannot eat normally and must be tube-fed. Legal advice is needed as to whether a living will in your state can include directions to forbid artificial provision of food and water, or whether doctors and medical facilities are required to continue providing nutrition and hydration. The rights of guardians and other representatives with respect to nutrition and hydration of incompetent patients are not legally settled. Again, your state's current laws must be consulted.

A related question is the "Do Not Resuscitate" order. The general medical policy is to perform cardio-pulmonary resuscitation (CPR) whenever patients have a heart attack or cease breathing. But CPR itself is a painful and risky business, and can result in further suffering and a prolonged death rather than an increased and improved lifespan. It may be possible for a competent individual to order his or her doctor not to perform CPR, or to designate someone else as a decision-maker about CPR.

Your clients must be informed about the risks and benefits of life support technology, and about the types of legal documents they can sign to make their wishes clear. The documents can be used to demonstrate a wish for maximum as well as minimum treatment. In practical terms, the cooperation of the patient's attending physician is essential, because the nursing home or hospital will probably listen to the doctor (and not necessarily to the patient or family). For non-emergency hospital and nursing home admissions, one factor in choosing a facility is whether its CPR and life support policy agrees with the patient's wishes. Also remember that a patient who wants maximum intervention may wind up living in a nursing home with limited capacity for medical treatment; by the time the ambulance or emergency medical technicians arrive, it may be too late.

Very ugly scenes often arise at the bedside if family members disagree about treatment of a dying or comatose family member. The person designated to make the decisions may have difficulty in getting the hospital or nursing home to comply with the decision — and may also face recriminations from family members who think a different course should have been taken. The social work or psychology background of the GCM in the planning team can be crucial in dealing with these severe problems.

WORKING WITH THE OLDER CLIENT

Once your planning team is operational, you will receive many referrals. There are many ways to attract older clients and caregivers of the elderly as clients. For instance, you can hone your speaking skills once again by presenting a program about insurance at a local senior center, self-help group of caregivers, state or local agency for aging, or religious or civic organization. Write an article or a regular column for a local newspaper. If local attorneys are speaking on elder law topics, ask if you can join them on the podium to discuss related issues. There is probably a local radio or TV program dealing with aging issues; volunteer to be a one-time or regular guest. (Be careful of call-in shows, though: it is tough to give good advice off the top of your head, and lay people often do not understand how to frame a question that accurately represents the real situation you would discover during an office interview.)

Be prepared to give extra time and a bountiful allowance of patience to your older clients. The tempo of post-retirement life is often slower than it was when your clients coped with demanding jobs and a houseful of kids. Your schedule is likely to be crammed with appointments, cold calls, continuing professional education, networking, and ever-present paperwork. Few of your older clients have such a crowded schedule. Do not make them feel that you are hurrying them out of the office or that you fail to value them as individuals and as clients. You do not want to be treated as a stereotype or crammed into a category; you want to be treated as an individual, and you want credit given for your strengths and allowances made for your limitations. Your elderly clients feel just the same way.

It does not take Sigmund Freud to tell you that you have feelings (loving, negative, or a mixture of both) about your own parents and grandparents. Recognize these feelings, but do not let them color your friendly yet professional attitude toward your older clients. Be prepared to be "adopted" as a surrogate son or daughter by older clients. This has its good and bad points. At least you will get some insights into the way things were done in the "good old days", and maybe some homemade cookies.

Before you start seeking elderly clients, make sure your office is friendly to them. Can you give clear directions to your office, and are parking spaces reserved for your office clearly marked for older clients who still drive? Can your office be reached by taxi or public transportation for those who do not drive any more? Is your office close to the elevator (with a large, clear sign on your office door), or can it only be reached by a dark, narrow flight of stairs? Are your building, your office, and the restrooms for clients accessible to someone who uses a cane, a walker, or a wheelchair? Do you have a speakerphone with an amplifier? A copier that enlarges? A TTY (telecommunications device for the deaf)? Does your office furniture include at least some firm, upholstered chairs with armrests that are easy for an old person to sit down in and rise from? Are the chairs close enough to your desk so a person with impaired sight or hearing can communicate with you? Are the other team members just as sensible about arranging their offices?

People over 65 do not lose their individuality simply by aging. They vary greatly in their physical and mental strengths and weaknesses, family situations, financial affluence, and wishes with respect to their assets. Your job is to find out what they possess, what their foreseeable personal needs are for the future, and how they would like to dispose of whatever property and funds remain after their death.

A complete elder care plan balances many elements: current tax savings against future estate tax; investment growth versus risk; and estate planning versus Medicaid planning. A complete elder care plan calls for frequent revision based on changes in the investment climate, tax and other laws affecting the elderly, and the client's health. Sensitive emotional issues, and the risk of vicious family conflict, must always be kept in mind. It is hard to imagine any one individual with all the necessary skills; it is far more likely that clients will get the smartest plan, the best follow-through, and the greatest degree of cost efficiency from a team of professionals working together, continuing to learn about elder care developments, and bolstering each other's skills.

Chapter 2

LIFE INSURANCE IN THE ELDER CARE PLAN

INTRODUCTION

You would not be reading this book if you didn't believe that life insurance has a valuable purpose to play in financial and estate planning! No doubt you are already familiar with the general techniques of using insurance to create an estate, meet the needs of the insured's surviving family, and provide liquidity pending settlement of the estate. This chapter briefly summarizes the major types of life coverage available, considered from the angle of the special needs of senior citizens and their families. Two types of coverage (second-to-die coverage and "living benefits" used to fund long-term care) are examined in detail because of their special applicability to the needs of pre-retirees and retirees. This chapter also summarizes the 1996 tax changes relating to these products.

Another issue relevant to life insurance planning for the elderly is the role of incapacity in leading to involuntary lapse. Recently, some states (such as Florida and Texas) have dealt with the potential for mental incapacity by requiring an additional grace period. These statutes require insurers to notify applicants of their right to designate someone who will receive notification if the policy seems about to lapse. Of course, the point is for the person who receives the notification to make sure that the premiums get paid and that no lapse occurs. Under a 1995 Texas law, an incapacitated insured person or that person's legal guardian can get a policy reinstated within one year of lapse, once the premium is paid with accrued interest.

In states that lack such a statutory provision, fiduciaries—and concerned friends and relatives even if they don't have a formal legal role—should monitor the status of policy payments and make sure that involuntary lapses do not occur through simple forgetfulness.

TYPES OF LIFE INSURANCE PRODUCTS

The life insurance industry has created a variety of products falling under the general heading of "life insurance", and advising the client about the selection of the right product or products is an important part of the planning process. Because the focus of this book is on the additional skills needed to serve the senior client, the types of insurance products applicable to clients of all ages will be discussed only briefly, with more detailed consideration given to products that have particular applicability to the senior citizen market.

Life insurance products can be analyzed in many ways. A threshold question is whether the policy is "participating" or "non-participating"; the holder of a "par" policy is entitled to policy dividends paid by the insurer out of its surplus earnings. The effect of policy dividends is to reduce the effective net cost of life insurance.

One of the most important considerations is who actually owns the policy. In a group policy (typically purchased by an employer), there is a single group policyholder, who negotiates with the insurance company. The various group members (typically, employees) receive a certificate showing their participation in the group, and thus, are sometimes called certificate holders.

An individual policy is owned by one person, who selects policy features such as size of the policy and whether riders will be attached. An individual policy can be purchased by an individual on his or her life, or by someone else who has an insurable interest in that person's life such as a spouse, a sibling, a child, a business partner, or a corporation for which the insured person performs vital services.

Another possibility is for one person or entity to purchase the policy, then transfer ownership to a second person or entity. This might be done to keep policy proceeds out of the estate of the insured person or to assist the insured in creating a charitable giving program or to further other planning objectives.

Another basic method of characterizing life insurance policies divides them into term policies and permanent insurance policies. Prior to 1980, endowment insurance (whose face amount is payable at a specified maturity date, or upon the death of the insured before this date) had a small but meaningful market share. Today's market is essentially divided between term insurance and permanent life insurance. In turn, each of these categories is divided into various plans.

Term Insurance

Term insurance provides pure insurance, with no investment element, either for a term of years or until the insured reaches a particular age such as age 65. Term insurance death benefits can be level, decreasing, or increasing depending on the purchaser's needs and financial condition. Decreasing term insurance is often used to secure payment of an indebtedness (such as a mortgage or consumer loan). As the balance of the indebtedness decreases, so does the amount of insurance. Increasing term insurance coverage increases either by a specified amount or in accordance with an economic index. This type of coverage might be selected by someone who feels that inflation will increase the financial needs of his or her beneficiaries.

A term policy that does not include renewal or conversion provisions will end at the expiration of the stated term, providing no further insurance coverage. Because renewal and conversion offer flexibility and greater access to insurance, policies containing these provisions are somewhat more expensive than those without them.

A renewable term policy gives the insured the option of renewing the policy at the end of the term, usually in the same amount and for the same term (or for a smaller amount and shorter term, but not a longer term and/or more coverage), with no requirement of proof of the continuing insurability of the insured. A re-entry term policy gives the insured the option of submitting proof of insurability in exchange for a lower premium rate. Typically, term policies either limit renewal to a specified age (e.g., no renewals after age 65) or limit the number of renewals (e.g., three renewals, but no more).

The term insurer is permitted to adjust the premium based on the insured's attained age at renewal, but not based on his or her medical condition at the time of renewal. The normal structure calls for a premium that is level throughout each term. Therefore, at a higher attained age for the new term, the premium may be much higher than during the initial term because the risk of death during the term is also much higher.

A conversion privilege allows a change from term to permanent life insurance coverage without proof of insurability, with the permanent life premium generally computed based on the insured's attained age at the time of the conversion. However, if the policy is one of the small minority that permits *original age conversion*, the premium for the permanent life policy obtained after the conversion will be calculated based on the insured's age when the original term policy was first purchased.

Typical policies limit conversion either in time (e.g. not after age 55 or age 65 or only during the first five years of a ten-year term) or in amount (e.g., only 50% of the face amount of the original term policy).

Because many policies are not available or renewable after age 65, and other policies can be obtained only at a high cost, term insurance is not always suitable for plans involving elderly clients, or for long-range plans involving middle-aged clients. One planning possibility for middle-aged clients is a term policy that is convertible to whole life insurance, with advice to the client to convert when it appears that affordable term insurance will cease to be readily available.

Generally speaking, term life insurance will not affect Medicaid planning. Although cash value is an asset for Medicaid purposes, term insurance has no cash value. Nearly all jurisdictions also take the position that purchasing term insurance is not a transfer, because there is no gift or below-cost element. In other words, the insurance purchaser buys insurance at its fair market value.

There is an exception to this rule, which may signal a new direction in state responses to Medicaid planning. In 1993, one state adopted a statute which treats a term insurance purchase made within 30 months of a Medicaid application as a transfer, unless the policy's death benefit is at least twice the sum of the premiums. This statute applies only to purchases after the effective date.

The purchase of a pre-need funeral policy will not be treated as a transfer, but if the funeral policy's benefits exceed the actual costs of the funeral, the extra benefits can be recovered by the state Medicaid agency.

Whole Life Insurance

The earliest whole life insurance products, unlike term insurance, were designed to provide permanent insurance lasting throughout the life of the insured person, as long as premium payments continued to be made. Although term insurance has only a pure insurance charac-ter, whole life insurance was designed to combine pure insurance with a savings element, so that the whole life policy's cash value can be recouped by surrendering the policy. The cash value can also be borrowed (although the amount of benefits payable on the death of the insured will be reduced by the balance of any policy loans remaining at death).

Even today, basic whole life products feature a level premium computed based on the age at which the policy is initially purchased. The significance of this method of setting premiums is that it provides a strong incentive to purchase insurance early so as to "lock in" the lower level premium rate. This factor is also significant in long-term care insurance which is also usually sold with a level premium.

The usual whole life policy calls for premium payments (generally made annually or quarterly) throughout the insured's lifetime. This mode of payment is called *continuous premium* or *straight life*. However, the entire premium for lifetime coverage can be paid over a shorter duration resulting in a "paid up" policy. Such premiums may be paid either over a certain number of payments (e.g., "20 pay" or "30 pay") or until a certain age (e.g., age 65). The entire premium can even be paid in a *single premium*. The typical reasons for using a payment form other than continuous premium is to allow rapid access to the policy's cash value or because a lump sum is available and the purchase of paid-up insurance fits well into the general financial plan.

Under a *modified-premium whole life policy*, the level premium is set below the normal level for a certain period of time (such as the first five years the policy is owned). Then, to compensate, the premium rises somewhat higher than the premium for continuous payment and remains at that level. This plan might be chosen by a young family that expects its expenses to decline and its income to increase based on the career progress of the parents. The face value of the policy does not change despite the fluctuations in the premium.

However, the face value of some basic whole life policies can be modified, providing for one or more decreases in coverage at specified times or at specified ages. Because coverage decreases, the premium is lower than if it remained level. Again, this plan might be suitable for a young family, unable to afford the amount of insurance it needs on conventional terms, and willing to make the assumption that coverage needs will decline as the children get older and become self-supporting. Older clients, however, may feel that a policy of this type will not provide a high enough death benefit to meet the needs of the surviving spouse.

Universal Life Insurance

The impetus behind the creation of universal life insurance was a desire to give the insured greater flexibility in selecting coverage terms and changing them as family needs change. The conventional whole-life premium is a single amount calculated based on mortality predictions as well as the insurer's experience with its investments and administrative expenses. Payment of this premium gives the insured access to cash values that grow in a predictable fashion.

On the other hand, the cash value as well as the premium and face amount of a universal life insurance policy can be altered at the insured's option. Within limits set by the insurer, the insured controls the size of the premium he or she will pay. Naturally, the larger the premium, the higher the cash value of the policy, given a steady death benefit amount. In order to preserve the treatment of the contract as one of insurance rather than as pure investment, the Internal Revenue Code limits the amount of cash value in relation to the face value of the universal life policy.

When each premium is paid, the insurer deducts charges for its administrative expenses and for predicted mortality costs. Deductions for older insureds will be greater because they are at higher risk of dying than younger insureds. The rest of the premium is credited to the policy's cash value, plus interest at a fluctuating market-based rate, subject to a minimum rate such as 4%.

If the insured chooses to decrease the face amount, it may be necessary for him or her to withdraw part of the cash value in order to comply with the Internal Revenue Code guidelines. Increases in face amount will not raise this problem, but it is likely that the insurer will demand evidence of continued insurability.

Universal life insurance may be suitable for a newly retired client who is keenly interested in financial planning and investments, and who is willing and able to spend time considering when it is appropriate to adjust the policy's premium and/or face value. Universal life insurance works best when interest rates are high, so that the insured benefits from the growth of the cash value enhanced by high interest rates. When interest rates are low, the cash value does not grow as fast.

Universal life insurance is probably not suitable for an older person or couple with health problems and some decline in mental acuity, because they need stability and financial predictability and have decreased or insufficient ability to determine when the policy parameters should be changed.

For example, consider POLICY A which is a universal life policy optimized for the needs of senior citizen retirees. The death benefit (which can be up to twice the single premium used to purchase the policy) can be accelerated and used to pay for nursing home, home health care (at 100% of the institutional benefit), or adult day care, and can be triggered by cognitive impairment as well as physical ill-health. Cash value can also be withdrawn, or loans taken, for medical care or any other purpose. The policy can be issued at ages to 80. The long-term care benefits can be as much as twice the premium paid over 24 months (or, if an option is elected, as much as four times the premium paid over 48 months). The guaranteed minimum rate of return is 4% while, as of September 1996, the current market rate was 6.25%.

Variable Life Insurance

Variable life insurance was developed to provide a life insurance product similar to variable annuities. In return for either a single premium or a continuing stream of level premiums, the insurer issuing a variable life insurance policy provides life insurance with a face amount and cash value which are both dependent on the investment performance of one or more special funds offered by the insurer. The insurer guarantees a "floor" below which the face amount will not fall (e.g., the original face amount of the policy), so the insured will always have some insurance protection but usually does not guarantee cash value, which may fall to zero if the investment account performs badly.

Usually the insurer maintains several accounts representing different investment philosophies (growth, high income, growth and income) and permits the policyowner to choose the account in which his or her premiums will be invested, and to switch between accounts under specified conditions.

Combination policies known as *variable universal life* or *flexible-premium variable life* are also available. These are extremely flexible products that permit the policyowner to control both the premium and the face amount of the policy as well as select the investment account whose success will determine the policy's cash value. Therefore, it should be noted that these products demand a great deal of attention from the insured in choosing and monitoring a policy.

Variable and variable universal life policies must be approached with caution when planning for the older clients. Although investment-oriented insurance did provide excellent results during the 1980's bull market, investment conditions are often unsettled and the greater risk inherent in investment-oriented insurance may in fact yield poorer results than a conventional whole life policy. In mid-1993, for instance, the median current interest rate on Universal Life policies was 7%. In early 1994, the current interest rate typically had fallen to about 6% — versus 9% for some conventional cash-value whole life policies. There is always a risk that an older client will eventually suffer mental impairment, making him or her incapable of making adjustments to the policy or choosing investment accounts. Furthermore, if the face value of the policy diminishes, the policy proceeds may not be adequate to meet the needs of the surviving spouse or other beneficiary[1].

Second-to-Die Insurance

Before 1981, estate planners faced many difficult choices in deciding how much property should be left to the surviving spouse. At that time, the marital deduction under the estate and gift tax rules was quite limited. When the Economic Recovery Tax Act of 1981 (ERTA) was passed, it revolutionized estate planning by creating an unlimited marital deduction for both gift and estate tax purposes. Now, the planner can advise the transfer of the entire estate to the surviving spouse without worrying about estate tax at the death of the first spouse. A similar lifetime transfer can be made without worrying about gift tax.

However, just because the "all to my spouse" estate plan or lifetime gift plan is possible does not mean that it is a good idea for every couple. Although avoiding or minimizing estate tax is an important planning objective, it is not the only thing that matters. Medicaid concerns must always be examined. The estate plan must reflect the testator's wishes as to who should receive income and for how long as well as who should receive immediate or deferred distributions of property.

Furthermore, saving estate tax today can create a large tax bill tomorrow. ERTA also created the "second estate" problem that occurs when a large estate passes tax-free to the surviving spouse who then invests it or has it managed professionally. When the surviving spouse dies, the estate may be much larger because of investment appreciation. Thus, a large estate tax liability is created because, unless the surviving spouse remarries, there is no spouse who can take advantage of the marital deduction. However, if the economy in general and the stock market in particular decline during the surviving spouse's remaining years, and medical costs increase, the second estate problem may, unfortunately, solve itself. The surviving spouse may find the estate heavily depleted rather than increased.

The problem can be avoided in many ways. First, part of the estate can be transferred during the lifetime of the first spouse to die, thus reducing his or her estate. Second, bequests can be made to children or other intended beneficiaries, up to the $600,000 limit (equalling the minimum taxable estate), with the balance left to the surviving spouse. Under this plan, the surviving spouse can make lifetime gifts or otherwise reduce his or her estate below $600,000. Either spouse can make charitable gifts or bequests to reduce the estate. Last, but not least, the couple can buy second-to-die life insurance (also called survivor life), which serves many objectives including providing cash to pay estate taxes.

Most couples can avoid paying any estate tax on the first and the second estate, either because the potential estate is small or by combining various estate planning techniques. However, if there is an estate tax to pay, the bill is likely to be heavy.

PLANNING TIP: Check with the lawyer and accountant in your planning team about state inheritance or estate taxes. Although these are smaller than the federal tax, they can reduce an estate and generate a need for liquidity — both of which can increase the need for insurance coverage.

Remember that Congress originally scheduled a decrease in estate tax rates. However, as part of the Revenue Reconciliation Act of 1993, the estate tax rates were not rolled back. Therefore, the marginal tax rate on an estate of $2.5 million-$3 million remains at 53%. Estates in excess of $3 million will have a marginal bracket of 55%. Higher estate taxation naturally makes estate planning more pressing.

The second-to-die policy is purchased on the joint lives of a married couple. However, no benefits are payable at the death of the first spouse to die. Instead, benefits are paid when the survivor dies. Because cash is available to pay estate tax, depletion of the second estate is avoided, and much more money is available for the second spouse's heirs.

Second-to-die policies frequently have attractively low premiums, because the insurer is accepting a fairly low risk (these policies are usually sold to healthy couples) and deferring the risk. In fact, the cost can be lower than the cost of a policy on just one spouse's life. Medical underwriting of these policies is usually limited, so insurance may be available even if one spouse is a substandard risk[2].

Second-to-die insurance works as part of a coordinated plan. It is an estate planning technique, not a substitute for life insurance on each spouse's life that is necessary to provide funds for the survivor to live on. Furthermore, if a second-to-die policy is chosen imprudently, your client or clients may be too old to be underwritten for a better substitute policy.

PLANNING TIP: An IRS Private Letter Ruling (9542037) states that exchanging one or more single life insurance policies for second-to-die insurance does not constitute a tax-free exchange under Code §1035, so it may be better to purchase a new second-to-die policy if one is needed, rather than make an exchange.

A wide choice of second-to-die policies is available: participating whole life, whole life reflecting interest rate changes, universal life, a combination of participating whole life and term. The policy can be purchased with a single premium or with continuing premiums, with the option of making a large payment to convert the policy to paid-up status. The best policy for your client is the one that is cost-effective, and will perform well in both economic upturns and difficult times. The policy should reflect the fact that lapse rates are much lower for second-to-die than for other life insurance policies; the insurer must have enough money available to cope with the higher persistency.

It is common for different carriers to offer dramatically different premiums for second-to-die coverage in the same case. At first glance, it might appear that the prudent strategy is to select the lowest ledger. Obviously, it is essential to select a financially strong insurer which perhaps may shift preference to a somewhat higher-priced policy. But it is also essential to examine the realism of the assumptions behind the price quote. In many cases, a low premium is based on unrealistically high investment returns. Thus, the insured may have to put a great deal of money into the policy in later years to maintain it, or the survivor may receive far less than the projected amount.

PLANNING TIP: Does the insurer indicate better results for its second-to-die policy than for its individual life policies? If so, it may be subsidizing the second-to-die product and may end the subsidy in the future, leading to a large premium increase[3].

A second-to-die policy is a life insurance policy, so the usual rules apply as to whether the policy itself will be included in the estate of either spouse. If either spouse owns the policy — or owns it and transfers it within three years of death — the policy will be included in that spouse's estate. Insurance benefits payable to an estate are also included in the estate. Therefore, the second-to-die policy should be payable to a named insured and not to an estate. Furthermore, you must consider life expectancy if you advise a client to buy such a policy. Even if he or she transfers it, it may be included in the estate if death comes within three years. A simple answer (if family and financial conditions permit this) is to have one of the couple's adult children — perhaps one who will serve as executor — buy and hold the policy.

Trust Techniques

If an irrevocable insurance trust fits into the plan, the trust can purchase and maintain the second-to-die policy. Some planners suggest combining a marital trust and a credit shelter trust.[4] The credit shelter trust is created under the residuary clause of each spouse's will. (The residuary clause copes with assets that are not specifically given to someone else. For instance, the will could provide bequests of $50,000 each to the spouse and two children, with the rest, or residue, of the estate placed in trust.)

The "credit shelter" trust provides that, when the first spouse dies, enough assets will be put into the trust to use up the unified credit against estate and gift tax (i.e., the trust "shelters" the amount eligible for the unified credit; under current law, that means $600,000). The trust also provides that trust assets will not be distributed until the second spouse dies. The rest of the estate can be left to the surviving spouse, protected by the marital deduction. The credit shelter trust can own the second-to-die policy, but the trust provisions should make it clear that the cash value of the policy will be completely unavailable to the surviving spouse. If the surviving spouse has access to the cash value, the policy is included in the estate of the first spouse to die, because the policy can be used to meet the family financial obligations of the first spouse to die.

Another possibility is for one spouse's employer to buy the second-to-die policy (e.g., if he or she is the business owner or a key executive); or, the policy can be included in a split dollar plan.

PLANNING TIP: The economic benefit cost of a split dollar plan goes up a great deal when the first spouse dies. To avoid this cost, the corporation could borrow heavily against the cash value once the first spouse dies, then transfer the policy to the credit shelter trust. More than likely the corporation will only be interested in doing this if the spouse is very important to the corporation.

Sample Second-to-Die Policies

POLICY A is a universal life policy sold at individual issue ages 18-85, joint equal ages 25-80, but is unavailable if the age difference between coinsureds is more than 25 years. The minimum face amount under this plan is $250,000, and the death benefit can be either level or increasing. There is no policy fee, and the target premium for nonsmokers is $12.96/$1,000 at age 55. The policy is subject to a minimum premium of $300 or the minimum annual premium per $1,000 (based on joint equal age) plus the premium for riders and for a substandard life. There is a 2% premium expense charge and a monthly administration fee is charged during the first seven policy years. To prevent lapse, the minimum annual premium must be paid for the first five years of the policy.

The interest rate is guaranteed to be at least 5.25%. When the plan was introduced, its current interest rate was 9%. Policy loans and partial withdrawals after the first year are permitted.

POLICY B combines whole life and additional term features. Insureds can pay additional premiums as inside or outside paid-up additions. The minimum amount is $100,000 (with a minimum of $1,000 each of whole life and term), available at joint equal ages 20-85. The policy can be issued to one standard risk and one nonsmoker, two standard risks, or two nonsmokers. Instead of an extra premium, applicants in substandard classes A-K and permanent flat ratings are subject to an age rate-up. There is an extra premium for temporary flat ratings. The policy is even available (albeit at an adjusted joint equal age) for one uninsurable spouse and one spouse who is younger than 76 and not rated. The policy pays dividends after the second year (with an extra dividend for policies over $1 million). The policy's guaranteed interest rate is 4.5%; loans can be taken at either an 8% fixed rate or a variable rate.

POLICY C is a participating whole life policy with a guaranteed level premium. It can be issued, with a minimum face amount of $250,000, up to a maximum age of 85, but the age difference between the insureds cannot exceed 26 years. Substandard classes are handled with an age rate-up. There is a $50 policy fee. The plan was launched with a 9.9% dividend rate and a guaranteed interest rate of 5.5%. Policy loans are subject to variable interest rate (8.86% when the plan began). The plan is not available if one of the lives is uninsurable. Individual term riders are not available, but a second death term rider is; the term portion of the plan can be converted to permanent insurance without evidence of insurability.

POLICY D combines a base plan, an annual renewable term rider, and paid-up additions. There are four classes: preferred, smoker, nonsmoker, and substandard. The policy is available at individual ages 15-80, joint equal age at issue to 85. At least $100,000 face value of base policy, $1,000 for the annual term rider, must be purchased. There is a $40 policy fee. The annual premium for nonsmokers at 55 is $17.03 per $1,000 in states allowing rates to differ for the two sexes, $17.20 in the states mandating unisex rates. Cash values do not change after the first death. The cash value can be taken in cash, used to convert the plan to a smaller paid-up policy, or borrowed (the rate on policy loans is a fixed 8%). There are seven dividend options (cash payment, premium reduction, purchase of term insurance on various conditions, accumulation earning interest).

POLICY E is an interest-sensitive whole life policy. There are several premium options (standard and preferred smoker and non-smoker) and four face amount patterns. The minimum issue amount is $500,000. There is no maximum amount. The policy can be issued to age 90 for standard risks. It is available with a non-spouse second life (e.g., for business succession planning). As of August, 1993, the current interest and dividend rate was 6.9%, but this rate was not guaranteed. Also as of this date, policy loans are available at a variable rate of 7.86%. Additional lump-sum contributions can be made, subject to a 5% load.

POLICY F is a variable universal life second-to-die policy, with 18 investment options (a fixed account, seven in-house variable funds, and 10 mutual funds). Its aim is to provide a guaranteed death benefit of $250,000 or more to high-worth individuals (i.e., those at high risk for estate taxation). The permissible issue ages are 30-90; the ages of the two insureds must not total more than 170 at issue.

The policy can be issued even if one spouse is uninsurable. A four-year term rider can be used to pay the estate taxes if the second spouse to die dies within four years of the issuance of the policy. There are surrender charges for the first 20 years of the policy. During the first decade, policy loans are available (at up to 90% of surrender value) at a 2% interest charge; there is no interest charge for loans after the tenth year.

A common feature in many second-to-die policies is the "exchange option", under which the policy can be split in two if the couple divorces, or if tax laws change to make the tax consequences of current second-to-die policies unfavorable. Some insurers will permit an unequal split (with the spouse with higher assets getting the larger policy); others insist on a 50-50 split.

LIVING BENEFITS (ACCELERATED BENEFITS)

Originally, life insurance policies served the single, simple purpose of providing survivors with cash for living expenses after the death of the insured person. Then, partially in response to criticisms that life insurance policies were poor investments, the insurance industry developed policies such as universal life and variable life that provided an easy way to invest while also securing life insurance coverage. In effect, ULI and VLI combine death benefits with investment benefits during the life of the insured person.

Some people feel that the next step is to make the death benefit more freely available to the insured person during his or her lifetime. To a certain extent, this can be done by policy loans — but this is not an option for a term policy, or a policy with small cash value (perhaps because it was recently purchased). Extensive life insurance coverage may mean that the family will be adequately provided for after the insured person's death. In the meantime, the family of an incapacitated or terminally ill person can be crippled by medical or nursing-home bills.

One possibility, known as "viatication" (from the Latin word for supplies taken along on a journey — in this case, the final journey) is for a terminally ill person to gain cash by the outright sale of a life insurance policy to an enterprise specializing in such transactions. Typically, anywhere from 60-80% of the face value of the policy can be realized, at the cost of losing the insurance protection. Although there is an obvious potential for abuse in this practice (and, generally, the companies doing it are not insurance companies, and therefore are not subject to regulation by state insurance departments), advocates believe that policyholders should have the maximum flexibility to use their insurance for health costs. Problems to be resolved include how much disclosure should be made to policyholders and to those who would be beneficiaries if the policy were not sold (protection of minor children is especially crucial); what happens if the insured and the policyholder are not the same person; the tax treatment of the sales proceeds; and whether the proceeds will be considered an asset to terminally ill Medicaid applicants or recipients (and, if so, whether the Medicaid agencies will force applicants to sell their policies and spend down the proceeds before the application is granted).

The policy sale option is not very relevant (though not necessarily useless) for senior citizens because the Medicare system does a pretty good job of taking care of the hospital and medical bills occasioned by a severe or terminal illness. Also note that the companies that buy policies usually limit their purchases to fairly large policies (at least $50,000); many people have smaller policies and still need cash immediately[5].

The companies handling these transactions ("viatical settlement companies") are usually not insurance companies, so they were not regulated by state insurance regulators. However, as viatication becomes more accepted, states will probably increase their degree of supervision.

Living Benefit Riders Since 1987

There is an increasing demand that the insurance industry itself do something to meet the needs of those with catastrophically high acute medical or nursing home bills. This demand is being met by development of living benefit or accelerated benefit riders for life insurance policies[6]. These riders pay part of the death benefit (usually 2% per month, perhaps subject to a dollar limit) to policyholders who choose this way of paying nursing home or other bills. Payment of benefits reduces the face amount and cash value of the policy. Under most living benefit riders, there is no requirement that the accelerated benefits be devoted to health costs — the funds can be used for general financial planning purposes.

This is a very new product. These riders were first noted in 1983, in South Africa. They next appeared in Britain in 1985. The first use in the United States seems to have been in 1987, when National Travelers permitted acceleration of life insurance benefits for long-term care (LTC) costs.

Figures from LIMRA and the American College show that 1991 was the peak year for introduction of ADB products, with 14 new products (representing a 52% market share) coming on-line, versus only one new product in 1989 and six each in 1990 and 1992. Their research shows that, as of April 30, 1992, there were 2,381,715 policies in force with ADB features, although only about 80,000 of these were triggered by the need for long-term care.

PRACTICE TIP: If your client is in need of funds for catastrophic medical expenses, yet does not have and cannot be underwritten for such a rider, it may be possible to enter into an extra contractual arrangement to accelerate benefits with the insurer. Insurers feel compassion for the critically ill and their financial problems — and anyway, the insurer can limit the payment based on the time value of money; if the person is that sick, the insurer would have to pay out the death benefit pretty soon anyway.

The variables involved with living benefit riders are:

(1)   Permissible entry age — can be anywhere from 65 to 80.

(2)   Type of policy for which this rider is offered — can be for any whole life policy; universal life policy; or universal life policy and interest-sensitive whole life.

(3)   Conditions triggering benefits — can be terminal illness; named catastrophic illness (usually including Alzheimer's Disease); or named catastrophic illness or need for custodial nursing-home care.

(4)   Maximum payout — can have a dollar limit; a percentage of the face value of the underlying policy; or no limit.

(5)   Whether the payout is made in a lump sum (more suitable for a terminal illness than for nursing home care) or over time.

PLANNING TIP: Of course, good claims service is an important factor in choosing among competing insurers. But it becomes crucial when benefits are needed *immediately* and the sick person does not have time to wait or strength to make repeated contacts with the insurer to collect the benefits.

(6)   Waiting period — for these benefits, there may be a prior hospitalization requirement or a "step-down" requirement; or, benefits may be delayed until nursing home confinement has continued for a certain period (e.g., 90 days).

(7)   Premium — usually 10-15% of the premium for the base coverage. Over the past several years several companies have announced that they will offer living benefits coverage on all new and existing policies as a no-additional-cost benefit, not an optional rider at extra cost[7]. Many companies treat the payout as a lien (not a policy loan), and charge interest on the policy amount, which becomes part of the lien.

Since most younger buyers of insurance have not yet purchased stand-alone LTC policies, it may be that these ADB riders to life insurance policies will be more attractive to younger buyers who are enhancing their life insurance coverage. The life insurance policy, unlike most LTC policies, offers cash value — which younger buyers often want to have available as a source of policy loans. Furthermore, the rider can be less expensive than a stand-alone LTC policy.

However, the insurance industry will have to be careful. The data has not yet been gathered to make fully valid actuarial calculations. Although the risk of adverse selection is lower for riders than for stand-alone LTC products, it is still meaningful. The risk of certain kinds of morbidity (such as heart attacks) among senior citizens is much higher than the risk of mortality; plans will have to be designed, and adapted as newer, better data is collected, to cope with the actuarial risk. And, of course, agents who are used to dealing only with life insurance concepts must understand the new riders, and be able to explain them well to prospects, who are by and large unfamiliar with this coverage.

Accelerated Death Benefits (ADB) and Viatication

Before the August, 1996 passage of the Health Insurance Portability and Accountability Act of 1996 (P.L. 104-191), accelerated death benefits (paid by the insurer that issued the life insurance policy whose benefits were being accelerated) and viatical settlements (paid by a third party settlement company in the business of purchasing insurance policies at a discount from terminally ill persons) were most commonly used by dying AIDS patients.

One effect of the 1996 legislation was to clarify some disputed tax issues. In effect, the act provides that long-term care benefits paid from contracts which were issued after 1996 and which meet the Internal Revenue Code's definition of a "qualified long term care contract" are received income tax free within certain limits. Basically, the act treats long-term care benefits as if received from an accident and health insurance policy.

The 1996 legislation also extends these benefits to a "chronically ill" person who is not terminally ill. In short, a person is chronically ill if he or she is severely cognitively impaired or unable to perform two or more activities of daily living without substantial assistance. Therefore, lifetime access of death benefits can become a mainstream planning device that can be taken into account if funds are needed to pay for home care, physical therapy, a nursing home, or other long-term care.

However, caution must be exercised. After all, the insured person bought the life insurance policy based on a planning need, usually a desire to provide for the financial security of a surviving spouse or companion. Unless there are factors that mean that financial imperative no longer exists, or unless the insured's need for long-term care is so urgent that funds must be found from any available source, accelerating death benefits or viaticating the policy will frustrate the original motive for buying the insurance.

Early in this decade, the viatication industry was a fairly small. However, the number of policies purchased and the face amount involved in the purchases has increased dramatically and is expected to continue to increase over the next several years, especially if the practice becomes more common for persons other than end-stage AIDS patients.

The New Rules

When a terminally ill or chronically ill individual (and not, for instance, a corporation that owns a key-person insurance policy) viaticates a policy or accelerates its death benefits, funds can be received tax-free. (In some circumstances, part of the funds will be taxable.)

The 1996 legislation defines a terminally ill person as one whose life expectancy is 24 months or less. (This is a longer time period than is used in some other contexts, where terminal illness is defined as a life expectancy of six months, 12 months or less.) As mentioned earlier, a person is chronically ill if he or she is severely cognitively impaired or unable to perform two or more activities of daily living without substantial assistance.

The Internal Revenue Code distinguishes between terminally and chronically ill persons for tax purposes. The terminally ill can receive the accelerated death benefits or viatical settlement free of income tax and use these funds for any purpose. However, amounts paid to a chronically ill individual are subject to the same limitations that apply to long-term care benefits. Generally, this is a $175 per day limitation. However, if actual costs for long-term care services exceeds this amount, the chronically ill individual may receive the cost amount tax free.

In most instances, the death benefit or viatical settlement will be received in lump-sum form. Under the 1996 legislation, the entire lump sum is tax-free for terminally ill persons. However, for chronically ill individuals who receive a continuing stream of payments the tax free amounts are limited to amounts of up to $175 per day or larger amounts that are equal to or less than the actual cost of care. But amounts over both $175 and the actual cost of care constitute taxable income.

When the transaction involves a third-party viatical settlement company and/or a viatical settlement broker, a viatical settlement provider must be licensed by the state in which the viator (person assigning the policy) lives. If the state doesn't have licensing rules for viatical settlement companies (and many states do not; this business is not heavily regulated, despite the potential for abuse), then the settlement provider must satisfy Sections 8 and 9 of the National Association of Insurance Commissioners (NAIC) Viatical Settlement Model Act and the corresponding Model Regulation dealing with the reasonableness of payments made pursuant to a viatical settlement.

Regulation of Living Benefit Riders

Some states take the position that no special permission or regulation of living benefit riders is necessary. Under this theory, living benefits are merely an extension of policy loans and the right to change the beneficiary designation. They are simply rights that the policyholder has as the owner of property and as a party to a contract with the insurer.

Other states have either adopted regulations or laws governing these riders, or are contemplating such action. The National Association of Insurance Commissioners (NAIC) has developed a model law and Connecticut has adopted a law similar to the NAIC's model, and Oregon used the NAIC model as a policy guideline. Alaska, Arizona, Colorado, Idaho, Illinois, Indiana, Kansas, Maine, Michigan, Minnesota, Mississippi, Missouri, Montana, New York, Oklahoma, South Dakota, Texas, and Virginia have adopted related laws and regulations.

Important issues confronting state legislatures include whether the state should impose minimum standards on the policies, how they should be advertised, and whether limitations should be placed on premiums and payout structures. Furthermore, it must be determined if the same rules should apply to individual and group policies such as group-term life insurance provided by employers. The employer, in this situation, is the actual owner of the policy.

Under the Model Regulation, which covers provisions of both individual and group policies (but does not cover products already regulated by the Long-Term Care Insurance Model Act), accelerated benefits are those payable to a policyowner or group plan certificate-holder, triggered by a single qualifying event. The Model Regulation specifies five types of qualifying events:

(1)   Terminal illness (one limiting the lifespan to the extent specified in the contract — e.g., to 24 months or less).

(2)   Need for extraordinary, life-preserving medical intervention such as an organ transplant or use of a life support system.

(3)   A condition that shortens lifespan drastically unless extensive medical treatment is provided — e.g., end-stage renal failure, AIDS, post-stroke neurological problems.

(4)   Qualifying event proposed by the insurer and approved by the state Insurance Commissioner.

(5)   Finally the most relevant event for our purposes is, "Any condition which usually requires continuous confinement in an eligible institution defined in the contract if the insured is expected to remain there for the rest of his or her life."

PLANNING TIP: This requirement could be problematic. Not only do some nursing home patients return to the community (or enter hospitals for acute treatment), but this provision could be used by alert Medicaid agencies to treat the insured person's home as having ceased to be a homestead, if the insured person collects benefits premised on leaving home for good.

The NAIC Model Regulation treats the accelerated benefits riders as primarily a mortality, not a morbidity risk, and thus properly regulated as life insurance, not accident and health insurance. The Model also requires consent of any assignee or irrevocable beneficiary before accelerating benefits. The insured person must be given the choice between a lump sum and periodic payout — but the benefit cannot be offered as a life annuity for the insured's lifetime. Nor may the insurer restrict the use of the proceeds by demanding that they be used to pay health care costs.

The question of disclosure is handled by requiring that the riders be described as "accelerated benefit" riders, and forbidding them to be called, or marketed as, LTC insurance. Furthermore, both at the time of policy application and when an application is made for accelerated benefits, the insured person must be warned to seek tax advice about the taxability of the benefits. Policy applicants must be warned in writing about the effect of benefit payments on cash value, death benefit, accumulation amount, premium, policy loans, and policy liens. If there is a premium for the coverage, the insurer must also give the policy applicant a numerical illustration (or example) showing the effect of paying the benefit on the cash value and other policy features.

PRACTICE TIP: Under the Model, agents must provide the disclosure form and the illustration with or before the application is given to the policy applicant, and the writing agent must sign the disclosure form along with the applicant. If the policy or rider is sold by direct response, the insurer must provide the disclosure form when the policy is delivered, with disclosure of a 30-day free look period.

Whenever a policyowner or certificate-holder applies to receive accelerated benefits, the insurer must disclose both to the policyowner/certificate-holder *and* any irrevocable beneficiary the effect of the payment — including a warning that acceleration may harm a Medicaid application, and a notice that tax advice is needed.

Premiums or cost of insurance charges are permitted for accelerated benefit premiums and riders (naturally — the insured is getting an additional benefit), but the charges must be actuarially justified and not excessive. The payment can be stated as the present value of the face amount, using "any applicable actuarial discount appropriate to the policy design", with an actuarially sound interest rate or interest rate methodology, not to exceed either the current maximum interest rate charged on policy loans, or the current yield on 90-day Treasury bills (whichever is greater). The same interest rate limitation is imposed on the interest charge the insurer accrues on the amount of the accelerated benefits paid out; and the interest rate on the part of the lien up to the cash value cannot exceed the contract's stated policy loan interest rate.

Although it is permissible to charge a premium, there is a trend for insurers to make ADB riders available without additional charge — either only on newly-issued policies, or on the existing policy base as well as policies issued after the date the company adopts the practice of offering ADB at no additional cost.

When an accelerated benefit is paid out, the insurer has two choices. First, cash value can be reduced, but no more than pro rata based on the percentage of benefits accelerated. The payment "may not be applied toward repaying an amount greater than a pro-rata portion of any outstanding policy loans."

The other choice is to treat the accelerated benefits, administrative expense charges, future premiums, and accrued interest all as a lien against the death benefit. In this case, the insurer is permitted to limit the benefit that can be accelerated to the amount by which the cash value exceeds these amounts plus other outstanding loans, and future policy loans can also be limited to excess cash value.

NAIC Rulemaking on Viatication

The National Association of Insurance Commissioners' (NAIC) Viatical Settlements Model Act was promulgated in January, 1994. It has been adopted, in whole or in part, in less than half the states: California, Indiana, Kansas, Louisiana, Minnesota, New York, North Carolina, North Dakota, Oregon, Pennsylvania, Vermont, Virginia, Washington, and Wisconsin; similar laws have been passed in New Mexico, Texas, and Utah.

The Model Act defines a viatical settlement broker as an individual or business entity that offers or advertises viatical settlements or connects settlement providers with potential viators, in return for compensation such as a fee or commission. Attorneys, accountants, and financial planners who are paid by the potential viator rather than the settlement provider do not fall within the definition.

It defines a viatical settlement contract as a written agreement establishing terms under which an insurance policy will be sold, assigned, or bequeathed for less than its expected death benefit. In other words, the provider's profit comes from the difference between the death benefit and the amount it pays the viator.

A viatical settlement provider is an individual or business entity who purchases more than one policy a year. The definition doesn't cover banks or savings and loan institutions, or the insurance company that issued the policy—it is subject to the Accelerated Death Benefits model rules.

The Model Act requires licensure of settlement providers, by the insurance commissioner, who has the power to revoke licenses if improprieties are detected. Viatical settlement contract forms must be filed in advance with the commissioner, who is deemed to approve of a contract if 60 days elapse without notification of disapproval. Potential grounds for disapproval include provisions that are unreasonable, contrary to the public interest, misleading, or unfair to the viator. The insurance commissioner's powers also extend to examining the business and financial affairs of licensees and license applicants. Once the license is granted, an annual report must be made to the commissioner.

Like most insurance Model Acts, this one contains disclosure provisions. The potential viator is entitled to these disclosures, not later than the date on which the contract is signed by all parties:

- Alternatives (such as accelerated death benefits and policy loans) to viatication that are available to terminally and chronically ill individuals

- The need to get advice about the tax consequences of the transaction (this provision pre-dates the 1996 legislation, but tax advice is still useful)

- The fact that viatical settlement proceeds are potentially subject to the claims of the viator's creditors

- The need for advice about the potential consequences of receiving the benefits on Medicaid eligibility (however, some states have ruled that the benefits are not assets for Medicaid purposes)

- The right to rescind the settlement contract within 30 days of the date all parties sign the contract, or within 15 days of receiving the proceeds — whichever comes first

- When the viator will receive the money. If the money is not paid on time, this renders the contract null and void.

The settlement provider has an obligation to get a written statement from a doctor that each applicant to viaticate is of sound mind and is not subject to compulsion or undue influence to enter into the transaction. The applicant must sign a statement (with witnesses) consenting to the transaction and disclosing the viator's medical condition, releasing medical records, and affirming that the viator understands the terms of the transaction and enters into it voluntarily.

All viatical settlement contracts must provide for unconditional refunds during a period of 15-30 days. Once the viator submits the necessary documents for viaticating the policy, the settlement provider has an obligation to put the settlement proceeds into an escrow or trust account approved by the state insurance commissioner, pending the policy issuer's acknowledgment of the transfer.

The NAIC Model Act gives state insurance commissioners the authority to promulgate standards in areas such as bonds, licensing, discount rates on viatication transactions, and fees paid to agents and brokers.

The Viatical Settlements Model Regulation has been adopted in only three states (North Carolina, Oregon, and Vermont), and has influenced the regulations of New York, Texas, and Washington. It's worth discussing because it includes some interesting provisions — even though they have not been widely adopted.

The Model Regulation contains a procedure for licensing viatical settlement brokers and providers. Brokers must maintain errors and omissions (E&O) policies in amounts reflecting their risk exposure. The license can be suspended, revoked, or non-renewed if the broker is guilty of fraud, dishonesty, misrepresentation in the license application, or attempting to place a viatical settlement with a non-licensed provider.

The Model Regulation also suggests the minimum percentage of the policy face value (net of any loans) that the viator should receive. If the viator's life expectancy is under six months, the percentage is 80%, declining as the life expectancy increases (70% for life expectancy of 6-12 months, 65% for 12-18 months, 60% if 18-24 months, and 50% if 24 months or more). The percentage can be reduced by 5% if the insurer does not have a high rating from rating services such as A.M. Best (i.e., if the settlement provider takes on extra risk because of the status of the issuer of the underlying insurance).

Another issue that is addressed is the manner of payment: proceeds are sent by wire transfer to the viator's account, or paid by certified check. The normal payment is a lump sum; periodic payments are only allowed if the viatical settlement provider buys an annuity or similar financial instrument is purchased from a bank or insurance company.

All advertisements for viatical settlements must be truthful, not misleading, and must disclose the time period from application to settlement offer and from settlement offer to receipt of funds. If an advertisement mentions dollar amounts that are available, it must disclose the average purchase price as a percentage of face value that viators have actually obtained from that provider in the past six months.

In addition to NAIC rulemaking, the industry trade group, the National Viatical Association (NVA), published its own model act and regulation in late 1996. The NVA says that in 1995, about 5,000 terminally ill persons viaticated about $400 million in insurance face value; in that year, only 300 people were involved in accessing about $25 million in death benefits. The NVA's estimate of 1996 viatical settlements is about $500 million.

Sample Living Benefits Riders and Policies

RIDER A can be purchased incident to a universal life policy at entry ages 20-75; the premium increases with age, but is a modest $3.47 per $1,000 at male entry age 60, with waiver of premium during the period of benefit payments and 90 days afterward. Up to 100% of the face value of the ULI policy can be paid out in accelerated benefits.

RIDER B can be purchased up to age 65 with any of the issuer's whole life policies, at a level cost of 12% of the whole life premium. Up to 30% of the face amount of the policy is payable in a lump sum on diagnosis of named catastrophic illnesses, including incapacitation by Alzheimer's disease, serious heart attack, or disabling stroke.

PLANNING TIP: This means that there is a likelihood of disagreement about the seriousness of a given person's condition, and whether it should trigger benefit payments.

RIDER C, available with all of the issuer's ULI and interest-sensitive whole life policies, has a level premium. Purchase is permitted up to age 75; the premium is $8.14 per $1,000 of face amount of life insurance. Up to 25% of the face amount is available in a lump sum upon diagnosis of Alzheimer's disease, heart attack, stroke, or other named catastrophic illness.

PLANNING TIP: The percentage limitation ensures that a balance will be struck between lifetime benefits and the benefits for survivors that are the original motivation for the creation of insurance plans.

RIDER D, available at issue ages 20-65 as a rider to a ULI policy of $50,000 or over, pays up to 50% of the face amount of the base policy, up to a maximum of $10,000 a month. The benefit can be accelerated at 2% of face amount per month for skilled nursing facility (SNF) or intermediate care facility (ICF) care, or 1% a month for purely custodial non-medical care or for home care (after 31 days of prior confinement in a nursing facility, or "stepping down" to custodial care within 31 days of receiving nursing care). The cost of the rider is about 10% of the base premium.

There is a 100-day waiting period for coverage, and the insured must hold the base policy for three years before making a claim for accelerated benefits. Cost-of-insurance charges are waived while accelerated payments are made; the issuer estimates that most insureds will be able to keep the policy in force to age 95 without further premium payments, based on the policy's cash value.

RIDER E is available on term, whole life, and universal life policies. A terminally ill person (life expectancy under 12 months) can receive one or more lump sums, with a minimum of $500 and a maximum of the smaller of $250,000 or 65% of the available amount (existing liens and policy loans reduce the available amount). The payout serves as a lien against the death benefit. The interest rate on the lien is the greater of the 90-day T-bill rate or Moody's Corporate Bond Yield Average. There is no premium for this rider, but an administrative charge of up to $250 can be imposed.

RIDERS F AND F PLUS are nursing home and home-care oriented. Purchasers aged 20-75 of ULI policies paying death benefits of $25,000 or more (no maximum) can buy either rider. Rider F pays up to 50% of the death benefit; Rider F Plus pays up to 100%. The cost of the rider is deducted from the account value. The monthly benefit for nursing home care is 2% of the first $150,000 of face amount, 0.5% of any excess over $150,000. There is no prior hospitalization requirement for nursing home care, but there is a 90-day waiting period. Home health care is also covered, at a rate of 50% of the benefits payable for nursing home care, and subject to the same 90-day waiting period and a three-day prior hospitalization or 20-day prior nursing home care requirement. Home health benefits are payable for up to six months per spell of illness, with a lifetime maximum of 24 months.

Accelerated benefits are treated as a no-interest first lien against the death benefit, not as a policy loan.

POLICY A combines interest-sensitive whole life and an accelerated benefit factor of 25% of the death benefit (plus 25% of any premiums paid after the insured becomes entitled to accelerated benefits, and 25% of unpaid premiums applying to the period before entitlement for accelerated benefits). In effect, this is a combination of two policies: the smaller one terminates when accelerated benefits become payable; the other continues in force. Acceleration is available for five named conditions: heart attack; stroke; coronary artery surgery; life-threatening cancer; and renal failure.

SELECTION AND ALTERATION OF THE BENEFICIARY: INSURANCE TRANSFERS

In the simplest case, an individual purchases a policy on his or her own life, makes all the premium payments, always has access to any cash value under the policy, and always controls the investment decisions to the extent permitted by the policy. He or she names a beneficiary and contingent beneficiary (who will be entitled to policy benefits only after the death of the initial beneficiary), and never changes the designation. One person, a group of persons, a corporation, an organization, or an estate can be named as primary or contingent beneficiary.

Even this simple case can create some problems. For instance, a married man could name "my wife" as the beneficiary, and "my children" as the contingent beneficiaries. At the time of the purchase of the policy, he could be married to Lisa, yet be married to Cathy at the time of his death or there could be two children when the policy is purchased, but four when he dies. This problem can be resolved by identifying the beneficiary by name instead of or in addition to title, by consulting state law to see what effect divorce has on beneficiary designation, and by carefully reviewing all financial consequences, including insurance implications, when divorce is being considered.

Furthermore, minor children have legal limitations on their ownership of property. To avoid the necessity of appointing a guardian for minors who are beneficiaries or contingent beneficiaries, the better method is to make an adult the beneficiary as guardian or custodian for the minors, or to specify that the benefits be paid to a trust for the minors. (Life insurance trusts in general are discussed in Chapter 11 in connection with other types of trust in the plan for senior citizen clients.)

The selected beneficiary will, of course, be someone the owner of the policy wants to benefit. Frequently, for senior citizen clients, the spouse will be chosen as beneficiary. It is especially important in this situation to choose contingent beneficiaries carefully — because it is not unlikely that the beneficiary spouse will predecease the insured spouse or that they will die at the same time or within so short a period of time that the surviving spouse will not have time to revise financial and insurance plans. Further, the surviving spouse (even if he or she has legal capacity) may be too confused to attend to insurance matters.

There are, however, some situations in which the spouse is not the appropriate beneficiary. For instance, the spouse could be a Medicaid beneficiary, or a nursing home resident likely to make a Medicaid application soon. In such cases, receiving a large sum of money from an insurance policy, or receiving significant additional income from settlement options, would probably make the receipt of Medicaid benefits impossible. The owner of the policy would probably be better advised to bypass the spouse and name a child, other relative or friend, or charity as the policy beneficiary.

Another reason to bypass the spouse as beneficiary is that the spouse may simply not need the insurance funds because he or she has ample personal funds or is well provided for under the other spouse's will while other family members may be badly off financially. However, remember that life insurance plays a very valuable role in providing liquidity. Even a wealthy widow or widower may suffer a temporary liquidity crisis when joint accounts are sealed after death and before the will is probated — a crisis that can be alleviated by receiving life insurance benefits.

For widowed, divorced, or single people, the choice of beneficiary can be more difficult. Policyowners with children often wish to benefit their children. A cohabitant or other companion, relatives such as siblings, nieces and nephews, or grandchildren, a friend, or a favored charity are other possibilities.

Under most life insurance policies, designation of a beneficiary is revocable. That is, the owner of the policy can change his or her mind about who should be the beneficiary, as often as he or she likes. Furthermore, the owner can exercise other incidents of ownership, such as borrowing against cash value, even at the risk of diminishing the benefits eventually available to the beneficiary. The person originally selected as beneficiary has no legal right to protest.

However, changing the beneficiary is a business transaction, and contractual capacity is required. Therefore, a person who is unconscious, mentally ill, or suffering from an illness such as Alzheimer's disease, and who lacks capacity, *cannot* change the beneficiary designation. Any of these fates may befall your senior citizen clients, so advise them of the possibility that a change in beneficiary designation might be impossible when it is required by good planning.

The policyowner can also make an irrevocable beneficiary designation. The effect of an irrevocable designation is to make the beneficiary a co-owner of the policy, whose consent is required before changing the beneficiary or exercising other incidents of ownership. (If the irrevocable beneficiary dies first, the policy terms usually used make the original policyowner who made the designation once again the sole owner of the policy.)

Note that the discussion above refers to the "policyowner." The simplest case is for the insured to purchase and own the policy on his or her own life. However, other mechanisms are possible. Anyone with an insurable interest (roughly speaking, a financial interest in the insured person's life) can buy a policy on another person's life. For instance, one spouse can buy a policy on the life of the other; children can insure their parents, or vice versa. In these cases, the person purchasing the policy is the owner and entitled to exercise the incidents of ownership (e.g., borrowing against cash value or designating or changing a beneficiary).

A life insurance policy is an item of property. Its owner can sell it or give it away. There are many reasons why this might be done. The Internal Revenue Code excludes from the federal gift tax gifts of up to $10,000 per year per donee (or $20,000 per year per donee if the donor's spouse joins in or consents to the gift). Giving a child an annual $10,000 or $20,000 gift with which to purchase insurance on the donor's life will provide a very significant benefit when the donor dies. Or, if the child has a young family and few assets, the parent/donor can give the money to pay insurance premiums to insure the child's own life, thus, providing security for the family. Of course the gift could be made directly, but a gift with equivalent "bang for the buck" would be more expensive and might give rise to an income tax liability. The parent could also leave money to the child by will, but that would reduce the estate available to the spouse or other beneficiaries.

Insurance gifts can also be an economical way to provide substantial tax-deductible benefits to a favorite charity. However, if this is your client's desire, make sure that he or she gets specialized tax advice since the law varies from state to state as to whether the lack of an insurable interest will affect the availability of a tax deduction associated with the transfer of a policy to a charity.

Perhaps the most common reason for transferring a life insurance policy is the desire to prevent the policy proceeds from being included in the estate of the insured for federal estate tax purposes. Proceeds will be included in the estate if they are made payable to the estate. This is not a problem in the small estate, but could be very expensive in an estate large enough to be subjected to federal estate tax.

Inclusion in the estate can be avoided if proceeds are payable to a named beneficiary such as a spouse, child, or friend — but only if the insured had no incidents of ownership in the policy at death, or at any time within three years before death. Some married couples cope with this requirement by purchasing policies on the lives of their spouses rather than their own lives; others, by transfer of the policy in the hope that death will occur more than three years after the transfer.

Another reason for transferring policies is Medicaid planning. A small amount of life insurance cash value is an exempt asset for Medicaid purposes. Ownership of a larger amount of cash value is likely to be treated as an excess resource that will delay the time at which Medicaid benefits are provided.

A couple's resources are assessed as part of a Medicaid application; transfer of an insurance policy from one spouse to another will not remove the cash value from this "snapshot." Transfer of the policy to the spouse might make the policy an excess asset if the second spouse makes a Medicaid application. Even if the transferee spouse tries to solve the problem by retransferring the policy to someone else, the retransfer might be considered in connection with the other spouse's Medicaid application.

TAX IMPLICATIONS OF LIFE INSURANCE

Life insurance is valuable as a way to create an "instant estate" when other financial assets are limited. Furthermore, Section 101 of the Internal Revenue Code gives favorable treatment to life insurance proceeds. If a beneficiary receives money under a life insurance contract by reason of the death of the insured person (as distinct from retirement benefits or payments under employment contracts that are merely *funded* by insurance), the actual death benefits paid will not be taxable income for the beneficiary. The entire amount of the death benefit, unreduced by income tax, can be used for family needs. This is generally true whether or not the beneficiary paid the premiums for the policy, as long as the beneficiary had an insurable interest in the life of the insured.

However, the general rule that proceeds are not taxable income to the beneficiary has several exceptions. One of them is the "transfer for value" rule of Code section 101(a)(2), under which proceeds of a policy that was transferred for value (e.g., sold, not given) will only be exempt from income taxation in an amount equal to the consideration paid by the transferee plus premiums paid by the transferee after the transfer. The rest of the proceeds are taxable income to the transferee. The transfer for value rule applies if only certain interests in a policy are transferred, but does not apply if the policy is transferred to the insured person, a partnership in which the insured is a partner or a corporation in which the insured is a shareholder or officer.

Although most life insurance benefits are paid in lump-sum form, this is not the sole permissible payment method. "Settlement options" are other methods of payment. The owner of the policy can elect the eventual form of payment; if no method of payment was chosen by the time the insured dies, the beneficiary has the right to choose the payment method. For instance, the policy proceeds can be left on deposit with the insurer, who pays interest to the beneficiary until payment of the proceeds is demanded. The proceeds (plus interest) can be disbursed in installments: perhaps a certain number of installments, installments of a fixed size, or installments over the lifetime of the beneficiary. A person who cannot or does not want to manage money may prefer a settlement option to receiving insurance proceeds in a lump sum which might be lost or mismanaged.

PRACTICE TIP: Before a client selects a settlement option, make sure he or she fully understands the Medicaid implication of the choice. In a state with a "medically needy" program, a settlement option that provides regular income could be a good idea. The lump sum would almost certainly limit Medicaid eligibility (unless it could be transferred before the penalty period); in a "medically needy" state, excess income can be "spent down" on medical care. But in an "income cap" state, *any* excess income makes Medicaid benefits unavailable, so income from a settlement option could be a real disadvantage.

For income tax purposes, the *interest* paid by the insurer on settlement options, as distinct from the death benefit itself, is taxable income to the beneficiary according to Code section 101(c). Therefore, Code sections 101(d)(1) and Regulations §1.101-4(a)(1)(i) provide that, unless the amount paid out is defined so that it cannot exceed the amount payable at the death of the insured, each payment made to the beneficiary must be prorated — divided into a taxable and a nontaxable component.

For these rules to be applicable, the benefits must be paid under a "life insurance contract." This is not a serious issue for conventional whole-life policies, but might be difficult for some universal and variable life insurance policies to meet.

The Code section 7702 definition, applicable to contracts issued after December 31, 1984, is a contract that is defined as life insurance under state law. Furthermore, throughout the duration of the contract, the policy must satisfy either the cash value accumulation test or both the guideline premium and cash value corridor tests. These tests, sometimes called the "TEFRA corridor" (TEFRA is a federal statute) are imposed to distinguish between policies that supplement true insurance benefits with investment aspects, and investments that have only a minimal insurance element.

PRACTICE TIP: Variable life insurance policies based on a segregated asset account are subject to further requirements, including the Code section 817(h)(1) diversification requirement, to count as insurance policies whose death benefits can be received free of income tax. Furthermore, a determination of whether a variable life policy continues to be life insurance under this definition must be made at least once a year, and each time the death benefit changes.

What happens if death benefits are paid under a policy, contract, or other arrangement that fails the tests for qualification as "life insurance", or under a variable life policy whose investments are not diversified as required by Section 817(h)? They constitute taxable income to the recipient. For the insurance company's record keeping, reporting, withholding, and deposit duties for these "failed" life insurance contracts, see Revenue Ruling 91-17, 1991-1 CB 190.

TAXATION OF TRANSFERS AND SURRENDERS

Under Code section 61, any receipt of funds that is not specifically excluded constitutes taxable income. Therefore, because there is no specific exclusion, a person who surrenders a life insurance policy and receives its cash value will usually have taxable income equal to the amount received minus the premiums or other consideration paid for the policy. (There might be other consideration if, for instance, the policy is purchased from a family member rather than directly from the insurer.) If the surrender of a life insurance policy results in a loss, the loss will not be deductible even if the policy was purchased as part of a business transaction.

PLANNING TIP: If a client who has plenty of life insurance wants to surrender a policy and invest the proceeds, or use them to purchase Medigap or LTC insurance, remind him or her that the transaction may generate taxable income, so only the after-tax amount can be used for these purposes.

This brings up the question of what happens when policies are exchanged, rather than surrendered. Code section 1035 provides that neither gain nor loss will be recognized if one annuity contract is exchanged for another; if an endowment contract is exchanged for an annuity contract or another endowment contract whose payments start no later than the payments under the original contract; or if a life insurance contract is exchanged for another life insurance contract, an endowment contract, or an annuity contract. In all these cases, the annuity can be either fixed or variable. See Rev. Rul. 68-235, 1968-1 CB 360 and Rev. Rul. 72-358, 1972-2 CB 473.

That means that taxable gain or loss will be recognized if an endowment contract is exchanged for a life insurance policy, or if an annuity is exchanged for a life insurance or endowment policy. The Code draws this distinction because, if these taxable exchanges were allowed tax-free, it would be possible to buy an endowment contract or annuity, then swap it for a life insurance policy whose proceeds would not be taxable income to their recipient—in short, taxation could be postponed indefinitely, a result disfavored by the Code.

TAX IMPLICATIONS OF LIFE INSURANCE FROM THE EMPLOYER

So far, this discussion has focused on individual coverage purchased by the insured or a member of the insured's family. After all, this is the area where the planning team can have the most impact, by informing clients of the need to purchase insurance or alter or supplement existing coverage. However, making a comprehensive plan requires understanding all the resources available to the client and family — including life insurance coverage provided by the employer. This topic will be summarized briefly here, but will not be explored in depth because the planning team usually can merely react to the existing coverage, not alter it.

PLANNING TIP: However, if your client is a senior executive, or an owner of a closely-held business, you may be able to recommend useful changes in employer-provided life insurance coverage.

Employees do not have taxable income when their employers pay the premiums on certain group-term life insurance policies. The employee will, however, have taxable income equal to any amount paid by the employer that exceeds the sum of premiums paid by the employee plus the cost of $50,000 worth of group-term life insurance. If the employer provides ordinary life insurance rather than group-term life insurance, the premiums paid by the employer will be taxable income for the employee under two circumstances:

- the employee has the right to designate the beneficiary

- the employer can designate the beneficiary, and names the spouse, dependents, or estate of the employee as beneficiary.

"Split dollar" insurance is a common employee benefit. In a split dollar plan, the premium for an insurance contract with investment elements is shared between employer and employee. Either the employer owns the policy and pays the entire premium (with the employee reimbursing the employer for the employee's share), or the employee owns the policy and the employer makes a no-interest or low-interest loan to the employee each year to pay premiums; the employee assigns the policy to the employer to secure the loans. Each year, the employer's share of the premium pays for the increased cash value of the policy; the employee pays the rest of the premium. When the insured employee dies, the employer gets the portion of the proceeds equal to the cash value; the beneficiary selected by the employee gets the remaining proceeds. Split dollar arrangements do subject the employee to income taxation on the one-year cost of term insurance as defined by the "P.S. 58" table issued by the IRS, minus the part of the premium paid by the employee.

INCIDENTAL LIFE INSURANCE
UNDER QUALIFIED PLANS

Many clients have insurance coverage they are unaware of, or have forgotten, provided as an incidental part of their pension or profit-sharing plans. These plans may provide life insurance, but, in order to retain their status as qualified plans (and the employer's ability to deduct contributions made to the plans), Code section 401 stipulates that insurance coverage must be merely incidental to the plan's primary purpose of providing retirement benefits. Rev. Rul. 68-453, 1968-2 CB 163 establishes a safe harbor under which life insurance will be incidental as long as the face amount of life insurance does not exceed 100 times the expected monthly benefit projected when the participant retires. Rev. Rul. 70-611, 1970-2 CB 89, Rev. Rul. 74-307, 1974-2 CB 126, and Rev. Rul. 66-143, 1966-1 CB 79 set out an alternate test based on the ratio between insurance premiums and employer contributions or total cost of all benefits.

The employee has taxable income equal to the cost of the "pure amount at risk" which is equal to the P.S. 58 rate multiplied by the face amount of the policy less the policy cash value at the end of the year.

Another issue to be addressed is the income tax treatment of life insurance contracts distributed by the employer to employees usually (though not necessarily) incident to retirement. The general rule is that the employee has taxable income equal to the cash value of the contract minus the employee's own basis in the contract. The employee's basis (tax cost) for the policy equals the P.S. 58 costs that the employee has already been taxed on, plus certain employer contributions.

The employee can avoid taxation when the contract is distributed by "rolling over" the contract to an annuity without life insurance elements, no later than 60 days after the distribution. However, the employee cannot roll over the contract into an IRA, because Code Section 408(a)(3) forbids IRAs to invest in life insurance contracts. Rev. Rul. 81-275, 1981-2 CB 92 clarifies that a life insurance contract cannot be rolled over into an IRA because the insurance contract is not a permissible IRA investment.

PROGRAMMING LIFE INSURANCE

Your special contribution to the planning team is to demonstrate how insurance (especially life insurance and health insurance) fits into the financial plan. In some ways, the task of insurance programming is easier for senior citizen clients than for their younger counterparts. For a younger client, death is often a remote contingency, and it is very difficult to determine what the family's needs will be when one of the parents dies. Will there be five children, ranging from infancy to age eight, or one "child" of thirty-five? What level of income will have to be replaced? Will the family have extensive assets or a large mortgage, heavy student loans, and significant consumer debt offset only by a small savings account?

For older clients, death within the next few years is much more likely, and clients are very aware of this fact. (For psychological reasons, however, they may resist taking practical steps to plan their estates or take care of their beneficiaries after their own deaths.) The planning perspective is much shorter-term.

Furthermore, the older person or couple is either retired or planning retirement, and has accumulated most or all investments. The rest of the lifetime will be devoted to husbanding these resources and spending will be more typical than saving. The level of retirement income is either known or somewhat predictable. Usually the couple's children will be grown and self-supporting, and the primary focus will be on providing income and resources for the surviving spouse. (If your client is a widow or widower, this objective no longer exists.)

In planning for a married couple, the clients and planner must determine what income and assets will be available to each spouse on the death of the other. The calculations must be done several times, based on several assumptions: that the husband will survive the wife, or vice versa; that the husband or wife will die at age 65, 70, 75, 80, or 85.

A plan that will meet the most demanding assumptions (that one spouse will die very soon, with no chance to accumulate further assets or do extensive financial planning, and be survived for many years by a spouse whose health deteriorates severely, or that both spouses will survive to old age but be very debilitated) will work even better under more favorable circumstances.

The next question is whether the expected income (including income from investing the assets) will be sufficient for the needs of the survivor, bearing in mind the strong possibility that the survivor will require some form of long-term care (at home, in a nursing home, or beginning in the community and then moving to a nursing home as dependency increases).

The factors to be considered include the level of social security benefits to be paid to the survivor; any death benefits payable by the deceased's employer or former employer; the survivor annuity payable under the deceased's pension plan, if any (unless the survivor annuity payment was waived to increase the size of the payments during the retiree's lifetime); payments to "buy out" a deceased business owner made by partners or by a closely held corporation; the surviving spouse's investment income deriving from personal and inherited assets; whether the survivor is an annuity investor; and the survivor's anticipated life expectancy and health condition. It takes more money to fund comfortable living for twenty years than for three!

The surviving spouse's own estate planning objectives must also be considered. If he or she insists on leaving an estate for children or other beneficiaries, then additional insurance coverage will be necessary. If the estate is likely to be very large, planning steps must be taken to soften or eliminate the impact of estate and inheritance taxes. On the other hand, if there are no beneficiaries each potential survivor feels strongly about, or if the potential beneficiaries are financially secure, it may be possible for the surviving spouse to gradually deplete the inherited assets over his or her remaining lifespan.

The next question is how much it will cost the survivor to live at the standard of living he or she wishes. Most senior citizens are homeowners with a small mortgage or mortgage-free, so housing expenses are relatively small. Expenses such as food, clothing, recreation, real estate taxes, and income tax can be reasonably easily estimated and adjusted for inflation over the expected lifespan of the surviving spouse. The real "joker in the pack" is the strong possibility that the survivor will require extensive health care that is not Medicare-covered.

One possibility, of course, if the client is insurable, is for the client to purchase long-term care (LTC) insurance, preferably LTC with adequate home-care benefits. But if the client's health precludes underwriting; if a policy is available but not affordable; or if the client refuses to buy LTC insurance, the potential cost of medical care must be factored into the equation.

After estimating the survivor's income, predictable lifespan, and predictable expenses, the planner must determine if there will be a shortfall. If so, life insurance on the life of the other spouse will be one of the major weapons to combat the shortfall. The first step is to review the existing coverage: term and whole life insurance purchased by the couple; group-term life insurance offered by the employer or former employer; insurance purchased by a partnership or corporation and benefiting the family of key individuals (as distinct from key person insurance benefiting the business).

Some older couples are actually overinsured, because they have a mortgage-free home and resources that are more than ample for a comfortable retirement and widowhood lifestyle. For these couples, life insurance cash value can be tapped to pay for long-term care; the diminution in benefits available at death is not severely deleterious, because there are other funds available. Life insurance policies can be converted to smaller paid-up policies and the funds that would otherwise be used to buy life insurance can be used to buy LTC and/or Medigap insurance. Owners of universal insurance or variable universal insurance policies can decrease their premium payments and apply the difference toward an investment program or health insurance. As long as the remaining death benefit is adequate, a portion of the death benefit may be accessible during the insured's lifetime to satisfy the expenses of long-term care or a terminal illness.

Other older couples have few other resources and little insurance; they need additional life insurance. The question then becomes what type of insurance. If they do not need access to cash value and if they are insurable at acceptable cost term insurance can be a good choice — provided that term insurance will be available and affordable throughout life. On the other hand, if the client is middle-aged and making long-range plans, conversion of existing term insurance to whole-life insurance can be an excellent move because it assures availability of insurance throughout life.

In other circumstances, whole life insurance is the better choice. As mentioned above, choosing universal, variable, or variable universal insurance always depends on a judgment that these forms of insurance are a good investment. For older clients, there is a further question: whether they are now capable of making informed investment judgments, are interested in active investing — and will continue to be in the future. If not, probably another form of insurance, combined with professionally-monitored investments, would be a better choice.

This discussion has been framed in terms of married couples, because the need for life insurance is keenest when the insured wishes to support a spouse and/or children. For a single or widowed person, unless there are young or disabled children in the picture, the need to insure his or her own life is less acute. However, a married couple's purchase of "second to die" insurance can be most useful if it is anticipated that a wealthy widow or widower will leave a potentially taxable estate.

Divorced or widowed people frequently want to benefit their children, and this can easily be done through insurance. Never-married or childless people may similarly wish to benefit friends, siblings, nieces and nephews, or charities. Small continuing premium payments can ensure significant provision for these beneficiaries, perhaps at lower cost than a lifetime giving program.

In summary, the question is whether existing life insurance coverage, taken in connection with other financial resources available after one spouse's death, will provide an acceptable lifestyle for the survivor. If not, the proper amount of coverage must be selected, and the couple's budget must be adjusted to take the insurance premiums into account. On the other hand, if the couple has been financially successful and made good investment choices, there may be ample funds even if existing life insurance coverage is reduced. In this case, the premium funds "freed up" can be invested to enhance the retirement and widowhood lifestyle. In many cases, the most prudent choice is to use these funds to enhance Medigap and LTC coverage to cope with the meaningful risk of expensive long-term care.

CHAPTER FOOTNOTES

1. See Dani L. Long and Gene A. Morton, *Principles of Life and Health Insurance*, 2d ed. (Life Management Inst. LOMA 1988), especially Chapter 3; Emmett J. Vaughan, *Fundamentals of Risk and Insurance* 5th ed. (John Wiley & Sons 1989), especially Chapter 12. For rates, see Andrew D. Gold, "Universal Life Policy Survey," *Best's Review*, July, 1993 p. 68; Mary Rowland, "Why Patience is the Best Policy," *New York Times* January 9, 1994 p. F17.

2. Roger L. Blease and Gary S. Pallay, "Survivorship Life Policy Survey," *Best's Review* August 1990 p. 76.

3. Karen P. Schaeffer makes this point in "Second-to-Die Plans: Why the Avalanche?" *Best's Review*, February 1990 p. 54.

4. "Estate Planning With a Second-to-Die Policy," *Life Association News*, August 1989 p. 66.

5. Tamar Lewin, "To the Dying, Life Policy Can Bring Money Now," *New York Times* March 5, 1990 p. A10; Cynthia Crosson, "NAIC in Final Vote on Viaticals, Assumption Re," *National Underwriter* December 13, 1993 p. 4.

6. Kenneth C. Klueh, "Putting LTC to the Test," *Best's Review* February 1989 p. 46; Rhona L. Ferling, "A Brave New Market," *Best's Review* February 1990 p. 44; Steven Brostoff, "Accelerated Benefit Plans Growing Fast," *National Underwriter* February 25, 1991 p. 3; Eric Weissman, "There's Nothing Fleeting About Accelerated Benefits," *Life Association News* February 15, 1993 p. 72.

7. Linda Koco, "Manhattan National Adds on Living Ben. Rider at No Cost," *National Underwriter* May 21, 1990 p. 7.

Chapter 3

MEDIGAP INSURANCE

Declining physical health and mental incapacity are not the universal fate of all older persons. However, all older persons are at risk for various acute or chronic conditions of the mind and body. The planning team must work with this fact, and make all decisions based on their impact on the possible future need for expensive care.

The entire planning team must work together, because the problem of funding health care is so complex. Many elements are involved, from Medicare and Medicaid to health care provided at home by agencies in the private for-profit sector and highly expensive nursing home care.

This chapter describes Medigap insurance. Medigap is private insurance designed to supplement the inadequacies of the Medicare program, and to relieve the elderly policyholders of part or all of their cost-sharing burden.

Chapters 4 and 5 describe long-term care (LTC) insurance. Originally limited to nursing home stays, LTC policies are responding to consumer demands and including increasing coverage of home health care for the chronically ill who do not want to — or need to — be institutionalized.

Medicare eligibility and coverage are described in Chapter 6. Medicaid and Medicaid planning strategies are discussed in Chapter 7.

INTEGRATING SOURCES OF HEALTH INSURANCE

For younger families, major financial challenges include career planning, making major purchases such as an automobile and a home, and financing the childrens' education. Older couples and single senior citizens face more sobering challenges: paying health-care costs and creating or preserving an estate.

A very confusing aspect of elder care planning is the fact that many sources of payment must be combined to provide complete health care coverage for the senior citizen. An important part of the planner's job includes becoming familiar with these sources of payment, keeping up with changes, teaching clients about them, and giving advice about preferable alternatives.

Medicare, the federal health care system for senior citizens, plays a major part in providing acute health care for the elderly. It also provides limited but still useful benefits for home care and skilled nursing facility (SNF) care. However, even within its own limitations, Medicare does not provide complete coverage.

Medicare beneficiaries must pay a monthly premium to get Part B benefits (doctor bills and related services). There is a deductible payable before Part B benefits begin and a significant deductible before Part A hospitalization benefits begin. Medicare beneficiaries are also required to make significant coinsurance payments. Sometimes Medicare beneficiaries have to pay "balance bills" which are the difference between a doctor's true charge and the amount of reimbursement that Medicare provides for the service. However, this is becoming a less significant factor because the Medicare system is phasing in limitations on reimbursement to doctors and on balance billing.

The insurance industry has responded to the deficiencies of the Medicare system by introducing "Medigap" insurance products, so that the risk of unpredictable and uncontrollable bills that are not covered by Medicare can be converted into a predictable and affordable series of insurance premiums.

HEALTH INSURANCE CONTINUATION COVERAGE

Employers are obligated to give retiring employees (as well as the divorcing spouses of employees; the surviving spouses of employees; and employees who are laid off) the chance to buy "continuation coverage." In effect, the ex-employee (or family member) "buys in" to the employer's group health plan. Especially for retirees younger than 65, who are not Medicare-eligible, continuation coverage is an important option, and buying this coverage is often a good use of funds.

Continuation coverage often ends when a retiree becomes eligible for Medicare, but a retiree's dependents may still have the right to continuation coverage for themselves.

"Continuation coverage" is usually referred to as "COBRA" coverage. (For Consolidated Omnibus Budget Reconciliation Act.) Employers are usually not required to allow continuation of coverage beyond 18 or 36 months, depending on the situation. The former employee or dependent is required to pay the full cost of the group coverage and may be charged an additional 2% for administration. Most employers track this closely because they want the coverage terminated at the earliest possible date. At best, it is an interim coverage for those who have a few more months until Medicare is available.

The spouse of a retired person who is still in the work force may have work-related health insurance that provides spousal coverage for the retiree during the "gap" period between retirement (and loss of health coverage as an active employee) or the end of continuation coverage and the beginning of Medicare eligibility.

Another possibility is for the retiree or person contemplating retirement to purchase individual health insurance. For example, affordable coverage may be available from a professional organization, a religious or philanthropic organization, or affinity group. Several states have passed statutes making it easier for health insurers to provide group coverage for older people.

Employers are not obligated to provide any health benefits for retired employees (or, for that matter, for active employees), but many (especially large corporations) do offer retiree health benefits. Retiree health benefits can be of substantial assistance to retirees with high medical bills. Very few employers include nursing home care in retiree health packages; and a controversial legal issue is the extent to which an employer can change its program of retiree health benefits (for example, by demanding that retirees pay part or an increased part of the cost of the plan) or terminate it entirely. ERISA, the federal pension and benefit law, requires pension benefits to vest (become irrevocable) after the employee has satisfied a tenure requirement. ERISA also sets the requirements for employers' payment of vested benefits. But employee welfare benefits (including health insurance and retiree health benefits) do not vest. If the employer reserves the right to amend or terminate these benefits, then it is lawful to cut back or end the benefits. Therefore, even a person who expects to retire and receive generous retiree coverage needs a contingency plan in case the employer is legally permitted to scale down or even eliminate the retiree health plan.

Most states require a conversion feature on group policies. The "conversion policy" may be a basic health policy only (basic usually includes coverage for only hospital confinement and surgery) or a basic and major medical policy (depends on state law) that is available (in a single or family plan) to individual employees who retire. These contracts are very expensive and the benefits are extremely limited. (An example might be 90 days of hospital expense at $50 per day, a surgical schedule with a $500 maximum, and a major medical policy with a lifetime individual maximum of $20,000.) Most state laws only require that the conversion policy be offered without addressing the question of cost or level of benefits. Insurance carriers do not want the business because only those who cannot get coverage elsewhere — because of health or other underwriting problems — will apply for the coverage. This means the company is almost guaranteed to lose money on these policies. In fact, they often include an additional charge to the employer at the end of the year for each conversion policy issued. A conversion policy is not a good answer to the problem, but it can be better than nothing for someone who has medical problems and nowhere else to turn.

In 1996, federal legislation was passed regarding "portability" of health insurance coverage when an employee changes jobs. However, both COBRA continuation coverage and portability relate only to insurance for acute health care. If the employer provides group long-term care insurance as an employee benefit, that coverage is not portable and the employer is not required to offer continuation coverage for it.

INTRODUCTION TO MEDIGAP INSURANCE

In a way, the entire Medicare system is a form of health insurance. Part of every dollar of Social Security tax deducted from a paycheck goes to fund the Medicare trust fund, and Medicare beneficiaries who elect Part B pay monthly premiums. However, it is not a very good insurance program because it leaves "policyholders" without coverage for many important types of medical care, it is expensive, and deductibles and coinsurance requirements are high. (Furthermore, the Omnibus Budget Reconciliation Act of 1993 (OBRA '93) requires active workers to pay much more Medicare tax, by imposing the tax on an unlimited amount of income.)

Congress made major changes in the law of Medigap policies in 1990 because the majority of senior citizens own at least one Medigap (Medicare supplement) policy to cope with the deficiencies of the Medicare system. Medigap policies cope with the Medicare system *on its own terms*. Thus, policyholders and prospects must be educated to realize that Medigap policies do *not* provide coverage for long-term chronic care, and that it is necessary to purchase a separate LTC policy to achieve such coverage.

Unfortunately, some unscrupulous fly-by-night operators entered the Medigap market, and attempted to sell policies that were over-priced, provided inappropriate coverage, or engaged in "twisting" or inducing policyholders to purchase expensive and duplicative coverage. Because of the vulnerability of the elderly to such manipulative devices, Medigap policies are now subject to extensive regulation, both on the federal and state levels.

Medigap insurance is an extremely popular product: according to the 1992 Medicare Current Beneficiary Survey, 78% of Medicare beneficiaries have Medigap insurance. About 25% of those with private coverage had more than one policy — e.g., more than one Medigap policy, or an employer group health plan plus one or more Medigap policies.

For 1992, the average annual Medigap premium was $914. However, in late 1995, the largest Medigap insurers announced that premiums would rise an average of about 30% in 1996 — ranging from 8% in Alaska to 40% in states such as Illinois, Ohio, and Oklahoma. The insurers blamed claims experience (especially increasing utilization of outpatient services) for the increase. Large premium increases were also announced for 1997.

Federal Regulation of Medigap Insurance

Medigap insurance has been subject to federal regulation since the 1980 "Baucus Amendment." The Baucus Amendment imposed standards to be met by any policy marketed as a Medicare supplementary policy. For instance, the Baucus Amendment permitted designing and marketing a policy limited to supplementing Medicare Part A, but forbade the insurer to describe or market the policy as a Medigap policy. The Baucus Amendment required all Medigap policies to supplement both parts of Medicare.

Because insurance regulation is traditionally the job of the state governments, the Baucus Amendment deferred to the standards set by the National Association of Insurance Commissioners (NAIC). States were allowed to adopt their own standards for Medigap policies, as long as they were *more* stringent than the federal standards and provided a higher degree of consumer protection. Policies that met all relevant standards were entitled to display a seal, and consumer education efforts focused on getting consumers to buy certified policies meeting the standards.

The status of Medigap insurance became confusing during the short life of the Medicare Catastrophic Coverage Act of 1988 (MCCA). This Act, which would have greatly expanded the benefits available under Medicare, was repealed in late 1989 before most of its provisions became effective. Many policyholders wondered whether they would need a Medigap policy at all, in light of the more generous new coverage. Many went on to drop their Medigap policies. Others, less energetic or more cynical, held on to the policies — which proved to be a wise decision after MCCA was repealed.

MCCA repeal was stressful for many senior citizens. Few wanted to pay an income tax surcharge to fund the expanded Medicare benefits, but most looked forward to increased benefits. It was also painful for health insurers, who face much greater Medigap liability as the Medicare program shrinks.

Legislative concern over potential consumer abuses (refusal to reinstate policies, profiteering) led to inclusion of Medigap provisions in P.L. 101-234, the federal statute that repealed MCCA. The NAIC was directed to develop a new set of standards for Medigap policies. This was done in December, 1989, and the new standards were "plugged in" to the Baucus Amendment as the new federal criteria for Medigap policies.

Nor was this the last change in Medigap requirements. The 1990 budget package, embodied in the Omnibus Budget Reconciliation Act of 1990 (P.L. 101-508), made very significant changes in the types of policies eligible for Medigap certification. Certification itself assumes additional significance: if a state has a certification program acceptable to the Department of Health and Human Services (HHS), selling an uncertified Medigap policy is an offense, subject to a fine of up to $25,000.[1]

Perhaps the most significant change was the requirement intended to limit duplication of policies, enacted in Section 4354 of the Omnibus Budget Reconciliation Act of 1990 (OBRA '90). The insurer must query any potential purchaser about his or her existing Medigap coverage; a civil monetary penalty (up to $15,000 for an individual, $25,000 for a company issuing the policy) and a jail term of up to five years can be imposed for selling a policy in violation of the new requirements.

The purchaser of a new Medigap policy must sign a statement on a form that, in effect, says that no one needs more than one Medigap policy; that Medicaid-eligible individuals generally do not need Medigap coverage; and that state consumer counseling may be available to give advice about wise purchase of Medigap insurance. (If the state does have a counseling program, the form may include the telephone number for the service.)

It is unlawful to sell the policy without getting the purchaser's statement about coverage. If he or she already has a Medigap policy, it is unlawful to sell another one *unless* the buyer indicates on the written statement that he or she is buying the new policy to replace the old one, and intends to terminate the old one as soon as the new policy becomes effective. The issuer or seller of the new policy must certify that, to the best of its knowledge, there will be no duplication of coverage once the replacement becomes effective.

The applicant must also sign a statement as to whether he or she is eligible for Medicaid. When a policyholder becomes eligible for Medicaid (for instance, after implementing a Medicaid plan or spending down), he or she has a right to notify the Medigap insurer, which then must suspend both premium collection and benefit payments (because Medicaid has assumed the functions of the Medigap policy).

If the applicant does decide to switch from one Medigap policy to another, the new insurer is obligated to waive the waiting periods, probationary periods, elimination periods, and preexisting condition limitations already undergone under the original policy. Nor may a Medigap issuer deny coverage or discriminate in premiums based on health status, claims experience, medical conditions, or medical treatment during the first six months when the applicant is a Medicare Part B beneficiary.[2]

The new requirements might be considered a program of mandatory "twisting" because the purchase of a new Medigap policy necessarily entails the termination of an old one. However, after OBRA '90, there will be less incentive to switch from one insurer to another, because policies will be far more standardized. Section 4351 of OBRA '90 directs the NAIC to create yet another set of Medigap standards. (See below.) These standards are explicitly aimed at reducing the number of potentially confusing policy variations, and at making it easier for consumers to make comparisons among rival policies.

All Medigap insurers must offer basic core benefits in the same format and using the same terminology. There are ten different Medigap packages (the core group of benefits, plus other combinations of benefits offered as separate benefit packages). A civil penalty of up to $25,000 can be imposed for non-compliance in policies issued after the effective date of the provision.

Under Section 4355 of OBRA '90, the minimum permitted loss ratio for individual Medigap policies is 65% (replacing the earlier 60% mandate) — and policyholders must be given a refund if their policies dip below the required loss ratio. All policies sold mail-order are deemed individual policies. The minimum required loss ratio for group policies is 75%. The 1990 legislation mandates that the states set up an approval process for premium increases, including public hearings before premiums can increase.

Medigap policies must be guaranteed renewable, with cancellation or non-renewal limited to material misrepresentation and non-payment of premiums. If the certificate holder of a group policy switches to another insurer, the replacement insurer must offer coverage to everyone covered under the old policy.[3]

Medigap insurers have every reason to be concerned by inflation in health care costs, and to seek ways to control costs. One possibility is to create incentives to use efficient health care providers. Section 4358 of OBRA '90 sets up a three-year (1992-94), 15-state demonstration project for "Medicare Select" policies (those limiting reimbursement to services provided by preferred providers or other networks aimed at controlling costs). (See below.) A preferred-provider policy that otherwise meets NAIC standards can be certified as a Medigap policy if it offers the full range of basic benefits through a network of providers that offers sufficient access and is subject to quality control requirements, and if policyholders have access to medically-necessary services outside the network if the network cannot provide the needed care.

As a result of the confusion caused by Medicare Catastrophic Care Act (MCCA) repeal, there are really five different sets of regulatory requirements:

(1) Policies sold before 1980 (before the Baucus Amendment and therefore not subject to it).

(2) Policies sold after 1980 but before 1988 ("pre-Catastrophic" policies).

(3) Policies sold in 1988-1989 (when policyholders and insurers based their expectations on expanded Medicare coverage provided by MCCA).

(4) Policies sold in 1990 and later (when expectations are based on MCCA repeal).

(5) Policies sold after the OBRA '90 effective date.

NAIC'S 1989 STANDARDS

The general trend of the 1989 National Association of Insurance Commissioner's (NAIC) standards was to require insurers to replace any benefits that were removed from a Medigap policy with Medicare Catastrophic Care Act (MCCA) in mind.

In general, the 1989 NAIC model did not make it necessary to enhance benefits over the pre-MCCA level. (Hence, the 1989 NAIC standards do not include long-term care (LTC) coverage, although states are permitted to impose such a requirement on Medigap policies.) However, there are some significant differences between the post-1990 and pre-1988 standards.

For post-MCCA policies, either the entire Part A deductible must be covered, or the policy must not cover any part of the deductible. For pre-1988 policies, it was permissible for an insurer to impose a $200 Part B deductible. Policies sold after MCCA repeal are not allowed to have a Part B deductible that is higher than the Medicare deductible figure of $100 ($75 prior to 1991). (However, insurers are not required to amend policies that were sold before 1988 to enhance the Part B coverage.) Before MCCA, insurers were allowed to limit their Part B liability to $5,000.

The 1989 NAIC standards mandate that post-repeal policies must subject the insurer to a risk of unlimited Part B payouts. This point is not addressed in the Omnibus Budget Reconciliation Act of 1990 (OBRA '90).

NAIC'S 1991 STANDARDS

After extensive meetings and discussions, the National Association of Insurance Commissioners (NAIC) promulgated an exposure draft of the Minimum Standards Model Act and implementing Model Regulation on May 16, 1991.

The Exposure Draft of the Model Act enhances the powers of state insurance commissioners: Section 3(D) of the Model Act permits commissioners to adopt regulations to conform state law to federal law and regulations, for instance by requiring refunds when policies fail to meet the mandated loss ratios; by publicizing loss ratios; holding public hearings before premium increases are granted; and setting standards for Medicare Select policies (discussed below). Section 6(B)(3) mandates disclosure by the issuer of "the existence of any automatic renewal premium increases based on the policyholder's age."

The most controversial materials can be found in the Exposure Draft of the Model Regulation to Implement the NAIC Medicare Supplement Insurance Minimum Standards Model Act. This is where the standards for the ten basic policies can be found.

Section 6 of the Model Regulation may also create turmoil within the insurance industry. Under the earlier version of the Model Regulation, Medigap policies were permitted to exclude ten types of treatment; now only five exclusions are permitted:

- Treatment of medical conditions caused by war, attempted suicide, intentionally self-inflicted injury, or aviation — but aviation injuries of fare-paying passengers *must* now be covered; the earlier draft allowed a comprehensive aviation exclusion.

- Cosmetic surgery

- Services provided by family members, of a type for which family members are usually not paid

- Eyeglasses, hearing aids, and exams to prescribe them

- "Rest cures, custodial care, transportation and routine physical examinations"

Section 8 of the Model Regulation sets the benefit standards for Medigap policies issued or delivered after the date that a state adopts the Model Act and its regulations. Section 8(A)(1) implements the Omnibus Budget Reconciliation Act of 1990's (OBRA '90) preexisting condition limitation. A Drafting Note to the Regulation advises states that have adopted the NAIC Individual Accident and Sickness Insurance Minimum Standards Model Act that this provision conflicts with the preexisting conditions language in the Accident and Sickness Insurance Act.

Under Section 8(A)(2) of the Model Regulation, the same basis must be used to indemnify sickness and accident losses; 8(A)(3) requires automatic adjustments of policy benefits whenever Medicare cost sharing (deductibles and copayments) changes. Insurers are permitted to modify their premiums corresponding to the changes in benefits. Section 8(A)(4) forbids insurers to terminate one spouse's coverage because the insured spouse's coverage terminates — unless the termination is for nonpayment of premiums.

Section 8(A)(5) enacts the OBRA '90 renewability provisions. That is, policies cannot be canceled or non-renewed for any reason other than nonpayment of premium or material misrepresentation; certificate holders under a group policy must be given access to comparable individual Medigap policies if the group policy is terminated by the group policyholder and is not replaced. Conversion must also be available for group members who terminate membership in the group. If a group policy is terminated but is replaced, the new policy cannot exclude as a preexisting condition anything that would have been covered under the first policy.

Core Benefits

The most significant change mandated by the Omnibus Budget Reconciliation Act of 1990 (OBRA '90) is the standardization of Medigap policies. Section 8(B) of the Model Regulation defines the standards for the "Basic Core Package" of benefits which must be offered in all Medigap policies. Furthermore, *every* insurer that sells Medigap policies must sell a policy or certificate that includes only the five basic core benefits:

- Coverage of Part A copayments for the 61st through 90th day of hospitalization in any Medicare benefit period.

- Coverage of Part A-eligible daily hospital charges during the lifetime reserve days. (See Chapter 6 for a discussion of these Medicare concepts.)

- Coverage of Part A-eligible expenses that are not covered by Medicare because the sick person has exhausted his or her lifetime reserve days; the Medigap policy must provide coverage subject to a lifetime maximum of 365 additional days.

- Coverage under Part A and Part B of the cost of three pints of blood.

- Coverage for Part B coinsurance (inside and outside the hospital), once the older patient has satisfied the Part B deductible.

Additional Benefits

The ten standard Medigap plans are limited to various combinations of the additional benefits permitted under the Model Regulation. Section 9(C) of the Model Regulation defines the eleven additional benefits that can be offered:

- Coverage of the entire Part A hospital deductible.

- Coverage of the coinsurance required for days 21-100 when a person receives skilled nursing home (SNF) benefits under Part A.

- Coverage of the Part B deductible.

- Coverage of 80% of the "balance billing" (within limits set by Medicare law) paid by Part B beneficiaries whose doctors do not accept assignment. (See Chapter 6.)

- Coverage of 100% of lawful balance billing.

- Coverage of 50% of outpatient prescription drug costs, subject to a $250 deductible with an annual maximum of $1,250 ("basic prescription drug benefit").

- Coverage of 50% of outpatient prescription drug costs, with a $250 deductible and a $3,000 annual maximum ("extended prescription drug benefit").

- Coverage of 80% of the Medicare-eligible costs of medically necessary emergency care when the insured is travelling outside the United States.

- Coverage of up to $120 a year for certain screening and preventive measures (e.g., flu vaccine; urinalysis for diabetes; thyroid function testing).

- Coverage for certain "short term, at-home assistance with activities of daily living" for people recovering from illness, injury, or surgery at home, in a relative's home, or in an institution (but not a hospital or skilled nursing facility), up to $1,600 a year, with not more than seven four-hour visits by caregivers in any week, with no more than $40 reimbursement per visit. The care must be received while the sick person is getting Medicare home care (or within eight weeks of the termination of Medicare home care) — but visits paid for by Medicare or other government programs cannot be covered under a Medigap policy; nor can care provided by family members or unpaid volunteers.

- Coverage of "innovative benefits" that are appropriate, cost-effective, and consistent with the goal of simplifying Medigap insurance — with prior approval by the state insurance commissioner.

The Ten Plans

Medigap insurers may *not* sell any Medigap policy other than the ten plans laid out in the Model Regulation.

- Plan A is the basic core benefit package. (See "Core Benefits" above.) The other nine plans are Plan A plus certain elements; all of them include the Part A deductible and medically necessary emergency care outside the United States.

- Plan B adds only the mandatory supplements to the basic core benefits.

- Plan C adds the Part B deductible and skilled nursing facility (SNF) care.

- Plan D adds SNF care and home care.

- Plan E adds SNF care and the Basic prescription drug benefit.

- Plan F adds SNF care, 80% of Part B balance billing, and home care.

- Plan G adds SNF care and preventive care.

- Plan H adds SNF care, the Part B deductible, and 100% of Part B balance billing.

- Plan I adds SNF care, 100% of the Part B balance billing, Basic prescription drug benefit, and home care.

- Plan J adds SNF care, the Part B deductible, 100% of Part B balance billing, the Extended prescription drug benefit, preventive care, and home care.

States have a degree of authority in determining which of the nine supplementary plans can be offered in the state. (All states must require that the basic core benefit package be offered.) However, no state is allowed to authorize any Medigap policy that is not one of the specified plans. This is a tremendous change in regulatory posture. Before, the focus was on setting limits on insurer conduct; now, the states have only the very limited discretion of authorizing some combination of the nine plans that are permitted in addition to the core plan.

In practice, the mere fact that a particular policy form is licensed for sale in a state does not always mean that the policy form is *available*. In particular, it can be difficult to find insurers that sell some of the more comprehensive forms — especially in states where the costs of medical care are particularly high.

Section 11 of the Model Regulation imposes an "open enrollment" requirement. That is, if an older person applies for a Medigap policy during the six-month period beginning with his or her enrollment in Medicare Part B, the insurer may not deny coverage or discriminate in pricing because of the applicant's "health status, claims experience, receipt of health care, or medical condition."

NAIC'S 1995 STANDARDS

The latest version of the Medicare Supplement Insurance Minimum Standards Model Act, dated April, 1995, has 11 sections:

- Definitions

- Applicability and Scope

- Standards for Policy Provisions

- Standards for Loss Ratios

- Disclosure (e.g., whether the policy covers deductibles and coinsurance; the extent to which it duplicates benefits available under Medicare)

- Availability of a Free Examination Period

- Obligation to File Advertisements With the Insurance Commissioner

- Administrative Procedures

- Penalties

- Severability (i.e., any invalid provisions will be severed, and the rest of the Act will remain in force)

- Effective Date.

The Medigap Model Act has been adopted in most states (Alabama, Arkansas, California, Colorado, Connecticut, Delaware, Georgia, Hawaii, Idaho, Illinois, Indiana, Kentucky, Louisiana, Maine, Maryland, Michigan, Mississippi, Missouri, Montana, Nebraska, New Hampshire, New Jersey, New Mexico, North Carolina, North Dakota, Ohio, Oklahoma, Oregon, Rhode Island, South Dakota, Tennessee, Texas, Utah, Washington, West Virginia, Wyoming). Related but not identical statutes have been adopted in Alaska, Arizona, Florida, Iowa, Kansas, Minnesota, New York, Pennsylvania, South Carolina,

Virginia, and Wisconsin. As of July, 1996, the Medigap Model Regulation had been adopted in all the states except California — and even California had related regulations.

Medigap disclosure is also subject to federal law. The Social Security Amendments of 1994 require that, for policies issued on or after August 11, 1995, newly-issued Medigap policies must disclose the extent to which the coverage duplicates Medicare benefits. The National Association of Insurance Commissioners (NAIC) has developed 10 standard disclosure statements, which have been approved by the Department of Health and Human Services (HHS).[4]

MEDIGAP CASES

Unfortunately, abusive Medigap marketing does occur and, if detected, can be expensive for the insurer. A vulnerable, aged, uneducated Georgia woman was sold a Medigap policy that was clearly unsuitable. Not only did it cost one-third of her income, but it was valueless in any event because she was eligible for Medicaid. She sued for fraud. The trial jury awarded her $250,000 as compensatory damages, and $15 million in punitive damages. The trial judge reduced the punitive damages to $12.5 million. The appellate court reduced the punitive damages again, to "only" $5 million. True, this was only one-third of the initial award, but it can hardly be considered a trivial sum.[5]

The insurer prevailed in a later Alabama case.[6] Charges that the company committed fraud and misrepresentation in connection with a Medigap policy were dismissed. The policy didn't cover the plaintiff's entire stay in a Skilled Nursing Facility, but neither did Medicare, because changes in the patient's physical therapy schedule prevented him from satisfying the SNF coverage criteria for the whole of his stay. The Alabama Supreme Court held that the insurer was not guilty of fraud. The agent who sold the policy said that it was better than the plaintiff's existing policy and would cover SNF care — but there was no fraud because neither statement was proved to be false.

MEDICARE SELECT

One approach that has been taken to reduce health care costs of group health insurance plans sponsored by employers is the "preferred provider organization." Insured employees are given financial incentives to get their medical care from an identified group of low-cost providers. Employees who are insured under these plans still have a free choice of health care providers, but if they go outside the "network" of preferred providers, they will bear a heavier cost-sharing burden.

Section 4358 of the Omnibus Budget Reconciliation Act of 1990 (OBRA '90) mandated a study of "Medicare Select" policies, which will apply the concept of a network of preferred providers to Medigap policies. The Secretary of Health and Human Services (HHS) has designated 15 states for a three-year pilot project under which Medicare Select policies will be issued beginning January 1, 1992. Premiums should be lower than those charged for regular Medigap coverage. People who buy Medicare Select policies will be fully covered for services provided by members of the restricted network of providers, but will be subject to copayment requirements if they go to a non-network provider in any circumstance other than an emergency, or for services that are medically necessary but not available within the network. The 15 states are Alabama, Arizona, California, Florida, Indiana, Kentucky, Michigan, Minnesota, Missouri, North Dakota, Ohio, Oregon, Texas, Washington, and Wisconsin.

Later, there was some change in the line-up of states. Oregon and Michigan could not find any insurers interested in selling Medicare Select policies, so they withdrew from the pilot project; Illinois and Massachusetts took their place.[7] In early 1993, the Health Care Financing Administration (HCFA) reported that there were 22 insurers in 10 states actually selling Medicare Select policies (the states were Alabama, Arizona, Florida, Indiana, Kentucky, Minnesota, Missouri, North Dakota, Texas, and Wisconsin). Medicare Select policies offered significant cost advantages, costing about 10-15% less than conventional Medigap policies.[8]

Legislation passed in 1995 (P.L. 104-18) extended the Medicare Select demonstration project to all 50 states, until December 31, 1997. Medicare Select policies will be permanently available nationwide as of June 30, 1998 unless the Secretary of HHS makes an official finding that Medicare Select did not produce either savings or improved access to care.

CHAPTER FOOTNOTES

1.   OBRA '90 Section 4353.

2.   OBRA '90 Section 4357.

3. OBRA '90 Section 4353.

4. See the HCFA Notice printed at 60 Fed. Reg. 30877 (June 12, 1995) and reprinted at CCH Medicare and Medicaid Guide ¶43,274.

5. *Life Insurance Co. of Georgia v. Johnson*, 64 U.S.L.W. 2348 (Ala. Nov. 17, 1995).

6. *George v. Associated Doctors Health & Life Ins. Co.*, CCH MEDICARE AND MEDICAID GUIDE ¶44,076 (Ala. 1996).

7. HCFA Notice, 58 *Federal Register* 35017 (June 30, 1993).

8. HCFA News Release, CCH Medicare/Medicaid Guide Report Letter #730, p. 12.

Chapter 4

LONG-TERM CARE INSURANCE

HOW SERIOUS IS THE PROBLEM?

In a nation with an aging population, and the medical profession's increasing ability both to treat the ailments of aging and to provide long-range palliative care for ailments that cannot be cured, the need for long-term care is bound to increase tremendously. It is very difficult to pay for this expensive care out-of-pocket. Until now, government programs (Medicare and Medicaid) have assumed much of the burden, and private long-term care insurance (LTC insurance) has been a minor factor. But as costs and utilization increase, and as the pressure to balance federal and state budgets increases, more and more attention is being devoted to private insurance.

Before 1996, the tax status of LTC insurance was ambiguous — which was another disincentive for affluent people to buy insurance for themselves, and for employers to offer LTC insurance as an employee benefit. In 1996, the Health Insurance Portability and Accountability Act of 1996 (P.L. 104-191) resolved some questions (inevitably creating others, however) and created a new category: the "qualified" LTC insurance policy. This chapter discusses the long-term care insurance provisions of the 1996 legislation, against a background of LTC insurance history and structure.

In 1992, there were close to eight million Americans over 15 who suffered disabilities in Activities of Daily Living (ADLs): close to three million who could not bathe unassisted, over two million who needed help with dressing and transferring from one place to another; more than a million needed assistance in using the toilet. About 4% of the overall population (3.2% of the male population, 4.8% of the female population) had health-related problems carrying out these basic tasks.

At that time, almost 11 million Americans (6% of the overall population, 4.9% of males, 7.0% of females) had limitations in Instrumental Activities of Daily Living (IADLs) — less dramatic, but still important, tasks like being able to cook, shop, or handle money.

An earlier (1984) survey showed that about a quarter of those age 65 and older had difficulty in doing heavy housework, and 19% had trouble walking. Eleven percent found it difficult to shop, and 10% had trouble bathing. Four percent needed help to use the toilet, and 2% had difficulty feeding themselves. Of course, there are many possible responses to an elderly person's need for help. Many people simply do not get any help, and they suffer and probably die prematurely. Others get informal and unpaid help from family and friends. The task of caring for a sick old person is tremendously difficult (both physically and emotionally) — especially because it never lets up. A caregiver must always worry that a person whose balance is poor will fall (risking a broken wrist or hip). A forgetful person can leave a stove on or a bathtub running — for hours at a time. An Alzheimer's patient can wander away, and have no idea of his or her name or how to get home.

Formal care is provided by home health agencies (HHAs), and can be paid for by Medicare, Medicaid, and private insurance, as well as out of the pockets of the elderly and their families. Nursing homes are not the only possible source of care for the impaired elderly; but in some cases, home care is not appropriate for the person's needs, or is not available in the necessary degree of intensity.

In 1993 there were about 32.5 million senior citizens enrolled in Medicare, and the program spent $129.4 billion on all services. About 10% of that went toward long-term care (3.3% to skilled nursing facilities, 7.5% to home care). The 1993 Medicaid spending on services was $101.7 billion — one-fourth of which went to nursing homes. Between 1980 and 1993, annual spending on home health care rose by an average of 19.1% nationwide. 1993 nursing home expenditures were about $66.2 billion — reflecting an average annual percent growth of 10.7% between 1980 and 1993.

In 1994, total health spending was $949.4 billion, of which consumers paid $488.1 billion, government sources paid $420.8 billion, and $40.4 billion came from other sources. Of this amount, about $72.3 billion went to nursing home care (private out-of-pocket spending approximately $26.85 billion, government $41.85 billion, private health insurance $2.2 billion, and other $1.4 billion), and a further $26.2 billion to home care (private out-of-pocket $6.1 billion, government spending $13.2 billion, private insurance $3.4 billion, other $3.5 billion). That adds up to $2648 per person ($66 per capita for home care, $227 for nursing home care). (This information comes from U.S. government sources, such as the Statistical Abstract of the United States and the Health Care Financing Review; all amounts are approximate, and may not add up because of rounding.)

On any given day, about 5% of the senior citizen population is confined to nursing homes. Understandably, the percentage increases with age; nearly a quarter of those over 85 live in nursing homes rather than in the community. About two-fifths of the elderly population will spend some time in a nursing home before dying. Only 20-25%, however, will spend more than a year in a nursing home.

As you would expect, the nursing home population is overwhelmingly elderly; only about 10% of the residents are under age 65. About 13% of the residents are in the age group 65-74. Another 13% are 75-79 years old.

Thus, nearly 65% of nursing home residents are over 80 — and nearly a quarter are over 90. Because the over-85 population is increasing rapidly, it is clear that more and more nursing home beds will be required to cope with the expectable influx. Furthermore, many nursing home residents are very severely debilitated and need a lot of care. More than a quarter are estimated to suffer from Alzheimer's Disease or other dementia; a further 13.7% suffer both from dementia and another mental illness; and 15.5% have some mental illness other than dementia.[1]

Projections have been made for nursing home use by people who reached age 65 in 1990 (that is, today's senior citizens, who are also in the prime market for long-term care insurance). It is estimated that, of this "cohort" (population group of approximately the same age), about 22% of males and 41% of females will spend at least three months in a nursing home at some point in their remaining life. An estimated 14% of males, and 31% of females, will spend at least a year in a nursing home; and 4% of males, 13% of females, will spend five or more years in a nursing home. The average duration of a custodial stay is estimated at 2.5 years.

GETTING INTO A NURSING HOME

It does not matter how much money you have. A nursing home is not like a hotel; you cannot just show up, book a room, and pay your bill.

There can be extensive red tape involved in getting into a nursing home (basically, a professional assessment to make sure that the person really needs nursing home care) — and significant waiting lists for good facilities. Making a Medicaid application is a complex process, and can be lengthy.

Getting into a nursing home is especially difficult for Medicaid patients. Nursing homes usually prefer private-pay patients. Except in unusual circumstances (for instance, in Minnesota, nursing homes are not allowed to charge more than the Medicaid rate, so they do not care about the source of payment), private-pay patients provide much more revenue for the nursing home, and much less hassle because there is less paperwork to fill out. In most states, the Medicaid reimbursement rates for nursing homes are lower than the Medicare rates — so, once again, the homes prefer Medicare patients. New York pays more for Medicaid than for Medicare, so this incentive is reversed there.

States vary widely in the way they pay nursing homes who care for Medicaid patients. Each system has its advantages and disadvantages. If the state pays a uniform rate for all patients, regardless of their condition, it is tough for a very sick Medicaid patient who needs a lot of care to find a nursing home bed. If the state pays on a "cost-plus" basis, nursing homes have an incentive to be wasteful in order to raise their costs and their profits. If it pays a higher rate for patients who are sicker and require more care, nursing homes may even discriminate against *healthier* patients in order to get more, more profitable heavy-care patients; or they may commit fraud by exaggerating the seriousness of their patients' conditions to get more reimbursement. Anyway, it seems crazy to give nursing homes an incentive to take such terrible care of their patients that they get sicker (and moved into a higher-paying category)!

It is fairly common for patients to enter as private-pay patients, then qualify for Medicaid by spending down their excess assets for nursing home care. However, as discussed in Chapter 7, some states do not allow "income spend-down." A person with income higher than the Medicaid income limit cannot get Medicaid, even if he or she has no excess assets, and even if he or she actually devotes the excess income to paying for medical care.

In these states, nursing homes may want to keep out patients whose resources are close to the spend-down level but whose income is too high (e.g., people with a moderate private pension and Social

Security) — because there is a real risk that they will use up their assets but still be unable to qualify for Medicaid. The nursing home then risks the bad publicity of evicting the residents, or going without full payment.

Private-pay patients can usually find a nursing home bed quickly. Waiting lists for Medicaid patients (especially heavy-care patients), can stretch for several months, even a year or more. The only opening for a Medicaid patient may be in a facility that is not convenient to visitors, or that does not provide quality care.

Ironically, many older patients remain in the hospital because they cannot go home, and because there is no institutional bed for them. Of course, hospital charges are even higher than nursing home charges. Sometimes Medicare or Medicaid pays the cost of these days — sometimes the hospital is stuck. In the latter situation, the state Medicaid authority has no incentive to shift the patient from the hospital bed to a less expensive nursing home bed, if the hospital has to absorb the cost of the "Administratively Necessary Days" but the Medicaid system has to pay for the nursing home care.[2]

LONG TERM CARE INSURANCE

When it comes to long-term custodial care, there are two basic care options: home care, provided by people with a variety of skills (people who provide basic tasks like shopping and cooking; professionals who provide health care, assess the older patient's needs, and oversee the implementation of the plan), and institutional care. Institutions, in turn, are divided into those that are purely residential and those that provide intermediate or skilled nursing care. Long-term care (LTC) insurance issuers differ in their approach to residential facilities. Some do not cover these facilities, viewing them as a substitute for ordinary homes; others do provide benefits for facilities that fit within the definition of "Alternate Levels of Care," such as facilities that combine individual rooms for elderly people with services such as shared meals and assistance with taking medication. The difference between intermediate and skilled care is that skilled care facilities provide more intensive professional services.

Medicare has limited coverage of home care and skilled nursing care. (See Chapter 6.) For intermediate-level custodial care, there are several payment options (which can occur together or be combined in an integrated plan). The very wealthy (or those who do not have good planning advice) pay the entire, and very substantial, cost of the care out of their own pockets. In the worst-case scenario, this results in depletion of all assets owned by the sick person and his or her family.

For those with fewer assets, or those who create a plan that takes full advantage of the legal planning options, Medicaid will pay the full cost of skilled or intermediate care for eligible individuals. (See Chapter 7.) However, there is a possibility that the healthy spouse will be sued for non-support during the Medicaid recipient's life, or that a lien will be placed on the Medicaid recipient's home. As discussed in Chapter 7, for Medicaid benefits received after October 1, 1993, there is also a possibility that the Medicaid agency will be entitled to recovery against other assets in the Medicaid beneficiary's estate — financial mechanisms such as trusts and annuities.

The past few years have seen an increasing number of (LTC) insurance policies being issued. There has also been significant expansion in the variety of choices of coverage, and important consumer protections have been added both by statutory requirement and by the companies themselves to improve the products. LTC insurance permits people to insure themselves against the heavy cost of custodial care — with no need to worry about the Medicaid impact of their financial planning tactics. However, LTC insurance can also be used as part of a Medicaid plan. Some life insurance policies also can be supplemented with living benefit riders.

At first, development of LTC insurance was slow. In 1984, there were only 16 insurers selling LTC policies; in 1987, there were 72 insurers in the LTC market; and in 1988, *Consumer Reports* talked to 81 insurers that were described as either having a LTC product or thinking of offering one. (Some of these insurers were planning to leave the LTC market.) *LAN's* annual surveys showed 17 companies offering LTC coverage in 1987, 43 selling individual and 11 selling group LTC policies in 1988, and 52 selling individual and 19 selling group LTC in 1989. At least seven companies also offered LTC riders to life or universal life insurance policies. (See the discussion of "living benefits" on page 36.)[3]

Health Insurance Association of America (HIAA) figures showed that more than 1.3 million LTC policies had been sold by mid-1989, by the 109 companies then selling such policies. Nearly all the policies were individual policies (88%). Although there were 35 employers offering LTC coverage as an employee benefit, they owned only 3% of the policies. Another 8% were sold to group associations, and only 1% were living-benefit riders to life insurance policies.

It takes several years to compile and interpret statistics, so the HIAA's February, 1993 report dealt with industry conditions at the end of 1991. As of that time, there was an average increase in sales of 31% in each year 1987-1991, resulting in overall sales of 2.4 million policies. The market was highly concentrated: the top 15 insurers sold 80% of all individual and association policies. Furthermore, individual and association policies constituted 85% of the market, with 6% deriving from riders to life insurance policies, and only 9% from employer-sponsored groups.

Between 1987 and the end of 1991, 45 companies stopped selling long-term care insurance, or stopped selling certain kinds of long-term care insurance (e.g., they dropped group coverage but maintained sales to individuals and associations). In late 1991, there were 135 companies selling long-term care insurance somewhere in the United States; in 1991, there was a net exit from the market, with 12 new companies entering to sell LTC insurance, but 22 companies dropping out. Thus, when the planner assesses competing policies, the questions to ask include not only which policy is best under current conditions, but which companies are likely to remain in the market throughout the purchaser's lifespan.[4]

According to the Health Insurance Association of America (HIAA)'s 1995 annual survey, there were only 118 companies selling LTC insurance in the United States in 1994, down from the 1990 peak of 143 companies. As of 1994, about 3.8 million LTC insurance policies had been sold. An average of 450,000 new policies were sold in each year between 1991 and 1994, and the average age of purchasers was 66.7 years old. On the average, policy sales increased 27% per year between 1987 and 1994. As of 1994, there were more than 400,000 persons covered by the 968 employer group LTC insurance plans — but sales of group policies declined 50% in 1994.

The LTC insurance market is highly concentrated: the top 13 companies shared 80% of the market. Of the 12 best-selling LTC insurance plans in 1995, all of them offered coverage of nursing home care, home care, and adult day care; eleven of the twelve offered benefits for alternate levels of care and respite services. All of them covered Alzheimer's Disease, provided nursing home care with no fixed maximum benefit, and were available to qualifying applicants aged 80 and over.[5]

Unlike health insurance for active employees, where "group" policies are typically owned by the employer, and paid for in whole or in part by the employer (and which are sold to the entire group with no attempt at medical underwriting), group LTC policies are nearly always paid for by the members of the group. Furthermore, because it is impossible for LTC insurers to spread risk the way group health insurers can, group LTC policies are only about 5% cheaper than individual policies. The differential for health policies is much greater.

Sometimes state regulation distinguishes between a "true group", which exists for other purposes and peripherally is involved in selling LTC insurance, and the "discretionary group" formed entirely for insurance-related purposes. State law may define long-term care insurance in a way that only true groups (those meeting state criteria such as number of members, activities other than insurance sales, record-keeping, annual meetings, etc.) are allowed to sell such policies. Not all states regulate the activities of out-of-state groups in selling LTC insurance to group members within the state. Groups — especially discretionary groups — may also be at risk for conflict of interest, because they receive revenue from group insurance sales. The risk is that they may sell the policy that is most beneficial to the group, not the one that is most beneficial to the group members.

LTC IS DIFFERENT

LTC insurance is a very special type of product, and one which insurers have to approach with caution. It is easy to estimate the cost of repairing or replacing a burned-out nine-room house in a particular neighborhood, or the insurance value of a "totaled" 1988 Nissan Sentra; and the law of large numbers will predict the number of fire losses in a city in a ten-year period.

In contrast, there are not enough LTC policyholders to make adequate predictions of how many of them will require institutional care (and how many of those will qualify under the terms of the policy), how long they will be in the nursing home or receiving home care benefits, and, most important of all, how much their care will cost. It is perfectly clear when there has been a fire in a house or store (though not necessarily whose fault it was), but it is not always clear whether an elderly person can or should go into a nursing home.

LTC insurers face serious problems of "adverse selection" (also called anti-selection) and "moral risk." Only a very small percentage of the population owns LTC insurance — and they are likely to be those who believe themselves at the greatest risk of institutionalization.

Moral risk, also known as induced demand, comes from the fact that the need for institutionalization is somewhat subjective. Some people are not receiving any care at all, despite their need for help with daily activities; others are receiving family or professional care at home, but would really benefit by moving to a nursing home. Some nursing home residents would really be better off in the community if adequate supportive services could be provided there. If the coverage is available, some people will enter nursing homes even though they would have stayed in the community had coverage been unavailable.

Insurers are caught in a dilemma when it come to policy design. If LTC insurance is marketed only to the elderly, then many policyholders will make claims shortly after purchasing the policy, preventing the broad spreading of risk that is the essence of insurance. At first glance, the solution is to spread the risk among a broader group of policyholders of varying ages.

The problem with that approach (aside from the sales problems discussed below) is that insurers cannot predict how much LTC costs will be in the distant future. Most LTC policies have an annual premium that remains stable throughout the life of the policy — so the insurer must set a premium level and stick to it. (Of course, most policies permit an increase in premiums throughout an entire class; but it is impossible to raise the premium of a level-premium policy in individual cases, based on age.) A consumer's decision to buy a policy at a particular time is really a decision that it is worthwhile paying premiums for more years in order to "lock in" the lower premium attributable to purchase at an earlier age.

If a 45-year-old buys a policy today, and maintains it until she enters a nursing home at age 72, the insurer can either offer her an affordable policy that provides a daily benefit that is far less than the real cost of nursing home care 27 years in the future — or provide significant inflation protection, at the cost of offering an unaffordable policy. The most common inflation protection provision offered by insurers is an annual 5% benefit increase, with a lifetime limit of 50% — a heavy burden for the insurer, although it may not be enough to make the policy responsive to real needs of the insured.[6]

Estimates by the Actuarial Research Corporation show that an older prospect would have to pay 30-40% more for an inflation-adjusted policy than one without indexing protection. Many customers would think that this is money well spent in light of the risk. However, younger buyers may have to pay four or even six times as much to get inflation protection, and it is unlikely that they can be induced to do so. For a younger family, trying to accumulate assets while satisfying day-to-day expenses (including other insurance coverage), LTC insurance is simply a very low priority.

REGULATION OF LTC INSURANCE

As it does for Medigap insurance (see Chapter 3), the National Association of Insurance Commissioners (NAIC) plays an important role in regulating LTC insurance. About half the states have their own LTC regulations, usually heavily influenced by the NAIC model. The NAIC defines LTC insurance as a policy offering coverage for at least twelve consecutive months (New Mexico's definition is coverage for at least six consecutive months), on an expense-incurred, indemnity, prepaid, or other basis, for medically necessary treatment or custodial care in a setting outside a hospital.

The state statutes regulate disclosure of the terms and conditions of LTC policies — usually by requiring a summary of coverage that sets out the policy terms and explains the difference between LTC and Medigap coverage. Consumers must be given information about: (1) policy limitations and exclusions, (2) deductibles and copayments, (3) the loss ratio for the policy, and (4) the policy's renewal provisions (including whether and when the insurer has the right to adjust the premiums).

About one-third of the states give LTC policy buyers a "free look" period of 10-30 days, during which the policy can be returned for a full refund if buyers decide they made a mistake in purchasing the coverage.

There are four possible types of renewal provisions for LTC policies:

(1)   The least protection for policyholders is provided by the "optionally renewable" policy, which gives the insurer the decision as to whether or not to renew a policy when its term expires.

(2)   A "conditionally renewable" policy allows the insurer to deny renewal to an entire class of policyholders, to stop selling LTC coverage in a geographic area, or to refuse individual policyholders renewal based on factors other than the state of their health. Thus, if a policy is condition-

ally renewable, the insurer cannot turn down an individual's renewal application based on deterioration in his or her health. Several states (for instance, Arizona, Florida, Hawaii, Idaho, Indiana, Illinois, Iowa, Louisiana, Minnesota, Nebraska, North Carolina, Oklahoma, South Carolina, Virginia, and Washington) require policies to be at least conditionally renewable.

(3)   If the policy is "guaranteed renewable", the policyholder is automatically entitled to renewal if he or she wants to renew an expired policy. However, the insurer retains the right to raise premiums on a class basis. This is by far the most common renewal provision used by insurers. The NAIC Model Regulation §6(A)(1) (a provision adopted by many states) requires long-term care insurance policies to be either guaranteed renewable or non-cancellable. The NAIC has discussed making it mandatory that all policies be non-cancellable (i.e., that rate increases would not be permitted); the industry has protested the potential loss of all flexibility in adjusting premiums to prevailing costs and conditions.

(4)   If the policy is non-cancellable, the policyholder is entitled to unlimited renewal whenever the policy expires, at no increase in premiums. Some consumer advocates want to impose a requirement of non-cancellability on all LTC policies. However, if they win, it will not benefit the elderly as a whole, because premium rates of all policyholders would have to be set high enough to deal with renewals by very sick 90-year-olds.

Another variable is that some policies limit inflation protection, either to a certain number of years (such as 10 years after purchase of the policy) or to a certain age (such as 70 or 80). Some policies are available with lifetime inflation protection, or inflation protection to age 85. Inflation protection may also have a percentage limit per year, for the lifetime of the policy, or both (e.g., a maximum of 5% per year, 50% overall).

Section 11 of the NAIC Model Regulation (7/93 version) requires inflation protection to be offered in all long-term care insurance policies. Policyholders (and individuals who are certificate-holders in group policies) must have access to benefit levels with the option of increasing "meaningfully." Meaningful increases are defined as enhanced benefits of at least 5% compounded per year without new proof of insurability (this option lapses if it is not exercised); or coverage of a percentage of actual or reasonable charges of long-term care, without a maximum "ceiling" amount imposed. The standardized disclosure form (Outline of Coverage) given to applicants must compare the effects of having inflation protection versus not having inflation protection on benefits payable under the policy. Inflation protection must be offered in true long-term care insurance policies, but the offer is not mandatory for life insurance Accelerated Death Benefit (ADB) riders.

PRIOR HOSPITALIZATION AND STEP-DOWN PROVISIONS

The very first LTC policies were offered before the Medicare Catastrophic Coverage Act was passed, and therefore followed the Medicare Part A definition of "skilled care" and imposed a "prior hospitalization" requirement. That is, nursing home care would not be covered under the policy unless the policyholder had been discharged from a hospital — after a hospital confinement of at least three days — not more than 30 days before entering the nursing home. The Medicare Catastrophic Coverage Act removed the prior hospitalization requirement from the Medicare law. Now the Medicare Catastrophic Coverage Act has been repealed, and the Medicare prior-hospitalization requirement has been reinstated. Therefore, an important function of LTC insurance, from the consumer's perspective, is providing nursing home benefits to people who are not entitled to Medicare nursing home benefits because they enter the nursing home directly from the community, without being hospitalized first.

Some LTC policies included a "step-down" requirement instead of, or in addition to, a prior hospitalization requirement. Under a step-down provision, benefits will not be paid for custodial care unless the policyholder first was treated in a skilled nursing facility and was discharged when his or her need for care was reduced. In other words, benefits will not be paid for residential care facilities unless there was prior treatment in an intermediate care facility.

Although these provisions reduce the cost of LTC policies, they make it less likely that policyholders will collect benefits, and may lead to a false sense of security. After all, the primary motive for buying an LTC policy is to get care that is not covered by Medicare or Medigap policies. Section 6(B)(3) of the NAIC Model Act forbids policies to "provide coverage for skilled nursing care only or provide significantly more coverage for skilled care in a facility than coverage for lower levels of care." It also forbids eligibility for institutional care to depend on receipt of a higher level of institutional care. In general, prior institutionalization requirements (e.g., home care) are forbidden, but prior institutionalization requirements can be imposed on post-confinement, post-acute care, and recuperative benefits, and on waiver of premium, as long as adequate disclosure is provided. Furthermore, if non-institutional benefits are subject to a prior institutionalization requirement, 30 days is the longest institutional stay that can be required as a condition of receiving benefits. Some states have imposed limitations on step-down provisions and prior hospitalization requirements (e.g., Florida, Illinois, Maryland, Kentucky, Louisiana, Michigan, New Mexico, North Dakota, Oregon, South Carolina, West Virginia).

The current generation of LTC policies usually do not include prior hospitalization or step-down requirements; but many people own older policies with these limitations. It is hard to advise them what to do. They may be medically disqualified from buying a more protective policy; and they are older than when they bought the now-outmoded policy, so their premium for a new-generation policy would be higher. Furthermore, the preexisting-condition limitation on the new policy may represent a significant portion of the life expectancy of the older person seeking improved LTC insurance.

Eligibility for benefits under an LTC insurance policy depends on satisfying the triggering requirements ("triggers") of the policy. Qualified policies under the Health Insurance Portability and Accountability Act of 1996 (see page 103) must have *both* ADL and cognitive impairment triggers.

ADL triggers relate to the insured person's inability to perform activities of daily living (ADLs), basic functions such as toileting, bathing, and self-feeding, without assistance. In other words, if the policy requires dependency in two out of six ADLs, a person who is no longer able to perform those ADLs independently can collect benefits.

A cognitive impairment trigger relates to having Alzheimer's Disease or a similar impairment that requires the individual to have supervision to protect him- or herself or to protect others. Cognitive impairment triggers work quite differently from ADL triggers, because an Alzheimer's patient or other cognitively impaired person may have the ability to perform ADLs (although they may be performed at inappropriate times or places). However, benefits are required because, without supervision, the impaired person may eat poisonous substances, accidentally start fires, wander into traffic, or cause other problems.

The NAIC Model Regulation §5(L) (followed by many state insurance laws) states that policy exclusions for "mental or nervous disorders" can only include "neurosis, psychoneurosis, psychopathy, psychosis, or mental or emotional disease or disorder." What this means in practical terms is that long-term care insurance policies cannot use a mental illness exclusion to avoid paying benefits for Alzheimer's Disease, which is an organic illness of the brain, not an emotional illness of the mind.

However, there may be other provisions within a long-term care insurance policy that may prevent Alzheimer's Disease patients from accessing benefits. If the policy is triggered by a doctor's certification of "medical necessity" for the benefits, the Alzheimer's patient's often-vigorous physical health may prevent benefit availability.

WAITING PERIODS AND PREEXISTING CONDITION LIMITATIONS

The insurance contract can work only if there is a balance of risk accepted both by insurer and insured. Nobody would buy insurance if they believed that it was *impossible* ever to collect benefits; they must believe that benefits will be paid if and when they fall within the terms of the policy. Insurers must believe that they will have a broad spectrum of insureds, some of whom will collect small benefits, some large benefits, some none at all. Benefits must be payable over a long period, not all at once. One way this balance is struck is through the preexisting condition/waiting period provision, which deters consumers from waiting until they *know* they need immediate treatment before buying insurance.

Usually, an LTC policy will define a preexisting condition as one which was treated by a doctor, or one which has the presence of symptoms which would induce an ordinary, prudent person to consult a doctor. The preexisting condition provision is used to cope with the problem of people who defer or cannot afford medical treatment for a problem which has already manifested itself. A certain waiting period is imposed (e.g., six months) *after* coverage becomes effective. Once this period elapses, the insurer can no longer claim that the condition for which benefits are sought is a preexisting one so that the treatment is excluded by the policy.

Preexisting condition limitations create a lot of problems in employer group policies, because it is very common for a new employee to make a claim which is denied on the grounds that the condition preexisted the coverage under the group policy. The problems are even greater in LTC policies, where so many claims are made for slow-developing diseases such as cancer and conditions such as Alzheimer's Disease where symptoms may exist for a long time before a definitive diagnosis is made. Courts have not had much to say about these issues. However, the 1985 *Brock* case from Georgia[7] forbade an insurer to disallow Alzheimer's disease as a preexisting condition under a policy that covered preexisting conditions after a two-year waiting period. The case did uphold a "step-down" provision in the same policy (requiring prior hospitalization before paying nursing home benefits), even though the plaintiff charged that the provision should be declared void because it violates public policy.

Some state legislatures, concerned because preexisting condition limitations make it much harder for the elderly to collect insurance benefits (or to change policies if they are dissatisfied with a policy they have already purchased), have imposed limitations on policies sold within their states. For instance, the definition of preexisting condition given above may be enacted into law as the most stringent permissible definition. Insurers can use a definition that offers a higher degree of consumer protection, if they prefer. The longest permissible waiting period may be defined as six months (for someone who was over 65 when the policy became effective) or 24 months (for younger insureds). Most of the states have statutes controlling waiting periods and preexisting condition provisions. Some of these statutes also forbid the imposition of a new waiting period if the insured converts an LTC policy to another form of policy offered by the same insurer (e.g., switching from a group to an individual policy). NAIC Model Act §6(b)(2) forbids a new waiting period if existing coverage is converted or replaced by another policy from the same company — but a new waiting period can be required if the insured person voluntarily upgrades the policy by adding more benefits.

INCONTESTABILITY PROVISIONS AND POST-CLAIMS UNDERWRITING

Section 7 of the NAIC Model Act, adopted in December, 1992, states that during the first six months an LTC policy is in effect, the insurer has the right to rescind the policy, or deny a claim that would otherwise by valid, if the insurer is able to show that the insured person made a misrepresentation that was material to the insurer's accepting the coverage in the first place. After the policy has been in effect for six months, but before two years of effectiveness has elapsed, the insurer can rescind or deny an otherwise valid claim only if it can show misrepresentation that was both material to accepting the application and relating to the condition for which the insured person attempts to access benefits.

The policy becomes incontestable after two years. That is, mere misrepresentation does not permit contest of a policy — the insurer must be able to show that "the insured knowingly and intentionally misrepresented relevant facts relating to the insured's health."

This leads directly to the question of underwriting. It is in the best interests of all for insurers to gather appropriate information, and to make valid decisions about which applications should be accepted, which should be refused. An industry practice that attracted much negative comment was "post-claims underwriting": accepting all applications without inquiry into the applicant's health status. If and when the insured made a claim, the insurer might "discover" that the application should never have been accepted in the first place. The accrued premiums would be repaid — but the insured person would not have the insurance protection he or she contracted for.

To avert this unfair practice, §9 of the Model Regulation requires all applications (except applications for guaranteed-issue policies) to contain questions designed to discover the applicant's true health status. It must be disclosed that untrue or incorrect statements on the application can result in denial of benefits or loss of coverage. If a policy is issued to an applicant aged 80 or older (most companies won't sell at such an advanced age), the insurer must get either medical records, a report of a physical examination, an assessment of the applicant's functional condition, or a statement from the applicant's doctor.

RESPONSE TO CONSUMER CONCERNS

The insurance industry is sensitive to criticisms from the elderly and their advocates, and responds by constantly updating and upgrading policies. (There is an upside and a downside to this: consumers become uncertain, and are inclined to wait — perhaps too long — if they feel that later policies will provide much more protection or cost-effectiveness than those currently available.)

In response to criticisms of the high lapse rate (40-80% of LTC policies lapse), some companies offer nonforfeiture benefits using concepts derived from anti-lapse provisions of life insurance policies. For instance, a percentage can be instituted for a "reduced pay-up." If the percentage is 3%, and the policy was maintained for 10 years before lapse, the insured may be granted an indemnity equal to 30% of the indemnity of a policy maintained in full force. An "extended-term" option extends an extra month of coverage for every year the policy was in force before lapse. The policy may contain a death benefit if the insured dies, for instance, between the ages of 60 and 70. (In a sense, this is the converse of the life insurance policy with living benefits, discussed in Chapter 2.) The idea of cash value LTC insurance is also being explored, but the idea is in its infancy.

Some insurers offer single-premium LTC policies — which certainly eliminates any risk of future price increases!

Perhaps, after 1996's ban on Medicaid transfers, older people will take funds that they planned to transfer and use them to buy single-premium LTC insurance policies, thus satisfying the objective of reducing the potentially taxable estate and securing the availability of care — with no risk of federal prosecution for criminalized transfers. Because it is possible to make very large withdrawals from pension plans in the years 1997-1999 without triggering an excise tax penalty, pension plans may also be sources of funds for lump-sum LTC insurance premium payments.

Section 8 of the NAIC Model Act requires some type of nonforfeiture benefit, but does not specify its form: all LTC policies (as well as certificates for group policies) must provide for "nonforfeiture benefits to the defaulting or surrendering policyholder or certificate-holder." Each state insurance commissioner is given responsibility for specifying the form which nonforfeiture benefits will be permitted to take within the state.

It should be noted that nonforfeiture provisions, like inflation protection, greatly increase LTC premiums. (See page 132.)

Model Regulation §7 deals with a related problem by seeking to control unintentional lapses. Each insured person must designate someone, such as a child or DPA agent, to receive additional notice if the policy is about to lapse for non-payment. If the potential lapse is caused by the insured person's forgetfulness, the designated person can make sure that the premium gets paid and the coverage is saved. LTC policies can also be reinstated at any time within five months after a lapse caused by the insured person's cognitive impairment.

NAIC STANDARDS

Although NAIC standards do not have the same legal stature in the LTC context as they do for Medigap insurance (where Congress has delegated to NAIC the power to set enforceable standards for Medigap policies), nevertheless they are important and influential. In response to industry changes, and the demands of consumers and legislators, the NAIC has constantly fine-tuned its Long-Term Care Insurance Model Act and Regulation.

The 1990 version contains provisions to prohibit post-claims underwriting (i.e., the practice of accepting applications — and premiums — without investigation of the applicant's medical condition, followed by rejection of claims because of medical conditions not disclosed by the applicant, because they were not inquired about by the insurer). Applications conforming to the NAIC Model must include clearly-written questions about the applicant's health and physical condition, with specific disclosure of the insurer's right to deny benefits and rescind policies for untrue statements on applications. Insurers must maintain records of rescission, and report them annually to state regulators.

Coverage of home care under LTC policies is discussed below. The NAIC Model does not require LTC policies to include a home care component; however, no policy including home care may include a step-down requirement. Home health benefits may not reduce the duration of institutional benefits provided under the policy; and any home care benefit must include services provided by custodial care workers and agencies that are not certified by Medicare.

There are tradeoffs involved in this requirement. Permitting benefits to be paid for care provided by those who are not registered nurses or licensed practical nurses, or by agencies that do not have Medicare certification, is a cost-saving device. Nonetheless, there is a risk that the quality of care will not be adequate without the safeguards of licensure and Medicare certification.

The Model Act and Model Regulations were revised in July, 1993. Since the 1990 version, the Model Act was amended most dramatically by the adoption of §7 (incontestability; see "Incontestability Provisions And Post-Claims Underwriting" above) and §8 (nonforfeiture benefits; see "Response To Consumer Concerns" above). Less dramatic changes were also made in the Model Regulation. In September, 1992, §16 of the Model Regulation was amended to require reporting of loss ratios on all policies (group as well as individual), setting an NAIC requirement of a 60% loss ratio; the "Drafting Note" points out that states may want to set the loss ratio above 60% for group policies.

December, 1992 amendments changed the Model Regulation requirements for notice to third parties (to prevent involuntary lapse) and disclosure of premiums. Section 20(C), on the responsibilities of associations with respect to LTC policies, was also added at that time.

LATER NAIC RULEMAKING

Subsequent to the January, 1993 Model Act and Model Regulation provisions "built in" to policies that are qualified under the Health Insurance Portability and Accountability Act of 1996, the NAIC has taken further actions.

The Model Regulation was amended in June, 1994, to restrict increases in premium rates for LTC insurance policies. Model Act §6(F) now provides that the initial premium for the policy cannot be increased in the first four years. Subsequent increases are restricted, based on the age of the insured. Premiums cannot increase more than a total of 25% in a four-year period (insureds under 65). They cannot increase more than 15% in a five-year period for insureds aged 65-80, or more than 10% in a five-year period for insureds aged 80 or over.

Another June, 1994 amendment of the Model Act, this time in §9, permits state insurance commissioners to establish minimum standards for market practices, premium rate stabilization, agent compensation, agent testing, reporting practices, and penalties within the LTC insurance market.

Model Regulation §5(E) defines cognitive impairment as "a deficiency in a person's short or long-term memory, orientation as to person place and time, deductive or abstract reasoning, or judgment as it relates to safety awareness."

Under Model Regulation §11, inflation protection must be offered as an option: i.e., the benefit level must be adjustable to cope with reasonably anticipated increases in the costs of securing long-term care. The insurer must disclose the anticipated additional premiums needed to pay for inflation protection. There are three permissible methods for insurers to offer inflation protection:

- All insureds receive automatic annual increases in benefit levels (compounded annually, 5% or more) — unless they actively reject this option (to reduce the premium).

- The periodic right to increase the benefit levels without proof of insurability; this option expires once the insured rejects an opportunity to increase coverage.

- The insurer can set the benefit level as a specified percentage of the actual cost of care, or a specified percentage of a schedule of reasonable charges, with no maximum.

Changes to the Model Regulation were adopted in March, 1995. A new §21 was adopted, dealing with gauging the suitability of a policy to the applicant's needs. All companies are obligated to have standards for judging whether purchase of an LTC insurance policy (or replacement of one policy by another) is consonant with the applicant's financial goals, existing insurance portfolio, and ability to pay, based on the size of the premium, the applicant's income and assets, and expected changes in income and assets.

All applicants must fill out a standardized personal worksheet at or before the time of the formal application. The disclosure form explaining the policy provisions is given to the applicant at the same time. The NAIC's Worksheet form says that "If you are buying this policy to protect your assets and your assets are less than $30,000, you may wish to consider other options for financing your long-term care" — although it does not mention Medicaid, or any other option, by name. (After January 1, 1997, Medicaid planning options are limited.)

If an applicant chooses to apply for a policy that does not fit the suitability guidelines, the Model Regulation gives the insurer two options: either reject the application on that basis, or send the applicant a form letter that allows the applicant to assent to the purchase despite its unsuitability under the guidelines. A policy can lawfully be issued to an "unsuitable" applicant who requests the policy and who meets medical underwriting standards.

The current version of Model Regulation §12 contains the requirements for application forms. A warning must be given about the consequences of replacing an LTC insurance policy with another, or replacing an accident and health policy with an LTC insurance policy, and the insurer must check to see that the policy applied for does not duplicate existing insurance. Furthermore, it is considered abusive to sell an LTC insurance policy to an individual who is a Medicaid beneficiary or who is Medicaid-eligible.

Model Regulation §23, the nonforfeiture provision, was also adopted in March 1995. (It should be noted that no state has fully adopted this NAIC requirement.) It mandates that all LTC insurance policies (but not life insurance accelerated death benefit provisions or riders) must offer a nonforfeiture option, defined as paid-up, shortened benefit period coverage after a lapse, with a credit for 100% of premiums paid. The nonforfeiture benefit must begin no later than the end of the third year after the policy date, although a later onset (ten years after the policy is first in force, or three years after it ceases to be subject to attained age rating) is permissible for policies using attained age rating.

So far, nonforfeiture options have not been very popular with consumers: only about 1.6% of individual purchasers in Massachusetts opt for this benefit, probably because it requires a premium increase of about 40%. Older purchasers of LTC insurance may also feel that they will soon be accessing benefits, and are not at high risk of forfeiture.[8]

The Model Regulation contains four appendices. Appendix A is used by insurance companies to report all instances in which they have rescinded LTC policies within the regulating state. (Voluntary rescission by the insured does not have to be reported on this form.) Appendix B is the form for the personal worksheet used to collect information about applicants' ability to comprehend the transaction, their health status, and the suitability of the policy for their needs. Appendix C is the standard disclosure form, and Appendix D is a response letter that applicants can use to demonstrate their informed intention to purchase a policy despite its lack of conformity to suitability guidelines.

In September, 1995, a new §24 was adopted, covering standards for benefit triggers. All LTC insurance policies must be triggered both by cognitive impairment and by dependency in three out of six ADLs, and can have other triggers at the option of the insurer. The Model Regulation defines dependency in a particular ADL as either a need for hands-on assistance with that task, or with a need for supervision or "verbal cueing" while the task is performed, for the safety of the insured or other people. (See page 105 below, however: note that the Health Insurance Portability and Accountability Act of 1996 requires benefits to be triggered by two out of five or six ADLs, and requiring dependency in three ADLs prevents a policy from being tax-qualified.)

The outline of coverage requirement (§25) was also amended in September of 1995. The standard format for the outline of coverage must be printed in 10-point or larger type, and must disclose that the policy is indeed one of long-term care insurance (and not a Medigap policy). The outline of coverage discloses basic information such as the benefits provided under the policy, its limitations and exclusions, the premium, and the relationship between its benefits and the projected cost of care. The outline of coverage explains when the policy can be returned for a refund, and conditions for continuing or discontinuing it. There must be an explicit disclosure that Alzheimer's Disease is covered (i.e., that it is deemed to be an organic illness rather than an excluded psychological disorder).

NEW FEDERAL RULES

The Health Insurance Portability and Accountability Act of 1996, P.L. 104-191, deals primarily with portability of acute-care health insurance for active employees. However, the 1996 legislation also contains provisions dealing with long-term care insurance, accelerated death benefits, and viatical settlements. The provisions about LTC insurance are found in Subtitle C of the statute (§§321-327), which enacts a new Internal Revenue Code section, §7702B.

Before the Health Insurance Portability and Accountability Act of 1996, there were serious unresolved questions about the tax status of both long-term care and long-term care insurance. It was not clear whether all costs of long-term care could be deducted as medical expenses; an argument could be made that expenses (such as board and lodging within a care facility) that replaced ordinary living expenses would not be deductible.

Thanks to the 1996 legislation, it is now clear that long-term care expenses are deductible as medical expenses. (Of course, taxpayers do not derive any actual deduction except to the extent that the total of all their allowable health care-related expenses exceeds 7.5% of their adjusted gross income.)

Before the Health Insurance Portability and Accountability Act of 1996, this ambiguity made it impossible to be sure whether LTC insurance premiums could be deducted on equal terms with acute health insurance premiums — or whether benefits received under an LTC insurance policy would be excludable from taxable income on the grounds that they were received under a policy of accident and health insurance. The 1996 legislation once again comes to the rescue: LTC insurance benefits are excluded from taxable income (within limits), and LTC insurance premiums are treated as health insurance premiums, whether they are paid by the employer or by an individual (although, as discussed below, the individual's deduction is limited).

This factor may spur an increase in group LTC sales, now that employers know that they can get a tax deduction for providing LTC insurance to employees and their dependents. (However, the Health Insurance Portability and Accountability Act of 1996 says that LTC insurance cannot be included in cafeteria plans and if LTC insurance is provided under a flexible spending account by an employer it will be included in the employee's income.)

Tax benefits under the Health Insurance Portability and Accountability Act of 1996 are available for a "qualified long-term care insurance contract." Policies issued before 1997 which were in compliance with the state law regarding long-term care policies are automatically "grandfathered in." Policies issued in and after 1997 must meet several requirements to be treated as qualified contracts:

- The policy does nothing but provide long-term care insurance — most saliently, it cannot have any cash value, although a refund can be provided at the insured's death or on cancellation or surrender of the policy.

- The policy must not duplicate Medicare benefits.

- It must cover only "qualified long-term care services."

- The recipients of these services must be "chronically ill individuals."

- The policy must satisfy specified NAIC consumer protection requirements, following the January 1993 NAIC rules (as discussed on page 99, above, there are later NAIC rules that have not been read into the Health Insurance Portability and Accountability Act of 1996).

It is not illegal to sell LTC insurance policies that are not qualified contracts under the Health Insurance Portability and Accountability Act of 1996; the only difference is that tax benefits are not guaranteed unless the policy is a qualified contract. The effect of the qualified contract rules will be to make LTC insurance policies somewhat more uniform than in the past. However, there is wide latitude for qualified contracts to take many forms. Although Congress chose to make Medigap insurance a standardized, commodity product, it has not done so with LTC insurance.

The Health Insurance Portability and Accountability Act of 1996 contains a window period of slightly more than one year, from August 21, 1996 to January 1, 1998, for tax-free exchange of old policies for new compliant policies. (Any "boot," or compensation other than a new policy received in exchange for the old one, will be taxed.)

This could be a good option if the old policy is an early-generation LTC insurance policy that provides fewer benefits or is more restrictive than later policies. There is also another option: to exchange, on a tax-free basis, an old policy for a qualified LTC insurance policy. The exchange must be completed within 60 days.

Services and Recipients

The Health Insurance Portability and Accountability Act of 1996 defines "qualified long-term care services" as "necessary diagnostic, preventive, therapeutic, curing, treating, mitigating, and rehabilitative services, and maintenance or personal care services" that a "chronically ill individual" receives under a care plan that is prescribed by a doctor, nurse, or other licensed health care practitioner.

In other words, then, the services must be necessary, but they need not be acute-care services — chronic and custodial care services are covered, and there is no need for the recipient of the services to show potential for improvement rather than mere maintenance of health status.

A chronically ill individual is a person who has been certified by a licensed health practitioner as either cognitively impaired or ADL-dependent. For Health Insurance Portability and Accountability Act of 1996 purposes, someone who has a "severe" cognitive impairment is chronically ill if he or she needs substantial supervision to prevent threats to his or her own safety, or the safety of other people. ("Severe" is not defined for this purpose in the statute, and the legislative history doesn't have anything to say either.) Furthermore, a licensed health professional must have certified the presence of a severe cognitive impairment at some time within the 12-month period preceding the application for benefits.

ADL dependency means that the insured has been certified by a health professional as having been unable to perform two or more ADLs without substantial assistance from another individual. The inability to handle daily tasks unassisted must be "due to a loss of functional capacity." The inability to perform ADLs must be certified as lasting "for a period of at least 90 days." The legislative history is helpful here: it says that the 90 day requirement is not a waiting period (i.e., it is not necessary to wait 90 days after the certification to begin collecting policy benefits under a qualified contract). Presumably, the requirement was added to distinguish between a genuine, ongoing loss of capacity and a temporary problem.

Under the law prior to the Health Insurance Portability and Accountability Act of 1996, policies that contained an ADL trigger could choose both the activities treated as ADLs, and the number of dependencies required to trigger coverage. The 1996 legislation requires that all qualified long-term care insurance contracts refer to either five or six of a standard list of ADLs:

- eating

- toileting

- transferring (e.g., from bed to chair)

- bathing

- dressing

- continence

Furthermore, coverage must be triggered by two ADL dependencies out of five or six — not three.

In sum, qualified long-term care insurance contracts must have both an ADL and a cognitive impairment trigger, not just one. Furthermore, the insurer's ability to define ADLs, and to select ADLs for coverage, is severely constrained.

Benefit Limits

The general rule under the Health Insurance Portability and Accountability Act of 1996 is that benefits received from a qualified long-term care insurance contract are "accident and health" benefits, and therefore are not taxed. However, there are limitations imposed by the 1996 legislation on this general rule of non-taxability. There is a "per diem limitation" of $175/day in 1997. This amount will be adjusted upward in each later year to account for inflation. If policy benefits are received that are greater than $175/day, the excess is still tax-free — provided that the benefit does not exceed the actual cost of LTC services provided to the insured.

In other words, if the benefit is $150/day, it is tax-free (even if it is greater than the actual cost of care). If the benefit is $200 a day, and the cost of care is $210, then the benefit is also tax-free. But if the insured receives an amount that exceeds both the actual cost of care and $175/day (as adjusted for inflation), then he or she will have taxable income.

If there are multiple sources of reimbursement (more than one insurance policy, or insurance plus Medicare, for example), the per diem limitation is computed by subtracting total reimbursement from all sources from the actual cost of care. If multiple parties are involved, everyone who receives indemnity benefits on behalf of a single insured is treated as only one person. The per diem limitation is allocated first to the insured, then to the others. The 1996 legislation mandates that regulations be drafted to explain how the allocation should be performed.

Limitations on the Deduction

Determining what part of the LTC insurance premium will be deductible (if any) depends on two factors: whether the individual is self-employed or an employee or retiree, and on his or her age.

Self-employed people are in a far better position to deduct LTC insurance premiums. In 1997, the self-employed can deduct 40% of their LTC insurance premiums and/or acute health insurance premiums. The percentage that can be deducted phases upward gradually, reaching 80% in 2006. Furthermore, some experts feel that the rest of the premium can be treated like an employed person's premium, and added to the total of health-care costs that can be deducted to the extent they exceed 7.5% of AGI.

For other people, the "eligible long-term care insurance premium" can be treated as a potentially deductible health care cost for 1997 and later years. The amount of premium that can be aggregated with other health care costs depends on the age of the taxpayer for the particular tax year for which a deduction is sought. (It does not depend on the entry age at which the policy was purchased.)

For individuals who have attained the age of 40 or less, the maximum potential deduction is $200 a year. For individuals ages 41 though 50, the maximum is $375 a year. Persons ages 51 through 60 can apply up to $750 toward the deduction. There is a dramatic increase in potential deductibility for persons who are ages 61 through 70: $2000 a year. Persons over 70 can apply up to $2500 a year toward the deduction. Of course, if the actual premium is lower than the potentially deductible amount, only the actual premium is used in the calculation. The premium amounts will be adjusted for inflation in post-1997 years. These amounts apply per taxpayer, not per tax return — so they can be doubled if a married couple both buy policies and file joint returns.

These figures have some planning implications. Although the potentially deductible figures for persons under age 60 are small, they may in fact represent the entire premium — if the insured has modest requirements in an LTC insurance policy. Persons over 60, however, may find that the full deductible amount is still less than the premium, especially if they anticipate getting care in a high-cost area, or if they want a policy with a full panoply of features. In this instance, the tax benefits will not be the deciding factor. The sale will probably turn on the prospect's understanding of the need to ensure that quality long-term care will be available at need — and on his or her understanding of the increased difficulties in Medicaid planning in the post-Health Insurance Portability and Accountability Act of 1996 environment.

Of course, the potential tax deduction is greater for a self-employed person (because 40%-80% of the premium can be deducted — depending on the year — irrespective of whether the entrepreneurial taxpayer has any other deductible medical expenses), and this point is well worth mentioning in a discussion with a self-employed potential LTC insurance buyer.

Compliance with Other NAIC Rules

Qualified long-term care insurance contracts must comply with the NAIC preexisting condition limitation. That is, the most stringent preexisting condition limitation that can be applied to an LTC insurance policy is a six-month exclusion of conditions for which medical treatment or advice was recommended by or received from a health care provider during the six months before the policy's effective date. (This limitation does not preclude insurers from getting complete medical information from applicants, nor from carrying out medical underwriting.)

In a qualified level-premium LTC insurance policy, nonforfeiture benefits must be available as an option. The policyholder must be given a choice of reduced paid-up insurance, extended term insurance, shortened benefit period, and any other nonforfeiture option that has received approval. Furthermore, the insurer can alter the nonforfeiture benefit only to reflect changes in claims, persistency and interest as reflected in changes of rates for premium paying contracts.

Qualified long-term care insurance contracts must also abide by Model Act §6D, which forbids LTC insurance policies to impose a requirement of prior hospitalization before benefits can be used. In other words, even though certain Medicare benefits depend on the patients' having spent at least three days in the hospital, LTC insurance policies must make it possible for a person to collect benefits even if he or she has not been hospitalized first. Step-down requirements are also forbidden: i.e., the policy cannot base eligibility for a lower level of care on previous use of a higher level of care. A prior institutionalization requirement (i.e., receiving care in a hospital or nursing home instead of at home) can be imposed, but only for waiver of premium, post-confinement, post-acute care, and recuperative benefits, and those benefits must be described in a clearly labeled, separate paragraph within the contract.

From the consumer's viewpoint, greater access to insurance benefits without various limitations is very important — because usually what happens is that a person's condition deteriorates over time, requiring a gradual increase in the use of long-term care services. It's possible to imagine the opposite scenario (for instance, a broken hip, followed by convalescence, followed by return to more or less normal functioning) but it is less likely to occur.

Various provisions of the January, 1993 version of the NAIC Model Regulation are also mandatory for qualified contracts:

- •   §7A (policies must be either guaranteed renewable or noncancellable).

- §7B (limitations and exclusions that are permitted — i.e., preexisting conditions, mental illness, but Alzheimer's Disease is considered an organic illness, attempted suicide and self-inflicted injury, treatment provided in government facilities).

- §7C (extension of benefits).

- §7D (insured's right to continue or convert coverage).

- §7E (discontinuance and replacement of policies).

- §8 (insured's right to designate an agent, who will be notified in time to prevent unintended lapse).

- §9 (mandatory disclosures — e.g., terms of renewability; effect of riders and endorsements; terms of preexisting condition limitations; benefit triggers).

- §10 (post-claims underwriting forbidden — other than guaranteed-issue contracts, all applications must collect adequate medical information, and must disclose that benefits can be denied, or policies rescinded, if the applicant misrepresents medical facts).

- §11 (minimum standards — if home care is covered, it must not be conditioned on the need for skilled care, or on prior institutionalization).

- §12 (inflation protection must be offered as an option — but the applicant can signal rejection of this option by a separate signature on the application itself, or on a separate form.

- §23 (preexisting condition limitations and waiting periods are not allowed in replacement policies).

Requirements for Home Office Conduct

In addition to defining the parameters of the qualified long-term care insurance policy that is eligible for tax-favored treatment, the Health Insurance Portability and Accountability Act of 1996 also imposes tax penalties on issuers of qualified contracts that fail to abide by the mandatory standards for marketing and disclosure. The penalty is $100 per insured per day, although the penalty can be reduced or waived if the insurer acted with reasonable cause and was not willfully neglectful (for instance, if the insurer acted in accordance with a reasonable but incorrect interpretation of the 1996 legislation). Penalty reductions can be granted "to the extent that payment of the tax would be excessive relative to the failure involved."

The insurer must satisfy these Model Act provisions:

- §6F (30-day free look; if an application is denied, the refund of any deposit must be made within 30 days of the denial).

- §6G (obligation to supply an outline of coverage, in the standard format prescribed by the state's insurance commissioner, at the time of initial solicitation).

- §6H (obligation to issue descriptive certificates to individuals participating in a group LTC insurance plan).

- §6I (requirement of providing a policy summary).

- §6J (obligation to furnish a monthly report of payments made and effect on the underlying policy, whenever accelerated death benefits are being paid out).

- §7 (period of incontestability — i.e., a policy can be rescinded, or a claim denied, based on misrepresentation material to acceptance of an application, within six months; if the policy has been in force for six months-two years, rescission or claim denial requires misrepresentation material to coverage and also involving the condition for which benefits are sought; after two years, the policy is contestable only because of the insured's knowing and intentional misrepresentation).

The insurer also must comply with many of the provisions of the Model Regulation, or face the $100 daily tax:

- §13 (application forms and replacement coverage).

- §14 (annual reporting; an additional report, once a year or more frequently, must also be rendered disclosing claim denials other than those denied based on preexisting conditions or failure to satisfy a waiting period).

- §20 (requirement of filing marketing materials with state regulators).

- §21 (marketing standards).

- §22 (suitability).

- §24 (standard format for the outline of coverage).

- §25 (mandate to deliver a shopper's guide on request).

PURCHASE PATTERNS

In 1992, a study, "Who Buys LTC?" was published. The study, commissioned by HIAA and carried out by Lifeplans, a consulting firm, looked at LTC insurance purchasing behavior and trends in 1990. It is informative to note what the average purchase and purchasing motivation were, although the elapse of even a few years means that the benefit amounts are likely to be too low for contemporary needs.

The typical insurance purchaser was a 68-year-old married woman; almost three-quarters of purchasers either lived with a spouse or with a spouse and other people (e.g., parents living with their grown children). Income of purchasers was fairly evenly divided: 18% had incomes below $15,000 a year, 11% income between $15,000-$19,000, 13% over $20,000 but less than $25,000, and so forth. Only 21% had income of $50,000 a year or more.

The typical policy covered all levels of institutional care (skilled, intermediate, and custodial) as well as home care, adult day care, alternate levels of care (specialized housing), and respite for caregivers. However, the average benefit level was not very high: $80 a day for institutional care, $40 a day for home care. The policies typically sold by the 15 carriers that captured 80% of the market had all three possible benefit triggers: certification of medical necessity for long-term care; ADL limitations; and cognitive impairment.

Purchasers' motivations were very significant: 30% said they bought LTC insurance to avoid becoming dependent; 14% wanted to protect their assets; 6% had a similar motive, to avoid losing their life savings; and 8% wanted to maintain their standard of living and protect it against high levels of health care costs.

A sophisticated study published in 1995[9] says that the amount of insurance purchased was most dependent on income, not the amount of assets — people studied tended to buy only enough insurance to cover the expected Medicaid penalty period. Men tended to buy more coverage than women, and more coverage was purchased in states that were active in pursuing Medicaid estate recoveries.

THE PUBLIC-PRIVATE PARTNERSHIP EXPERIMENT

The Robert Wood Johnson Foundation launched a fascinating experiment in 1989. Eight states (California, Connecticut, Indiana, Massachusetts, New Jersey, New York, Oregon, and Wisconsin) got foundation grants to test a system for coordinating LTC insurance and Medicaid. The theory was that people could buy private insurance; when private insurance coverage was exhausted, they would automatically qualify for Medicaid benefits, even if they had more assets than the Medicaid program would otherwise permit. (See Chapter 7 for a discussion of Medicaid asset rules.)

The states adopted different methods of linking insurance and public benefits: for instance, individuals could purchase $1 of coverage for each $1 of assets they wished to shelter, or could purchase a stipulated amount of coverage in return for a promise of Medicaid eligibility if the coverage was exhausted.

The experiment must be judged a failure. Although a few of the test states did bring policies to the market, the policies were not very popular — perhaps because the public, which finds LTC insurance difficult to understand and depressing to think about, found the "Partnership" policies even harder to understand. In the early 1990s, several states (Colorado, Illinois, Iowa, Missouri, North Dakota) passed laws to study public-private partnerships, or to put them into operation.

However, the most crucial factor in dooming the Robert Wood Johnson experiment was Congress. The Omnibus Budget Reconciliation Act of 1993 (OBRA '93) requires states to seek estate recoveries from the estates of persons who own public-private partnership LTC policies. This means that buying one of these policies will *not* succeed in preserving the estate — which was the underlying reason why people would want the policies in the first place.

Five states (California, Connecticut, Indiana, Iowa, and New York) are "grandfathered in" because they had Medicaid plan amendments authorizing Robert Wood Johnson policies before OBRA '93 was passed. In these states, public-private partnership policies can still be sold; the "grandfathering" effect is not limited to policies that were sold before OBRA '93. But if other states go ahead and set up a public-private partnership, the policies will not protect estates against Medicaid recovery.[10]

THE EMPLOYER'S ROLE IN LTC

Another solution to the problem might be to get employers involved. After all, hardly anyone would have health insurance if they had to pay 100% of the premium out of pocket. Some insurers do sell group LTC coverage, and state retirement systems (Alaska, Maryland, Ohio) and some very large employers (e.g., American Express, John Hancock Mutual Life Insurance, Procter & Gamble, Eastman Kodak, IBM) do offer some degree of employment-related group LTC coverage.

Although the employee pays the full premium under many plans, the employer is able to negotiate favorable terms for the employee group. Coverage may also be available for employees' dependent parents, even if they are not active or retired employees of the employer sponsoring the group. According to John Hancock Financial Services figures, a 60-year-old IBM employee will pay about $1,000 a year as a premium for a policy with a $150-a-day nursing home benefit. At 70, the premium is over $2,000; at age 72, the premium is $3,028. This is a heavy cost — but quite economical compared to the $3,900 premium for an individual policy. The IBM plan also has a "cash value" feature, so that a policy that would otherwise lapse can be transformed to a smaller paid-up policy. This feature requires a 10-20% increase in the premium.[11]

HIAA examined the problem in its 1989 report, "Long-Term Care: An Emerging Employer Concern," based on a 1988 symposium at which 140 employers, insurers, and policymakers discussed the issue that has been called "the employee benefit of the 21st century."

Employers have concerns other than cost that keep them from offering LTC insurance. They do not know how their plans should allocate resources between nursing home benefits and home care. (See page 102 for discussion of tax issues.) (From the insurer's viewpoint, Rev. Rul. 89-43, Mar. 22, 1989, makes it clear that LTC insurance reserves and earnings on these reserves get the same favorable treatment as life policy reserves.) Employers are not sure how to "shop" for long-term care services, and do not know how to choose appropriate services or what costs should be.

Coopers & Lybrand partner Joseph Rosmann contributed some interesting insights to the symposium, noting that employees must be motivated to enroll in LTC plans, and that this can best be done by presenting it as a financial benefit (a savings mechanism) rather than a type of catastrophic health care coverage (which is unlikely to appeal to the younger workers who are the key to the actuarial soundness of the plan). He suggested that a new type of plan, which permits employees to "mix and match" benefits, and to tailor protection to income stages, would be more attractive.

A later HIAA survey (this one published in January, 1991) showed that 153 employers either offered or planned to offer long-term care insurance; most of the plans were quite recent, having been added since 1989. There were about 80,000 covered employees, with an average age of 43. Later figures from HIAA show 135 employers offering the coverage, but only 5-15% of eligible employees electing the coverage. The most common factor cited is lack of information, but perhaps workers in their 40s and 50s think that long-term care is too remote a contingency to concern themselves with; they may also find the insurance unaffordable, even given the savings obtainable with group coverage and low entry ages.

A small study (31 public and private employers) done in 1993 showed that the most popular program signed up 25% of eligible workers; the least popular, not a single employee or retiree. The average was 7% of eligible workers. Enrollment rates for retirees (who would be expected to have more interest in long-term care insurance — but perhaps less available cash to pay premiums) ranged from less than 1% to 11%; the average was 4.4%.

According to the Life Insurance Marketing and Research Association (LIMRA), annualized new premium in group LTC went up 40% between 1991 and 1993. In 1991, 92 new employer groups, with about 50,000 participants, were added; in 1992, 213 new groups and about 67,000 participants were added, so that there were 410 active employer groups, with more than a quarter of a million participants, in 1992.[12]

It is worthwhile including a discussion of this topic with your employer clients and prospects — but note that employers are usually looking for ways to terminate health benefits or shift costs to employees — not looking for new benefits to offer, however helpful they would be to employees!

Associations can be excellent prospects for group LTC (especially since, as mentioned above, they can save substantial revenue from the group policy). Furthermore, the prospecting process can remind the group's officers and members that their personal insurance portfolios are deficient — and that you are a knowledgeable and service-oriented purveyor.

HOME CARE IN LTC POLICIES

When most people think about long-term care, they think of nursing homes. However, there is an increasing trend to provide intensive long-term care "in the community." For example, visiting nurses could provide health care, while homemakers take care of services such as cleaning the house and cooking meals, and aides assist the elderly person with ADLs.

There are two arguments in favor of home care: that it enhances the quality of life of the recipient of the care, and that it saves money. However, only the former argument is valid. As long as the providers of care, not those who pay, decide how much care costs, there is no limit to the amount that home care can cost! Furthermore, there are legitimate economies of scale that can be realized in a nursing-home setting. A physical therapist who has to travel from client to client cannot see as many clients as one who can work with several at one time in a nursing home, then move on to another group of patients in the same nursing home.

There is a corresponding trend toward including home-care benefits in LTC policies. Usually, if home care is covered, the home care daily benefit will be 50% of the daily benefit for institutional care. (Therefore, especially if the policy has weak inflation protection, the insured may have a substantial out-of-pocket cost for home care despite receiving policy benefits.) Some policies also vary their home care coverage depending on the type of home care. For instance, the policy might provide coverage of 80% of the cost of skilled home care (e.g., care from a nurse or physical therapist), up to a maximum of $75/day, but only 50% of the cost of custodial home care (such as care provided by a nurse's aide or housekeeper), up to the daily maximum of $75.

Increasingly, it is an oversimplification to talk about home care benefits in LTC policies. Instead, it makes more sense to discuss home and community-based benefits, because there is a trend to include coverage of:

- Adult day care.

- Bed holds (when a nursing home resident must be hospitalized temporarily, or takes a short vacation from the nursing home).

- Case management services.

- Specialized housing.

- Respite care for the caregiver.

Section 10 of the NAIC Model Regulation sets standards for home and community-based benefits, if they are offered. (Under the NAIC Model Act and Regulations, it is permissible to sell a policy that is limited to institutional benefits and does not offer home care — but it is impermissible to sell one that is limited to *skilled* nursing care.) The home care benefit must be at least 50% of the institutional benefit. Home health benefits can be added to institutional benefits in determining if the maximum coverage has been exhausted. Policies that do include home care coverage must cover adult day care.

Certain restrictive provisions are forbidden: for instance, insurers cannot limit payment of home care benefits to persons who would need to go to a skilled nursing home if they could not get home care. Nor can it be required that the insured person use institutional care before collecting home health benefits. (Although some people do use home care after a hospital discharge, most people stay at home as long as they can, so they typically move from home to an institution, not the other way around.) Insurance benefits must be provided when the lowest-cost provider who can render the services adequately is involved: it is forbidden to require a Medicare-certified home health agency, or care from a registered nurse or therapist, when a less-skilled, lower-cost provider would be adequate for the patient's needs. Personal care services from home health aides must be covered if the policy includes home care at all.

Home care benefits in LTC policies are problematic. It is hard to distinguish between medical needs and social needs, between necessary and optional activities, and between special needs and the normal functions of everyday life that are usually not covered by insurance. Insurers do not want to pay for services that, absent insurance, would be provided free by relatives or friends; but the elderly do not want to impose on relatives and friends for services that can be provided more consistently by paid providers. Clearly, success in selling policies including meaningful home-care benefits depends on the insurers' instituting "gatekeeper" and monitoring mechanisms. However, these mechanisms involve a great deal of work, and can be expensive to administer. They are also resented by policyholders and their families.

CHAPTER FOOTNOTES

1. These figures come from Erik Eckholm, "An Aging Nation Grapples With Caring for the Frail," *New York Times* March 17, 1990 p. . Al and Joshua M. Wiener, "Which Way for LTC Financing?" *Generations* Spring 1990 p. 5.

2. Reimbursement and AND problems are discussed in "Nursing Homes: Admission Problems for Medicaid Recipients and Attempts to Solve Them," GAO/HRD-90-135 (September 1990).

3. Chuck Jones, "LAN's Third Annual Long-Term Care Survey," May 1989.

4. Chuck Jones, "LTC Market Growing But Many Issues Unresolved," LAN December 1989 p. 27; Susan Van Gelder and Diane Johnson, "Long-Term Care Insurance: A Market Update," HIAA, January 1991; Khurshid Ahmad et.al., "Long Term Care: An Insurance Industry Perspective," 48 *J. Am. Soc. CLU / ChFC* 62 (March 1992); "LTC Insurance Rapidly Evolves," (no by-line), *LTC News & Comment* May 1993 p. 9.

5. See Matthew P. Schwartz, "Fewer Companies in Market, but LTC Sales Grow," *National Underwriter* (Life/Health Edition) May 8, 1995 at 3; Frederick Schmitt, "HIAA Expects Long-Term Care Sales to Rebound," *National Underwriter* (Life/ Health Edition) May 13, 1996 at 1.

6. Social scientists Alice Rivlin and Joshua Wiener make this point in their book, *Caring for the Disabled Elderly: Who Will Pay?*, published by the Brookings Institute in 1988.

7. *Brock v. Guaranty Trust Life Insurance Co.*, 175 Ga.App. 275, 333 S.E.2d 158 (1985).

8. Jim Connolly, "Why Aren't Consumers Buying More LTC Policies?" *National Underwriter* (Life/Health Edition) July 31, 1995 p. 2.

9. Nanda Kumar et.al., "Understanding the Factors Behind the Decision to Purchase Varying Amounts of Long Term Care Insurance," 29 *Health Services Research* 653 (February 1995).

10. For the history of the Robert Wood Johnson experiment, see GAO/HRD-90-154, "Long-Term Care Insurance: Proposals to Link Private Insurance and Medicaid Need Close Scrutiny," (September 1990). The OBRA '93 section is §13612(a). For historical perspective, see "Connecticut to Test Long-Term Benefits Plan," *National Underwriter* September 18, 1989 p. 25; Matthew Schwartz, "Insurers Launch Conn. LTC Program," *National Underwriter* January 6, 1992 p. 3, and Alan M. Kunerth, "Timely Medicine for the LTC Crisis," *Best's Review* January 1992 p. 34. For the New York program, see Milt Freudenheim, "Medicaid Plan Promotes Nursing-Home Insurance," *New York Times* May 3, 1992 p. A1. *LTC News & Comment* has good coverage of the evolution of public-private partnerships: see, e.g., news item, "Update on Connecticut Partnership," January 1993 p. 1; news item, "Connecticut Partnership Update," June 1993 p. 12; Kevin J. Mahoney, "California's Partnership Sets New Standards," May 1993 p. 7; and C. Jean Blaser, "Illinois Partnership in Motion," July 1993 p. 7.

11. Mary Rowland, "Group Policies, Long-Term Care," *New York Times* October 21, 1990 p. F17.

12. For HIAA study, see news item, *Wall Street Journal*, July 15, 1991 p. B1; for 1993 study, see Phoebe S. Liebig, "Employer LTC Plans Fail to Live Up to Expected Enrollments," *LTC News & Comment* May 1993 p. 11. LIMRA figures are found in Matthew P. Schwartz, "Insurers Reluctant to Sell Group LTC," *National Underwriter* May 3, 1993 p. 7.

Chapter 5

HOW WELL DOES LONG-TERM CARE INSURANCE WORK?

In the early to mid-1980s, the most cogent criticism of long-term care (LTC) products was that virtually no one had access to any type of LTC product! Today, however, many insurers have entered the field, and criticisms center around factors of cost and policy design rather than availability.

In January, 1990, for example, Families USA Foundation released a report, "The Unaffordability of Nursing Home Insurance", prepared in collaboration with United Seniors Health Cooperative's James P. Firman and Susan Polniaszek. Their objective was to determine what percentage of the 22 million members of the prime market for LTC insurance (those aged 65-79) could afford the top-quality policies being marketed nationwide by leading insurance companies. (As a comparison point, 1.3 million LTC policies had been sold as of June 1989; probably most, but not all, were purchased by people over 65.)

The policies studied were sold by A+ or A-rated companies; had a minimum benefit period of 2 years; provided either $110 per day without inflation protection, or $80 per day with automatic escalation in light of inflation; did not have a prior hospitalization or step-down requirement; and did not have a deductible period in excess of 90-100 days. For a 67-year-old insured, 1990 premiums at the nine companies studied averaged $1,346 per year for the minimum recommended plan, ranging from a low of $690 to a high of $2,749. (The policies that were analyzed were less comprehensive — and thus less expensive — than the minimum plan recommended by *Consumer Reports*, which suggested a deductible of only 20 days and a guarantee of at least four years' benefits. Such a policy would be even less affordable than those criticized by the study.)

The standard of affordability assumed that older customers can afford to spend up to 10% of their income and available assets for the combination of LTC premiums and medical expenses not covered by insurance. This reflects an assumption that a certain degree of asset liquidation can and should take place, and it was quantified by treating the assets as an annuity.

Even under this assumption (which would be unacceptable to many older consumers), the study found that only about one-sixth of Americans age 65-79 can afford the average cost of the high-quality policies studied. In fact, about three-quarters of Americans in this age group cannot afford even the lowest priced policies meeting the survey standards. Moreover, the older a person is (and therefore the greater the risk of institutionalization), the less likely he or she is to be able to afford a policy.

An earlier publication by Mr. Firman of the United Seniors Health Cooperative (monograph, *"Private Long-Term Care Insurance: How Well is it Meeting Consumer Needs and Public Policy Concerns?"*, September, 1988) addressed another criticism of LTC insurance: that policy design prevents those who *can* afford such coverage, and who are aware of the need and purchase LTC policies, from collecting benefits. The study, performed between April and July 1988, analyzed 77 LTC policies and policy options offered by 21 companies selling in the District of Columbia area. Eighty-two percent of the policies and options had such severe restrictions (prior hospitalization and step-down, for instance) that the probability of NOT collecting any benefits under the policy was 61%. Only 18% of the plans and options gave policyholders as much as a 50/50 chance of collecting benefits. The most common policy structure was a $50 per day indemnity; even if collected, this amount would not pay all or even a substantial portion of the cost of care in many institutions.

U.S. Seniors Health Cooperative also looked at home care insurance in a March, 1990 study authored by Susan Polniaszek: "Will Your Insurance Pay If You Need Home Care? An Analysis of Major Long-Term Care Insurance Policies." The Study's conclusion was that only one of the nine major insurers whose policies on sale January 1, 1990 were examined provided an adequate home care benefit. The Amex policy was the only one found not to be deficient. It offered home care triggered by two ADL deficiencies or cognitive impairment, and could be purchased with benefits for 2, 3, or 4 years or for lifetime, subject to a 20 day deductible in a 60-day period or a 100 day deductible within

300 days. Coverage included skilled, health aide, and personal care, adult day care and respite care, reimbursed at 80% of the charge up to a daily limit.

The other eight were defective because of their step-down requirements or because of an overly restrictive definition based on medical necessity rather than the patient's need for assistance with the activities of daily living (ADLs). (According to this study, there are more than 1.6 million senior citizens who are impaired in at least two ADLs, and who live in the community rather than in nursing homes. A study using 1985 costs showed an average out-of-pocket expense on home care ranging from $2,000 to $8,000 a year per home care recipient.) Seven of the nine policies also offered too limited a duration of care. The study defined the average need as 4.5 weekly home care visits for a period of 5-10 years.

However, as discussed above, NAIC standards and many state laws forbid step-downs, and strict medical necessity triggers are being replaced by ADL and/or cognitive impairment triggers, so these concerns may be outdated.

In 1993, Families USA and HIAA debated affordability. Families USA's latest report found that only 15% of senior citizens could afford LTC insurance with low premiums and high copayments. If the opposite approach is taken — more insurance, and therefore lower copayments — Families USA said that only 3% of senior citizens would be able to afford the coverage. This time, their affordability standard was a premium less than or equal to 5% of income, and copayments not in excess of the insured person's income.

HIAA reported that its calculations showed that 60% of the elderly could afford to buy and maintain LTC insurance, noting that almost two-thirds of policyholders paid less than $1,000 a year for their coverage.

The various affordability studies have been criticized as methodologically flawed. The studies do not always use the same policy, or even the same type of policy, for analysis. Affordability is often set at an arbitrary percentage level of income, ignoring the role of pricing in demand. Perhaps, with better information, potential buyers would be able to distinguish between superior and inferior policies, and would be able to determine if they should buy LTC coverage, and if so, which policy.[1]

The essence of the need for home care is that the recipients suffer from one or more chronic diseases, such as arthritis, high blood pressure, and diabetes; the problem is not a flareup of acute disease but limitations in strength and mobility. Thus, an individual may desire home care (and purchase a policy that he or she believes has adequate home care benefits) under circumstances that would not trigger payment of benefits under a policy that requires that the home care be "medically necessary."

It is a tough call. Insurers want to design a practical, financially sustainable product that can be sold at affordable prices. One way to do this is to install "gatekeeper" mechanisms such as professional assessment and medical necessity qualifications. The problem of induced demand becomes severe when the policy provides benefits based on ADL limitations. On the other hand, consumers want and deserve meaningful protection. Every LTC policy must be designed, and modified as necessary, to strike the balance.

POLICY PROVISIONS

Actuary Kenneth Klueh summarizes typical LTC insurance policy provisions as follows:[2]

(1) Benefit is typically in indemnity form (usually ranging from $25-100), although a developing type of policy provides both home and institutional care on a service basis, with coverage by calendar year rather than spell of illness, subject to a 100-day waiting period (to coordinate with Medicare skilled nursing home coverage). Some innovative policies use concepts drawn from disability insurance (based on ADL limitations, stressing the needs of the client rather than dollar amounts) rather than from life or health insurance. As an example, some policies treat the benefit as a "pot of money," so that if the insured person uses benefits on a particular day that are below the maximum, the difference can be applied later to other benefits.

(2) Premium is typically level.

(3) Maximum issue age is usually 80-85.

(4) Guaranteed renewability is standard.

(5)   Three major patterns in waiting periods are found: no waiting period; 20 days; 100 days.

(6)   Policies typically cover Alzheimer's Disease but exclude mental illnesses that do not have an organic component.

(7)   Usually, if the patient enters and leaves the nursing home, then returns in less than six months, benefits will be granted without imposing a second waiting period or a second requirement of hospitalization.

(8)   As discussed above, newer policies seldom include a prior hospitalization or step-down requirement. If there is a prior hospitalization requirement, the insured must usually enter the nursing home within 30 days of hospital discharge to collect LTC benefits. Although NAIC rules and many state laws forbid it for newer policies, it was common in older policies for home care coverage to include a requirement of prior nursing home institutionalization — a provision that may make it hard for many insureds who still maintain the old policies to get home care benefits, because people usually want home care as soon as they become ill or frail, to keep them out of nursing homes. It is much less common for people to enter a nursing home, be discharged after a brief stay, then go home (and get home care) than for people to get home care until they are no longer able to be cared for adequately in the community, then enter a nursing home for the balance of their lives.

(9)   The policy usually has a maximum covered length of stay (e.g., 2-10 years) and is usually subject to a lifetime maximum.

(10)   The daily benefit for home care, adult day care, and respite care is usually limited to 50% of the daily benefit for nursing home care.

(11)   Waiver of premium (usually after 90, 120, or 180 days) is a typical provision.

LTC policies cover care in skilled nursing facilities, and usually they cover care in intermediate-care facilities as well. Some policies cover residential care (in facilities that are keyed to supervising the frail elderly and helping them with ordinary activities, not to medical care). An important question is the extent and type of benefits that the policy will cover when provided at home. Visiting nurses' services are usually covered, as are those of physical and speech therapists. Occupational therapy and homemaker services, adult day care, and respite care, are less common. Coverage of these services can be very worthwhile for some insureds.

An important recent development is geriatric case management or care management. (The term "case management" is often used to refer to gatekeeper mechanisms; "care management" is more oriented toward meeting the needs of the elderly and their families, less oriented toward saving money for the insurer.) The case or care manager's job is to assess the needs of the elderly person and develop and coordinate an ongoing program of services to meet those needs. A very wide variety of services is available to the elderly from the public sector (Medicaid; Medicare; programs run by states and cities), from philanthropic organizations, and from private-sector businesses. A good case or care manager can find the right mix of services for each client. Often, the services will include some that are available free or at low cost — so that a package that provides superior care, and has the desirable effect of keeping the elderly person at home as long a possible, can save the insurer a great deal of money (because few of the services are provided under the policy, or they are provided by low-cost rather than high-cost providers).

So far, comparatively few LTC policies include case or care management — but it is likely that this will become more common in the future. Good management can be the difference between an unhappy elderly person inappropriately institutionalized (at very high cost) and a happy elderly person staying at home and receiving appropriate care and saving money.[3] The problem for the industry (as well as for government and policyholders) will be if home care costs rise to the level of institutional costs, or even surpass them. Then the choice will be whether to provide insurance or public benefits for home care (if this is the older person's preference) even if cost savings could be obtained by forcing institutionalization.

An increasing trend is the use of LTC riders to other life, disability, or health insurance policies, or to annuities, especially for those who cannot afford or are unwilling to purchase a stand-alone LTC policy. Riders can fill the bill if you have a client who wants to buy LTC coverage but is medically unqualified (some programs knock out 40-50% of applicants for underwriting reasons.[4] In addition, various benefits are offered as riders to stand-alone LTC benefits; for instance, waiver of premium during confinement in a nursing home.

SAMPLE POLICIES

NOTE: All policies are qualified (e.g., are triggered by cognitive impairment AND dependency in 2/5 or 2/6 ADLs).

POLICY A reflects growing interest in assisted living facilities (housing units that provide some ADL assistance, but not full-scale medicalized care) by insuring the full cost of assisted living stays on a parity with nursing home institutionalization. This is an institution-focused policy, so home care benefits are available only as a rider. All policyholders are also entitled to information and referral services under the policy even if they are not entitled to make a claim. The policy can be purchased covering two, three, four, or six years of care (but not lifetime benefits); daily benefits range from $30-$250, but are limited to $150/day if the insured is between ages 80-84.

POLICY B concentrates on alternatives to nursing home institutionalization, and pays 100% of the maximum daily policy benefit when the insured resides in an assisted living or personal care facility — even if the daily benefit exceeds the actual cost of staying in the facility. The policy also covers adult day care, hospice care, respite care, "bed holds" (paying to keep the nursing home bed available when the insured is hospitalized), and alternate plan of care services.

POLICY C uses the "pool of money" approach for nursing home, home care, adult day care, and alternate care (assisted living services). The available benefit levels are $50-$200 a day, and the available durations of benefits are two-five years or lifetime. There is no separate maximum per benefit, so benefits can be accessed throughout the entire continuum of care.

POLICY D covers nursing home care, home care (up to 100% of the cost of home care, with a limit of 50% of the daily nursing home benefit), plus hospice care at home for the terminally ill and adult day care. Up to 100% of the cost of assisted living facility residence, up to a maximum of 50% of the daily nursing home benefit, is covered. If the insured is in a hospital, medically ready for nursing home placement but no bed is available, the policy will cover the full cost of the hospital stay up to 100% of the daily nursing home benefit. The policy also covers 20 days worth of bed holds, 20 days of respite care, and reimburses a geriatric care manager up to the cost of two days of nursing home care. The available benefit periods are three years, five years, and lifetime; the benefit periods for home care and nursing home care are integrated. Available waiting periods are 20 days, 60 days, and 100 days. The policy is issued at ages 40-79.

POLICY E is a fixed-dollar indemnity policy, which pays the level of benefit selected by the insured for each day of nursing home institutionalization. The policy also covers up to 100% of the cost (limited to 50% of the benefit amount) for home care (by a registered or practical nurse or physical, occupational, or speech therapist). Adult day care and residence in assisted living facilities are also covered, but only 80% of the cost with a limitation of 50% of the daily nursing home benefit amount. The benefit period is three years (comprising both home care and nursing home care). Available waiting periods are 30 and 100 days, and immediate coverage with no waiting period. The insurer has a case manager whose services can be covered (annual limit: twice the nursing home indemnity amount). Up to 14 bed-hold days per year, and respite care up to 14 times the nursing home indemnity amount, are also covered. However, hospice benefits are not available, and the option to enhance home care coverage to 100% of the nursing home amount is not available. All costs of hospital care while awaiting nursing home placement are covered. The policy can be issued at ages 45-84, although options are limited for applicants over 80.

IDENTIFYING AND SOLVING MARKETING PROBLEMS

The optimist's view is that Americans who do not have LTC insurance make up a vast, untapped market. The pessimist's view is that the small extent of coverage must indicate widespread resistance to acquiring such coverage. Whichever view you take, one problem — which you can easily overcome — is widespread *ignorance* about LTC insurance. Surveys have showed that many Americans erroneously believe that Medicare will meet any need they encounter for long-term custodial care. Some people may have heard about the passage of the Medicare Catastrophic Coverage Act (and erroneously assumed that it would add long-term care coverage to Medicare), but not about its repeal.

Denial is a severe problem. Understandably, people prefer not to think about age, debility, incapacity, and social isolation. It will take all your tact to make them face these ugly prospects. At least you have useful tools to offer them.

You may also have willing prospects who want LTC insurance, but are uninsurable for medical reasons; or prospects who can secure a policy, but do not think they can find the cash to pay for it. After all, they have their other expenses to meet — including the expense of their other insurance policies. It may be possible to reallocate insurance within their portfolio, or to find a policy that is less expensive than their current coverage, yet is more suitable for their needs (consonant, of course, with state anti-twisting regulations).

A July, 1987 survey of 226 financial planners (70% of whom sold insurance products) revealed that, although the majority of the respondents sold life, disability, and health products, only one-third sold LTC insurance. Nearly all of them assessed their clients' life insurance coverage as a part of creating a financial plan. About a third felt their clients were adequately covered in this area; 55.7% felt their clients were underinsured; and 11.2% felt they were overinsured. If this perception is correct, some funds can be transferred from life insurance to LTC without impairing the life coverage that is required by the financial plan. LTC insurance was the factor *least* often considered by survey respondents. Only 38% included this type of coverage in their plan, and none of them believed their clients had too much LTC insurance. In fact, 96.2% believed their clients were underinsured in this regard.

Yet 84% of the planners strongly agreed that the cost of catastrophic illness is a major national problem, and only 31% "strongly agreed" that their clients' private resources would stretch far enough to cover long-term catastrophic illness. Fifty-four percent "strongly disagreed" with this proposition. Eighty-six percent agreed that planning for long-term catastrophic illness is an important function of the financial planner — but 75% "strongly disagreed" with the proposition that planners already give sufficient attention to this crucial problem. Two-thirds stated that their clients are not generally aware of the availability of LTC policies; and opinion was divided about whether clients perceive a need for LTC insurance (54% strongly disagreed with this statement; 19% were neutral; 27% very much agreed) and whether clients think LTC insurance is worth what it costs (33% strongly disagreed; 42% were neutral; 26% strongly agreed).

The planners' own feelings about LTC insurance were quite different. When asked whether they think this coverage is "probably not worth the cost", 56% strongly disagreed, 32% were neutral, and only 13% strongly agreed. Seventy percent strongly agreed that most adults should maintain LTC insurance (only 13% strongly disagreed); yet only two-thirds disagreed with the statement that their clients do not need LTC insurance. Only one-third of the respondents stated affirmatively that they themselves are familiar with the "typical provisions of various LTC insurance policies"; half strongly disagreed with this statement. As you would expect, 58% strongly agreed with the statement that private insurance is the best way to fund chronic care; 59% strongly disagreed with the statement that government programs are the best way to cope with this terrible problem.[5] A study commissioned by CNA, and released in December, 1996 showed that survey respondents had little insight into how much long-term care really costs, and they also overestimated the cost of such coverage (which CNA estimated at $125/month on the average).

Planners have evolved various rules of thumb for marketing LTC coverage. Remember, these are only rules of thumb; you may be able to prove every one of them wrong in your own career!

(1)   Clients under 50 are usually not interested in buying LTC insurance; other family needs are much more pressing, and old age seems very far away. This could change if employers adopt LTC insurance more widely.

(2)   Clients with income under $20,000 probably cannot afford LTC premiums. NOTE: Under the NAIC Model Act, purchase of LTC insurance is not considered suitable for persons with assets under $30,000.

(3)   In effect, LTC insurance operates to protect clients' assets from "spend-down" if they must be institutionalized. Therefore, the asset level matters. Some planners feel that assets below $50,000 cannot economically be protected by LTC insurance. Others feel that, for married couples having assets that are less than twice the state's spousal protection asset limit, the best strategy is to divide the assets between the two spouses, then rely on the Medicaid spousal protection provisions. Another viewpoint is that, for assets over $400,000, clients can afford to self-insure and pay for care from their own assets.

(4)   As discussed above, one way to use LTC insurance is as a "buffer" for Medicaid-oriented transfers; in that case, three years' worth of coverage is ample, and the policy can be dropped once the Medicaid application is approved.

(5)   Another possibility, if clients are interested in LTC insurance but think it is too expensive, is for them to assume part of the risk, by buying a less expensive policy with benefits less extensive than full coverage for an indefinite term. They might also accept a larger deductible or more coinsurance as a trade-off.

(6)   Explore your clients' wishes with regard to leaving an estate. For some, it is crucial to leave money to a spouse or to children. Others, perhaps widowed, childless, or estranged from relatives, are much more willing to use or even deplete their assets for nursing home care.

Actuary Bertram Pike analyzes the special aspects of group LTC as follows:[6]

(1)   Underwriting data is not yet complete, and probably will not be for five or ten years — so a badly-designed product may put the insurer at risk for many years to come. It is very hard to make design changes if they would result in different plans based on when employees enrolled.

(2)   There are significant claim lags — today's enrollees probably will not be entering nursing homes for many years.

(3)   Although this is a group product, individual underwriting standards will probably be required.

(4)   A reinsurance treaty is an important protection for the issuer.[7]

(5)   Certain issues of policy interpretation remain unresolved — and, remember, courts and legislators are very sympathetic to the elderly and quick to assume that underwriting and sales abuses have occurred.

(6)   LTC policies are nonpar, so the insurer does not have a cushion of dividends to cope with negative trends in the economy or in health care costs.

(7)   The insurer may have to maintain a constant program of education and encouragement to keep insured employees from dropping their LTC coverage (especially in an employee-pay-all plan). Usually, this is the employer's job.

The public/private initiatives described above usually include a component of consumer education.

UNDERWRITING AND PRICING ISSUES

LTC insurance underwriting is a difficult and highly significant task. Premiums are usually age-based rather than based on health status, so it is extremely important that proper underwriting be done to identify applicants whose health condition (whether physical or cognitive) precludes the issuance of a policy. It is also important that the information be gathered at the application stage, because "post-claims underwriting" (accepting all applications, then canceling policies when claims are made) is forbidden by NAIC rules that have been adopted by most states.

Proper underwriting data is also important within the LTC insurance insurer's operations, because premiums must be set so that the company's products are competitive, but also so that adequate reserves are available as claims are made, and so that the product is a profitable one for the issuer.

A report by Margaret Czellecz, "Underwriting Individual Long Term Care Insurance," published as a pamphlet by the Duncanson & Holt Group in 1993, describes conditions that are normally screened out right away when they are disclosed on the application: e.g., AIDS, Alzheimer's Disease; stroke with residuals within the past three years. Arthritis, breast cancer more than five years earlier, adult-onset diabetes, heart bypass three years earlier, are probably acceptable, although with some degree of additional medical underwriting.

Typically, either the agent completes the application, based on information from the prospect, or the prospect completes the application and the agent then forwards it to the insurer. Follow-up telephone interviews are commonly done to confirm the hard data on the application and assess the client's home life, availability of supportive services, and other measures of ability to function. An Attending Physician's Statement (APS) from the applicant's own doctor is requested if ambiguities remain after a telephone interview. Some companies require an APS from all applicants over 70. For applicants aged 80 or over, NAIC standards mandate either an APS, physical examination by the insurer's doctor, assessment of functional capacity, or submission of medical records.

Most insurers will decline an application if the applicant uses a cane; some will accept the application if a cane is used only occasionally, or as part of recovery from an accident. Although some companies decline LTC insurance applications showing three or more conditions, others will accept an applicant whose multiple conditions do not restrict his or her activities.

Underwriters often disfavor applications from residents of retirement communities; use of services such as adult day care or Meals on Wheels is likely to result in declination. However, a borderline case might be underwritten if a healthy spouse, who can provide supportive services, applies for a policy at the same time.

A 1995 survey done by Connecticut's Cologne Life Reinsurance Co.[8] shows that 97% of the insurers responding to the survey used cognitive and lifestyle factors in underwriting, in addition to more conventional measures of health status. This survey found that the individual purchaser averaged 67.5 years of age (versus only 42.5 in the group market). Nearly all (85% of the companies responding to the survey) used telephone follow-up to applications; about 80% required APS.

About a third of those responding (large rather than small insurers) had a paramedic perform a cognitive assessment of applicants. Less than one-quarter of the respondents used the Short Portable Mental Status Questionnaire or Mini Mental Status examinations (two common psychological tests). Nearly all companies used tests of recall of words and numbers to test cognitive status. All respondents asked about applicants' ability to perform ADLs; most asked about "instrumental activities of daily living" such as shopping, cooking, and handling money.

Research done by a team of social scientists[9] projects that about 12% of age-65 LTC insurance applicants would probably be rejected because of recent hospitalization, fairly recent nursing home use, or cognitive or functional limitations. A further 10.9% would possibly be rejected because of other health problems. At age 75, 20.3% would probably be rejected, and 10.3% possibly rejected.

Thus, the team estimates that about 15.8% of remaining nursing home use at age 65 would not be insurable by private companies; at age 75, about 27.1% of remaining nursing home use would not be insurable. (Remaining nursing home use is nursing home use occurring after the application for the policy.)

Economic as well as health factors preclude the sale of LTC insurance policies to the entire senior citizen population. However, there is a correlation between poor health and low income, so many of the individuals unable to afford coverage would also be ineligible for coverage because of health reasons.

Premiums and Pricing

HIAA figures (discussed in the May, 1993 issue of *LTC News & Comment*) show that for a four-year policy, with a 20-day elimination period and $80/$40 day benefit, the basic premium would be $477 for purchase at age 50. Adding 5% compound inflation protection would raise the premium to $852; inflation protection plus nonforfeiture features would make the premium $1,252, or about triple the base premium. At purchase age 65, for the same benefit plan, the premium would go from $1,103 (basic) to $1,781 (basic plus inflation protection), to $2,525 (basic, inflation protection, nonforfeiture). Corresponding figures at purchase age 79 are $3,989, $5,627, and $7,675 per year. Clearly, then, although the effect lessens over time, adding features does make the policy more expensive.

Later LIMRA figures suggest that the average LTC insurance premium, nationwide, is $1500 at age 65 (for a standard risk; $150-$200 can be subtracted if the purchaser is a preferred risk), $2000 at age 75, and $3000 at age 80 — but these figures are quite different from HIAA estimates of 1994 premiums. The HIAA estimate is $397 a year at age 50 for a four-year policy providing $100 a day institutional, $50/day home care benefit, with a 20-day elimination period; the same policy would cost $1050 at age 65, $4512 at age 79.[10]

A 1997 article by Richard T. Grote and Peter B. Wetzel[11] says that inflation riders increase the premium of an LTC insurance policy anywhere from 25-60% (depending on factors such as the percentage of inflation protection offered, and whether it is simple or compounded), and nonforfeiture benefits increase the premium 30-40%. Nevertheless, this article contains financial projections suggesting that an affluent elderly person who pays $3,100 a year for an LTC insurance policy with a $36,000 annual maximum benefit will be able to pass along a larger estate than an elderly person who invests $600,000 of his or her assets to produce $36,000 in income — and that the estate planning result is better when LTC insurance is purchased than when it is not, even if the senior citizen never requires long-term care.

SUMMARY

For the middle- and upper-income elderly, the risk of nursing home confinement or a need for lengthy home care could mean spending at least $30,000 a year, and possibly $75,000 or more a year, for a period of several years. In an extreme case, LTC could be required for more than a decade. Insurers see this unfortunate fact as a situation in which risk can beneficially be shifted via insurance. Federal and state Medicaid authorities see it as a crisis, and see the need for enlisting the private sector in finding a solution.

Before 1996, the purchase of LTC insurance was suitable for two general planning strategies. The first coordinated private coverage with Medicaid, by using the LTC insurance benefits to pay for care during the Medicaid penalty period. Users of this strategy entered nursing homes as private-pay patients and later converted to Medicaid — and therefore had the wider range of choices available to private-pay patients. (Those who enter nursing homes as Medicaid patients have to accept the first Medicaid bed that becomes available, even if it is not in the most convenient or highest-quality local facility.) The second strategy was entirely private-sector-oriented, and bypassed Medicaid in favor of using the insurance to protect assets from depletion.

As discussed in Chapter 7, the Health Insurance Portability and Accountability Act of 1996 has altered the Medicaid planning process. Therefore, private-sector solutions seem more attractive than ever before. A fully-insured senior citizen has access to the full panoply of choices. He or she can select any facility, with no need to worry about whether Medicaid beds are available. If he or she prefers home care, and home care is medically suitable, then there will be no pressure for inappropriate institutionalization.

CHAPTER FOOTNOTES

1.   For the affordability debate, see Ian Olgeirson, "Two Health Groups Clash Over Issue of Affordability of Nursing-Home Care," *Wall Street Journal* 2/5/93 p. B7; Marc A. Cohen and A.K. Nanda Kumar, "Affordability and Demand for LTC Insurance," *LTC News & Comment* February 1993 p. 5.

2.   "Putting LTC to the Test," *Best's Review* February 1989 p. 46. Mr. Klueh is Senior Vice President and chief actuary of Baltimore's Monumental Life; Ronald D. Hagen, "Long-Term Health Care," 42 *J. American Society CLU/ChFC* 62 (March 1992). Mr. Hagen estimates that the cost of an appropriate LTC policy will be approximately the same as the cost of insuring the family automobile.

3.   Carol Wechsler Blatter, "Putting the TLC in LTC." *Best's Review* December 1989 p. 21.

4.   See Linda Koco, "Develop More LTC Riders as Soon as Possible," *National Underwriter* October 29, 1990 p. 21.

5.   Peter W. Bacon et al., "Long-Term Catastrophic Care: A Financial Planning Perspective," *J. Risk & Insurance* 146 (March 1989).

6.   "Is Group LTC Your Cup of Tea?" *Best's Review* April 1990 p. 46.

7.   Also see Gary Corliss, "Reinsurance: The Key to LTC," *Best's Review* June 1993 p. 41.

8.   See Barry D. Eagle, "Lifestyle, Mental Factors Key to LTC Underwriting," *Best's Review* August 1996 p. 71.

9.   Christopher M. Murtaugh, Peter Kemper, and Brenda C. Spillman, "Risky Business: Long-Term Care Insurance Underwriting," *Inquiry* 271 (Fall 1995); also see Nancy Ann Jeffrey, "Insurance Won't Patch Hole in Medicaid Safety Net," *Wall Street Journal* November 17, 1995 at C1.

10.   The figures come from Alan C. Kifer, "Offer Clients Coverage in Growing LTC Market," *Best's Review* April 1996 p. 80 and Frederick Schmitt, "HIAA Expects LTC Sales to Rebound," *National Underwriter* (Life/Health Edition) May 13, 1996 p. 11.

11.   "Long-Term Care Insurance Provides Powerful Protection," *Trusts & Estates* January 1997 p. 59.

Chapter 6

MEDICARE

It is almost inevitable that your older clients will rack up high medical bills. Even a basically healthy elderly person is likely to need physical monitoring and preventive care. As physical health declines, there will be doctor bills and bills for prescription drugs, and could be a need for medical equipment such as walkers and wheelchairs, supplies such as incontinence pads, and short hospital stays.

In 1994 (the last year for which figures are available), total Medicare payments to health care providers aggregated $147.1 billion. About two-thirds ($94.2 billion) was paid under the Part A program, $52.9 billion under Part B. Also for 1994, average spending per Medicare enrollee was $4,301, but most of the spending was on account of the sickest enrollees. There were 18.6 million Medicare enrollees (the healthy aged) for whom no Medicare payments were made, and payments on behalf of about one-third of all enrollees were under $500.

Another way of analyzing spending is that 51.7% of all Medicare outlays went toward inpatient hospitalization, 4.1% to skilled nursing facilities (SNFs), 8.6% to home health agencies (HHAs), 26.3% to doctors, and 9.3% to outpatient services.

Medicare pays a lot of money to cope with these acute health needs. However, Medicare does not pay every dollar of the senior citizen's bill. There are extensive deductibles and coinsurance requirements. Although the federal government and some state governments have placed limits on the practice, in some circumstances doctors are allowed to charge more ("balance bill") than the Medicare charge for a particular service. If a doctor is allowed to "balance bill", the insured is required to pay the "balance" of the doctor's bill not paid by Medicare.

As you have read dozens of times in this book in various contexts, Medicare does not pay for long-term custodial care. People who need extensive home care, or who need to enter a nursing home for more than a 100-day recuperative stay after hospitalization, or who go straight from the community into a nursing home, have several options, all with disadvantages. These options are: (1) private payment (with the attendant risk of depleting all accumulated savings); (2) Medicaid; and (3) long-term care insurance (which can be expensive, and whose benefits are not always available when chronic care is required).

On the individual level, planning for the cost of health care is a difficult challenge. On the societal level, it is nothing short of awesome.

THE ROLE OF MEDICARE IN PLANNING FOR THE OLDER CLIENT

When the Medicare program was signed into law in 1965, it was intended to be a complete solution to the problem of the high medical bills that were such a source of anxiety to elderly Americans in the 1960s. Unfortunately, for many reasons, the Medicare program failed to live up to this objective. Medicare costs the federal government much more than anticipated, because of failure to control the cost of medical care. (The states pay for part of the cost of Medicaid, for the indigent and medically indigent, but the federal government pays for Medicare without state help.)

Medicare also costs *beneficiaries* much more than anticipated. Medicare beneficiaries must pay a monthly premium (usually deducted from their Social Security checks) for Part B coverage. (See below for a discussion of Parts A and B.) Before they collect Medicare benefits, they must cover deductibles, and they are also responsible for coinsurance amounts. For many senior citizens, these financial responsibilities are very burdensome. Ironically, the elderly now spend *more* for their share of medical care than they did before the Medicare program was created.

Part of Medicare's funding comes from a tax imposed on workers and their employers. The Medicare Hospital Insurance (HI) tax is collected at the same time, and in the same way, as the FICA (Social Security) tax. The HI tax rate is 1.45% each on employers and employees. Beginning in 1994, all earned income, regardless of amount, is subject to the Medicare tax. Prior to 1994, the tax was limited to a maximum earnings base (the maximum amount of annual earnings subject to tax). The maximum earnings base was $135,000 in 1993.

Yet, no matter how expensive Medicare is for taxpayers and for elderly Medicare beneficiaries, it is still not a complete program, and it ignores many of the real needs of the senior citizen population. Medicare is oriented toward "heroic" acute-care medicine — short-term treatments designed to cure a condition and restore the patient to full health.

Although elderly people do have acute-care needs (such as treatment of pneumonia, heart attacks, or broken hips), many of them suffer from chronic illnesses. Nothing can be done to cure them, or even to improve their condition; yet, a great deal can be done to keep their condition from deteriorating further, and to make them more comfortable and improve their ability to do basic daily tasks.

Medicare does not even provide complete coverage of all acute illnesses. Medicare covers hospitalization for up to 90 days in each "spell of illness"; and each patient has 60 "lifetime reserve days" which can be used if hospitalization lasts 91 or more days. (Coinsurance is higher for lifetime reserve days than for other hospital days.) Once all the reserve days are used up, Medicare stops paying hospital bills.

For 1997, senior citizens have to pay a monthly premium of $43.80 for Medicare Part B coverage (comprising doctors' bills and related services). Before they collect any Part B benefits, they must pay a $100 annual deductible. Although most senior citizens are automatically eligible for Part A coverage (hospitalization), for various technical reasons some are not. They can purchase Part A coverage voluntarily by paying a premium. For 1997, the basic Part A premium is $311 a month. However, a special relief provision reduces the premium to $187 a month for certain individuals with 30 quarters of Social Security coverage and some of their family members. If they are "Qualified Medicare Beneficiaries" (meeting the federal definition of those who are too poor to get private coverage), the state Medicaid system has an obligation to pay their premiums and copayment obligations.

In 1997, a Part A patient must pay a $760 deductible before receiving Part A hospitalization benefits. There is no coinsurance for the first 60 days of hospital care, but there is a $190 daily coinsurance requirement for hospital days 61-90 and $380 a day for the lifetime reserve days. (Because the Diagnosis Related Group system compensates hospitals on the basis of the patient's diagnosis, not the actual number of days of hospitalization, patients are being discharged faster. It is uncommon for a person to be hospitalized for more than 90 days at a stretch.)

Medicare does not cover long-term custodial care, and this is one of the biggest obstacles to selling long-term care (LTC) insurance. Many middle-aged and older people do not think they need LTC insurance because they expect Medicare to pay the cost of nursing home care. Medicare, however, covers care in a "skilled nursing facility" only, and coverage is limited to 100 days in each "spell of illness." (These terms will be defined below.) Even this limited coverage is not complete: for days 21-100 of covered skilled nursing home care, the Medicare beneficiary must pay coinsurance of $95 per day (1997 figure).

People who qualify and apply for Medicare benefits for skilled care are frequently turned down; but, if they have a good lawyer (and you can recommend one, if you work with a good planning team), and the determination to pursue their claim, they usually win an administrative appeal and succeed in getting the benefits.

PLANNING TIP: Inform your policyholders about the availability of Medicare skilled-care benefits, home-care benefits (discussed below), and appeals. After all, the cost of three months in a nursing home could add up to at least $10,000, or even $20,000. Winning the Medicare hearing means that the policyholder and family save money (bearing the coinsurance requirement in mind), get the care they need, and defer either using their hard-earned assets to pay for care or applying for Medicaid.

Because Medicare focuses on acute treatment, it specifically excludes most preventive medicine, check-ups, and para-medical services that many older people need to stay healthy and active (such as the foot care that prevents gangrene; eyeglasses (except after cataract surgery); hearing aids). Nor does Medicare pay for prescriptions drugs, insulin or over-the-counter drugs, incontinency pads, and other supplies (even though these are a major expense for many senior citizens).

To sum up, the need for Medigap insurance arises because the Medicare system fails senior citizens in many ways:

(1)   It forces them to pay deductibles and coinsurance.

(2)   It subjects them to the risk of having to pay hundreds of dollars a day for the full cost of hospitalization once the 90 days per "spell of illness" and the lifetime reserve days run out.

(3)　It pays only part of each doctor bill: elderly patients (or their Medigap insurers) often have to pay the rest.

(4)　It deprives senior citizens of coverage for needed preventive and maintenance services.

The need for LTC insurance arises because, except for the limited "skilled nursing care" coverage discussed below, Medicare does not cover nursing home care.

MEDICARE ELIGIBILITY

The Medicare program covers people over 65 (regardless of their income and/or assets), as well as certain disabled individuals under 65. The Medicare program does not provide medical care directly. Instead, it either pays doctors and hospitals directly for their services, or reimburses older patients who have paid bills themselves.

Medicare is divided into Part A, which provides hospitalization, some skilled nursing care, hospice care, and a limited amount of home health care; and Part B, which pays doctors for their services.

Everyone age 65 and over entitled to a Social Security check is automatically enrolled in Part A, and there is no specific requirement for premium payments (although, in a sense, part of every FICA deduction from an employee's paycheck goes to fund Medicare, including Part A). People age 65 and over who do not receive Social Security checks — such as those who are deferring retirement — also get Part A coverage without premium payments, but they must make an application.

A dependent or survivor of a person entitled to Part A, or a dependent of a person under age 65 who is entitled to Social Security retirement or disability benefits, is also eligible for Part A benefits if such dependent or survivor is at least 65 years old.

A Social Security disability beneficiary is covered under Medicare after entitlement to disability benefits for 24 months or more. Those covered include disabled workers at any age, disabled widows and widowers age 50 or over, and beneficiaries age 18 or older who receive benefits because of disability beginning before age 22.

PLANNING TIP: Eligibility for Medicare depends on age, not income or status as a retiree. Therefore, people who retire before age

65 are not covered (unless they qualify under the Medicare definition of disability). Spouses *younger* than 65 of retirees over 65 are also not covered. When you do a plan for people in this situation, investigate whether the employer provides adequate retiree health benefits (and whether the employer is likely to reduce or eliminate the benefits in the future), whether continuation coverage is worthwhile, and whether the individuals involved must strengthen their individual health insurance coverage.

Anyone who receives Part A coverage also gets Part B coverage unless he or she rejects it. The difference is that Part B (Medical Insurance) carries a monthly premium, which can either be deducted from the Social Security check, paid from a group plan (e.g., an employer's plan, if a person over 65 is still working), or billed every quarter to the beneficiary.

PART A HOSPITAL COVERAGE

A Medicare beneficiary is entitled to inpatient hospital care for up to 90 days in each "benefit period." The 90-day benefit period begins again with each "spell of illness." A "benefit period" begins the day a patient is admitted to a hospital. It ends when the patient has been in neither a hospital nor a facility primarily furnishing skilled nursing or rehabilitative services for 60 straight days. There is no limit on the number of 90-day benefit periods a person can have in his or her lifetime (except in the case of hospitalization for mental illness).

If the patient is hospitalized more than 90 days in a spell of illness, he or she must use lifetime reserve days; once the 60 lifetime reserve days are used up, the patient (or the patient's insurer) must pay in full for the hospital care. The patient's lifetime reserve is not renewable.

Medicare does not start to pay until the Part A deductible has been satisfied. There is no coinsurance for the first 60 days of hospitalization in a spell of illness; coinsurance is required at one level for days 61-90 ($190 a day in 1997), and at a higher level for the lifetime reserve days ($380 a day in 1997).

Originally, Medicare payments were made to hospitals (and nursing homes) on a "cost-plus" basis. This system encouraged waste because the more health facilities spent, the more they were paid by Medicare. A new system, the DRG (Diagnosis Related Group), was phased in in 1983. Now, hospitals are paid a flat fee for each Medicare patient, based on the patient's initial diagnosis. Theoretically, this will encourage greater efficiency, because the hospital makes more money if it can cure the patient and discharge him or her faster. The risk is that hospitals now have an incentive for undertreatment rather than wasteful overtreatment.

This is kept in check by federal laws against "dumping" patients, and by a requirement that all Medicare patients are entitled to "discharge planning." That is, the hospital must notify patients of their right to a written discharge plan that advises them about available health resources (such as nursing homes and home care) appropriate for their needs. If a patient thinks a discharge is premature, he or she is entitled to appeal it.

PLANNING TIP: An important function of the elder-care planning team is informing the elderly and their families about their right to discharge planning; explaining the discharge planning documents; giving independent advice about post-discharge alternatives: and, if necessary, vigorously handling the appeal.

PART A HOSPITAL BENEFITS

The following inpatient hospital services are covered under Part A:

- Bed and board in a semi-private room (two to four beds). Medicare will pay the cost of a private room only if it is required for medical reasons. If the patient requests a private room, Medicare will pay the cost of semi-private accommodations; the patient must pay the extra charge for the private room.

- All meals, including special diets.

- Nursing services provided by or under the supervision of licensed nursing personnel (other than services of a private duty nurse or attendant).

- Services of the hospital's medical social workers.

- Use of regular hospital equipment, supplies and appliances, such as oxygen tents, wheel chairs, crutches, casts, surgical dressings, and splints when routinely furnished by the hospital to all patients Certain equipment, sup-

plies and appliances used by the patient in the hospital
continue to be covered after the patient has been discharged. Examples are a cardiac pacemaker and an artificial limb.

- Drugs and biologicals ordinarily furnished by the hospital.

- Diagnostic or therapeutic items and services ordinarily
  furnished by the hospital or by others, under arrangements made with the hospital.

- Operating and recovery room costs, including hospital
  costs for anesthesia services.

- Services of interns and residents in training under an
  approved teaching program.

- Blood transfusions, after the first three pints.

- X-rays and other radiology services, including radiation
  therapy, billed by the hospital.

- Lab tests.

- Respiratory or inhalation therapy.

- Independent clinical laboratory services under arrangement with the hospital.

- Cost of special care units, such as an intensive care unit,
  coronary care unit, etc.

- Rehabilitation services, such as physical therapy, occupational therapy, and speech pathology services.

- Appliances (such as pacemakers, colostomy fittings, and
  artificial limbs) which are permanently installed while in
  the hospital.

- Lung and heart-lung transplants.

SKILLED NURSING FACILITY CARE
UNDER MEDICARE

Although Medicare does not provide long-term chronic care in a nursing home for patients who are frail but not acutely ill, it does provide a certain amount of recuperative care for patients who have been hospitalized. Medicare Part A pays for up to 100 days of skilled nursing facility (SNF) care per spell of illness, provided that a number of conditions are met:

(1)   The patient needs and is receiving "skilled services" — i.e., nursing care, physical therapy, etc., provided or supervised by professional nurses and/or therapists.

(2)   The SNF care starts within 30 days of the patient's discharge from a hospital (i.e., a person who goes directly to a nursing home from the community cannot get Part A SNF benefits).

(3)   The patient was in the hospital for at least three days before the discharge.

(4)   The patient's attending physician orders the care, and periodically re-certifies the need for the care.

The patient pays nothing for the first 20 days of covered services in each spell of illness; after 20 days, the patient pays coinsurance for each additional day, up to a maximum of 80 days. For a patient in a SNF in 1997, the coinsurance is $95 a day. Thus, a 100-day stay in a SNF during 1997 would cost the patient $7,680.

There is no lifetime limit on the amount of SNF care provided under Part A. Except for the coinsurance (which must be paid after the first 20 days in each spell of illness), the plan will pay the cost of 100 days of post-hospital care in each benefit period, regardless of how many benefit periods the person may have. After 100 days of coverage the patient must pay the full cost of SNF care.

The Medicare system defines a "skilled service" as one that is so inherently complex that professionals must be involved in it. This differs from simple custodial care of a person who needs help walking, dressing, or eating, but is not ill. After many, many court cases, it is an accepted principle of law that the need for skilled services includes monitoring the condition of a patient with many illnesses or conditions (for instance, a cancer patient who also has a bad heart and is diabetic). The patient as a whole must be considered; if a person's condition is unstable and could rapidly deteriorate, even services that would ordinarily be custodial could become skilled (and thus reimbursable by Medicare).

The federal regulations list examples of services that are defined as skilled services:

- Injections.

- Intravenous feeding.

- Inserting and changing catheters.

- Treating severe, widespread skin disorders such as bed-sores.

The federal regulations also list examples of personal care services that are *not* covered:

- Giving pills, cough syrups, other oral medications.

- Routine care of the skin.

- Maintenance of plaster casts.

- Turning patients in bed.

- Helping patients with normal daily activities such as walking and getting dressed.

Until 1983, nursing home patients faced a knotty Medicare problem. If they had to leave the nursing home to enter a hospital (say, after a stroke, fracture, or heart attack), then went back to the nursing home, they were often turned down for Part A benefits for later hospitalization. The theory was that they could never start a new "spell of illness" after the first hospitalization, because they were still "inpatients" in the nursing home (even though Medicare did not pay for that care). However, many court cases have held that a person who lives in a nursing home is not an "inpatient"; he or she simply goes home after hospitalization. Therefore, Part A hospital benefits can no longer be denied on this basis.[1]

PLANNING TIP: It can take the involvement of the entire care team to get SNF or home care services from Medicare. Your job is to inform patients of their rights under Medicare and under their health insurance or Medigap insurance. The geriatric care manager (GCM) informs patients and families of available programs in the area, and the advantages and defects of each program. The patient's attending physician must be reminded of the need to certify and re-certify the patient's requirement of skilled care.

Even if the patient is not applying for Medicaid, and has no intention of applying for Medicaid in the future, the laws of some states require *all* patients entering a nursing home to be assessed under Medicaid standards so they can be assigned to a utilization grouping based on their needs. It is up to the care team to make sure that this assessment is performed. It may also be necessary to teach doctors what language is required to guarantee that qualified patients receive Medicare benefits.

Last but not least, the attorney (or other appropriate representative) may have to demand a hearing if a Medicare Part A claim for skilled nursing care is turned down.

HOME HEALTH CARE UNDER PART A

Medicare home health care is a little-known benefit. Ironically, many of the bureaucrats administering the program are not familiar with the various court cases and administrative rulings that have expanded eligibility for this benefit. Therefore, it may be necessary to get a hearing to secure Part A home health care benefits. The effort is definitely worthwhile. In appropriate cases, Medicare will pay for thousands of dollars' worth of care that will greatly improve the patient's quality of life and delay institutionalization until the patient really needs to leave home and enter a nursing home.

PRACTICE TIP: New Jersey has had a statute since 1987 that provides legal aid for Medicare beneficiaries who are unfairly turned down for benefits they are entitled to. All other states, please copy!

Part A "home health services" are described as:

(1)   "Part-time or intermittent" (that is, not full-time) nursing care, physical therapy, or medical social services.

(2)   Provided or supervised by a registered nurse, therapist, or other appropriate professional. The care must require professional skills; care that can safely be performed by the patient, or by an unskilled person, does not fit the definition. However, if the patient's condition requires professional monitoring, otherwise unskilled care may become skilled.

(3)   Provided to a person who is "home-bound." A home-bound person need not be confined to bed, and can even leave home with help occasionally (for instance for medical treatment or to attend religious services). A person who is fully mobile or has only minor mobility limitations does not qualify.

(4)   Provided to a person who is under a doctor's care, based on the doctor's certification that home care (or outpatient care at a nursing home, hospital, or rehabilitation center, if care is required that calls for equipment that cannot be brought to the patient's home) is required. The doctor must draft a care plan, and bring it up to date periodically. The plan must be specific about why skilled care is required; what skilled services are needed; and how often and how long skilled care and services must be provided.

        PRACTICE TIP: One of the tasks of the geriatric care manager (GCM) or other advocates for the patient is to be sure the patient's doctor provides an adequate care plan, and recertifies the patient's eligibility as necessary (at least once every two months).

(5)   Provided *by* a licensed home health agency.

The patient pays nothing for home health visits, except he or she must pay a 20% coinsurance amount for durable medical equipment provided by home health agencies (except for the purchase of certain used items — for which the coinsurance is waived). Durable medical equipment includes iron lungs, oxygen tents, hospital beds and wheel-chairs.

The home health care covered by Medicare Part A must be *either* "part-time" (individuals who need full-time skilled care theoretically should be in a nursing home) or "intermittent" (for instance, an occasional catheter change or a nurse's assessment of how well a person is responding to medication). Until 1988, it was almost impossible to get meaningful Medicare Part A home health benefits because the Health Care Financing Administration (HCFA, the branch of the Department of Health and Human Services that administers Medicare) insisted that covered care would have to be *both* part-time *and* intermittent. However, in that year, the District Court for the District of Columbia told HCFA that "or" means "or", not "and" — so care that is either part-time or intermittent qualified.[2]

Another misinterpretation that has been struck down by a court was that home health care (especially physical therapy) was not available if the patient's condition was stable. In order to qualify for Medicare, the patient's condition does not have to improve; care for the chronically ill, or even the terminally ill, can be covered.

Furthermore, once a person qualifies for Part A home health care, Medicare will also pay for "home health aide" services on a part-time or intermittent basis. Home health aides are not professionals. They provide services such as bathing, feeding, colostomy care, turning patients in bed, and "hands-on personal care of the beneficiary or services which are needed to maintain the beneficiary's health or to facilitate treatment of the beneficiary's illness or injury."

The problem is that people who are qualified for Medicare Part A home health care often have a hard time receiving benefits. Home health agencies may refuse to provide the care because they are afraid that Medicare will deny reimbursement. The intermediaries who process the claims do not always understand the rules, and they are under heavy pressure to cut costs. The easiest way to do that is to deny benefits. Even HCFA bureaucrats and hearing officers do not always understand the rules.

HCFA's rulebook in this area is the Medicare Home Health Agency Manual (the "HIM 11"), and the relevant rules are found in Transmittal No. 222, dated April, 1989. Under these rules, coverage determinations must be based on a complete consideration of the situation of the individual applicant. It is no good to say that *every* elderly person with multiple sclerosis is ineligible, for example. Furthermore, it must be presumed that there is nobody at home who is qualified and willing to provide skilled home care (although an application can be denied if there really is someone at home who can provide skilled care — because, in that situation, it is not reasonable and necessary for Medicare to pay for the care).

According to the HIM-11, "intermittent" care means that the patient has a medically predictable need for occasional skilled nursing care — at least once every 60 days. Up to 28 hours per week of skilled and home aide care can be provided (as long as care is not provided on a daily basis); in fact, the fiscal intermediary can provide up to 35 hours of care per week in the appropriate case.

The HIM-11 definition of part-time care means up to 28 hours of skilled nursing and/or home health aide services per week (as long as the services add up to less than 8 hours a day). Up to 35 hours a week of services can be provided (as long as there is less than 8 hours a day of care), if the fiscal intermediary agrees after reviewing the documentation in the case.

"Part-time or intermittent" care usually means care less than seven days a week, but Medicare Part A can be required to pay for seven-day-a-week care for a short period of time, such as two to three weeks. In unusual cases, and if the doctor can make a compelling case, Part A will even pay for seven-day-a-week care for longer than three weeks.

Economic Implications of Medicare Home Care

Home care (for home-bound individuals) is one of the fastest-growing segments within the Medicare program. This is both a positive and a troubling development. Because most people strongly prefer to receive their care at home, expanded eligibility is a good thing — especially if it permits them to remain at home longer, thus reducing the number of capital-intensive nursing homes that must be built.

However, from the viewpoint of Medicare Part A's solvency and accounting soundness, the expansion of home care has a negative impact. The number of Medicare beneficiaries receiving home health services went from 1.7 million (in 1989) to 2.8 million (1994). Furthermore, during this period, the average number of home health visits per recipient more or less doubled: from 26 to 57 a year. The number of heavy-care home care recipients also approximately doubled. That is, in 1989, about 11% of the people who received Medicare home care got more than 60 visits per year, versus about 25% who got more than 60 annual visits in 1993.

Also in 1993, a study performed by HHS' Office of the Inspector General shows that most CHHAs (Certified Home Health Agencies doing business with Medicare) received about the same reimbursement per visit: between $56.06 and $60.06. However, reimbursement per CHHA patient showed dramatic variation, based on the number of visits that each CHHA deemed appropriate for its patient caseload. Reimbursement ranged from $1,534 per patient to $7,978 per patient. Although the quality of care and the beneficiary profile were fairly similar for all 6,803 HHAs studied, some of the agencies had two to four times as much staff as others, made five times as many visits, and got five times as much reimbursement per patient.[3]

President Clinton's budget proposal, announced in January, 1997, called for transfer of Medicare home care from Part A to Part B — which would make the Part A financial statements look healthier, but would not, of course, cut the actual cost of providing this benefit. As this Third Edition went to press, it was unclear if the transfer would be implemented.

MEDICARE PART B

Medicare Part B, in contrast to Part A, pays doctor bills. It also covers certain outpatient hospital services, artificial limbs and other prosthetic devices, ambulance services, and certain drugs that are administered by doctors.

The Health Care Financing Administration sets a "reasonable and customary" charge for each physician service (e.g., office visit to cardiologist; ophthalmologist's post-surgical visit to a hospitalized cataract patient). In response to criticisms that the fee schedule gives financial incentives for surgery and other interventions, but penalizes doctors who take the time to talk to their patients and provide needed health education and preventive services, a new payment system, the Resource-Based Relative Value Scale (RBRVS) is being phased in over a five-year period beginning in 1992. The changed payment system will probably cut payments to surgeons and radiologists, but pay more to family practitioners. Various technical changes in the reimbursement system were made by the Omnibus Budget Reconciliation Act of 1990 and Omnibus Budget Reconciliation Act of 1993.

Medicare beneficiaries are responsible for a $100 annual Part B deductible. Once the deductible has been satisfied, Medicare pays 80% of its reasonable and customary charge for covered services. More than three-quarters of Medicare claims are "assigned" (also called "on assignment"). Patients "assign" their right to collect benefits to their doctors, and the doctors submit their assigned claims direct to Medicare, and bill their patients for the 20% coinsurance amount. Medicare "participating physicians" agree to accept assignment on all their Medicare claims, and agree not to charge Medicare patients more than the reasonable and customary charge set by Medicare.

Doctors decide whether or not to accept assignment. Until September 1, 1990, doctors billed Medicare patients directly for unassigned claims; the patients then applied to Medicare for reimbursement, again at the level of 80% of the reasonable and customary charge after satisfaction of the deductible.

After September 1, 1990, doctors are responsible for handling the paperwork on all Medicare claims, assigned or unassigned. Not everyone thinks this will benefit the elderly. Although many elderly people were confused by lengthy Medicare forms, at least they had an incentive to file promptly to get their money back. Doctors can be tardy, and sloppy, about filing, resulting in unnecessary delays, denials and hearings.[4]

Federal law imposes a cap on the level of fees that can be charged to Medicare patients, and doctors who overcharge are subject to federal sanctions, including fines.[5] Furthermore, several states in the Northeast (Massachusetts, Vermont, Rhode Island, Connecticut, New York) either require all doctors who treat Medicare patients to accept assignment, or forbid or limit "balance billing" (the practice of charging Medicare patients more than the reasonable and customary charge).

MEDICARE PART B BENEFITS

The following services are among those covered under Part B of Medicare:

- Doctors' services. This includes the cost of house calls, office visits, and doctors' services in a hospital or other institution. It includes the fees of physicians, surgeons, pathologists, radiologists, anesthesiologists, psychiatrists, and osteopaths.

- Services from certain specially qualified practitioners who are not physicians but are approved by Medicare, including certified registered nurse anesthetists, certified nurse midwifes, clinical psychologists, clinical social workers (other than in a hospital), physician assistants, and nurse practitioners and clinical nurse specialists in collaboration with a physician.

- Services of clinical psychologists are covered if they would otherwise be covered if furnished by a physician (or as an incident to a physician's service).

- Services by licensed chiropractors for manual manipulation of the spine to correct a subluxation that is demonstrated by X-ray.

- Fees of podiatrists, including fees for the treatment of plantar warts, but not for routine foot care.

- The cost of diagnosis and treatment of eye and ear ailments, including an optometrist's treatment of aphakia.

- Plastic surgery for repair of an accidental injury, an impaired limb or a malformed part of the body.

- Radiological or pathological services furnished by a physician to a hospital inpatient.

- The cost of blood clotting factors and supplies necessary for the self-administration of the clotting factor.

- (As of February, 1995) Lung transplants and heart-lung transplants.

- Certain immuno-suppressive drugs given in conjunction with organ transplants.

- Vaccination against influenza; hepatitis B vaccination for persons at moderate or high risk of infection.

- Outpatient physical therapy and speech pathology services received as part of a patient's treatment in a doctor's office or as an outpatient of a participating hospital, skilled nursing facility, or home health agency; or approved clinic, rehabilitative agency, or public health agency, if the services are furnished under a plan established by a physician or physical therapist. Payment for services of independent physical therapists is limited to a maximum of $900 in approved charges in any one year. Services of independent occupational therapists are covered up to a maximum of $900 in a calendar year.

- Services and supplies relating to a physician's services and hospital services rendered to outpatients; this includes drugs and biologicals which cannot be self-administered.

- Dentist's bills for jaw or facial bone surgery, whether required because of accident or disease. Also covered are hospital stays warranted by the severity of the noncovered dental procedure, and services provided by dentists which would be covered under current law when provided by a physician.

- The cost of psychiatric treatment outside a hospital for mental, psychoneurotic or personality disorders, but with 50% coinsurance instead of the usual 20% (except that the latter applies when services are provided on a hospital-outpatient basis if, in the absence of treatment outside a hospital, hospitalization would have been required).

- An unlimited number of home health services each calendar year. A doctor must certify to the need for the home visits. These home visits are covered under Part A unless the person only has Part B coverage (and then under that program).

- Radiation therapy with X-ray, radium or radioactive isotopes.

- Surgical dressings, splints, casts and other devices for reduction of fractures and dislocations; rental or purchase of durable medical equipment, such as iron lungs, oxygen tents, hospital beds and wheel chairs, for use in the patient's home; prosthetic devices, such as artificial heart valves or synthetic arteries, designed to replace part or all of an internal organ (but not false teeth, hearing aids, or eyeglasses); braces, artificial limbs, artificial eyes (but not orthopedic shoes).

- Ambulance service if the patient's condition does not permit the use of other methods of transportation.

- Comprehensive outpatient rehabilitation facility service performed by a doctor or other qualified professionals in a qualified facility.

- Certified nurse-midwife services.

- Screening pap smears for early detection of cervical cancer.

- Screening mammography, which is defined as a radiologic procedure provided to a woman for the early detection of breast cancer, including a physician's interpretation of the results of the procedure.

- The cost of an injectable drug approved for the treatment of a bone fracture related to post-menopausal osteoporosis under the following conditions: (1) the patient's attending physician certifies the patient is unable to learn the skills needed to self-administer, or is physically or mentally incapable of self-administering, the drug, and (2) the patient meets the requirements for Medicare coverage of home health services.

- One pair of eyeglasses following cataract surgery.

- Oral cancer drugs in certain cases, beginning January 1, 1994.

The following items and services are *not covered* under Part B:

- Routine physical check-ups, eyeglasses (except after cataract surgery), hearing aids (and examinations for same).

- Most immunizing vaccines.

- Ordinary dental care and dentures.

- Cosmetic plastic surgery.

- Services required as a result of war.

- Acupuncture.

- Drugs and medicines the patient buys with or without a doctor's prescription.

MEDICARE AND OTHER FORMS OF INSURANCE

Medicare is designed to be merely the "secondary payor" in any situation in which another form of health insurance (such as an employer's coverage of an older employee; liability insurance) could cover. Under federal law, the general rule is that the other plan is the primary payor, and Medicare is the secondary payor — even if the other plan is drafted to make Medicare primarily responsible.

If an employer has more than 20 employees, and provides health insurance, the employer's plan is generally the primary payor (and Medicare is only the secondary payor) for employees age 65 and over and for the Medicare-eligible spouses of active employees (whatever the age of the working spouse). That is, employers do not have the right to draft the plan to put Medicare on the hook. However, employees can choose to be covered by the employer plan (with Medicare as a secondary payor) or to drop out of the employer plan and be covered by Medicare (without the employer plan acting as a backup).[6]

Medicare secondary payments are limited to the lowest of: (1) the amount actually charged by the health care provider, minus amounts paid by an employer or other plan, (2) the amount Medicare would pay if the service were excluded from the employer's plan, (3) the *higher* of the amount allowable under the employer's plan, or the Medicare reimbursement for the service (both calculated without regard to deductibles or coinsurance), and (4) for assigned claims only — but remember that most claims are assigned — the Medicare reasonable and customary charge minus the amount paid by the employer's plan.

For Part A and other claims that are not based on a reasonable charge, the Medicare payment is limited to the lower of the gross Medicare payment minus deductible and coinsurance, or the gross Medicare payment minus the amount paid by the employer's plan.

Under federal law[7] employers' contracts with health-care providers must obligate the provider not to charge more than the Medicare reasonable and customary charge, even if the employer's plan, and not Medicare, pays the bills.

If Medicare covers only part of an older employee's claim, the employee is entitled to get Part A inpatient hospital benefits first, then SNF care, with other Part A benefits restored last. If only part of a bill that includes both Part A and Part B claims is covered, the beneficiary is entitled to Part A benefits first (until the applicable

benefit is exhausted), then Part B benefits if he or she is entitled
to any balance. If a bill includes both Medicare-covered services
and items that are exempt from Medicare, and it is impossible to
allocate payment under an employer plan between covered and
non-covered services, Health Care Financing Administration policy
calls for dividing the employer plan's payment in the same proportion as the bill (e.g., if the employer pays $200 of a $500 bill, $100
of which is for non-Medicare-covered services, 20%, or $40, of the
employer payment is deemed to be for the non-covered services).[8]
See page 236 for a discussion of coordination of employer's retiree
health benefits and Medicare; the rules are somewhat different
than the rules for active employees over 65.

Medicare coverage is also secondary to payment to be received
from liability or other forms of insurance.[9] Sometimes Medicare
payments are "conditional": Medicare pays because a Medicare claim
is submitted without mention of the other insurer, or Medicare pays
because the insurer fails to pay promptly. The beneficiary must refund
the conditional Medicare payment when the other payment is received. No one is entitled to a windfall profit for being injured after age
65.

Medicare will pay the portion of the bill that the elderly injured
person would be responsible for because of the *other* insurance
policy's deductible and coinsurance provisions (but the senior
citizen remains liable for the Medicare deductible and coinsurance).[10] For instance, assume that a Medicare beneficiary suffers
minor injuries in an automobile accident, and is treated in the
emergency room at a cost of $300. The no-fault insurance policy has
a $1,000 deductible, so the accident victim cannot recover under
the no-fault policy; instead, the injured person can have the
hospital send the $300 bill to Medicare.

MEDICARE ADMINISTRATION

Although the Health Care Financing Administration sets Medicare policy, it does not handle the actual paperwork; this task is
delegated to insurance companies. The insurance companies that
handle Part A claims are called "intermediaries." There were 44
intermediaries nationwide in July, 1996. There were also one or two
"carriers" for each state to cope with Part B claims.[11] Improvements in
computer systems — and mergers between insurers — resulted in a
contraction in the number of Medicare contractors (intermediaries
and carriers).

The intermediaries and carriers are not just paper pushers; their job is to review Medicare claims and prevent waste and fraud by eliminating improper claims. They handle claims processing (including review of claims for propriety) and payment safeguards (checking to see that home health care agencies and outpatient services that bill on a cost-plus basis do not overstate their costs, and making sure that Medicare does not pay claims where it is only a secondary payor).

PLANNING TIP: Advise your clients who are older employees that expenses can be counted toward the Medicare deductibles even if they are paid by the employer's plan instead of from the employee's own pocket.

The carriers' job also includes checking Part B claims to see that the services provided were reasonable and medically necessary. Intermediaries review some Part A claims for the same purpose, but they do not check to see that claims for inpatient care of Medicare beneficiaries are appropriate or medically necessary. Instead, the hospitals have Peer Review Organizations (PROs) that sign contracts with the Health Care Financing Administration to perform this function.

Part A claims are sent by the health care provider to the intermediary. The provider agrees to accept the intermediary's determination of how much should be paid under the claim. The Medicare beneficiary agrees to be responsible for the deductibles and coinsurance as required by Medicare. As described above, since September 1, 1990, doctors have been responsible for filing all Part B claims, whether assigned or unassigned. However, some carriers announced that they would continue to accept their pre-existing forms, not just the official HCFA-1500 (the standard Medicare claim form), for an undefined transition period. Furthermore, at least one carrier, New York's Empire Blue Cross-Blue Shield, announced that it would continue to accept filings made by Medicare beneficiaries rather than their doctors.[12]

WAIVER OF LIABILITY

The waiver of liability concept protects Medicare beneficiaries (and their health and Medigap insurers) in situations in which a claim is rejected under circumstances when the beneficiary is not at fault — typically, because neither the beneficiary nor the health care provider should have known that the claim would be rejected. In this circumstance, the beneficiary is "held harmless" (does not have to pay). Either Medicare pays, or the health care provider is stuck (if the provider knew or should have known that the claim was not covered, but the beneficiary did not have this knowledge).[13]

Medicare beneficiaries are not entitled to waiver of liability if they were given a written notice from the health care provider, the provider's own utilization review committee, a PRO, a carrier, or an intermediary, that the care was not covered. If the beneficiary gets such a notice on one occasion, he or she will not be entitled to waiver of liability for any future claims that are the same or reasonably comparable — unless, of course, the beneficiary protested the earlier denial and won.

MEDICARE MANAGED CARE

Medicare managed care, usually in the form of risk HMOs, has been available since 1985, but few Medicare beneficiaries took advantage of this option until the 1990s. In 1993, about 6% of all Medicare beneficiaries, approximately 2.1 million people, were enrolled in managed care plans. In 1994, 2.9 million people (7.8% of the Medicare population) were managed care users. As of August, 1995, 2.8 million people, 7% of the Medicare population (as compared to 25% of the general population) got their care through HMOs.

1994 is the last year for which complete cost figures have been analyzed. In that year, the Medicare system made managed care payments of $14.8 billion, representing about 20% of all Medicare payments. Part A managed care payments were $8.1 billion; Part B payments were $6.7 billion. (Although overall Medicare spending is concentrated on institutions, it makes sense that Part B would take a bigger chunk of managed care spending, because so much of HMO expenditure goes to the physicians who staff HMOs.)[14]

By September, 1996, about one-eighth of the Medicare population, or 4.5 million people, were enrolled in managed care plans. At that time, about one-fourth of the overall U.S. population participated in a managed care plan, so there is much room for growth in the Medicare managed care sector.

Nearly all Medicare managed care takes the form of the "risk" HMO. Other Medicare managed care forms include "cost" HMOs, which are entitled to additional HCFA funds in years in which their costs are especially high, and POS (point of service) HMOs that provide some reimbursement when members seek medical care outside the network. There are now 325 Medicare managed care providers; 234 of them are risk HMOs. In 1992, there were 96 HMOs with risk contracts and 77 with cost contracts, versus 110 and 85 respectively in 1993, and 153 risk and 86 cost HMOs in 1994. For 1995, there were 183 risk and 87 cost HMOs. In other words, the number of cost HMOs has essentially remained the same, while the number of risk HMOs has more than doubled.

A risk HMO enters into a contract with the Health Care Financing Agency (HCFA) under which HCFA pays a capitation amount equal to 95% of the average cost of providing health care to an approximately matched population of Medicare beneficiaries with similar health characteristics.

The risk element is that HCFA will not make any additional payments if the HMO spends more than the capitation amount to treat its patients. There is also a limitation on a risk HMOs profits: it is supposed to make a refund to HCFA, or extend additional benefits to its participants, if its costs are particularly low.

In general Medicare managed care patients are subject to "lock-in." That is, when they sign up with the HMO, they agree to accept care from the HMO in lieu of all other Medicare services. In a conventional risk HMO, patients must pay the full cost of non-emergency care that they choose to receive outside the HMO network (for instance, if they want to maintain a treatment relationship with a particular specialist).

Medicare beneficiaries are allowed to enroll in a managed care plan at any time — there is no specific open enrollment period. HMO marketing efforts are subject to strict policing by HCFA, and potential HMO members are entitled to disclosure of what the plan provides, what it costs, and what its administrative, grievance, and disenrollment procedures are.

Usually, HMO membership appears to be free, because the managed care patient continues to pay his or her Medicare Part B premium, but for most people the premium is deducted automatically from the Social Security check. Although it is not illegal for HMOs to charge a separate premium of their own, most do not do so. Usually, though not mandatorily, Medicare HMOs provide coverage of Medicare copayments, so participants will not have to pay out-of-pocket for Medicare deductibles and coinsurance. Another advantage is that Medicare HMOs frequently offer their members benefits — such as prescription drug coverage and preventive care — that do not appear in the conventional fee-for-service Medicare program. Thus, many

HMO enrollees can avoid the separate expense of Medicare supplementary insurance.

There is no specific disenrollment season for Medicare managed care, either: managed care beneficiaries can disenroll by notifying the HMO. They can either enroll in another HMO (in most markets, Medicare beneficiaries have a choice of at least two HMOs, and some have access to many more) or return to the ordinary Medicare fee-for-service system.

Potential Problems

In surveys performed by HCFA's Office of the Inspector General, nearly all Medicare HMO members express satisfaction with the quality of care they receive.[15]

Other studies also report that most Medicare enrollees in HMOs were adequately served by managed care (although naturally persons who disenrolled from Medicare HMOs expressed lower satisfaction than those who remained). (It is, however, possible that they are satisfied because they deal with polite, friendly people, and not necessarily because their care is of good quality.)

The American Managed Care and Review Association commissioned a report,"Managed Care Can Save Medicare: Achieving High Quality and Low Costs Through Managed Care," prepared by Health Care Strategy Associates Inc. and published in June, 1995. The conclusion of this report is that HMOs perform well for Medicare beneficiaries, especially because HMOs have more quality assurance measures and stress preventive care more than fee-for-service plans. However, some public health physicians have published articles criticizing the availability and quality of managed care, especially for the most vulnerable populations (the oldest, frailest, and poorest members of the managed care population).

MEDICARE HEARINGS AND APPEALS

There are four levels of review within the Medicare system. Beneficiaries do *not* automatically get hearings; they must request the review, within the appropriate timetable. The intermediary or carrier's initial determination can always be reviewed; after that, the beneficiary's rights depend on the type of claim and the amount of money involved.

Some claims are heard by hospital Peer Review Organizations; some by Administrative Law Judges (who work for the Social Security Administration, not for the Health Care Financing Administration); some by the Department of Health and Human Services (HHS); and some can be brought in court and heard by judges. However, it is a long, hard road to court, and claimants must "exhaust their remedies" (i.e., go through all the required stages of administrative review) before filing a lawsuit.

CHAPTER FOOTNOTES

1. The cases include *Kron v. Heckler*, Medicare/Medicaid Guide (CCH) Para. 33, 105 (E.D. La. 1983), *Henningson v. Hecker*, MMG Para. 33, 476 (N.D. Ia. 1983), and *Mayburg v. Sec'y of HHS*, 740 F.2d 100 (1st Cir. 1984).

2. *Duggan v. Bowen*, MMG Para. 37,220 (D.D.C. 1988).

3. This financial data derives from GAO/HEHS-96-19, "Medicare: Home Health Utilization Expands While Program Controls Deteriorate," (Mar. 1, 1996) and OIG Report No. OEI-04-93-00260, "Variations Among Home Health Agencies in Medicare Payments for Home Health Services," (July 1, 1995).

4. The paperwork requirement was imposed by OBRA '89 (the 1989 budget bill), P.L. 100-203.

5. See 42 USC Sections 1395(b)(4), 1394u(j). Doctors protested that the cap was unconstitutional, but constitutionality was upheld by *Isaacs v. U.S.*, MMG ¶37,235 (D. Ariz. 1987).

6. See CCH's *Medicare Explained* 1990 Para. 439.

7. Added by H.R. 3299 (1989).

8. See Medicare Intermediary Manual Section 3489.7; Medicare Carrier Manual Section 3335.8.

9. 42 USC Section 1395y(b)(1).

10. Medicare Intermediary Manual Section 3489.5.

11. HHS Press Release August 8, 1995; See CCH MMG ¶13,310.35.

12. See Leonard Sloane, "New Rule on Medicare Paper Work," *New York Times* August 11, 1990 p. 30.

13. The waiver of liability concept is enacted in 42 USC Section 1395.

14. GAO/HEHS-96-63, "Medicare HMOs: Rapid Enrollment Growth Concentrated in Selected States," (Jan. 18, 1996), MMG ¶44,028. Detailed tables showing risk HMO enrollment broken down by age group, sex, state, and county can be found in a news

release by HCFA's Office of Managed Care, CCH MEDICARE AND MEDICAID GUIDE ¶43,604 (Sep. 7, 1995), with corrections at CCH MEDICARE AND MEDICAID GUIDE ¶43,656, Sep. 26, 1995); Health Care Financing Review Medicare and Medicaid Statistical Supplement, 1996, especially pp. 7, 25, 29, 30, 125, 127, and 133.

15. HCFA's Office of the Inspector General publishes annual reports about HMOs; also see Peter T. Kilborn, "Tucson H.M.O.s May Offer Model for Medicare's Future," *New York Times* March 26, 1996 p. A1, and Linda Koco, "Why Seniors Join Medicare Risk HMOs: The Benefits," *National Underwriter* (Life/Health Edition) January 8, 1996 p. 13.

Chapter 7

MEDICAID PLANNING FOR THE OLDER CLIENT

The first edition of this book, published in 1992, contained a brief, simplified explanation of the difficult, convoluted Medicaid rules. In 1993, the Medicaid rules were rendered even more complex and harder to understand by the Omnibus Budget Reconciliation Act of 1993, which aimed at closing loopholes and making Medicaid planning harder and less worthwhile for affluent persons. These changes were duly reflected in the second edition of this work.

Now you have the third edition, published in 1997, in your hands. A major watershed was reached in 1996, when Congress passed a law making certain Medicaid-oriented transfers a criminal offense. Clearly, the risk of prosecution is a far greater disincentive to Medicaid planning than earlier changes, which merely restricted eligibility.

However, the criminalization statute contains exemptions for certain transactions that were also exempt under the earlier versions of the law. Therefore, in order to understand the post-1996 rules, it is first necessary to understand the earlier set of rules and how they evolved. Furthermore, efforts are underway either to repeal the criminalization statute, or to get a court judgment declaring it unconstitutional. If these efforts succeed, the earlier rules may have been reinstated by the time your clients seek Medicaid benefits.

In 1965, Congress passed laws establishing two medical-care systems for vulnerable groups: Medicare for those over 65 (later expanded to cover certain disabled persons), and Medicaid for the "indigent": those at or below the poverty level. Although some people advocated the establishment of the national health system that would cover all Americans, Congress decided that this was inappropriate.

The Medicare system, although established as a complete solution to the medical problems of the elderly, falls short of its promise in two respects. First of all, it is expensive for senior citizens: they have a significant "cost-sharing" burden in the form of monthly Part B premiums, deductibles, and coinsurance. The Omnibus Budget Reconciliation Acts of 1990 and 1993 also expanded the Medicare burden of "junior citizens" in the workforce, by increasing the amount of income on which they must pay a tax used to support the Medicare system.

Second, Medicare pays for acute care only, such as hospitalization, visits to a doctor's office, medical tests, and a limited amount of skilled nursing care for recuperation from acute illness. Medicare also has a limited benefit for home health care.

PLANNING TIP: If the client does meet Medicare's restrictive coverage requirements, the planning team should actively pursue the skilled nursing and home care benefits; a little persistence can pay off in benefits worth thousands of dollars.

Medicare does not pay for chronic, custodial nursing home care or extended, long-term home care. If someone enters a nursing home but does not need "skilled care" as defined by Medicare, or enters a nursing home and needs skilled care but has used up the Medicare Part A benefit, that person has very few choices, most of them disagreeable:

(1)   Probably the least disagreeable choice is collecting benefits under a long-term care (LTC) insurance policy. However, this is more likely to benefit future senior citizens than today's cohort. LTC insurance is a fairly new product, and most of today's senior citizens have little or no LTC coverage.

(2)   Many people simply do without necessary care, and experience unnecessary suffering until their premature death, because they cannot afford the care they need.

(3)   Other senior citizens pay privately for their nursing home care. Nursing facilities are very expensive: the average cost nationwide is at least $30,000 a year, and many facilities charge more than $50,000 a year. Some even charge over $100,000 a year!

(4)   Once the resources of a private-pay nursing home patient are depleted, the only refuge is Medicaid. Depletion of resources means that there will be no inheritance for the Medicaid beneficiary's spouse or children. If he or she has

a spouse living in the community (outside a nursing home), the spouse may be short of funds — or even reduced to poverty. Tragically, some people even deplete resources that the Medicaid system would allow them to keep, and allow the spouse in the community to suffer deprivation that is not required by the Medicaid system, because they do not "know the ropes" and do not have appropriate professional advice.

Eligibility for Medicaid depends on meeting the system's criteria (discussed below). Some senior citizens (or middle-aged people contemplating future senior citizen status) make Medicaid plans by structuring their income and transferring resources to fit the definition. Medicaid planning is controversial. Some people feel that it is improper, or unethical, to take advantage of what they see as loopholes. Others feel that it is unfair to divert resources that are intended for the poor.

Medicaid planning can be risky. A person or couple could transfer resources to children or grandchildren as part of a Medicaid plan, only to find that they *do not* need nursing home care. The result could be serious financial trouble, or a decline in the standard of living of the person or couple. In addition, the Medicaid rules could change so that the planning steps do not have the desired effect of securing Medicaid eligibility.

Major changes were made in 1993 by the Omnibus Budget Reconciliation Act of 1993 (OBRA '93) (Public Law 103-66). OBRA '93 does several things to make it harder to qualify for Medicaid:

- It extends the look-back period from 30 months in all cases, to 36 months for most transactions, and to 60 months for some transactions involving irrevocable trusts.

- It removes the "cap" on the penalty period. Under earlier law, the longest possible waiting period generated by a transfer of assets would be 30 months. But, for Medicaid benefits received after October 1, 1993, OBRA '93 permits a penalty period of any length.

- It makes it clear that if there is a series of transfers, they will be treated in the way that creates the longest possible penalty period, not the shortest one.

- States now must impose transfer penalties on people who get Medicaid institutional care, and can impose transfer penalties on people who get Medicaid home care.

One major reason that people who are not indigent by ordinary definitions want to make Medicaid plans is to preserve their assets so that they can be inherited by their spouses, children, or other intended heirs. OBRA '93 spikes these guns, too. Under earlier law, the only way state Medicaid agencies could seek repayment after a Medicaid beneficiary's death was to place a lien on his or her home. As described on page 178, there were (and still are) limitations on the circumstances in which liens could be placed, and in which they could be enforced; people making Medicaid plans could (and still can) transfer their homesteads to avoid the imposition of a lien. The homestead recovery rules survive OBRA '93. States have also been given much wider powers of recovery. They can collect against the Medicaid beneficiary's entire estate, including his or her share of "financial assets" such as trusts. The Secretary of the Department of Health and Human Services (HHS) has the power to prescribe rules about what constitutes a "financial asset." It's possible that annuities will be placed in this category.

The planning team must make a determination about what is, or is not, proper and ethical behavior in giving advice to clients. It is crucial to keep in touch with Medicaid developments. Each client must assess his or her personal risk of needing chronic care; the likely timing of this need; whether LTC insurance is a good buy; and whether he or she wants to make transfers with a Medicaid motivation. The planning team must advise the client of the potential risks, including the risk that the local Medicaid agency will be entitled to recover the cost of care from the Medicaid recipient's estate after his or her death.

HISTORY AND POLITICS

The Medicare system is fully funded and administered by the federal government. Therefore, there is a single set of Medicare rules for the whole country. The states do not have either a financial or an advisory role in administering Medicare.

The Medicaid situation is completely different. The Medicaid system is funded by both federal and state contributions, and states have a lot of discretion in setting the terms of their own Medicaid programs. Each state must have a Medicaid plan that is subject to federal approval and minimum federal standards (including federally-imposed ceilings), but there really are fifty different permutations of eligibility rules and services provided by Medicaid. All state Medicaid plans must include certain services mandated by the federal government; these services include skilled nursing home care and home health care for people who would otherwise be confined to skilled nursing homes. If they want to, states can choose to add other services, such as care in intermediate-level nursing homes and case management services.

Furthermore, the federal restraints on state Medicaid plans divide the state Medicaid plans into many categories — categories which determine the income, resource, and transfer limitations your clients will be subject to if they want to apply for Medicaid.

The SSI system (Supplemental Security Income — a federal welfare program for the aged, blind, and disabled) plays an important role in Medicaid, because many of the standards used by SSI are applied to Medicaid, even if the Medicaid applicant or beneficiary is not poor enough to qualify under SSI's very restrictive standards.

SSI VS. 209(b)

One way to analyze state Medicaid programs is to divide them into "SSI" and "209(b)" states. The SSI states (nearly all of the states fit into this category) use eligibility standards for Medicaid that derive from the SSI program.

However, twelve states take the position that using SSI criteria would be too expensive because too many people would qualify for Medicaid. These states are allowed to use criteria that are more restrictive than the SSI rules. However, they cannot use rules that are more restrictive than their own Medicaid rules as they existed on January 1, 1972, or more liberal than the SSI rules or the rules the states have for their own programs for supplementing the SSI benefits of elderly and disabled people.[1]

CATEGORICALLY AND MEDICALLY NEEDY

The federal government requires all state Medicaid plans to cover the "categorically needy." These are people who fall into a specified category, such as those receiving SSI payments.

Since 1986[2] the Medicaid system has included "optionally categorically needy" beneficiaries. That is, states have the option of giving Medicaid benefits to elderly people whose resources do not exceed either the SSI limit or the limit for the medically needy program (see below) and whose income is not higher than 100% of the federally-defined poverty level. The federal poverty level is quite a bit higher than the income limits permitted under the rules for the "categorically needy", so the effect of the 1986 change is to make more elderly people (in states that include the "optionally categorically needy" in their Medicaid plans) eligible for Medicaid. (A state that grants Medicaid to the optionally categorically needy can set an income limit that is somewhere between the SSI income limit and the poverty level — but not a level higher than the poverty line.)

Thirty-five states also provide Medicaid benefits for the "medically needy": people who are not poverty-stricken under the usual definitions, but who have medical bills that exceed their ability to pay. States set their own income and resource standards for the medically needy, which must be at least as generous as those allowed for categorically needy or optionally categorically needy but cannot exceed federal guidelines.

For instance, the income level permitted for medically needy Medicaid beneficiaries cannot be more than an amount calculated based on the benefit level of other federal programs.

PRACTICE TIP: Medically needy Medicaid beneficiaries *must* be allowed to "spend down" their excess income by incurring medical bills. But states that do not have a medically needy program (many of them located in the South and West) do not have to allow income spend-down; they can deny a Medicaid application just because someone has a few dollars of extra income, even if his or her family is reduced to poverty by high medical bills.

The way the income spend-down process works for the "medically needy" is that the state sets a "medically needy income level" which Medicaid beneficiaries are allowed to keep. The beneficiary is also allowed to keep a small allowance for personal needs, and to use part of his or her income for the support of spouse and dependents. In order to receive Medicaid, the beneficiary must spend the rest of his or her income on medical care.

For single people, the determination of income is pretty straightforward. For married couples, questions arise as to whether income belongs to the spouse entering the nursing home (or already in the nursing home), to both spouses jointly, or only to the spouse who remains in the community.

The basic rule is the "name on the instrument" rule: if the check is payable to Jack, the income is his; if it is payable to Ethel, the income is hers; if it is payable to both of them jointly, or if it is impossible to tell, half is considered to belong to each spouse. Income from a trust is attributed to the spouses based on the terms of the trust; if it is joint income, or ownership is impossible to analyze, half is considered to belong to each.

PRACTICE TIP: The spouse in the nursing home is allowed to demand a hearing, and prove that income that is assigned to him or her for Medicaid purposes really belongs to the other spouse. But the spouse in the community does *not* have a right to prove this.

The Medicare Catastrophic Coverage Act of 1988[3] added a class of what might be called "part-time" Medicaid beneficiaries. These QMBs (for Qualified Medicare Beneficiaries) are entitled to Medicare Part A benefits, and fit within specified income and resource limits, even if they are not eligible for full Medicaid coverage. The state Medicaid program is obligated to "buy-in" Medicare for QMBs: that is, the Medicaid program pays the Part B premium and the Medicare deductibles and coinsurance (see Chapter 6) for the QMBs, but does not otherwise provide them with medical services.

PLANNING TIP: The federal Medicaid rules contain a complex series of provisions dealing with people who would be eligible for Medicaid except for certain cost-of-living and related increases in their Social Security and other benefits. If you have a client who is close to Medicaid eligibility limits, get specialized professional advice as to whether your client is Medicaid-eligible under one of these provisions.

Once a person becomes eligible for Medicaid, he or she is expected to devote *all* income, except for a small personal allowance (about a dollar a day) and an allowance for the spouse or dependents (discussed below), to the cost of medical care. Each state has a "methodology" for determining exactly how much income a Medicaid beneficiary must devote to this purpose. If you want to learn the rules in detail, a cooperative attorney or bureaucrat might be able to show you the ropes or get you a copy of the relevant Medicaid Manual.

Make sure you keep up to date! State policy is expressed in changes to the Manual, or in interoffice memos called Transmittals. One of the really frustrating things about Medicaid is that state agencies also develop informal policies which affect clients' eligibility, but which are not published anyplace, much less distributed to elder law attorneys and advocates for the elderly for use in planning.

ASSETS, AVAILABILITY AND TRANSFER

As discussed above, one of the most important considerations in Medicaid eligibility is income. However, from the planning point of view, assets (resources) and transfers are at least as important.

Because the Medicaid program was originally designed as a poverty program, not a program to provide nursing home care for the aged, eligibility is based on having extremely limited resources. Medicaid beneficiaries were originally allowed to own certain "exempt resources" that were not counted in determining eligibility — a house, basic household goods such as furniture, a car, and a small burial fund — plus only a very limited amount of "nonexempt resources." (The current SSI standards do not permit non-exempt resources above $2,000 for an individual or $3,000 for a couple; all other resources are "excess" resources, which must be "spent down" on medical care before Medicaid benefits can be granted.)

Furthermore, under the Medicaid law as originally drafted, the assets of *both* spouses were supposed to be applied to the care of the first spouse to get sick. The only exceptions were the assets (such as a homestead) specifically defined as exempt, and assets that were not "available" to the Medicaid applicant. This could create an intolerable situation. Fortunately, in 1988, the law was changed (as described below) to provide significant financial protection for the non-institutionalized spouse.

If the key to eligibility was a shortage of "available" assets on the date of the application, it was easy enough to find loopholes. People simply waited until they realized they might need Medicaid, then either transferred their assets (for example, making a gift to a son or daughter) or made them "unavailable" by putting them in a trust that they could not control. The Medicaid system responded in two different ways to plug the loopholes. First, there are restrictions on transfers: making transfers during the "look-back" period (described below) will delay or prevent Medicaid eligibility. Second, restrictions have been placed on the use of trusts in Medicaid planning.

THE LOOK-BACK PERIOD

In determining Medicaid eligibility, not only does a state Medicaid agency look at current income and assets; it also examines transfers that were made during a period of 36 months before the Medicaid application. For transfers made into an irrevocable trust, from which the transferor cannot receive income and cannot take back any part of the trust principal, the look-back period is 60 months. (If a person makes a Medicaid application before being institutionalized, the period is counted back from the date of institutionalization, not the date of the application.) Before OBRA '93, the look-back period for all kinds of transfers was 30 months. Maybe it is a coincidence that some studies show that the average nursing home stay is two and a half years — maybe not! Medicaid eligibility can be denied, based on transfers that are not otherwise exempted by law, during the look-back period.

A "transfer" is an outright gift, or an exchange for something worth less than the full value of the transferred property. For instance, if a client owns an art collection appraised at $50,000, and "sells" it to his daughter for $1,000, there has been a transfer of $49,000. Simply spending money to buy things at market value does not constitute a transfer, and the Medicaid system looks at assets and transfers, but not household budgeting. Medicaid eligibility cannot be denied if a person or couple has a somewhat extravagant lifestyle (frequent vacations, dinners out, theater and sports tickets), but can be denied if they accumulate assets such as savings accounts and securities.

The penalty period is calculated by determining whether there have been any non-exempt transfers during the look-back period. If there were no transfers, or if all transfers occurred before the look-back period, or if all transfers were exempt (e.g., transfers between spouses), then there will be no penalty period. Otherwise, the penalty period equals the amount of the transfer, divided by the state's official published figure for the cost of private-pay care. Say, for example, that $75,000 was transferred, and the cost of care is $3,000 per month. The transfer will give rise to a 25-month penalty period.

Before OBRA '93, the penalty period was "capped": the longest possible penalty period was 30 months, regardless of the size of the transfer. Many people felt that it was a reasonable trade-off: make a big transfer, then wait out the waiting period (knowing that it would not exceed two and a half years), or keep enough in reserve to pay privately for care during the penalty period.

OBRA '93 removed the cap, and a post-October 1, 1993 transfer can give rise to a penalty period of any length. If the transfer was $750,000 instead of $75,000, and the cost of care is set at $5,000 a month, the transfer will create a 150-month penalty period — not very practical as a planning alternative!

Before OBRA '93, states *had* to impose transfer penalties on "institutionalized persons": those who received either Medicaid nursing home benefits, or Medicaid home care under a waiver program. (Waivers are issued by the Health Care Financing Administration, exempting state Medicaid plans from certain technical requirements.) OBRA '93 makes it clear that states also have the option of imposing transfer penalties when Medicaid home care is received under non-waiver programs.

PLANNING TIP: If a state does impose transfer penalties for non-waivered home care, the nursing home figures will still be used, even though the actual cost of home care is likely to be lower. So a person who transfers $30,000 where the cost of nursing home care is officially reported at $4,000 a month will have a penalty period of seven months (fractional months are rounded down), yet he or she may be spending only $1,000 a month on home care during the penalty period.

PLANNING TIP: If a person uses both Medicaid home care and nursing home care, the penalty period will be divided between the two. In effect, the penalty assessed for one kind of care will be "credited" when the other kind of care is used. Similarly, OBRA '93 permits the penalty period to be apportioned between spouses if both spouses get Medicaid benefits. After all, transfers by each spouse affected the other spouse's eligibility for Medicaid.

TREATMENT OF TRUSTS

In 1985, the Comprehensive Omnibus Budget Reconciliation Act (COBRA) added new limitations on "Medicaid qualifying trusts." These are trusts that are *intended* to qualify someone for Medicaid, but because of COBRA, they have turned out to be *disqualifying* trusts. A Medicaid qualifying trust is a trust set up by an individual for his or her own benefit, or by one spouse for the benefit of the other spouse, that has other characteristics:

(1)   The Medicaid applicant is, or could be, a beneficiary of part or all of the trust payments.

(2)   The trustee of the trust has the discretion to determine the level of trust payments; the payment level is not fixed by the terms of the trust.

If a trust is a Medicaid-qualifying trust, then the *maximum* amount that the trustee could possibly distribute to the Medicaid applicant is considered an available asset. This is true even if the trustee never lets the applicant have a single penny; it is also true whether or not the applicant has the right to cancel the trust and take back the trust principal.

OBRA '93 also made significant changes in the Medicaid treatment of trusts. For new trusts, the "Medicaid qualifying trust" rules have been abolished — but they remain in effect for trusts set up before August 24, 1993 (the date OBRA '93 was enacted, in contrast to its October 1, 1993 effective date).

Under the OBRA '93 rules, most *inter vivos* (living) trusts are divided into three categories:

- *Revocable trusts.* Just as under earlier Medicaid law, all income received from the trust is treated as available income, and will probably have to be spent down. Income paid to someone else (for instance, a child who is also a trust beneficiary) is treated as a transfer made by the Medicaid applicant, giving rise to a penalty period. The trust principal is considered an available asset for the creator of the trust, because he or she has the right to revoke the trust and take back part or all of the principal.

- *Irrevocable trusts — creator can get income and / or principal from the trust.* Whatever the creator actually does get from the trust is available for Medicaid purposes; anything going to anyone else counts as a transfer, but principal that remains in the trust is not considered available to the creator.

- *Irrevocable trusts — creator cannot get income or principal from the trust; neither can the creator's spouse.* For instance, a wealthy person might place money into a trust which makes quarterly payments to that person's children for ten years, at which time the trust assets are distributed to the creator's grandchildren, with no income going to the creator and no way for the trustee to return part of the trust corpus to the creator. In this case, trust income and principal are not considered available to the creator for Medicaid purposes, but the look-back period for this type of transfer is stretched out to 60 months, not the normal 36-month period.

PLANNING TIP: Special, more lenient rules are applied to testamentary trusts (trusts created under the will of someone else, benefiting the Medicaid applicant or recipient), and to trusts administered by a charitable organization into which assets of a disabled person (of any age) are deposited. Relief is also available for trusts set up by parents, grandparents, guardians, and courts to benefit disabled persons under 65, so clients who are concerned about the needs of a disabled child may be able to set up a trust to provide small comforts for the child without jeopardizing the child's entitlement to Supplementary Security Income (SSI) and Medicaid benefits. However, the trust corpus must revert to the state after the disabled child's death; it cannot go back to the family if this relief provision is to be used.

PROTECTING THE SPOUSE

When one spouse enters a nursing home, it is an emotional challenge to the other spouse, who must cope with a new form of marital relationship and the other spouse's devastating illness. It is also an economic challenge to the non-institutionalized spouse, who must somehow survive on whatever is left over after the other spouse pays huge medical bills as a private-pay patient or to satisfy Medicaid spend-down requirements.

Before the passage of new laws in 1988, the "community spouse" was frequently reduced to financial desperation. In a typical case, most of the couple's assets would be in the husband's name or jointly held; the wife would have few resources of her own. Most of their post-retirement income would derive from his pension and Social Security benefits. If he got sick first, then most or all of the couple's income and assets would be devoted to his care; the wife would somehow have to pay her rent, utility bills, food bills, and other expenses, including her own needs for health care. (Ironically, if she needed to enter a nursing home, Medicaid eligibility would be no problem, because she was without significant income or assets.) The one bright spot was that sometimes the at-home spouse could sue the institutionalized spouse for non-support, and a sympathetic judge would award part of the couple's income to the at-home spouse.

This tragic situation was greatly improved by provisions of the Medicare Catastrophic Coverage Act of 1988 (MCCA). Instead of making transfers far in advance, without being able to predict when, or even whether, nursing home care would be needed, now people can wait until institutionalization is imminent, then make specifically exempted transfers to make sure that the at-home spouse will be protected.

The law includes provision for a spousal income allowance: the at-home spouse is entitled to maintain the level of income determined by the state, even if his or her spouse is a Medicaid beneficiary who is required to apply nearly all of his or her income to medical costs. If the at-home spouse's personal income is lower than the permitted amount, the at-home spouse can demand enough of the institutionalized spouse's income to make up the difference. The state Medicaid system must let the at-home spouse keep at least $815 a month, and may allow an income allowance of as much as $1565 a month (both of these amounts are adjusted to keep up with inflation). For 1997, the corresponding figures are $1,295 (minimum) and $1,975 (maximum).

PLANNING TIP: The income allowance represents income *after* taxes and after health insurance premiums — so the at-home spouse should be encouraged to maintain adequate health insurance, including Medigap and LTC insurance where appropriate, to take care of his or her own health needs.

Furthermore, in high cost areas, the at-home spouse is entitled to retain even more income, as an "excess shelter allowance." It may even be possible to get a court order that the at-home spouse needs even more income; the institutionalized spouse's Medicaid eligibility will not be affected if he or she complies with the court order and makes support payments to the at-home spouse.

RESOURCES FOR THE AT-HOME SPOUSE

In addition to transfers already made (carefully!) as part of a long-range Medicaid plan, certain transfers of resources can be made to the at-home spouse without affecting Medicaid eligibility. The state sets a resource allowance that the at-home spouse can keep, within limits set by Congress. The resource allowance must be set at a level of at least $12,000, and can be as much as $60,000 (again, the numbers are inflation-indexed: the minimum permitted resource allowance for 1997 is $15,804; the maximum for that year is $79,020).

In practice, the way this works is that all of the couple's assets (including amounts previously transferred by one spouse to the other) are evaluated when a Medicaid application is made. The at-home spouse is allowed to retain the amount of the resource allowance. If he or she does not have personal resources in this amount, the Medicaid applicant spouse can transfer the amount required to make up the difference without losing Medicaid eligibility. (The at-home spouse can also keep one-half of the couple's total resources, if this amount is greater than the state's resource allowance but less than $60,000 as adjusted for inflation.)

Furthermore, if the couple has lots of resources but low income, it may be possible to make an even larger transfer of resources from the Medicaid applicant spouse to the at-home spouse to make sure that the at-home spouse has the level of income guaranteed by MCCA.

PLANNING TIP: In most states, it is not clear how high the extra transfer can be, or how it should be made. If the state will accept the theory that enough assets should be transferred to yield the missing income, the transfer can be very large indeed, given the low interest rates paid on investments in the mid-1990s. If the rate of interest is set at 2%, then fifty times the income shortfall could be transferred to the community spouse. However, in 1993, Iowa ruled that this is not the correct method.[4] Instead, the Iowa court held that the sick spouse should transfer enough money to buy a single-premium life annuity that will yield the necessary income; it is not permissible to transfer low-interest-yielding bank accounts or Certificates of Deposit for this purpose. Clients in other states making Medicaid plans might consider the purchase of a single-premium annuity for this purpose, on the assumption that other states might follow Iowa's lead.

"INCOME-FIRST" AND SPLIMPA

There are many state-to-state variations in the way Medicaid rules are drafted and interpreted. It is clear that federal law requires all Medicaid systems to have "spousal protection" provisions. That is, if the healthy spouse's personal income and assets fall below the amount incorporated into state law, the spouse in the nursing home can make a one-time transfer of assets, and a monthly transfer of income, to bring the at-home spouse up to the required financial levels.

In other words, at the simplest level, if the state sets the resource allowance at $50,000, and the at-home spouse's resources are calculated to be only $25,000, the nursing home spouse can transfer $25,000 of his or her own resources to the at-home spouse. If the state sets the income allowance at $750 a month, and the at-home spouse's individual income is only $500 a month, the nursing home spouse can give him or her $250 a month, thus reducing the amount that the nursing home spouse has to spend down as a condition of continued Medicaid eligibility.

This shifting of funds is not forbidden by Medicaid law; in fact, it is not even considered a transfer that gives rise to a penalty period. Therefore, it does not affect the sick spouse's Medicaid eligibility, and it cannot be treated as criminal transfer under the Health Insurance Portability and Accountability Act of 1996 (P.L. 104-191) (see page 179).

What if the nursing home spouse has a high level of resources, but a low income — or has a high level of resources, and wants to shift as many of them as possible to the healthy at-home spouse? Depending on the facts of the case, and on local interpretations of Medicaid law, it may be possible to transfer enough resources to the at-home spouse to generate enough income to bring the community spouse up to the income level. In other words, if the at-home spouse is entitled to $200 a month more income, it may be possible to transfer additional resources to him or her, sufficient to generate $200 a month income.

Depending on the state, different methods may work. From the planner's point of view, the best-case scenario is simply to be able to transfer a lot of assets, thus keeping them within the family. Furthermore, there are many investments (e.g., money market funds; Certificates of Deposit) that pay a low rate of return. If the at-home spouse is entitled to an extra $200 a month, for instance ($2,400 a year), and interest rates for safe investments are 4% a year, then it would be necessary to transfer $60,000 (25 x $2,400) to provide the extra income.

Some states will allow extra funds to be transferred to the at-home spouse, but not in the form of a lump sum. Instead, they permit the SPLIMPA approach (Single Premium Life IMmediate Payment Annuity). That is, the nursing home spouse purchases a commercial annuity large enough to generate the required additional income. This approach can provide needed extra income for the at-home spouse, but does not give him or her full discretion and control over resources, the way that an outright transfer would do.

Whenever an annuity is used in Medicaid planning, it is vital to make sure that the annuity is actuarially sound: i.e., it reflects a reasonable estimate of the annuitant's life expectancy, so the payments to be received are reasonably proportionate to the value of the purchase price. If the annuity is not actuarially sound, it is more likely that some transfer element will be seen in the transaction.

DUTIES BETWEEN SPOUSES

The Medicaid system takes the vow "for better or for worse" very seriously. Each spouse has an obligation to support the other; it is a unisex obligation, not just one that runs from husband to wife. Theoretically, the at-home spouse who has more income that the spousal income allowance is supposed to contribute some of the excess to the state Medicaid authority to pay for the institutionalized spouse's medical care. (Medicaid agency manuals suggest that 25% is the proper figure.) Theoretically, the Medicaid agency has the right to sue the at-home spouse for nonsupport, although staff shortages and public relations concerns make this option somewhere between theoretical and nonexistent. Does this contradict the discussion above regarding relief for the spouse in the community? No, because there are two sets of Medicaid rules: one which determines a person's initial eligibility for Medicaid, another which sets out that person's rights and obligations once he or she becomes a Medicaid beneficiary. After eligibility is established, there is the question of whether either spouse is entitled to support from the other.

MCCA also requires the at-home spouse to disclose his or her income and resources to the Medicaid agency. Under MCCA's "just say no" provision, the applicant can be denied Medicaid benefits if the at-home spouse refuses to provide this information, but *cannot* be denied eligibility if the at-home spouse provides the information but refuses to contribute assets over and above the resource limitation to the Medicaid agency to pay for the sick spouse's care. However, the Medicaid agency has the right to sue for non-support. So far, this is a very uncommon event (if it happens at all), but it may become more common as states try to accommodate a growing Medicaid case load to a shrinking state treasury.

The Medicaid implications of a very special asset — the family home — are discussed below. Here, just note that, under certain circumstances, the Medicaid agency can impose a lien on the home (with legal limits on when the lien can be enforced). This will affect

Medicaid planning and will also alter the estate plan, if it is no longer possible for the Medicaid recipient to leave the house to the heir he or she has chosen.

ESTATE RECOVERIES AFTER OBRA '93

People who receive Medicaid benefits after October 1, 1993 face another disincentive. The homestead recovery rules continue to be in force, and state Medicaid agencies have additional, much broader, recovery powers. For one thing, the homestead provisions apply only to people who received Medicaid after reaching age 65. The broader estate recovery rules apply to everyone receiving Medicaid benefits at age 55 or older. States can seek estate recovery for any Medicaid services, including home care services.

Most crucially, the recovery can be sought against the entire "estate" of the deceased Medicaid recipient, including assets that were not considered available in determining eligibility — for instance, the corpus of an irrevocable trust. The estate also includes items such as joint accounts and jointly held real estate — but only up to the extent of the Medicaid beneficiary's interest in the property.

PLANNING TIP: If a client's reason for wanting to make a Medicaid plan was to preserve assets to be inherited by family members or friends, this provision is likely to make the plan unworkable. At the very least, the amount to be inherited will be reduced (which may mean that the client should buy more life insurance to replace the amount recovered by the state). If Medicaid planning is undesirable, the client should consider saving more money (to pay privately for care); research the availability and financial stability of Continuing Care Retirement Communities (that combine residential and recreational services with nursing care); purchase long-term care insurance; or combine these strategies.

CRIMINAL PENALTIES FOR
MEDICAID-ORIENTED TRANSFERS

An obscure provision of the Health Insurance Portability and Accountability Act of 1996 (P.L. 104-191) imposes criminal penalties on certain Medicaid-motivated transfers. The provision is brief, poorly written, and has no legislative history, so it's not very clear what it means or how it will be applied. It isn't even clear which member of Congress initially added the provision to the bill, or which members supported and which opposed it.

Section 217 of the Health Insurance Portability and Accountability Act of 1996 amends the federal Medicare fraud statute to impose a misdemeanor penalty of up to one year in prison, a $10,000 fine, or both, on anyone who "knowingly and willfully disposes of assets (including by any transfer in trust) in order for an individual to become eligible for medical assistance under a state plan under title XIX if disposing of the assets results in the imposition of a period of ineligibility for such assistance under section 1917(c)."

Elements of the Crime

Medical assistance under a state plan under title XIX means Medicaid. That's clear enough; the problem is interpreting the rest of the provision. Three things must occur for the statute to be violated:

(1)   Knowing and willful disposition of assets.

(2)   Disposition in order to become eligible for Medicaid.

(3)   There must be a penalty period — i.e., the disposition must be a non-exempt transfer under the Medicaid rules, which are found in Section 1917(c) of the Social Security Act.

Criminalization under the 1996 legislation does not apply to transfers that are very remote in time (more than 36 months, or more than 60 months for a transfer involving an irrevocable trust from which the Medicaid applicant cannot receive benefits) — because those transfers are not taken into account in the Medicaid application process, and therefore do not give rise to any penalty period.

Several problems are obvious at the outset. If a penalty period is imposed, then the applicant will be denied Medicaid benefits, or will receive them after a delay. Why make it a crime to make an ineffective attempt to get Medicaid benefits inappropriately, but not a crime to arrange the transaction so that Medicaid benefits are granted immediately? (Imposing criminal penalties after benefits are denied does not constitute double jeopardy, because that refers to imposing two *criminal* penalties on the same conduct, not a criminal penalty plus a civil penalty.)

The 1996 legislation is ambiguous: what does it mean for a penalty period to be "imposed?" One theory is that the penalty period is imposed automatically whenever there is a transfer. Another theory is that the penalty period is imposed by the state Medicaid agency when an application is made. If this interpretation is correct, there's a simple strategy for avoiding criminal liability: simply defer the Medicaid application until after the expiration of the penalty period. Of course, this means that there must be money available to "wait out" the time when a penalty would be imposed.

Another problem is that the 1996 legislation uses the phrase "disposes of an asset," which is not found anywhere else in the Medicaid law. It probably means the same thing as "transferring" an asset: i.e., either giving the asset away or receiving less than its full market value.

Nor is it clear what it means for a transfer to be made "in order" to qualify for Medicaid benefits. Does that mean that there is no crime unless Medicaid was the sole motivation for disposing of the assets — or that a crime can be committed if a transfer is part of a full-scale financial plan that has many objectives (wise management of assets, saving current income tax, saving estate tax, transmitting assets within the family in accordance with the senior citizen's wishes, and potential Medicaid eligibility)? Perhaps a defendant could be acquitted by testifying that he or she didn't even know about Medicaid planning until he or she needed long-term care — and certainly didn't know about Medicaid planning at the time of the transfer, which was made for non-Medicaid reasons.

Exempt Transactions

Section 217 of the Health Insurance Portability and Accountability Act of 1996 took effect on January 1, 1997, so transfers made before that date cannot be subjected to criminal penalties. Nor is a criminal penalty imposed if the transfer is exempt under §1917(c) and therefore does not result in a period of ineligibility. For this purpose, transfers are exempt if:

- One spouse transfers assets to the other spouse. In some states, such as New York, as soon as the sick spouse becomes eligible for Medicaid, the healthy spouse who received the transfers can re-transfer the money or property to someone else (such as the couple's children) without impairing the sick spouse's Medicaid eligibility.

- One spouse transfers the assets not directly to the other spouse, but to someone else for the "sole benefit" of the other spouse. It's not clear what "sole benefit" means, but it probably means either that someone else manages the money for the transferee spouse, or that a trust is set up that has the transferee spouse as its sole beneficiary. Clearly, if there are other beneficiaries, the trust is not for the transferee spouse's sole benefit. If the trust lasts for the transferee spouse's lifetime, and its funds are then paid over to someone else, perhaps the state Medicaid agency could argue that the trust is not for the spouse's sole benefit.

- The assets are transferred to the Medicaid applicant's child, if the child is a minor, blind, or disabled. In practical terms, elderly Medicaid applicants usually do not have minor children. However, some of them do have blind or otherwise handicapped children, and planning for the children's future (including their own eligibility for Medicaid, Supplemental Security Income, Social Security disability benefits, or other government benefits) is very important to them.

Under the Medicaid system, the personal residence is entitled to special protection as a homestead. The value of the residence is not counted in determining Medicaid eligibility. However, if the Medicaid applicant qualifies for Medicaid benefits, and dies after receiving the benefits, the state Medicaid agency that provided the benefits is entitled to recover the value of the benefits from the recipient's estate. The agency can't undertake this collection effort as long as the recipient's spouse, or minor, blind, or disabled child continues to live in the home — but this right of estate recovery can make it impossible for a Medicaid recipient to leave his or her home to a child, friend, or other intended beneficiary.

However, under §1917(c), a Medicaid applicant can transfer his or her interest in the homestead without giving rise to a penalty period, if the transfer is made to:

- The applicant's spouse.

- The applicant's minor, blind, or disabled child.

- A brother or sister who had an equity interest in the property for at least one year before the Medicaid application (e.g., two sisters inherit their parent's house; one sister transfers her interest in the property to her sibling before making a Medicaid application).

- A "caregiver child" who lived in the home for at least two years. The policy rationale for this exemption is that the child presumably provided care that made it possible to defer the Medicaid application.

Under §1917(c), penalties are not imposed if the Medicaid applicant makes a "satisfactory showing" under federal regulations that the applicant did not intend to give away the assets, but intended to sell the assets at their fair market value, or at least to get value in return. (So far, however, the Department of Health and Human Services has not published regulations on this subject.)

There is no penalty if the assets were transferred exclusively for a purpose other than qualifying for Medicaid. In other words, the transferor had only ONE motivation, and that motivation did not involve Medicaid. This exemption is not available to the ordinary planning client who tries to meet many financial objectives with the plan.

State Medicaid agencies can draft their own procedures (as long as the procedures conform to federal law) to grant Medicaid benefits if denying the benefits because of transfers would result in "extreme hardship." So far, few states have taken advantage of this opportunity; the ones who have usually took a hard line, defining "extreme hardship" very restrictively (for instance, a situation in which the applicant would become homeless or unable to purchase food, not just a situation in which the applicant's estate plan is frustrated).

Last but not least, there is no penalty under §1917(c) if the assets are returned to the transferor. Before the 1996 legislation, this exception was seldom used — because returning the assets would naturally have the effect of disqualifying the applicant (because he or she now has excess assets). But if returning the assets means that Medicaid benefits will be denied, but criminal penalties will not be imposed, the trade-off is worthwhile!

Effect of the Provision

Of course, the criminalization provision raised a storm of protest from elder law attorneys. In January, 1997, Representative LaTourette introduced a bill simply to repeal the Health Insurance Portability and Accountability Act of 1996 criminalization provision; when this book went to press, his bill was still pending.

There was also a possibility that declaratory judgment actions would be filed, asking the federal courts to interpret the ambiguous terms in the 1996 legislation. Certainly, if any attempts are made to prosecute anyone under the statute, cases will be litigated and appeals will be filed. There is always the possibility that ambiguities will be clarified — and it will be absolutely clear that transfer-based Medicaid planning is illegal — not quite the result that elder law attorneys want!

It is very unlikely that the 1996 legislation will ever be used to send elderly Medicaid applicants to prison. For one thing, convicts have a constitutional right to adequate medical care, so the federal government would have to spend more money to imprison and provide medical care to the applicants that it would have cost simply to grant them Medicaid benefits.

In all probability, the criminalization provision was passed strictly in order to create a "chilling effect." That is, if no one is quite sure what the provision means — and if attorneys and other planners are afraid of being prosecuted for aiding and abetting a crime! — then people will refrain from making Medicaid-oriented transfers (even if the transfers might fit within an exception and thus not be illegal). Furthermore, the elderly who need medical care may end up suffering additional hardships, or even losing their homes, if they are afraid to apply for Medicaid benefits.

If they are nursing home residents, there is an additional complicating factor. Medicaid pays nursing homes much less than the rates that private patients pay, so it is understandable that nursing homes prefer private-pay to Medicaid patients. The nursing homes therefore have no incentive to encourage patients to apply for Medicaid, or to educate them about Medicaid or assist them in appealing Medicaid denials (unless, of course, the patients are totally out of money and the facility's only choice is between Medicaid payment and no payment).

Planning Possibilities After the Health Insurance
Portability and Accountability Act of 1996

The criminalization provision appears in the same federal statute as the new tax and other incentives for the private purchase of long-term care (LTC) insurance. It seems clear that Congress wants both to discourage transfer-based Medicaid planning and to encourage private-sector solutions such as insurance purchases. Clearly, for planning clients who are insurable, and who have enough cash to buy the insurance, then LTC insurance can be a far better option than Medicaid planning.

There are various ways to find cash for premiums, if the client's budget is tight. Perhaps the client's children can contribute (especially since the insurance has the side effect of preserving the parent's assets so they can be inherited by the children). The client may wish to continue working a little longer, deferring the initial pension payment and receiving enhanced pension (and Social Security) checks because of the delay. Perhaps the client can sell some of the stock in his or her portfolio, and use the proceeds to pay for care. (This is not a transfer, because the stock is sold at its fair market value, and proceeds are used to purchase a commercial product, not given away.)

The advantage of private-sector planning is especially great because Congress may impose further restrictions on the Medicaid program. Quality care may become more difficult than ever to obtain through the Medicaid system, especially if there are drastic budget cuts or if states are granted full discretion over their Medicaid programs (and are no longer subject to federal minimum requirements). For example, states might be allowed to stop providing home care or even nursing home care for impaired senior citizens. It won't matter if you qualify for a Medicaid program, if the entire program has been discontinued!

Even under current conditions, for those who are uninsurable, or for those who are committed to making transfers for other reasons (compelling needs of family members; estate planning; income tax savings; desire to make gifts that are not subject to gift tax), it may still be possible to carry out the elder care plan without engaging in a criminal transfer.

In essence, the crime consists of applying for Medicaid during a penalty period. Therefore, if the application is delayed until after the penalty has expired, there should be no problem. If less than half of a person's excess assets are given away, and the rest is retained to pay privately for nursing home care, it should be quite possible to defer the application until after the expiration of the penalty period.

Planners should concentrate on transfers that are exempt under §1917(c), and therefore are not criminalized: for instance, transfers between spouses, and exempt transfers of the home.

MEDICAID AND NURSING HOME ACCESS

Yet another area in which state Medicaid agencies have discretion is in setting the level and method of determining how much reimbursement nursing homes will receive for Medicaid patients. The rates have one thing in common, though: most of them are much lower than the rates nursing homes can get from "private-pay" patients (those who use their own funds, insurance benefits, or a combination of the two, rather than Medicaid). There is no requirement that nursing homes participate in Medicaid; most of them do, because the high cost of care makes it likely that patients will begin as private-pay patients and later shift to Medicaid. But a nursing home participating in Medicaid does not have to make all its beds available for Medicaid; it can have some Medicaid beds and some private-pay beds.

Nursing homes are generally administered to select the "case mix" (mixture of patients) that will be the most profitable. This depends on local Medicaid reimbursement policies and whether there are plenty of nursing home beds in the area or only a few. If there is no real competition, nursing homes will not be restrained by market forces. Minnesota has a state law forbidding nursing homes from charging private-pay patients more than the Medicaid rate, and Connecticut imposes a "cap" on the difference between private-pay and Medicaid rates. Nursing homes in other states can set their own rates. Usually, Medicaid rates are a lot lower than Medicare skilled nursing facility (SNF) rates, so nursing homes would rather have Medicare patients — but in New York, Medicaid pays more, so the opposite wish prevails.

Some state Medicaid plans pay a flat daily rate to nursing homes, which means they prefer "light care" patients (who are less expensive to take care of). Others pay a rate based on the intensity of care, so "high care" patients are more profitable. That can make it tough to find a bed for a patient who needs the kind of care that is least well rewarded by the state Medicaid plan.

All these factors determine whether a suitable nursing home bed will be available when it is needed, or if there will be a waiting period for certain types of care. Usually, it is much easier to "place" a private-pay patient than a Medicaid patient; waiting lists of over a year have been reported in some areas for some types of Medicaid patients.

DISCRIMINATION; CONTRACT ISSUES

There is no outright federal ban on nursing home discrimination against would-be residents who are already on Medicaid. Nursing homes can avoid participating in the Medicaid system. Unless there is a state law against Medicaid discrimination, the nursing home can also refuse to admit a person who is a Medicaid beneficiary.

However, if a person becomes a resident of a nursing home, starts out by paying privately, and exhausts all excess resources and therefore becomes eligible for Medicaid, it is against federal law for the nursing home to evict the person merely because the method of payment has changed from private payment to Medicaid. If the person can no longer pay the nursing home's charges, but is not eligible for Medicaid, the nursing home can evict the patient. This is a real risk for people in states with no "medically needy" Medicaid program who do not fit the "categorically needy" or "optionally categorically needy" definition.

The relationship between a nursing home and its residents is a contractual one, with the nursing home contract setting out rights and responsibilities of both parties. Federal and state law contain lengthy "bills of rights" for nursing home residents, and it is worthwhile for an attorney to review the contract prior to nursing home placement. In some cases, unfair provisions can be negotiated out; or, the nursing home resident may be entitled to damages for breach of contract or if the contract contains illegal provisions.

Since 1987, federal law has included limitations on certain types of contract provisions that affect Medicaid patients[5]:

(1)   It is illegal for nursing home contracts to force residents to give up their right to receive Medicare or Medicaid. In fact, nursing homes are legally required to counsel residents about the availability of these benefits.

(2)   It is illegal to force a relative or friend to make a personal guarantee of payments in order to get someone into a nursing home. It is permitted to require a person who is in charge of the potential resident's funds (such as a

guardian, or the holder of a durable power of attorney) to make a commitment to apply the resident's own funds to pay nursing home bills.

(3)   "Medicaid supplementation" is illegal — the nursing home cannot require a person or a person's family to pay more than the Medicaid rate in order to get a Medicaid-eligible person admitted to the nursing home.

PRACTICE TIP: Geriatric care managers are valuable team members because they know so much about nursing homes, and can serve as advocates for the rights of clients who become nursing home residents.

OTHER MEDICAID QUESTIONS

This discussion merely scratches the surface of a very complex subject. It focuses on what a person has to do to become eligible for Medicaid. Other issues arise because the Medicaid system requires periodic recertification of Medicaid eligibility. Changes in financial status (such as receiving an inheritance, or a cost-of-living increase in a pension or Social Security) or changes in medical status (i.e., the individual is discharged from the nursing home, but has to return after deteriorating health) can affect Medicaid eligibility.

The Medicaid rules are so complex and change so often that misunderstandings often occur — even among the people whose job it is to administer the system. If you have a client who is turned down for Medicaid, consult the lawyer on your planning team. It is very likely that your client is entitled to a hearing to protest the denial — and more than possible that, under the rules as properly interpreted, your client in fact qualifies for Medicaid benefits.

CHAPTER FOOTNOTES

1.   As of November, 1996 the 209(b) states are Connecticut, Hawaii, Illinois, Indiana, Minnesota, Missouri, New Hampshire, North Carolina, North Dakota, Ohio, Oklahoma, and Virginia. The other states are SSI states.

2.   OBRA '86 (P.L. 99-509) Section 9402.

3.   P.L. 100-360 Section 301. The actual provisions dealing with catastrophic health care coverage were repealed, but the statute's Medicaid provisions remain in force.

4.   *Ford v. Iowa Department of Human Services*, 500 NW2d 26 (Iowa Supreme Court 1993).

5.   OBRA '87 Section 4211.

Chapter 8

THE FAMILY HOME: A SPECIAL RESOURCE

The sentimental value of "Home Sweet Home" is undisputed. A central part of the American Dream is owning one's own home. A majority of America's senior citizens are homeowners, and most of them own their homes free and clear. For many families, home equity is by far their greatest asset, and the home is the most expensive purchase the family ever makes. Therefore, even if there were no emotional elements involved, the family home would have to figure largely in an older person's or older couple's lifetime and estate plan.

One reason for the purchase of the "rose covered cottage" is to have a good place to raise a family; another is to have a comfortable place to retire. Yet the same house (or condominium unit) may not be suitable for both purposes. Choosing a home for a young family includes consideration of having enough room for growing kids and being close to schools and sports facilities. An older couple may find the home too big now that they are "empty nesters", and may find the school and the mall to be excessively noisy neighbors.

Therefore, a strategy that appeals to many older clients is to put the old home on the market, take advantage of the tax benefits described below, then use the proceeds of the sale to buy a suitable home for the post-retirement years. Their choice can be a unit in a retirement community or life-care community, or simply a smaller home in a nice quiet neighborhood. This time, closeness to basic shopping and medical care will be important in the choice of location.

PLANNING TIP: Maybe older clients should not be too quick to move out of that big, old, rambling house. Economic conditions, or divorce, may make grown offspring want to return to the family nest. Even if this is not true, extra rooms can make it possible for older people to avoid institutionalization by hiring a live-in home attendant. If needs are not that great — or the budget is not that large — extra room can permit the older homeowner to participate in a home-sharing program under which a younger person gets free rent in exchange for home chores and companionship for a lonely elder.

For most of American history, buying a home was a significant personal step, but did not have much investment significance, because home prices remained fairly stable. A hyperactive housing market in the 1970s and 1980s changed all this, and many families found that the value of their home soared, giving them access to credit (via home equity loans and credit lines) and making large sums of money available after a home sale.

The downside of this phenomenon was that many potential first-time home buyers found it impossible to afford a home or get a mortgage (forcing some of them back to live with their parents). In the 1990s, the housing market has certainly cooled down, and prices have declined severely in many areas. If your clients live in one of these areas, you must remind them that their home equity — and the amount they can expect to realize if they do sell the home — have declined. You will need to come up with a contingency plan to safeguard their standard of living.

OLDER CLIENT HOME STRATEGIES

Your older clients can:

(1)   Stay put, and plan to leave the home to a child or grandchild as a major part of their estate. This may not be necessary if the kids are already homeowners. It may not be practical — the estate may have to be divided among three kids and five grandchildren (making the only practical possibility selling the house and dividing the sales proceeds). It may not even be possible if health care costs require drastic financial steps.

(2)   Stay put, and fix up the home so that it is suitable for the needs of older people. If climbing stairs is a problem, it may be possible to install a small elevator or a stair lift. It might make sense to install an extra powder room (so there will not be a flight of stairs between a person who finds it hard to walk and the bathroom), widen doorways and install a wheelchair ramp, install special safety devices in kitchen and bathroom, or even move the bed-

room into the downstairs dining room and close off some upstairs rooms. Spending money for these purposes can have positive tax and Medicaid consequences. (See below.)

(3)   Remain in the home, but transfer its ownership as part of a Medicaid plan. (See below.)

(4)   Engage in an intrafamily (within the family) transaction, such as a sale-leaseback. These are sophisticated strategies. Do not even think of recommending them to a client without intensive tax advice!

(5)   The spouse remaining in the community draws on home equity to pay for nursing home care for the institutionalized spouse.

(6)   As discussed above, the home can be sold, and sales proceeds applied to the cost of entering a retirement or life-care community. Or, the older person or couple can move to rented accommodations, or move in with a family member, and invest the proceeds of the home sale. The investment income, in turn, can be used for other living expenses, or can be accumulated to become part of the estate. There may be a special housing project for senior renters in the area, with federal, state, or private sponsorship. Although these projects do not provide health services, they may have special services such as monitoring and congregate dining facilities for those who are no longer interested in or capable of doing their own cooking.

(7)   On the other hand, a family member or friend can move in with the older person or couple, and take care them and the house, in return for free housing or with the understanding that the house will be transferred to, or left to, the caregiver.

Which strategy is best? Not only must you make an assessment about the state of the economy, and where it is headed — you must also be capable of *listening* to your clients in a patient and compassionate manner. Sure, it may be sensible to move into a little efficiency apartment. But that "smart move" could also mean the sacrifice of fifty years of memories. One child's expectation of inheritance can create difficulties for parents who really prefer another estate plan. And remember, especially when something as meaningful as a home is involved, tax savings are not everything. A plan that costs more in tax terms can be worthwhile in emotional terms.

TAX BREAKS ON HOME SALES

Under Section 1034 of the Tax Code, a person who sells a home (that is, a personal residence, not an investment property) and buys another, more expensive home within two years may defer the income tax on the profit on the sale of the first home. In other words, someone who buys a home in 1975 for $100,000, and sells it in 1990 for $200,000 (at a time when the basis, or tax value, of the home is $133,000) has $67,000 of profits. Normally, the $67,000 would be taxable income. However, if the homeowner buys a home that costs more than $200,000 during the two years before or after the home sale, tax on the profit is deferred. Theoretically, the "rollover" process would stop when the taxpayer stops buying new homes and becomes a renter or otherwise ceases to be a homeowner.

PRACTICE TIP: If a married couple sells a home, intending to buy another one, but one spouse dies before the replacement purchase, the surviving spouse is still entitled to the "rollover" provisions of Code Section 1034.[1]

The Tax Code contains a special tax relief provision for those who sell a home when they are age 55 or over. Under Code Section 121, an over-55 homeowner gets a once-in-a-lifetime chance to receive up to $125,000 in home-sale profits free of income tax, whether or not another home is purchased. (The Section 1034 rollover and the Section 121 tax break can be used in the same transaction, if there are more than $125,000 in profits to protect and the criteria for purchasing a more expensive home are met.) Section 121 treatment is not automatic: the taxpayer must make an election, using IRS Form 2119.

If one spouse is age 55 or over and the other is younger, they can still make the election as long as they file a joint income tax return and own the property as joint tenants, by the entireties (a special form of joint tenancy between married couples that exists in some states), or if it is community property. If the home was owned by only one spouse, the other spouse can give his or her consent on the couple's joint tax return, and the owner-spouse can make the full election (after all, a single person can make a full election). However, a married person who files a separate return can only get an exclusion of $62,500. If the home is joint property, but the joint tenants are not a married couple (for instance, if the home is owned by a brother and sister), *each* joint owner can get a full $125,000 election.

Because it is a one-time election, if one spouse makes an election (even if he or she was single at the time, or married to someone else), the other spouse cannot make a later election — even if they file separate tax returns. If two people, each of whom owns a home, marry, then the couple can make *one* election to exclude gain on the sale of one home — not both homes.[2]

Code Section 121's basic rule is that the taxpayer must have lived in the home for at least three years out of the five years before the sale. (After all, this is a rule for principal residences, not for vacation homes or investment properties.) However, for sales after September 30, 1988, there is a special relief provision for nursing home residents. As long as they lived in the home for *one* out of the five years before the sale, and spent the rest of the time in a licensed nursing home because they were unable to care for themselves, the election is still available.

Also note that improvements made to the home for medical purposes (such as a stair lift or a lap pool prescribed by a doctor as therapy for arthritis — not a recreational swimming pool) may give rise to a deduction. The whole cost cannot be deducted at once — it must be spread out over the life of the improvement. There is no deduction, however, if the improvement increases the value of the home (such as adding an extra bathroom required by market conditions).

The extra tax boost may be the deciding factor for older homeowners who want to modify the house to suit present or projected medical needs, but are afraid that the changes will make the house worth less on the resale market.

When the Third Edition went to press in early 1997, President Clinton's budget proposal called for making the Section 121 exclusion even more comprehensive. If this proposal is adopted, then few or no senior citizens would face any capital gains tax at all on home sale profits.

FAMILY HOMES AND MEDICAID

It would be tragic if families were to lose their home simply because a parent or spouse is sick or debilitated enough to need nursing home care. Some people — because they do not have access to good advice, or because they refuse to accept Medicaid benefits (which they consider "charity") — actually do sell the family home and use the proceeds to pay for nursing home care. But there are almost no circumstances under which this would be mandated by the Medicaid system.

Under Medicaid, a "homestead" is an exempt asset that is not counted in determining whether the Medicaid applicant has excess assets. A "homestead" is defined as a family home plus the land it rests on. (Normal household furniture and effects are also exempt.) This is true even if the homestead is an expensive one; even if it was recently purchased; and even if it was, in fact, purchased as part of a Medicaid plan — as long as it really does belong to the applicant.

One of the first steps in Medicaid planning, then, is to determine if clients who are not homeowners should buy a house. It is not necessarily a good idea for everybody. Your clients may not have enough cash to buy a house outright, and may not qualify for a mortgage. Even if the finances are not a problem, there is a lot of hassle involved in home ownership.

If they are already homeowners, does the home need repairs or improvements? Fixing that wheezy, energy-inefficient furnace, putting in those storm windows, and modernizing the kitchen makes the home more convenient and livable and increases its resale value. It also turns funds that might otherwise be excess assets for Medicaid purposes into an exempt asset. Spending the money this way does not count as a transfer, because a transfer involves giving something away or getting less than the market price for it; paying market price for goods or services does not fit this definition.

Once a person enters a nursing home (whether as a private-pay patient or as a Medicaid applicant or beneficiary), the home remains exempt as long as the institutionalized person's spouse, minor child, or disabled child continues to live there. (Of course, few senior citizens have minor children; usually their children have grown up.)

If the homeowner never married, or is divorced or widowed, the home remains a homestead as long as it is possible that the owner can be discharged from the nursing home and return home. State rules differ on the medical standards for determining when it is impossible to return home. Sometimes a mere statement of intention to return will keep the property in homestead status; sometimes the Medicaid agency must prove that return is impossible; and sometimes the

Medicaid beneficiary must offer medical evidence of ability to return. In practice, it is rare for a state Medicaid agency to try to force an unmarried institutionalized person to sell his or her home. (It is a somewhat different matter after the institutionalized person dies. See below.)

In fact, an allowance for upkeep of the homestead may be allowed. If it is, the Medicaid recipient can devote part of his or her income to keeping the homestead in livable condition. As discussed in Chapter 7, Medicaid beneficiaries must devote their entire income, except for permissible deductions (such as a personal needs allowance and allowances for dependents) to paying for nursing home care.

TRANSFERS OF A HOME

As discussed in Chapter 7, Medicaid eligibility can be delayed or prevented if the applicant makes transfers during the penalty period. If a homestead is exempt, can the applicant transfer it without affecting eligibility? One theory is that exempt assets are completely outside the Medicaid system. Owning a homestead does not affect eligibility, and *transferring* a homestead should not affect eligibility. The other theory is that Medicaid protects the homestead only while it is owned by the applicant, and the property loses its homestead status after it is transferred. Before 1988, some states followed each of these theories (with various confusing elaborations along the way).

In 1988, the federal rules were changed, imposing uniformity on the process. Under these rules, some transfers of homesteads can be made without affecting Medicaid eligibility. The homestead can be transferred to:

- The homeowner's spouse.

- The homeowner's minor, blind, or disabled child.

- The homeowner's "caregiver child": that is, a son or daughter who lived with the homeowner in the home for at least two years, and provided personal care that delayed the need for institutionalization. (It is up to the state Medicaid agency to decide whether an alleged caregiver child really did provide the necessary standard of care.)

- The homeowner's brother or sister who is part-owner of the home *and* lived there for more than a year before institutionalization of the homeowner.

Other transfers are not exempt, and are subject to the usual penalty period. Why make a transfer, when ownership of the home will not impair Medicaid eligibility? The primary reason is to avoid the imposition of liens and recoupment, described below.

Because of confusing 1989 federal statutory changes, it is very unclear whether a spouse of an institutionalized homeowner who is also the transferee of the homestead has the right to give it or otherwise transfer it to someone else (e.g,. a child or other family member) without affecting the Medicaid eligibility of the transferor. The planning team must take a very careful look at current state Medicaid regulations, case law, and the unwritten policies of the Medicaid agency before including a "re-transfer" in the Medicaid plan.

LIENS AND RECOUPMENT

Federal Medicaid rules allow a state to impose a lien on the real estate (including the homestead) of a Medicaid beneficiary for benefits that were properly paid to an eligible person who was 55 or over when the benefits were received. (No matter how much personal property the recipient had, the lien applies only to real estate.) The lien "attaches" to the real estate, and when the real estate is sold, the Medicaid agency gets the part of the proceeds representing its lien.

Liens can be imposed only if the beneficiary was getting Medicaid nursing home care, and only if the agency holds a hearing (giving proper notice to the beneficiary) and determines that the beneficiary will never be able to leave the nursing home and live in the homestead once again. (This is slightly different, but related, to the question of whether the homestead is exempt when a person's Medicaid eligibility is being determined.)

Some states have adopted statutes saying that there will be *no* Medicaid liens, or limiting the circumstances in which liens will be allowed. In the other states, federal law imposes limitations on the creation and enforcement of liens. A lien cannot be placed on the property as long as the Medicaid recipient's spouse, minor child, disabled child, or sibling with an equity interest who lived there for a year continues to live in the home. (No exception is made for a "caregiver child.")

Even if a lien has been properly placed on a homestead, the Medicaid agency may have a long wait before it can collect. The lien can be enforced if the homeowner voluntarily sells the property — but the Medicaid agency cannot enforce the lien during the lifetime of the Medicaid recipient's surviving spouse. Recovery will not be allowed if the Medicaid recipient has minor or disabled children, or as long as caregiver children continue to live in the homestead.

In March, 1995, the Health Care Financing Administration's (HCFA) Office of the Inspector General issued a report stating that 27 states had programs seeking recovery from the estates of deceased Medicaid beneficiaries, 12 more states had plans to set up their own recovery programs, and another 16 states planned to hire a consultant to study the feasibility of creating a recovery program. (In 1993, only 14 states made a practice of filing liens.) Only 10 states went after the estates of widows or widowers who survived spouses who received Medicaid; the other states felt that those cases were too complex to monitor. For 1995, nationwide estate recoveries added up to $85 million; about one-quarter of the total came from just one state, California.

Federal law allows recovery against the entire estate, but some states have either passed statutes or have policies limiting recovery to the probate estate. What this means is that anything that passes directly to a joint tenant, or is placed in a revocable trust or otherwise escapes the probate process, will also be exempt from Medicaid estate recovery.

As discussed in Chapter 7, the homestead provisions still remain valid after OBRA '93. However, the homestead is no longer the only possible source of estate recovery — a factor that must be taken into account in planning.

HOMESTEAD TRANSFERS AFTER 1996 LEGISLATION

As discussed in Chapter 7, transfers are criminal under the Health Insurance Portability and Accountability Act of 1996 only if they give rise to a penalty period. Therefore, a transfer that is exempt under 42 USC §1917(c), and does not give rise to a penalty period, cannot be criminal. This means that pre-January 1, 1997 homestead transfers are not criminal. It also means that a Medicaid applicant's homestead transfer that occurred *before* the lookback period is not criminal. Last but not least, a transfer from one spouse to another, a transfer to a minor, blind, or disabled child, to a caregiver child, or to a sibling with an equity interest in the home who resided there for at least one year, is not criminal either.

USING HOME EQUITY TO PAY FOR NURSING HOME COSTS

Many people, at all points on the political spectrum, dislike the use of Medicaid planning to get public benefits for the middle and upper-income elderly. Some conservatives are angry because they believe that the private sector, not the government, should provide this care. Some liberals are angry because they believe that the limited funds of the poverty program should be devoted to the "truly needy." Furthermore, both state and federal governments face severe fiscal pressure, and it is likely that cuts will be made in the Medicaid program. So, for practical as well as political reasons, alternatives to Medicaid must be found, and every long-range care plan must make provision for these alternatives.

One proposal that is often made is that senior citizens should use their home equity as a source of funds for nursing home care.

PLANNING TIP: If your clients are still employed and making long-range plans, or are recently retired with substantial pension income, suggest that they consider opening a home equity credit line (while their eligibility is still good) — and suggest that they not use it! That way, the credit line can be tapped if and when medical bills or other emergencies arise. No interest will be charged until credit is obtained (although there may be application or maintenance charges). A possible disadvantage is that the credit line might be treated as an actual, not just a potential, debt when your clients apply for other forms of credit and could lead to a turndown on the grounds that they are overextended even though they have few real debts.

Under a reverse mortgage, a senior citizen-homeowner enters into an agreement with a lender (usually a bank; the state may have a guarantee program to encourage use of this option). Under the plan, the senior citizen receives regular payments (sometimes in the form of an annuity). At the end of the loan term, or upon the homeowner's death (or the death of both homeowner spouses), the lender has an equity interest based on the amount provided to the homeowner. Sometimes the arrangement is drafted to give the lender an "equity kicker": a share in the appreciation in the home's value. (But you can bet your boots the lender will not agree to be liable for a decline in the home's value.)

So far, many scholars have written analyses of the strengths and weaknesses of reverse mortgages, but few reverse mortgages have actually been written. One study estimates that reverse mortgages tend to provide $6,000-$7,800 income a year. The advantage to the homeowner is that these payments are not considered "income" for Medicaid or SSI purposes, because the arrangement is considered a loan. Note, however, that $6,000, or even $7,800, a year would only pay for a few months' nursing home care for an institutionalized person — although it could be very useful in hiring home care attendants to supplement any home care provided under public benefit programs. The payment would be higher if the loan were written for a short term (such as five years).

The reverse mortgage will probably have the effect of forcing the sale of the home after the death of the mortgagor-spouses (in order to pay off the mortgage) unless there are plenty of other liquid assets such as insurance. This can be a severe problem if the parents' estate planning goal includes leaving the home to their offspring. It is not a problem if there are no children; the children are already homeowners; the children live so far away that the home would not be a useful inheritance; the parents and children are estranged; or if there are other estate planning goals.

The Truth in Lending Act (15 USC §1502(bb) defines a reverse mortgage as a nonrecourse transaction that secures one or more advances of credit from lender to homeowner. Repayment is not due until the consumer dies, vacates the home, or transfers the dwelling. Homeowners who enter into reverse mortgages are entitled to Truth in Lending disclosures for adjustable-rate mortgages. The disclosures must be based on a "total annual loan cost rate," not an "annual interest rate," because all closing and associated loan costs are included in the opening balance, with the result that if the homeowner leaves the property only a few years after getting the mortgage, the costs will not yet have been fully amortized, and the effective interest rate will be much higher than the nominal interest rate.

The FHA has a Home Equity Conversion Mortgage program under which federal insurance is available for five types of mortgages available to persons over 62 who own houses or condominiums. The FHA-insured "tenure plan" mortgage provides a fixed life annuity (terminable if the owner leaves the property). The "term plan" provides a fixed annuity for a term of years. A "line of credit plan" sets up a line of credit that does not provide funds immediately, but only on request of the homeowner. (The other two FHA-approved plans combine aspects of these plans.) FHA-insured reverse mortgages are limited to $155,250. The percentage of the home value that can be borrowed is proportional to the borrower's age: the maximum is 26% for a 65-year-old, 39% for a 75-year-old, and 56% for an 85-year-old. (The percentage increases rather than decreases with age, because the lender expects to extend credit for a shorter time to an older person because of his or her limited life expectancy.)

The Federal National Mortgage Association ("Fannie Mae") has its own reverse mortgage program, the Home Keeper Mortgage, available in denominations of up to $207,000. Fannie Mae maintains a toll-free number, (800) 572-4562, for information on reverse mortgages and a list of participating local lenders.

Although the reverse mortgage lender is usually a bank, this is not necessarily the case. Some states (such as Illinois and Tennessee) have programs under which state housing agencies make loans directly to older homeowners, with no bank involvement.[3]

Housing values reached a peak in many parts of the country in the 1980s, then declined in the 1990s. As a result, many senior citizens had a great deal less home equity in the 1990s, simply because the paper value of their homes had gone down, although no real changes occurred in their living situations. The amounts obtainable under reverse mortgages also declined correspondingly.

INTRAFAMILY TRANSACTIONS

Some wealthy clients, who are also high-bracket taxpayers (or whose children are fortunate enough to fall into this category), may be helped by intrafamily transactions involving the family home.

One possibility is for the older generation to sell (not transfer) their home to the younger generation. In a sale-leaseback transaction, the elders continue to live in the home and pay rent to the "youngsters." The house is removed from the potentially taxable estate, and the older generation, which is obligated to pay rent, gets a large sum of money (or continuing payments under a purchase-money mortgage). Depending on the way the figures work out, the mortgage payments from the children may be larger than the rent payments, so the older generation gets some net income. The parents will probably have a profit from the home sale — but they can use the Section 121 exclusion to shield the first $125,000 of it.

PRACTICE TIP: Although the Code *taxes* gain on profits earned by selling personal residences, it does not allow a deduction for losses on such sales.

Another possibility is a "gift-leaseback" where the home is given to the children, then rented from them. In this case, it is very likely that gift tax will be due, or that the giver/leaser will use up part of the unified gift and estate tax credit, which can lead to a bigger estate tax bite in the future. New Chapter 14 of the Tax Code, added by the Omnibus Budget Reconciliation Act of 1990, must be consulted with regard to gift tax and valuation issues in these intrafamily transactions.

To be valid, and obtain the estate tax and other desired advantages, the leaseback transaction must be a real one, based on prevailing market values.[4] In Medicaid terms, a sale-leaseback (at market rates) is not a transfer, because the buyer/child pays a fair price for the assets. However, the parent no longer has the exempt asset, and does have non-exempt sales proceeds until and unless they are spent for medical care or other purposes. (On the other hand, there is no longer a risk of a Medicaid lien, because the home no longer belongs to the parent and potential Medicaid applicant.) A gift-leaseback definitely is a transfer. If it can be made before the penalty period starts to run, there will be no Medicaid effect; but if the family guesses wrong, the gift will impair Medicaid eligibility.

Another possibility is a "split-interest" transaction, under which parent and child join in purchasing a home or other interest. The twist is that the parent buys a life interest in the property (the right to live there, or otherwise use the property, for life, or for the joint lives of two spouses). The child buys the remainder interest — the right to the property after the older generation's life or lives. Or, for assets already owned by the parent, the remainder interest can be given or sold to the child.

The purpose of the transaction is to remove the asset from the parent's estate, but still allow the parent to use the asset. In order to keep the remainder asset out of the parent's estate, the child must pay the full value of the remainder interest; if the child pays less, or nothing, the parent has made a gift (which may be taxable) equal to the shortfall. Valuation of remainders must be done according to the IRS' official unisex life expectancy tables, and under the Chapter 14 rules.

As this brief summary shows, intrafamily transactions are big-league estate planning techniques. These transactions will probably have a negative Medicaid impact, so they should either be done far enough in advance so that it is predictable that the penalty period will expire before a Medicaid application is made — or be limited to families whose wealth means that qualifying for Medicaid is very unlikely, and saving estate tax is a major financial objective.

PRTs AND QPRTs

Affluent older people need to plan to avoid estate taxes, and estate planning frequently involves a gifting program involving outright transfers or transfers into trusts, with the objective of removing valuable assets from the potentially taxable estate. Abusive transactions, especially abusive intra-family transactions, have long been a Congressional target. The tax rules for these transactions are complex, and change frequently as Congress (and the IRS, which writes the Regulations) try to plug loopholes.

In 1990, Congress added Chapter 14 to the Internal Revenue Code, with the effect of preventing certain intra-family and small business transactions from being used to remove assets from the estate and save gift taxes. Chapter 14 does not apply to Personal Residence Trusts (PRTs) and Qualified Personal Residence Trusts (QPRTs). (The main difference between the two is that a PRT contains the grantor's one or two personal residences and nothing else; a QPRT can also contain a small amount of cash to be used, for instance, to maintain the property and pay real estate taxes.)

The grantor of one of these trusts places ownership of the house(s) in a trust. The trust is written to give the grantor the right to continue to live in the house for a term of years, after which time ownership reverts to the grantor's children or other desired transferees.

Obviously, then, the grantor has made a gift to the children. How valuable is the gift, for gift tax purposes? The IRS' actuarial valuation tables are used to determine the value of the remainder (which is what the grantor has given away — he or she still has the right of occupancy). The gift is a gift of a future interest (it does not take effect until the term of years ends), so it doesn't qualify for the $10,000 per donee annual exclusion.

If the grantor is still alive at the end of the term, and still wants to remain in the house (instead, say, of moving to a retirement community or nursing home), he or she can remain there, but must pay a fair market rent to the remainderman (who is now the owner). In fact, in order to remove the house from the estate of the former homeowner, he or she must *survive* the term of the trust.

The IRS published a set of proposed Regulations dealing with QPRTs in April, 1996. Under these rules, a trust created on or after May 16, 1996 can be treated as a QPRT only if the trust documents are specifically drafted to forbid the trust from selling or transferring the house(s) in the trust to the grantor, his or her spouse, or any entity (such as a corporation or another trust) controlled by the grantor or grantor's spouse.

The reason for the proposals is that some grantors abused the process by placing their homes into a trust, then buying the homes back and leaving them to their heirs — so that the heirs would get a basis (tax value) as of the grantor's death, not the usually lower basis for a gift, which is calculated as of the time the grantor originally purchased the house. The lower the basis, the higher the taxable profits if the heirs or donees sell the house.

CHAPTER FOOTNOTES

1. TAMRA (1988) Section 6002.

2. Reg. Section 1.121-2(b).

3. Recent articles about reverse mortgages: see, e.g., Jay Romano, "For Reverse Mortgages, A Fannie Mae Imprimatur," *New York Times* June 23, 1996 p. B3; June Fletcher, "Reverse Mortgages Reverse the Fortunes of Seniors," *Wall Street Journal* November 29, 1996 p. C1; Jay Romano, "Getting a Reverse Mortgage," *New York Times* December 22, 1996 p. F3.

4. As an example of an arrangement that did not pass muster for tax purposes, see *Maxwell v. Comm'r of Internal Revenue*, #92-4230 (2d Cir. 1993). Mrs. Maxwell entered into a purported sale-leaseback of her house, and granted a mortgage to her son and daughter-in-law. No money changed hands: the mortgage payments, which were never made, equalled twice the annual exclusion, so she "gave" this amount to her son and daughter-in-law each year. Her will called for forgiveness of the ostensible mortgage balance remaining at her death.

Chapter 9

RETIREMENT PLANNING

The typical family faces many planning problems in its life cycle: career planning (including planning for downturns and saving enough to withstand a potential layoff); buying a house, car, and other major consumer durables; college tuition for the kids; and retirement planning. The young family's task is to accumulate enough resources so that retirement will be pleasant and comfortable, and so that there will be enough resources for the surviving spouse and an estate to leave to the children.

The traditional way to think of retirement security is as a "three-legged stool": the retiree relies on Social Security benefits, pension benefits paid by the employer, and on his or her own savings and investments. Clearly, as the baby boom generation moves toward retirement, some changes must be made on both the personal and the societal levels. Baby boomers are not very good at saving, but they must be prepared to have personal resources to supplement the endangered Social Security system. It is possible that in the early twenty-first century, income taxes will increase dramatically (to balance the budget), FICA taxes will increase dramatically (to prevent the demise of the Social Security system)—or both. A greater tax burden would make it harder than ever to save.

Economist and Merrill Lynch consultant Douglas Bernheim prepares a retirement index each year showing the percentage that various groups have saved relative to the amount they would need for an economically secure retirement (100%). The 1996 index for all baby boomer households is 35.9% (i.e., they have an average of only about one-third of what they need). Those who have pension plans fare best, at 51.1%. Surprisingly, income doesn't make much difference: Boomer households with incomes under $60,000 have an index of 31.9%, and those with incomes over $60,000 have an index of only 42.9%.

According to Bernheim's calculations, for the 17.5 expected years of retirement, at age 55 a couple with annual income of $75,000 would need to have saved $209,646 (if they have access to a pension) or $295,314 (without a pension). By age 65, the same couple would have to have put away $329,309 and $451,355, respectively. Of course, many couples have accumulated far less than that at age 65. For a more affluent couple, with earnings of $150,000, maintenance of their lifestyle after retirement would call for $468,837 at age 55 (with a pension) or $674,139 (age 55, no pension). The goal for age 65 in this scenario is $820,215 (pension) or $1,104,981 (no pension).[1] Some observers cite with alarm some recent trends that are likely to make pensions an even smaller factor in retirement planning:

(1)   Fewer factory jobs, which traditionally included meaningful pension plans in the compensation package.

(2)   More service jobs, many of which do not carry any pension coverage.

(3)   A shift from defined benefit to defined contribution plans, particularly 401(k) plans. This often means a smaller pension. A Wyatt Corporation survey showed an average 28% income replacement for individuals who received benefits under a defined benefit plan after retiring with average earnings of $15,000, versus 19% income replacement from a defined contribution plan. (Furthermore, the employee assumes the investment risk under defined contribution plans — and these are risky days indeed for investors.)

(4)   Unlike Social Security, many pension plans are not inflation-indexed.[2]

There is not much you as a financial advisor can do about Social Security benefits (although you can give advice about whether to defer retirement and the onset of benefits, or claim them early), but you have a major role to play in informing future retirees about the choices that the employer offers them. We have come a long way since the days when the retiree got nothing but a gold watch and a handshake. But it takes plenty of information and good judgment to decide whether to take advantage of an early retirement "window" or continue in a job that may be terminated due to a corporate merger or an economic downturn.

It is hard to decide whether to retire at age 63 or 71. If the employer offers a choice, there are complex factors involved in deciding between a lump sum pension and a pension paid in annuity form; and, if a lump sum payout is chosen, investment savvy is essential.

PLANNING TIP: Elder lawyers often recommend the lump sum pension, which offers greater Medicaid planning opportunities by transferring part or all of the lump sum before the Medicaid lookback period begins (thus avoiding criminalization of the transfer—see Chapter 7). Furthermore, there may be more than two choices: even an annuity pension is payable in various forms (although the non-employee spouse's consent is generally required for forms other than the joint and survivor annuity).

Of course, professional advice is needed for investment planning for the retiree just as much as for the active worker. It is also important for a working couple to coordinate their benefits. There can be problems if one spouse retires and wants to move to a leisure-oriented or retirement community, while the other spouse wants to stay put and stay at work.

Part of your role as advisor is to inform your clients of the public benefits (including Medicare) to which they are entitled, and how to use insurance and investments to "fill in the gaps." For instance, retirees are entitled to buy a certain amount of "continuation coverage" health insurance when they retire, and many employers provide "retiree health benefits" as part of their health insurance plan for employees. However, each individual retirement plan must be examined without preconceived notions. Many people retire early and do not bother to purchase continuation coverage, or exhaust their own coverage before they turn 65 and become eligible for Medicare. (Spouses and some other family members have an independent entitlement to buy continuation coverage.) If they have retiree health benefits, or if they are covered under a still-working spouse's family health benefits, they should not need additional coverage; if not, or if the ex-employer terminates retiree health benefits, such individuals need private health insurance.

There are special challenges in working with the self-employed professional (lawyer, doctor, CPA, business consultant) or the entrepreneur. They are responsible for setting up their own retirement plans (which may have to cover their employees as well) — not just for making decisions about the wise use of a preexisting plan. Your task includes helping them set up a cost-effective plan that provides significant retirement income — and advising them about wise investment of Keogh plan money and how and when to withdraw Keogh funds for the best investment results at the lowest obtainable tax cost.

A Keogh plan (also known as an HR 10 plan) is a qualified retirement plan that covers one or more self-employed individuals. Initially, Keogh plans were subject to tax rules entirely different from the rules covering conventional pension plans, and provided far less opportunity to accumulate significant retirement benefits. Current Keogh rules are almost identical to the rules for plans maintained by corporations for their employees (although some differences still exist).

When advising the self-employed person, the key is to determine the extent to which post-retirement income is expected to approach pre-retirement income. It may be necessary to start reducing lifestyle during the pre-retirement years in order to fund larger retirement benefits. Also note that the tax code requires employers and professionals to be more generous to their employees if they are more generous to themselves!

LIFE EXPECTANCY AND INFLATION

The challenge of planning retirement cannot be taken lightly. A great deal is at stake. There is an increasing trend toward earlier retirement (either because companies use early retirement incentives to cut the payroll, or because people are less compelled by the "work ethic" and more interested in retiring while they are healthy enough to enjoy leisure). Lifespans are also increasing. The two trends, taken together, make it possible for post-employment life to last as long as work life.

In 1900, life expectancy at birth was 47 years; by 1990, life expectancy at birth had soared to 75 years. But that is only part of the story. Sound retirement planning requires consideration of the individual's remaining life expectancy at age 65. A person who reaches 65 naturally did not succumb to childhood diseases or early adulthood accidents, and in fact is a sturdy sort of person with an advanced life expectancy. For men born in 1900, life expectancy at age 65 was 78; for women born in the same year, it was 81. The figures have increased slowly but steadily. Those who reached 65 in 1985 have a life expectancy of 80 years (for men) and 84 years (for women). For those born in

1940 (and probably just starting to think about retirement planning), life expectancy at 65 is 81 and 86, respectively. Estimates for those born in 1990, who reach age 65, are a life expectancy of 83 years (male) and 89 years (female).

In 1995, the over-65 population of the United States had reached approximately 33,532,000, and was projected to be close to 35 million in 2000. Also in 1995, 30% of the total over-65 population was between ages 65-69, with 26% aged 70-74, 20% 75-79, 13% 80-84, and 11% 85 and over. The proportions of "young-old" to "old-old" are demographically very significant, because most of the "young-old" are healthy and live independently, but the degree of debility and the need for services increases in each "sector" of the senior population.

Life expectancy at birth was 72.5 years for men in 1995, and 79.3 years for women. As for the future, demographers project that in 2000, a male's life expectancy will be 73 years and a female's will be 79.9 years. The projection for 2005 is 73.5 and 80.2 years respectively, and 74.1 years and 80.6 years respectively in 2010. The difference in life expectancy, reinforced by the prevalence of couples in which the husband is older than the wife, means that most married couples will have to plan for a significant period (10 years or more) of widowhood for the wife.

In any population, life expectancy represents an average figure for everyone at birth. It takes into account those who succumb to childhood diseases, gang warfare, automobile accidents, and diseases typical of adulthood. People who live to be 65 have already proved that they are sturdy enough to survive these challenges, so life expectancy at age 65 is significant. In 1993, the last year for which complete figures have been compiled, life expectancy at 65 was 15.3 years for men, 18.9 years for women.

In 1996, less than one out of every 100 Americans was aged 90 or over—but there were nevertheless 1.37 million members of this, the fastest-growing group in the population. In 1940, only 7% of 65-year-olds lived to be 90. In 1940, one out of every seven senior citizens did so. In 1980, one-fourth of those who reached age 65 also managed to reach age 90—and in 1995, 41% of those who lived to 65 lived to be 90.

The planning implications are immense. Clients who reach 65 have a four-in-ten chance of living an additional 25 years or more (and an estimated 50-50 chance in the year 2000). This must color their plans (are they willing to play golf for 25 straight years?) and their projections for the amount of resources they will need. In particular, if they elect a 10-year term for a pension or investment annuity, the probability of outliving the income is very great. Even if they pick a 20-year term, there is a significant risk of outliving the income.

In other words, a retirement of 20 years can be expected, and a retirement of 25, or even 30 years, is more than possible. That is a lot of income to assure, and a lot of difficult long-range planning decisions to make. Another implication of these figures is a "double whammy." Women have a longer life expectancy than men, and also tend to marry men who are older than they are. Therefore, widowhood of at least a decade is a reasonable planning assumption.

Keep in mind the impact of inflation. Although inflation is no longer the raging monster it was in the seventies and early eighties, even a moderate 5% inflation rate will result in prices doubling about every fifteen years. As noted above, retirees can expect fifteen years of retirement as practically a given — and so can expect prices to double. Prices may double again if they survive retirement by thirty years. Furthermore, inflation in medical costs (a major financial planning factor for the elderly) is higher than the rate of inflation in general. In short, today's healthy assets and ample income may become very insufficient over the course of a prolonged retirement.

A traditional concern of retirement planning is to help retirees who have fixed incomes that do not keep up with inflation. Many pension plans do provide for cost-of-living adjustments (COLAs), which lessen this problem, and Social Security benefits are adjusted upward to keep pace with inflation. As discussed in Chapter 10, "Special Investment Needs of the Older Client," inflation protection is an important investment goal. However, if the investment climate is poor, a retiree with a fixed income may actually be better off than one whose pension is linked to the pension plan's investment success, or the performance of the stock market — if the variable amount is lower than the fixed one.

You can expect the value of a client's investments to grow during the post-retirement years, so it may be possible to withdraw as much as 5% of the portfolio each year and still prevent it from running out within 30 years. However, a more conservative theory is that withdrawals should be limited to about 4% a year (reflecting historical results of a conservative balanced portfolio), to prevent depletion.[3]

Another way to look at it: the client must retire with a fund of 20-25 times the amount of annual income he or she needs to supplement Social Security.

Another planning approach comes from the investment firm T. Rowe Price. This approach assumes that the goal of retirement planning is to replace 75% of income before retirement. (Many plans are constructed on a more conservative assumption of 70% replacement of income.) It also assumes that 8% of pretax income will be invested every year for retirement, and that retirees will use up their accumulated savings and investments during a 25-year retirement. T. Rowe Price has compiled tables to see if the retirement fund is large enough to generate the required post-retirement income.

For instance, 10 years before scheduled retirement, conservative investors should have accumulated 6.76 times their annual income in the retirement fund. Investors who will accept a moderate degree of risk need 5.58 times annual income under this model; aggressive investors need 4.63 times annual income—in other words, a client who earns $100,000 a year and who subscribes to this model should have at least $463,000 saved for retirement. Five years before retirement, the Price model suggests that conservative investors should have 8.9 times annual earnings in the retirement fund; the multiple is 7.73 for moderate-risk investors, and 6.75 for aggressive investors. In the year of retirement, the fund should represent 9.57-11.4 times annual earnings, depending on how aggressive the client's investment style is.[4]

SOCIAL SECURITY

The Social Security system is politically powerful — so powerful that beneficiaries have received cost-of-living increases (COLAs) almost every year, no matter how severe the government's fiscal problems have been. However, the "flip side" is that employers and employees pay far larger Social Security (FICA) taxes than were ever envisioned when the Social Security system was created as part of the New Deal.

Social Security benefits are a very important source of income for the elderly, but they must be supplemented for the individual to maintain a comfortable lifestyle. An "average" worker, who retires at Normal Retirement Age under Social Security (currently age 65), will receive a benefit that replaces about 42% of his or her earlier wage.

People who earn above-average incomes get a lower "replacement rate" and, therefore, must either cut their expenses dramatically, or have plenty of pension and investment income. According to the Social Security Administration's own figures, Social Security benefits in 1986 represented only 21% of the income of retirees with more than $20,000 annual income. However, Social Security provided more income than private pensions (at 19%). More than a third of retirees' incomes (34%) came from their investments — and 24% was earned income, because many retirees take post-retirement jobs, either because they are bored being out of the work force or they need extra income.[5]

PLANNING TIP: Point out to your clients that two-income couples have an especially great need for post-retirement income. The Social Security system was created at a time when the average couple consisted of a working male and a housewife. There is a maximum family benefit under Social Security that could limit the amount of benefits available to a two-earner couple.

Social Security Terminology and Computations

Almost all workers in the United States are covered by Social Security, and have been covered throughout their working life. Some work, however, is specifically excluded by law, and other types of work are covered only under certain conditions. Among those excluded are federal employees hired before 1984, some domestic workers, some workers involved in family employment, and some employees of state and local governments.

There are several conditions imposed before a person can receive a full Social Security retirement benefit (called the PIA, for Primary Insurance Amount). Some people who do not meet these conditions are entitled to receive a reduced Social Security benefit. A few people (such as some people who defer retirement) are entitled to an enhanced benefit. The benefit payable to the spouse of the worker is also defined as a percentage of the worker's PIA. If both spouses work, the second spouse to retire must choose between collecting benefits as a worker, based on his or her earnings record, or as a spouse, based on the other spouse's earnings record; you cannot collect both. Furthermore, if both spouses had high earnings, benefits for the second spouse to retire may be limited by the family maximum. The Social Security system also provides benefits for the disabled, and for survivors of insured workers, but a detailed explanation of these benefits is beyond the scope of this book.

FICA taxes are "regressive" taxes. Instead of being assessed on a worker's entire income, or on the income above an exempt minimum amount, FICA taxes are assessed from the first dollar of employment income up to a maximum ($65,400 in 1997). In any given year, nobody pays FICA taxes on income above that year's maximum. (The maximum also changes almost every year.) In effect, then, people who earn very little pay a fairly high percentage of their income in FICA taxes. People who earn a lot pay a small percentage. The Social Security benefit depends on many factors, including the relationship between the worker's earnings and tax payments in each year he or she worked to the average earnings and payments.

Just to make things more complicated, different calculation formulas are used depending on the worker's date of birth. However, because of the political power of senior citizens, benefit levels cannot be reduced for those already collecting benefits.

The Social Security benefit, or PIA, depends on:

(1)   The worker's date of birth.

(2)   The worker's Average Indexed Monthly Earnings (AIME). The AIME is based on Social Security earnings after 1950 (or after the year the worker reached age 21, if later), and is based on the worker's earnings record after wages have been indexed. The indexing process is carried out for each year the worker was employed, ending in his or her "indexing year", two years before he or she either reaches age 62, or dies or becomes disabled before reaching age 62. Indexing creates an earnings history which more accurately reflects the value of the worker's actual earnings in comparison to the national average wage level at the time of eligibility.

(3)   The worker's Primary Insurance Amount (PIA). The PIA is determined by applying a formula to the person's AIME. Where first eligibility is in calendar year 1997, the PIA is the sum of three separate percentages of portions of the AIME. It is found by taking 90% of the first $455 of the AIME, 32% of the AIME between $455 and $2,741, and 15% of any AIME exceeding $2,741.

As an additional complication, a slightly different method, the Average Monthly Wage Method, is mandatory for those who reached age 62 before 1979. Those who reached age 62 between 1979 and 1983 can choose either a slightly modified Average Monthly Wage Method or the AIME computation, whichever yields a higher benefit.

Understandably, most people shrink from trying to calculate their own eventual Social Security benefits.

MARKETING TIP: As a simple but sobering exercise, show your clients the *maximum* monthly PIA ($1,326 in 1997) and maximum family benefit ($2,320 in 1997), and explain that very few people qualify for maximum benefits because they require earning the FICA maximum ($65,400 in 1997) in each year. (For individuals who reach age 62 or die in 1997, the maximum family benefit equals 150% of the first $581 of PIA, plus 272% of PIA between $581 and $839, 34% of PIA between $839 and $1094, and 175% of any remaining PIA. They probably would not want to be restricted to the maximum benefit, much less the benefit they will receive. One rule of thumb is that a 70% replacement level of preretirement earnings is a minimum for comfortable retirement.

In 1997, Social Security beneficiaries received a 2.9% cost-of-living benefit increase. The average monthly Social Security retirement benefit increased to $745. The average benefit for a couple, both of whom count as retired workers, is $1,256.

The Contract with America Advancement Act of 1996 (P.L. 104-121) increases the annual earnings limit that beneficiaries may earn without a reduction in Social Security benefits to $13,500 in 1997, $14,500 in 1998, $15,500 in 1999, $17,000 in 2,000, $25,000 in 2001 and $30,000 in 2002.

For 1997, a beneficiary age 65 through 69 may earn up to $1,125 a month in the *initial year of retirement* without a reduction in benefits ($720 a month if the beneficiary is under age 65). However, a beneficiary will lose a whole month's Social Security benefit if earnings exceed the monthly limit by even $1.

An annual earnings limit applies to beneficiaries after their initial year of retirement. For 1997, benefits are reduced if a beneficiary is under age 70 but over age 65 for the whole year and earnings exceed $13,500, or a beneficiary is under age 65 for the whole year and earnings exceed $8,640. Benefits are reduced by $1 for every $3 of earnings over $13,500 for a beneficiary over age 65 through 69 in 1997. If more than $8,640 is earned in 1997 by a beneficiary under age 65 for the entire year, $1 of benefits will ordinarily be lost for each $2 of earnings over $8,640.

A person can check on his or her Social Security earnings record and receive an estimate of future Social Security benefits by filling out Form SSA-7004-SM (Request for Earnings and Benefit Estimate Statement). This form can be picked up at any Social Security office or by calling the Social Security Administration's toll-free number, 1-800-772-1213. A statement of total wages and self-employment income credited to the earnings record and an estimate of current Social Security disability and survivor benefits and future retirement benefits will be mailed to the individual. If all earnings have not been credited, contact a Social Security office and ask how to go about correcting the records. While there are specific time limits for correcting an earnings record, an earnings record can be corrected at any time if the amount of wages entered on the Social Security Administration records is less than the correct amounts paid to an individual by an employer.

Since 1995, the Social Security Administration has been providing a PEBES (Personal Earnings and Benefit Estimate Statement) automatically to all workers when they reach age 60 (prime retirement-planning age).

Normal Retirement Age

Originally, the Normal Retirement Age under the Social Security system was 65, with the option of retiring at 62 and receiving a decreased benefit. (Even earlier retirement is possible for disabled persons, but an additional set of requirements is imposed.) Unfortunately, it became common for people to be fired outright or forced to retire merely because they reached age 65. There have been many changes in society. People are living longer and staying healthier, and the Age Discrimination in Employment Act makes it illegal to fire a competent, qualified worker merely because of age.

Furthermore, an increasing proportion of the population consists of the elderly. That means that the proportion of retirees is increasing, while the proportion of active workers to support them in retirement is decreasing. Social Security is a "pay-as-you-go" system, where today's FICA taxes are used to pay benefits to today's retirees. It is not a funded system where each person's FICA taxes are kept in an account awaiting his or her retirement. To keep the system solvent (and to assure that there are plenty of trained, skillful workers with a good work attitude and self-discipline), it is essential to keep people working longer.

Those who retire at age 62 receive an actuarially reduced benefit — not just at age 62, but as long as they live and keep drawing benefits. The reduction equals about one-half percent of the worker's PIA for each month between the actual age of retirement and the Normal Retirement Age. In making the reduction, the worker's PIA must first be determined. The PIA is then reduced by 5/9 of 1% (1/180) for each of the first 36 months that the worker is under Normal Retirement Age when the benefits commence, and by 5/12 of 1% (1/240) for each such month in excess of 36. For workers reaching age 62 before the year 2000, the age 62 benefit is 80% of the worker's PIA.

In 1983, Congress increased the retirement age when unreduced benefits are available (presently age 65). Eventually, for workers reaching age 62 after 2022, the Normal Retirement Age will be 67. The increase in Normal Retirement Age is being phased in gradually in the interim. The Normal Retirement Age for people born in 1938, for instance, is 65 years and 2 months; 65 years and 4 months for those born in 1939, and so forth. The Normal Retirement Age is 66 for everyone born between 1943 and 1954.

After 1999, the increased retirement age will be reflected in decreased benefits for early retirement. For example, the age 62 benefit for a worker born in 1938 is 79.2% of the worker's PIA; the age 62 benefit for worker's born in 1943-1954 is 75% of the PIA; and the age 62 benefit for a worker born in 1960 and after is 70% of the PIA.

1996 federal legislation allows qualified plans to conform their Normal Retirement Ages to the Social Security provisions.

Those who reached age 62 before 1987 and retire late — after age 65 — receive a somewhat increased benefit. Each month of deferral between age 65 and age 70 results in an increased benefit of 1/12 of 3% of PIA (3% for each year): Deferring retirement past age 70 did not increase benefits any further. In order to provide an incentive for late retirement, a larger increase is being phased in between 1990 and 2009. For workers reaching age 62 in 2005 and after, deferral leads to an 8% increase in benefits for each year retirement is delayed.

PLANNING TIP: Calculations about retirement timing depend on the individual's life expectancy. It is impossible to be sure whether a person will live long enough to reap any advantage from delayed retirement. At least those who retire early have a "bird in the hand" — some benefits, even at a reduced level. Those who defer retirement purely to receive the higher benefit may die before "catching up" because they receive fewer Social Security checks.

Taxation of Benefits; Investment Effect

For nearly 40 years, Social Security benefit recipients did not have to pay federal income taxes on their benefits. However, in 1984, some Social Security benefits were made subject to federal tax. Many states also impose state income tax on all Social Security benefits. Beginning in 1994, beneficiaries whose income exceeds a "base amount" must include in gross income for tax purposes up to 85% of the Social Security benefit. About one-seventh of Social Security beneficiaries are affected by this change.

PLANNING TIP: The percentage of your clients who are affected will be much higher, because financial planning clients tend to be more affluent than the average senior citizen.

The income tax calculation depends on the computation of an adjusted income amount, which includes half the Social Security benefit, plus certain other taxable income, plus tax-exempt interest income and other miscellaneous adjustments. Where adjusted income is below $25,000 for a single taxpayer, or $32,000 for married taxpayers filing jointly, no part of the Social Security benefit is taxable. For adjusted income between $25,000 and $34,000 (single taxpayers) and $32,000-$44,000 (married taxpayers filing jointly), 50% of the Social Security benefit is taxable. For higher adjusted incomes, as much as 85% of the benefit may be taxable.

There are several implications that taxation of Social Security benefits have on a retirement plan. First, it is important for your clients to know whether they are likely to face this tax. If so, they will need extra cash to pay the tax (which should discourage them from tying up too much money in illiquid investments such as real estate and limited partnerships). Second, tax-exempt municipal bonds are an attractive investment to many senior citizens, because of the safety of the bonds, but too much municipal bond income could trigger a higher tax bill — not on the bond income itself, which remains tax-exempt, but on Social Security benefits. Part of the investment planner's job is to work out the numbers and calculate the after-tax effect of purchasing municipal bonds compared to that of purchasing taxable bonds of comparable safety and yield, or other possible investments such as certificates of deposit and stocks.

Third, remind clients that if they have additional taxes to pay on Social Security benefits, they must consider if their estimated tax payments are adequate. This is a "double whammy": the increase in tax rates under the Revenue Reconciliation Act of 1993 already required many higher-income taxpayers to beef up their quarterly estimated tax payments.

PRIVATE PENSIONS

The threshold question with respect to pensions is whether your client will be eligible for a pension at all. Federal law regulates many aspects of retirement plan financing and administration, but does not obligate employers to offer any kind of retirement plan. Many small companies do not, in fact, maintain such plans. Furthermore, some employees leave a job before they are entitled to participate in the plan, or before they are fully vested (see below) so that although they are entitled to a benefit, its amount is minuscule.

Pension plans are incredibly complex systems, subject to a multitude of federal requirements. However, within the bounds of those requirements, an almost infinite number of variations is possible. Eligibility for a pension depends on many things. Plans have rules governing who is eligible to participate — in general, any full-time employee over 21 who has worked for the employer for a year must be eligible. Vesting requirements are also important. Workers do not accrue pension rights immediately. Until they have worked for a specified period of time (usually not exceeding seven years) they are only "partially vested." That is, they are not entitled to the full amount in their account, or to a full pension, only to part of the account or pension. Once they become fully vested, they are entitled to the full account or the full pension *at normal retirement age*.

This is important because many people leave jobs, or change jobs, voluntarily or involuntarily. A person may be laid off at age 43, when he or she is fully vested, then get another job and become vested in that job's pension plan. Some plans will allow the worker to receive the pension in a lump sum when he or she leaves the first job; however, most do not allow this until retirement age.

The design of a plan will determine what the employee is entitled to receive. The most basic distinction is between a "defined contribution" and a "defined benefit" plan. In a defined contribution plan, each employee has an individual account. The employer makes a contribution each year, as required by the plan terms — for instance, a percentage of the employee's salary. If the employee leaves the job and is entitled to the vested portion of the account, he or she must include the entire amount in income upon distribution — unless it can be rolled over into an IRA, or into another employer's qualified plan, so that taxation is deferred until distributions begin.

An employer who maintains a defined benefit plan has a single account for all participants. An actuary advises the employer how much must be contributed to fund the plan so that each participant will be able, at retirement, to receive the level of retirement benefits described by the plan. There is no "account" for a participant to receive on leaving the plan, or when the employer or the retirement plan falls into financial difficulties. That is why defined benefit, but not defined contribution, plans are insured by the Pension Benefit Guaranty Corporation (PBGC), a federal agency. The size of the defined benefit depends on factors such as the employee's age at retirement, number of years of service with the employer, and the salary level reached. Sometimes plan benefits are based on the final year's salary, sometimes on the average salary for the entire career or for a certain number of years (e.g., three or five), or sometimes on the highest three or five years' compensation.

The risk structure in each case is different. A retiree from a defined contribution plan knows how large the account is, but does not know how large a retirement income it can provide (whether the plan continues to invest the funds, paying the retiree an annuity, or whether the retiree takes a lump sum and invests it). An increasing trend is to let active participants in defined contribution plans have some degree of control over the investment of their accounts; typically, they will be given a choice of several investment vehicles, such as guaranteed investment contracts, stocks, and bonds, as well as the limited ability to reallocate assets after the initial choice.[6]

A retiree from a defined benefit plan knows what his or her retirement income will be — but, because the benefit amount is usually fixed and thus without inflation protection, cannot be sure that the pension will keep up with inflation or provide an adequate sum for comfortable retirement. The amount of a retiree's retirement check from a defined contribution plan depends on the plan's investment success (and his or her own investment success, to the extent that the employee controls investment of the account, or assumes the investment burden after retiring). In an era characterized by a booming stock market, retirees from defined contribution plans often stay well ahead of inflation. It remains to be seen how they will do when the market is more bearish.

Timing Retirement

To a large extent, the timing of retirement is a personal choice. Is the person eager and excited about the job, or dragging into the office each day? Is continuing to work medically burdensome (which could compel early retirement)? A healthier person might want to work longer; on the other hand, a vigorous person might want to retire and enjoy several years of travel, fishing, camping, golf, tennis, and other sports activities.

The wishes and needs of other family members must be considered. Does the employee want to help a son or daughter with child care while the son or daughter works? Does the employee have a spouse, and if so, does the spouse want to retire or continue working? For instance, a 64-year-old man offered an attractive retirement package might have a 59-year-old wife who returned to the work world after years of childrearing and who is beginning to get major raises and promotions. She may prefer to stay at work — and will not be available to travel with her husband, or to keep him company.

Some people greatly enjoy a leisurely existence; others are bored and frustrated. A job provides much more than a paycheck. Co-workers are a kind of family. The routine of working structures the day and the work world provides challenges that may be missing after retirement. Make sure your clients think long and hard about whether, just because they can afford to retire, they will enjoy retirement. Maybe switching to a part-time schedule or a less demanding job is a better choice than retirement.

In the 1990s, many early retirees discovered that their choices were problematic. Some people took early retirement packages, confidently expecting to be hired in new jobs. But the economic forces that impelled their ex-employers to downsize also affected other potential employers. Older job applicants often encounter prejudice. Even if they have a legally sustainable case of age discrimination, few of them have the anger, energy, and stamina to pursue their claims.

Furthermore, falling interest rates paid on safe investments such as bank accounts, money market accounts, and certificates of deposit mean that many early retirees have far less income than they counted on when they made projections based on the high interest rates prevailing in the early 1980s.[7] This is not to say that early retirement is always a bad choice—only that early retirement incentives must be examined with great care.

Of course, the decision to retire is neither irrevocable nor irreversible. Sometimes the employee can be re-hired by the same company (though seldom in the same job).

PLANNING TIP: Watch out: If an employee retires, then returns to work at the same company, the likely result is that pension payments will be suspended, and the individual will also lose Social Security benefits because of excess income (unless he or she is over 70, when benefits are not reduced on account of earned income). If the new job pays a lot less than the old job, the rehired worker may end up losing money.

Other jobs may be available although, once again, a decline in pay or prestige is common. There are ample opportunities for volunteer work. Some retirees who always wanted to write, paint, sculpt, or start their own businesses take advantage of retirement to finally satisfy these dreams.

PRACTICE TIP: Remind your clients that, if they start to collect Social Security benefits, the general rule is that they will lose $1 in benefits for each $3 in income above the permitted amount earned before reaching age 70. That could be a reason to restrict post-retirement earnings, or to take a volunteer assignment rather than a job. (Every retiree gets a grace year — usually the year of retirement — in which excess earnings will be disregarded for Social Security benefit purposes; however, don't forget that in 1996 Congress phased in a schedule of increasing permitted earnings.)

Naturally, the decision of when to retire is also largely a financial decision. Your client must determine *when* retirement will yield the most favorable financial consequences and the best after-tax income. Frequently, companies that want to downsize offer a "retirement window" designed to motivate employees to take early retirement. In this instance, the client may have a valuable opportunity to negotiate "outplacement," including a discussion of continuation coverage and retiree health benefits. It is more likely that the benefit package will be fixed and no variation will be possible, but even in this case the client must understand all the implications of accepting the package (such as taxation, and availability of health benefits until Medicare eligibility at 65).

Sometimes the client may feel that the early retirement package is offered as a disguised form of age discrimination — forcing him or her out of a job he or she wants to keep. In that case, an attorney should be consulted about the possibility of bringing an Age Discrimination in Employment Act (ADEA) suit. Certainly, the employee must not accept the early retirement package — which often includes signing away the right to sue under the ADEA — without understanding and assessing the legal consequences of the choice. A later federal law, the Older Workers Benefit Protection Act (Public Law 101-433, signed into law on October 16, 1990), amended the ADEA and limited the extent to which companies can offer voluntary early retirement incentives to older employees.

Annuity or Lump Sum?

Since the effective date of the Retirement Equity Act of 1984, which was designed to protect the surviving spouses of employees, the normal form of pension payment for married plan participants is the "joint and survivor annuity." A joint and survivor annuity is an annuity for the life of the participant with a survivor annuity for the life of the spouse. The employer can reduce the spouse's survivor annuity, but not to less than 50% of the initial annuity payment. Employers differ widely in their practices with respect to reducing the survivor annuity; some subsidize the survivor annuity by making the initial payment for a joint and survivor annuity with a 50% survivor annuity only 5% less than the payment for a single-life annuity. Certain pension plans must offer pension payments in joint and survivor annuity form (or single annuity form for unmarried participants) in order to retain the tax-favored treatment afforded such plans.

If a married employee wants a form of payout other than a joint and survivor annuity, the spouse must express his or her written consent to the alternative form of payment (because choosing another form of payment could leave the spouse with limited income after the employee's death). However, if the spouse is expected to die first (e.g., the spouse is older than the employee, or is in bad health) it may make sense to take the single-life annuity.

PLANNING TIP: A choice some couples may prefer is "pension max": this arrangement involves collecting the benefit in single-life annuity form (thus increasing the size of each pension check) and using some of the extra money to purchase insurance on the life of the employee, naming the spouse as beneficiary and naming children, or other people the potential retiree wants to leave money to, as contingent beneficiaries. (Of course, this strategy will work only if the employee is insurable at affordable rates.) Typically, the surviving spouse receives the insurance proceeds, ensuring at least a degree of financial security after the employee's death. Furthermore, if the spouse dies first, or after the death of both spouses, the insurance can provide benefits for the contingent beneficiaries or the heirs of the employee and spouse. This can be a more favorable outcome for the family than the single life annuity which ends with the death of the spouse(s). Of course, as with all strategies involving life insurance, if you expect a taxable estate, consider taking steps to keep the insurance proceeds out of the estate. "Pension max" is not perfect: If the insurance policy is investment-oriented, it may have a disappointing return. Also, the surviving spouse will lose the benefit of any pension COLAs payable under the annuity pension option and may also lose access to retiree health benefits under the employer's plan.

Payment Choices

In a defined contribution plan, the employee's benefit is based upon his or her account balance. In a defined benefit plan, an employer is permitted to calculate the benefit under two types of formulas: a fixed benefit ($x per month; x% of the salary reached after y years of working for the employer) or a unit benefit which is based on the employee's length of service with the employer ($x or y% of average compensation for every month worked for the employer). Once the benefit to which the retiree is entitled is known, the next question is how it will be paid out.

Employers do not have to offer any payment option other than the single-life and joint and survivor annuity, but they can offer several others if they want, such as:

- An annuity for a term of years (not to exceed the life expectancy of the joint annuity beneficiaries);

- An annuity for the lifetime of the employee;

- A commercial annuity purchased from an insurance company using the benefits due to the employee; or

- Payment in a lump sum.

Within limits set by the Internal Revenue Code and ERISA, the income paid to retirees may fluctuate based on the plan's investment success, or may include cost of living increases.

How much difference does it make how the benefit is paid out? According to figures provided by Lipper Analytical Services,[8] a person who retired at a salary of $100,000 a year could expect a single-life annuity payment of $4,000 a month. If the company's joint and survivor annuity paid the same benefit to the survivor as to the first life, the payment would be $3,120 a month. However, if the benefit was reduced, and the company provided a 75% survivor annuity, the payment would be $3,320 a month during the first life, $2,490 during the spouse's life. A 50% survivor annuity would yield $3,520 a month during the first life, $1,760 a month to the survivor for life. A single-life annuity, 10 years certain, would pay $3,640 a year; in effect, this is lower than the simple single-life annuity, because of the "insurance" effect of the 10 guaranteed payments.

Which Choice is Better?

Taking the pension payout in the form of a lump sum gives the employee greater flexibility to invest (or the option to purchase his or her own commercial annuity, if better deals are available from other insurers).[9] A young, vigorous retiree may want to use a lump sum to start a business. An older or frail retiree may want the money to enter a life-care community or retirement community. Retirees of any age may want a lump sum to pay off the mortgage and make home improvements — or to purchase a home, if they rented a house or apartment before retirement.

The employee may look forward to active supervision of an investment portfolio if he believes his investments will yield higher returns than the conservative management style of the pension fund or commercial annuity. Or, the employee may plan to get professional management of the lump sum, for the same reason. Thus, the choice of a lump sum rather than continuing payouts (from plans that offer a lump sum option) has important practical consequences. It also has important tax consequences.

PLANNING TIP: If an employee does not want a lump sum, the plan generally cannot make him or her "cash out" unless his or her vested balance is less than $3,500. Factors in the decision include:

- How severe is the risk of incapacity? The retiree should not be placed in a situation where he or she has a lump sum but no steady income and is incapable of managing money.

- Does the retiree intend, even post-1997, to engage in transfers for Medicaid planning (in which case a lump sum is better)?

- Does the retiree live in a state that makes Medicaid available to the "medically needy?" If not, it is likely that excess income (whether from a pension or investments) will block Medicaid eligibility — which could be the deciding factor as to whether LTC insurance is appropriate for the retiree.

- Is the retiree married? If so, and if the other spouse has significant pension rights, it might make sense for one spouse to take a pension in lump sum form, the other in annuity form.

- What is the retiree's investment track record? If he or she has no significant investment experience, or has a record of making bad choices, then it is unlikely that he or she will turn into an investment genius post-retirement.

- Does the employer's annuity plan offer COLAs?

- How does the return on the employer's plan compare to returns of commercial annuities? What are the investment assumptions of the employer's plan, and how do they compare to the competition?

- What are the after-tax results of taking the lump sum and investing it (based on reasonable projections of investment results), with and without averaging, versus the after-tax income from the annuity form of payment?[10]

Taxation of Retirement Benefits

The Internal Revenue Code gives businesses very substantial incentives for setting up and maintaining qualified plans. Employer contributions to such plans are tax deductible (within limits specified by the Code and its regulations). Top executives like these plans because they can set aside enough for substantial income after retirement — even though the tax laws require that they make comparable provisions for rank-and-file employees.

Employees have an incentive to want deferred compensation (in the form of qualified retirement plans) to replace a certain amount of current compensation, because they are not taxed when the employer's contributions go into the plan, nor are they taxed currently on the appreciation in the plan — taxation is generally deferred until they draw benefits from the plan.

Favorable treatment is granted precisely in order to create incentives for funding of retirement savings. The motivation was strongest before the 1981 tax act (ERTA '81) reduced the highest tax rates, and especially before TRA '86 chopped both tax rates and the number of brackets. With fewer tax brackets and the ones that remain closer together — even after OBRA '93 — there is less incentive to find ways to shift income to lower brackets. Before 1986, one of the most important issues to be considered was whether part of a client's retirement benefit could be treated as a capital gain and taxed at a lower rate than ordinary income. (This is still an important consideration for clients who were born before January 1, 1936 and, under grandfather provisions, may continue to use a 20% capital gains rate. See "Special Rules for Capital Gains," below.) In 1986, the preferential rate for capital gains was eliminated. In 1990, it was restored, but in a way that had little impact for most taxpayers because the difference between ordinary income and capital gains tax rates was small. The picture changed again when the Revenue Reconciliation Act of 1993 raised the maximum income tax rate on ordinary income to 39.6%, while the maximum capital gains rate remained at 28%. The change gave high-income taxpayers a more meaningful incentive for seeking capital gains instead of boosting their ordinary income.

The qualified plan provisions of the Code are designed to encourage employers to contribute to funds that are used for *retirement*. Limitations are placed on employers' ability to dip into pension funds for other purposes (although, as explained on page 237, employers can invade certain overfunded plans to pay for retiree health benefits). Limitations are also placed on employees' ability to dip into retirement funds (including IRAs and Keogh plans) during their work life. Under Code section 72(t), a 10% penalty tax is imposed on "premature withdrawals"—generally withdrawals before age 59½. Exceptions to the premature withdrawal penalty include payments made upon the disability or death of the plan participant.

PLANNING TIP: Companies that are downscaling often offer early retirement incentives. Payments to employees who separate from service after attaining age 55 are not subject to the penalty tax. If your client is not yet age 55, the penalty can be avoided by (1) receiving the distribution in a series of substantially equal payments to be made over the life or life expectancy of the employee (or the employee and a beneficiary), or (2) rolling over the unwanted distribution into an IRA or into a new employer's qualified plan. Legal or accounting advice as the rollover rules should be obtained.

Until 1997, a 15% tax was imposed on excess distributions, defined as either distributions in a calendar year totalling in excess of $155,000 (in 1996, as adjusted for inflation) or, in the case of a lump sum for which special averaging is elected, $775,000 (in 1996, as adjusted for inflation).

As part of the Small Business Job Protection Act of 1996, Congress returned to pre-1986 law and suspended the 15% excise tax on excessive distributions for the years 1997, 1998, and 1999. In other words, while a retiree who draws a six- or seven-figure sum from a pension plan is likely to face a major income tax bill and the loss of tax-deferred growth, he or she will not have to pay an excise tax in addition to the income tax during 1997 through 1999.

Even though excessive distributions are not penalized, excessive accumulation within the estate continues to be penalized by a 15% excise tax, which was not repealed in 1996. This penalty tax is imposed on excessive accumulations of retirement benefits at the death of the participant. An excess accumulation is one that has a present value (measured either on the date of death or on an alternate valuation date permitted for estate tax purposes) in excess of the amount needed to yield a pension of a specified amount a year for each year of the deceased person's actuarially predictable lifespan in the year he or she died. The specified amount is adjusted each year for changes in the cost of living ($155,000 for 1996, $160,000 for 1997). The calculation is based on age at death, using IRS valuation tables.

Before 1986, plan participants were given a free choice: either start drawing their pension early, or at normal retirement age (and start paying income tax on the payments!) or stay at work and defer distributions from the plan. In 1986, however, tax policy changed. Pensions were supposed to be used for lifetime needs, not to create an estate for transmission to future generations; therefore, a 50% excise tax was imposed on individuals who failed to take minimum distributions. Generally, distributions had to begin no later than April 1 of the year after the year in which the individual reached age 70 1/2—even if he or she continued to be employed.

The Small Business Job Protection Act of 1996 reinstated the choice for most employees who are still working at age 70-1/2 to delay distribution until retirement; however, more-than-5% owners and IRA owners must still begin distributions by April 1 of the year after reaching age 70-1/2.

If your client is healthy and mentally active, and wants to stay at work, this is a tax incentive to do so. He or she can continue to draw a salary, but defer the receipt of the pension until after retirement, when presumably the tax bracket will be lower. The plan must increase the pension actuarially to account for the fact that payments begin later, so will continue for a shorter time.

Under Code section 401(a)(9)(B), minimum distributions are still required upon the death of the participant. If the participant dies after annuity payments have already begun, the survivor part of the joint and survivor annuity is paid to the survivor (or the pension stops, if the participant was single, or was married and a single-life annuity was properly elected).

If the participant dies before annuity payments began, and also before the plan's earliest retirement age, then the annuity paid to the survivor must equal the joint and survivor annuity that would have been paid if the participant had stopped working at the date of death, but had lived to the earliest retirement age, retired with a joint and survivor annuity, and then died. The employer is allowed to defer actual payment of the annuity to the survivor until the plan's earliest retirement age—which could be many years after the employee's death.

Where the participant dies after the earliest retirement age, but before actually retiring and collecting benefits, then the benefit to the survivor must be at least as great as the joint and survivor annuity that would have been payable if the participant had retired the day before his or her death.

With respect to the taxation of plan benefits, the general rule is that every dollar that goes into or comes out of a qualified plan is supposed to be taxed only once; thus, any amounts that were taxable (i.e., not deductible) when they went into the plan are generally not taxed when they come out.

Taxation of Annuities

Before 1996, income taxation of pension benefits received in annuity form was more or less identical to taxation of investment annuity payments. Another SBJPA '96 change simplifies tax calculations for pension benefits in annuity form. It is still necessary to calculate investment in the contract and an exclusion ratio, but for payouts with a start date after November 18, 1996, the employee's investment in the contract equals his or her after-tax contributions to the plan, minus any amount that has already been received before the start date, but was not included in his or her gross income.

The exclusion ratio is calculated using a simple table based on the annuitant's age when payments start. It is no longer necessary to use the IRS' lengthy and cumbersome actuarial tables. If the annuity is payable for a term of years, it is assumed that payments will be made for 120 months (10-year term), 240 months (20-year term), or corresponding amounts for a different term.

For lifetime annuities, and for people whose pension start date occurs before they reach age 55, the calculation simply assumes that the pension will be paid for 30 years (i.e., 360 payments will be made)—no matter how old the early retiree actually is, or what his or her predictable life expectancy may be.

The assumption is that 310 payments will be made for persons aged over 55 but under 60 at the start date; 260 payments for those aged over 60 but under 65 at the start date, 210 payments for those aged over 65 but under 70, and 160 payments for those who start payments at age 70 or over. (Remember that people who want to remain at work may defer the first distribution until April 1 of the year after retirement.)

Taxation of Lump Sums

If the participant has no investment in the contract, the basic rule is that he or she will have taxable income each year equal to the benefits received from the plan in the year of distribution. In other words, a monthly pension of $800 yields taxable income of $9,600; four withdrawals from an IRA of $2,000 each in a single year means taxable income of $8,000. Under this rule, receipt of a lump sum of $329,714 would result in taxable income of $329,714 if the tax law did not provide some relief in the form of "forward averaging."

Generally, people born before January 1, 1936 (or their beneficiaries and estates) can choose either five-year forward averaging or ten-year forward averaging of lump sum distributions. If five-year forward averaging is elected, current year tax rates are used. The rates prevailing in 1986 are used for ten-year forward averaging.

PRACTICE TIP: Forward averaging is available only to those who were plan participants for five or more years before the year the distribution is made (unless the distribution is made to a beneficiary or estate of a deceased plan participant). This can be a problem for middle-aged and older employees who lost their jobs due to economic conditions or mergers, and found another job — but were plan participants for only a couple of years before retirement.

To be eligible for special averaging under Code section 402(d)(4), a lump sum distribution must:

- Come from a qualified plan trust or annuity;

- Constitute the whole balance to the employee's credit under the plan;

- Be made in one taxable year of the recipient; and

- Be payable on account of the employee's attainment of age 59½, separation from service (in the case of an employee only), disability (in the case of a self-employed person only), or death.

Five-year forward averaging may be elected only if a lump sum distribution is received after the employee attains age 59½, and the employee treats all amounts received during the year in the same manner. Under five-year forward averaging, the lump sum is subjected to certain adjustments and treated as if it were paid to the recipient in five equal annual installments. The recipient's income tax on the lump sum is computed at the rate for an unmarried taxpayer who is not a head of household (i.e., at a higher amount than a married taxpayer filing a joint return). However, it is important to note that the recipient does not get five years to pay the tax — he or she is taxed, in the year the lump sum is received; however, the amount of the tax is equal to five times the tax on one-fifth the lump sum (at the single taxpayers' rate).

The advantage of 5-year forward averaging is that the tax on five times one-fifth the adjusted amount is likely to be lower than the tax on the entire amount, because some of the income will be shifted to a lower tax bracket. Note that, since 1986, and even after the tax changes in 1993, there are fewer tax brackets and not as much difference between the bottom and top as before 1986. The only way to tell if five-year averaging is worthwhile is for a to make computations assuming it is elected, and assuming it is forgone (IRS Publication 575 contains worksheets for 5-year averaging). Five-year averaging can be used only once (even if an employee gets lump sums from more than one plan), and it cannot be used if any part of the lump sum has been rolled over to an IRA or a qualified plan (because that would give the employee too many tax breaks).

The election to take five-year averaging is made on Form 4972. This same form is also used to elect ten-year forward averaging, which is based on making a different set of adjustments and paying ten times the tax on one-tenth the lump sum. Ten-year forward averaging is unavailable to taxpayers who were born after 1935; furthermore, ten-year averaging requires five years of plan participation, can be used only once after 1986, and is also denied if part of the lump sum is rolled over.

The Small Business Job Protection Act of 1996 (P.L. 104-188), eliminates the five-year averaging option beginning after 1999. The theory is that people who are entitled to receive a lump sum, but don't want to pay a lot of income tax, can handle the tax problem by rolling over the unwanted lump sum into an IRA (or into another qualified plan, if they are eligible to join another plan that accepts contributions).

The delayed effective date provides a planning window; for tax years 1997, 1998, and 1999, five-year averaging is still permitted. After 1999, ten-year averaging will still be allowed, but only for people born before 1936; thus, the large baby boom generation will not have access to it.

Special Rules for Capital Gains

Special rules apply to the portion of a lump sum distribution allocable to service before 1974 by employees who were born before January 1, 1936.

This group of older employees can elect to treat the portion of the plan distribution attributable to pre-1974 contributions as capital gains taxed at a flat rate of 20%. Forward averaging may be elected for the post-1973 portion. Tax advice from an attorney or accountant may be necessary for a client in this situation; the capital gains rules are complex and interact in subtle ways with the other rules for taxation of benefits. These rules were unaffected by SBJPA '96.

Taxation of IRA Benefits

There is a penalty if IRA funds are tapped before age 59½ (with certain exceptions, such as disability, death, or a lifetime annuity payout). But there is also a penalty if they are tapped too late. In general, distributions from an IRA must begin by April 1 of the year after the account-holder reaches age 70½ (unlike those from an employer's pension plan, which may be delayed until retirement). A penalty is imposed unless at least a minimum distribution is made each year.

PLANNING TIP: If the IRA account-holder wants more money, he or she can withdraw up to the full balance remaining in the account after age 59½ without penalty (and, of course, will be subject to income tax on the amount withdrawn). However, if there is plenty of other income, but the account-holder wants to leave more money in the estate, a child or even grandchild can be named as joint beneficiary, and payments calculated based on the joint lives. This "stretching out" of payments is limited by the incidental benefit rule, which provides that the life expectancy of a nonspouse beneficiary is limited to that of an individual 10 years younger than the account-holder.

Minimum distributions are also required upon the death of the IRA account-holder, and are generally determined in a manner similar to the method used for qualified plans. However, the surviving spouse of the IRA account-holder has one major advantage over the surviving spouse of a qualified plan participant: the surviving spouse of the IRA account-holder may elect to treat the IRA as his or her own and distributions can then be postponed until the surviving spouse attains age 70½.

Amounts remaining in the IRA at the death of the account-holder become part of his or her estate and are potentially subject to estate tax. If they are made payable to the surviving spouse, they may qualify for the marital deduction. However, the payments would still be subject to income tax.

PENSION WITHHOLDING

For taxable distributions made from qualified plans, income tax generally must be withheld at a 20% rate. The most typical distribution subject to this requirement is a lump-sum distribution. This requirement speeds up the collection of income tax, but does not increase the amount of tax imposed on distributions. The withholding requirement applies to situations in which an individual actually receives money from a retirement plan; it is not imposed on trustee-to-trustee IRA transfers, such as those made when a person wants to change the way in which an IRA is invested.

Withholding also does not apply to nontaxable distributions, to installment payments made for a term of 10 years or more, nor to annuity payments for the employee's life or the joint lives of an employee and spouse.

PLANNING TIP: Remind clients that they may be able to decrease their quarterly estimated tax payments if withholding is taken from their pension distributions.

If, on the other hand, the client wishes to avoid withholding, this can be done by means of a direct rollover either to an IRA or to another qualified plan. A direct rollover is an eligible rollover distribution that is paid directly to a retirement plan for the benefit of the distributee. Under earlier law, rollovers were allowed only if at least 50% of the balance in the pension account was distributed; current law allows a rollover of any amount. Rollovers are not allowed for nontaxable distributions, required minimum distributions, annuity payments, or installment payments.

RETIREE HEALTH BENEFITS

According to "Retirement Benefits of American Workers," a study published by the Department of Labor in 1996, only 4.7 million out of the 17.4 million retirees age 55 and over were given access to retiree health benefits by their former employers, as compared to 37% of retirees who had such health benefits in 1988, and 27% in 1994. The average premium for the coverage was $840 a year, as compared to $778 a year (in constant dollars) in 1988.

In 1995, 41% of employers provided health coverage for their early retirees, and 35% covered employees who retired when Medicare-eligible. According to the Foster Higgins 1995 National Survey of Employer-Sponsored Health Plans, companies with over 500 employees paid 9.5% more for retiree health coverage in 1995 than in 1994— a rate of cost increase well above that for employer health care costs in general.

To employees, retiree health benefits are particularly crucial during the years between early retirement and Medicare eligibility. Although retirees can buy continuation coverage, they may neglect to do so, and if they retire more than 18 months before becoming Medicare-eligible, the employer is permitted to terminate the continuation coverage. Because of employees' personal preferences, and corporate attempts to downsize via early retirement incentives, about 39% of those who receive retiree health benefits are under 65.[11] In contrast, a Hewitt Associates' survey of 463 medium and large businesses showed that 69% of the respondents provide retiree health benefits (but 9% provide coverage only to those who retire early, not those who retire at the normal age).[12]

The costs of providing health benefits to retirees are even greater than those of providing benefits to active workers — because older people are more likely to need medical care than younger people; and because bad health is one of the factors that impels a person to choose early retirement. The Schwartz article cited in footnote 12, above, shows the cost of providing retiree health benefits at about 1.1% of the active payroll, representing 2% of pretax profit and about one-half a percent of equity in the corporations.

Okay to Drop or Change the Plan?

Employers, understandably, are looking for ways to reduce their retiree health care costs. The simplest alternative would be simply to terminate the retiree coverage. Whether this can be done lawfully depends on many factors. The most significant question is whether the employer can be held to have a contractual obligation to provide the benefits, and to continue to provide them in the future. A collective bargaining agreement would certainly be such a contract (although the bargaining unit includes only active, not retired, employees); so would a Summary Plan Description or other plan document if it obligates the employer to provide lifetime benefits or to refrain from modifying the terms of the plan.

Sometimes the argument is made that the promise of retiree health benefits is part of the unspoken employment contract between employer and worker and therefore cannot be modified by the employer after the services have been provided — but even if this argument is accepted, it will not stop an employer from maintaining benefits for those who are already retired but denying benefits to future retirees who are currently actively employed. Furthermore, if an employer states explicitly that it retains the right unilaterally to modify or terminate the retiree health plan, most courts will permit the employer to carry out its stated intentions.

Ironically, Congress has passed statutes that, in effect, give retirees of bankrupt companies a greater measure of benefit protection than retirees of solvent companies: A Chapter 11 filer can modify its retiree health plan only if it demonstrates to the satisfaction of the bankruptcy court that it needs to save that money to stave off liquidation.

Cost-Cutting Mechanisms

Employers are more likely to modify a retiree health benefit plan than to do away with it altogether. One popular choice is to mandate cost-sharing by beneficiaries, or to increase the retirees' obligations in terms of premiums, deductibles, and coinsurance.

Another possibility is to design a retiree health plan as either a "defined benefit" or "defined contribution" type of plan, set up similarly to pension plans of those types. Instead of promising to cover a retiree's entire health bill, or the bill after satisfaction of deductibles and coinsurance, the employer may obligate itself to pay only a certain amount for retiree health coverage (so that the retiree gets whatever coverage that level of funding will purchase) or set benefits in a way that takes length of service into account. For instance, the employer might pay a basic level of 50% of the premium for those who retire at normal retirement age, plus an additional 2% of the premium for every additional year of service — with a higher degree of copayment expected of early retirees. A "cash cap" plan obligates the employer to maintain its current level of effort, and also assume cost increases in the future, but not beyond a specified level (e.g., spending $1,500 per year per retiree) that is communicated to the employees.[13]

Coordination With Medicare

An important question is how the retiree health plan interacts with Medicare. Federal law mandates that, for active workers (even those over 65), Medicare is only a secondary payor; the employer's plan is the primary payor. However, for retirees over 65, Medicare becomes the primary payor, and the employer's plan is secondary. There are four major approaches to Medicare coordination:

- The Medigap plan covers Medicare deductibles and coinsurance and certain medically needed services excluded by Medicare — for instance, preventive care and checkups (perhaps subject to a deductible and its own coinsurance requirement, e.g., paying 80% of the Medigap amount).

- A coordination plan uses traditional insurance methodology, and treats Medicare much the same way one insurer treats coordination with another insurer's coverage. The plan pays the smaller of its own regular benefit, calculated as if Medicare were not in the picture, or the retiree's covered expense minus Medicare reimbursement. If the coordination plan does not impose deductibles and coinsurance on the retiree, it will be more expensive for the employer than the other types of plans, which factor in retiree cost-sharing.

- An exclusion (or expense carve-out) plan applies the plan's deductibles and coinsurance to the amount of the covered expenses minus Medicare reimbursement. That is to say, Medicare reimbursement is considered first; deductibles and coinsurance are limited to the portion of the bill not covered by Medicare.

- A carve-out (or benefit carve-out) plan takes the opposite tack: the deductibles and coinsurance are applied to the entire bill, then Medicare reimbursement is credited, and only then does the retiree health plan pick up the rest of the tab. This method makes the benefit carve-out plan the least expensive option for the employer.

Employers may be able to cut the cost of retiree health care, without limiting the benefits available to retirees, by using general cost-cutting techniques such as the "PPO," or preferred provider organization. A PPO consists of health care providers who agree to provide health care at reduced rates for group members. Group members, in turn, are provided more reimbursement from the plan if they receive their care from the preferred providers than if they receive their care from others.

Case management is the process of reviewing high-cost claims (such as those generated by a person who has suffered a crippling accident) and finding lower-cost alternatives, such as home care and rehabilitation to restore a higher degree of physical function. Case management can cut costs while it improves the quality of life of the sick person.

The retirees' cost sharing burden (deductibles and coinsurance) can be re-adjusted periodically to keep pace with inflation, so that the employer's burden remains the same in real dollars. If the employer has trouble finding appropriately skilled younger employees, and thus wants to keep older employees from retiring as long as they can be effective at work, the employer's share of retiree health costs can be tied to the length of employment — full retiree health coverage for those who worked for the employer for 30 years, scaling down to 60% or 50% coverage for those with shorter periods of employment. (In effect, employers who use this method are creating their own counterpart of Social Security's incentives for deferred retirement.)

Raiding the Piggy Bank?

Under the Omnibus Budget Reconciliation Act of 1990 (Public Law 101-508), and under certain limited and specified circumstances, employers have the right to transfer assets from overfunded defined benefit pension plans (but not multiemployer plans) to health benefit accounts known as "401(h) accounts." The employer can make only one transfer a year, not to exceed the amount needed to pay "qualified current retiree health benefit liabilities." The transferred assets, and income from the transferred assets, must be devoted exclusively for paying qualified current retiree health liabilities for rank and file employees (not merely business owners or major stockholders). Furthermore, the employer must keep up at least a minimum level of retiree health benefit payments for four years after the transfer. If it turns out that not all the transferred funds are used during the tax year to pay qualified current retiree health liabilities, the unused part must be given back to the pension plan. The employer does not have to pay income tax on the retransferred assets, but does have to pay the 20% excise tax on reversions. After 1990, employers cannot make a contribution to a 401(h) account, or to a welfare benefit fund, for the part of the employer's retiree health benefit obligation paid for out of transferred assets.

The OBRA '90 provision changed prior tax law, under which a transfer of this type would have generated a 15% penalty excise tax on the reversion to the employer and might even have resulted in the disqualification of the plan. The tax provision initially ended in 1995, but was extended; thus, transfers were allowed beginning with the 1990 tax year, but not for tax years beginning after December 31, 2000. (However, presumably if the provision succeeds in making retiree health benefits more accessible to workers — and in cutting federal Medicare and Medicaid costs — it will continue to be extended.)

Funded or Pay-as-You Go?

One major problem with paying retiree health benefits is that very few companies fund these benefits in advance. Federal law imposes elaborate funding and vesting requirements on qualified retirement plans. No employer can get away with ignoring the need to pay pension benefits until workers retire, then claim that there is no money in the kitty for their pensions! However, technically speaking, under ERISA retiree health benefits (like health benefits for active workers) are "welfare benefits," not "pension benefits," and thus there is no legal requirement for advance funding and the benefits do not vest. When companies do not fund the benefits in advance, they do not take an accounting charge for the reserved money and their earnings record looks rosier.

All that is changing, because FASB (the Financial Accounting Standards Board, the group that prescribes uniform standards for accounting) decided that, starting in 1993, employers would be required to make actuarially sound estimates of their eventual cost of providing retiree health benefits, amortize the cost of a period of years, and take an annual deduction against earnings representing a share of the overall retiree health benefit cost. (The 1993 effective date was for employers of 500 or more; smaller companies were given an extra year to comply.)

The initial effect of this type of a change is a decrease in company earnings (because a new, and probably large, charge must be made against each year's earnings). The probable effect for many companies will be that, if earnings must be affected anyway, they might as well establish an actual pre-funding account to diminish the practical impact of paying retiree health benefits as the very large baby boom group of employees starts to retire.[14]

Continuation Coverage for Retirees and Families

As noted above, only about one-third of U.S. workers have access to retiree health benefits — but, unless the employer suspends the retiree health plan, coverage continues for life. All U.S. workers whose employers have 20 or more employees have access to "continuation coverage," which provides up to 36 months of benefits for individuals and families who lose coverage under an employer's health plan. However, employers differ in the amount of cost-sharing required under retiree health plans. Under continuation coverage, the employee or family member must, in effect, take over the entire premium for the coverage (in addition, the employer can impose a service charge which is not permitted to exceed 2%).

Continuation coverage, which was added to federal law by the Consolidated Omnibus Budget Reconciliation Act of 1985 (COBRA), can be purchased by employees or their families whenever a "triggering event" occurs. Triggering events include being fired (for any reason except serious misconduct), being laid off, having working hours reduced below the limit for health coverage, divorcing or legally separating from an employee who has health coverage, the employer's bankruptcy, and an employee's child losing qualification as a "dependent child" under the plan.

For our purposes, the most relevant triggering events are retirement (which entitles the retiree to purchase 18 months of continuation coverage personally) and the older person's becoming Medicare-eligible or dying (which entitles the former worker's spouse, and in some circumstances the children, to purchase 36 months of continuation coverage).

However, a retiree's continuation coverage period ends as soon as he or she becomes eligible for Medicare. Continuation coverage is required as a "last resort" for those who would otherwise lack access to affordable health insurance. The spouse may maintain continuation coverage even after the ex-worker becomes Medicare-eligible, as long as the spouse is not Medicare-eligible. Remember, Medicare, unlike Social Security or employer's health plans, does not provide spousal coverage!

The employer must notify employees and their families of their COBRA rights and must provide an "election period" of at least 60 days for the ex-employee or other eligible person to make the voluntary choice to purchase continuation coverage.

CHAPTER FOOTNOTES

1. Peter Passell, "You Saved, but They Didn't. So Now What?" *New York Times* July 7, 1996, Section 3, p. 1.

2. See Louis Uchitelle, "Company-Financed Pensions are Failing to Fulfill Promise," *New York Times* May 29, 1990 p. S1.

3. Jonathan Clements, "Can Retirement Savings Last 30 Years? Here's a Reality Check on Withdrawals," *Wall Street Journal* December 3, 1996 p. C1.

4. Jonathan Clements, "Retirement Honing: How Much Should You Have Saved for a Comfortable Life?" *Wall Street Journal* January 28, 1997 p. C1.

5. Karen Slater, "Social Security Records Deserve a Check in Planning Retirement," *Wall Street Journal* July 13, 1990 p. D1.

6. On G.I.C.s, see Deborah Rankin, "Junk Bond Anxiety Shakes the G.I.C.," *New York Times* May 27, 1990 p. F12; Earl C. Gottschalk Jr., "Guaranteed Investment Contracts Spook More Firms," *Wall Street Journal* December 10, 1990 p. C1. Your clients with several years to go before retirement may get some good tips from Ellen E. Schultz, "Taking Full Control of Retirement Funds," *Wall Street Journal* April 27, 1990 p. C1.

7. Pauline Yoshihashi and Peter Pae, "A Retirement Haven Struggles with Curse of Low Interest Rates," *Wall Street Journal* January 30, 1992 p. A1; Felicity Barringer, "As Interest Rates Are Cut, Retirees Are Stung," *New York Times* July 5, 1992 p. A12; Julie Amparano Lopez, "Many Early Retirees Find the Good Deals Not So Good After All," *Wall Street Journal* October 25, 1993 p. A1; Mary Rowland, "Early Retirement's Souring Side," *New York Times* February 20, 1994 p. F15.

8. Quoted in Mary Rowland, "The Many Faces of a Pension Plan," *New York Times* September 16, 1990 p. F13.

9. Karen Slater, "Special Annuity May Give Bigger Check," *Wall Street Journal* April 10, 1990 p. C1; Mary Rowland, "Planning to Collect in Retirement," *New York Times* December 12, 1993 p. F15 and "Prickly Decisions for Retirees," *New York Times* January 16, 1994 p. F15; Deborah Lohse, "For Some Retirees, Taking Out Funds in Periodic Payments May Make Sense," *Wall Street Journal* December 20, 1993 p. C1.

10. See Mary Rowland, "The Lure of the Lump Sum," *New York Times* January 28, 1990 p. F17.

11. For information about retiree health benefits, see "Employee Benefits: Extent of Companies' Retiree Health Coverage," GAO/HRD-90-92 (March 28, 1990); "Employee Benefits: Extent of Multiemployer Plan Retiree Health Coverage," GAO/HRD-90-132 (July 17, 1990); "Retiree Health Plans: Health Benefits Not Secure Under Employer-Based System," GAO/HRD-93-125 (July 1993); Milt Freudenheim, "Companies Moving to Reduce Benefits Promised to Retirees," *New York Times* January 24, 1992 p. A1 and "Health Limbo for Early Retirees," *New York Times* July 10, 1993 p. A39; Lee Berton, "Effects of New FASB Rule on Benefits for Retirees is Less Than Expected," *Wall Street Journal* December 12, 1993 p. A2.

12. Matthew Schwartz "Many Companies Have Begun to Make FASB Changes," *National Underwriter* (Life/Health Edition) October 29, 1990 p. 6.

13. Lisa S. Howard, "Consultant Tells How to Cut Retiree Costs," *National Underwriter* (Property/Casualty Edition) May 14, 1990 p. 23.

14. Milt Freudenheim, "New Rule on Benefits Approved," *New York Times* October 18, 1990 p. D1.

Chapter 10

SPECIAL INVESTMENT NEEDS
OF THE OLDER CLIENT

After retirement, most people have three sources of income: a private pension from the employer, Social Security benefits, and investment income. A comfortable life during retirement depends on having adequate income from all sources and maintaining income adequacy in the face of inflation. Yet, because of the possibility of a Medicaid application, older investors (or their representatives) must have the flexibility to alter investments that constitute excess assets or result in excess income that limits Medicaid eligibility.

This chapter describes your two main tasks: (1) determining the client's needs and (2) making recommendations to older investors as well as their attorneys-in-fact, trustees, conservators, and guardians. Depending on the client's abilities and wishes, your role can be very limited (if the client has a broad-scale plan and is willing and able to devote time and energy to monitoring it) or very sweeping (especially if you are licensed to sell securities, licensed as an investment advisor, or both).

CLIENT NEEDS

Your older clients can include the full spectrum, from a sophisticated financial executive planning early retirement to a 90-year-old with severe mental and physical limitations. This discussion will concentrate on the client whose ability or desire to undertake active investment management is limited, since techniques for dealing with a competent, knowledgeable, active 70-year-old would not differ significantly from those used with his or her 30-year-old counterpart.

When dealing with the older client, especially one who is or may become impaired, one threshold inquiry is, "what does the client seek to achieve through the financial plan?" (Does the client need more income now, for example, to help pay off the mortgage? Does the client wish to create an estate for the surviving spouse or the children, and if so, is it his or her intention to reduce any estate tax?) Every investment must be undertaken with a time horizon: for instance, observing a stock for a year, buying zero-coupon bonds for college tuition, or investing in a start-up industry that is expected to flourish within ten to fifteen years. Younger clients can have either a short or long time horizon; older clients usually want to liquidate earlier investments for current needs or to invest over a shorter time horizon (e.g., one to ten years). Older clients typically (but not always) want to receive high current income, to be spent for current needs or saved to pass along to heirs.

Older investors are usually less interested in growth (increase in value of investments over time). However, a "young-old" person may want to invest now for use in extreme old age, or an investor who is also engaged in estate planning may see an opportunity to turn a small investment into a large inheritance. Recommending appropriate investments depends on the client's comparative need for income and appreciation, and particularly on his or her need to preserve capital and tolerance (or intolerance) of risk.

In setting a time horizon, remember that even a person in his or her seventies may very feasibly survive for two more decades. Also explore the client's wishes and values. Some prefer to enhance their current lifestyle, even if this means liquidating some assets (at the risk that they will outlive their funds — especially if they encounter high health-care costs). Others prefer to keep assets intact, and to continue saving, minimizing current consumption in order to maximize family wealth. Once again, this strategy can backfire, if lifestyle compromises are severe enough to endanger health—or if having more money simply increases the amount that must be spent down before Medicaid benefits are available.

A typical challenge facing investors in their fifties and older is the prudent treatment of lump sums, such as early retirement incentives; lump-sum payouts from pension plans; withdrawals from 401(k) plans, IRAs, and Keogh plans; proceeds from the sale of the family home; and insurance benefits paid when a spouse dies. The typical solution is to convert the lump sum into a stream of income, either by investing in income-oriented vehicles or by purchasing an annuity. This is a typical solution because many older investors are no longer capable of active hands-on management of a large sum of money. Many more are capable of this task, but prefer to delegate it to professionals and enjoy the continuing income payments.

The client's health needs may affect income requirements both directly (money to pay bills) and indirectly (the Medicaid planning strategies described below). The client may wish to formally or informally designate someone else to make financial decisions, or a court may make a determination that the client's capacity to do business is impaired. The representative may need advice about the client's financial affairs and about investments that are suitable for a fiduciary.

RISK TOLERANCE

Although there is a range of personal needs and preferences, it is a fair generalization that elderly investors are risk-averse. Though a 65-year-old can reasonably expect to live for ten or even fifteen more years, the investment horizon is not unlimited. Older investors know that if they make a bad investment decision, or if investment conditions are unfavorable, they may not have time to make up any loss with better investments at better times. They also know that if investment income declines, they will not be able to rely on overtime hours at work or a Christmas bonus. Retirees are often in a lower tax bracket than they were before retirement so even a tax loss is not much consolation to a retiree who has lost money on an investment.

Current conditions tend to decrease risk tolerance even further. Many retirees are worried about the security of their pensions for a variety of reasons, including: insolvency of the employer, acquisition of the employer by another corporation, insolvency of the insurer making annuity payments, worthlessness of guaranteed insurance contracts, and poor investment performance of defined contribution plan accounts. In addition, younger retirees and pre-retirees have long-range concerns over the solvency of the Social Security trust fund.

If the other components of retirement income are at risk, older investors will guard the safety of their investment income even more zealously. If a prominent executive loses money on an investment, he or she may have to delay buying a yacht or decrease the size of the diamond in a spouse's Christmas present. If a retiree with a small pension and Social Security benefits sells stock at a loss or sees bond or annuity income drop, he or she may have to delay repairing the roof or cut down on the amount of fuel in the oil burner.

Your discussion with clients should include a full exploration of their personal values and investment priorities. One way to handle this is to ask them if they would invest at various hypothetical risk levels. The questions might be as follows: "Would you invest $100,000 with someone who promised a 15% return...if there was a 50% chance you would lose *some* of the $100,000, and a 10% chance you would lose *all* of it?"; "What would you do if you did lose the $100,000 — how would it affect your lifestyle?"; and "What would you do with the $15,000, if you did get it?"

Find out what the practical implications of losing money would be. Will it diminish the childrens' inheritance, or severely restrict the client's lifestyle here and now? Also attempt to determine what the psychological implications of a loss would be. It is reasonable to assume that older people who have lived through the Great Depression are apt to equate any loss with being completely wiped out.

You must discuss with them the historical equation: the safest investments typically offer the lowest yield, with riskier investments offering higher returns to tempt investors; however, "risk" has many facets. For example, (1) the client could lose part or all of the invested capital if the investment loses value or becomes worthless; (2) the client could earn a return that is less than he or she expected (an investment was yielding 11% when purchased, but the return declines to 6%) or less than he or she needs (total monthly income from all sources is insufficient to provide the lifestyle desired by the client); (3) the client may earn a high level of income, but later discover that what seemed like an impressive sum is feeble when it comes to coping with the cost of living, such as in the case of an inadequate pension benefit; (4) there is the tax risk that, upon distribution, a sum will generate heavy taxation to the recipient or in the estate; and (5) there is the Medicaid risk that the elderly and disabled must face — the risk that accumulated assets or current income will render the recipient ineligible for Medicaid, or will delay eligibility, forcing the recipient to pay heavily for nursing home or home care.

THE NEW ANATOMY OF RISK

There used to be some simple rules of thumb by which one could invest. One was that real estate was a good, safe investment "because they're not making it anymore." Another was that government bonds were rock-solid and a perfect choice for conservative investors and fiduciaries, especially tax-exempt municipal bonds. A third was that bank certificates of deposit and money market funds offered high income at virtually no risk. Finally, one other basic rule suggested that junk bonds were underpriced because there was little real risk in investing in low-rated corporate obligations.

The investment climate of the 1990s has become far more complex. The real estate industry experienced speculative overbuilding and business problems that led to a glut of office and retail space and made many residential properties unsaleable or saleable only at a severe loss. Interest rates declined, which is good for borrowers but bad for lenders (a category that includes bond and money market fund investors, bank depositors, and C.D. purchasers). As the utilization of junk bonds expanded beyond financing untried corporations to financing corporate takeover attempts, the number of junk bond defaults also grew. A combination of real estate and junk bond problems led certain insurers to fail or come close to failure, sapping investor confidence in products such as annuities.

In these perilous times, it is impossible to categorize individual investments as the "safest" or "riskiest" on the market. However, certain conclusions can be drawn about risk. (See page 259 for further discussion about selecting investments and combining investments into a diversified portfolio.) These conclusions are as follows:

- Federal government obligations remain extremely safe. If the U.S. government stops paying its obligations, investment safety will be the least of our problems. However, it is important to distinguish between direct government obligations (e.g., Treasury bonds and notes), those that are merely insured by the federal government (such as "Ginnie Maes," whose safety in turn depends on the size of the guarantee fund and the number of demands that will be placed on it), and those that merely have an implicit federal guarantee (e.g., "Fannie Maes" and "Freddie Macs"). Although the Government National Mortgage Association, Federal National Mortgage Association, and Federal Home Loan Mortgage Corporation (which insure Ginnie Maes, Fannie Maes, and Freddie Macs, respectively) are all federal agencies, only the Ginnie Maes are backed by the full faith and credit of the United States and, thus, are somewhat safer than their counterparts.

- Bonds issued by states and localities (often called municipal bonds or "munis") must be examined very carefully. The government entity issuing the bond can be creditworthy or a poor risk. Default is a real possibility for many issues. Municipal bonds are a traditional favorite for safety-oriented investors, especially those seeking tax-exempt income. However, two cautionary notes must be considered today. First, municipal bond purchasers must be able to make a reasonable assessment of the risk of their purchases. If the issuer is very hard-pressed for cash, it may pay such high rates, and its bonds may trade at such a heavy discount, that purchase is worthwhile for high current income even if the issuer eventually defaults. Second, the tax implications must be understood. Not all state and local government obligations provide tax-exempt income (the prospectus will indicate if the income is federally or state-taxable). In addition, municipal bond income may affect the taxability of a high-income senior citizen's Social Security benefits. This is an especially significant consideration after the Revenue Reconciliation Act of 1993, which raised tax rates for everyone and also increased the potentially taxable portion of the Social Security benefit from 50% to 85%.

Also note that certain municipal bonds are issued with guarantees from private insurers as an attempt to cope with variations in the credit-worthiness of issuers. Yet the insurers themselves vary in financial stability. Whenever an obligation is guaranteed (be it FDIC deposit insurance, PBGC guarantee of defined benefit pension plan payments, or a guaranteed municipal bond), the value of the guarantee depends on whether the guarantor will be able to satisfy all of its obligations in case of a widespread failure of the guaranteed items.

Usually bond purchasers invest in bonds (either government or corporate) because they are interested in the stream of income provided by the bonds. There are two major exceptions. Zero-coupon bonds are purchased at a deep discount by a person who wants to trade a comparatively small sum of money now for the promise of a larger sum in the future. A bond purchaser may also believe that various economic factors (especially interest rates) will lead the price of that particular bond to increase in the future, so that the bond purchaser can sell the bond at a profit. The same factors may lead to a *decrease* in bond prices. A bond owner who needs cash and liquidates part of a bond portfolio may experience losses on the sale of the bond, even if the bond is not in default and continues to make interest payments as scheduled. Older clients must be advised of this risk of loss unless they are certain that they will hold all bonds to maturity.

- Corporate bonds are issued by corporations that must borrow to meet their financial needs. The purchaser of a corporate bond is therefore making an assumption that the corporation will be able to keep making scheduled payments for the term of the bond — or that the bond was cheap enough, and its current yield high enough, to make it worthwhile to take the risk of default.

- A mutual fund may purchase a mixture of stocks, bonds, and other securities. Mutual funds are generally less risky than individual securities because they give investors the benefit of diversification. For example, a small investor could afford to buy only a few stocks or bonds; but the same investment in a mutual fund permits the investor to share in a portfolio with dozens or hundreds of securities. As discussed below on page 259, mutual funds have various objectives, and some mutual funds are more successful than others with similar objectives.

- Usually investors buy corporate securities (common and preferred stock, rights, warrants, and options) because they believe that the value of the securities will increase over time, and that the securities can either be sold at a profit or will enhance the net worth of the owner. Various theories have evolved as to why stock prices change. It is probable that both general economic factors and the prosperity of the individual corporation are involved, and that both determine whether purchase of a particular stock is likely to be a conservative or an aggressive and risky investment. Another motivation for buying certain stocks is to gain income. The issuer of preferred stock commits to a particular level of dividend before a dividend can be paid on common stock. Other stocks, such as utility stocks, have a history of paying high dividends. However, investors who turn to utility stocks must be aware that utilities, too, can encounter financial problems and lower or eliminate their dividends.[1] Securities other than stock (i.e., options, warrants, and rights) in effect are ways to speculate on price movements of the underlying stock. These tend to be much riskier than the underlying stock, although they do give investors the chance to earn a large

return on a small investment. There is also a significant
risk of losing the entire investment, or sometimes even
more than the amount invested. All things considered,
they are probably not appropriate in a senior citizen's
portfolio because they are too risky and require too much
hands-on management and monitoring.

In general, the stocks of well-established and pros-
perous corporations are usually considered "blue chips";
whereas the stocks of newer or more volatile corporations
are considered a much higher risk. However, large corporations can be victims of size and inertia, meaning that
they can become the subject of takeover battles that lead
to a lower stock price or, on a more basic level, they can
simply encounter financial problems. The inherent risk of
a stock investment depends on how long the stock will be
held before sale, as well as on stock market and economic
conditions at the time of purchase and sale.

- Real estate investments range from the safe to the highly
  speculative and risky. Home ownership is one type of real
  estate investment that is almost imperative for older
  investors because of the security of knowing they will
  have a place to live without rent fluctuations, and because
  of the Medicaid preferential treatment of the homestead.
  Investors can also buy raw land, or invest in residential or
  commercial property, as well as buy real estate or mortgage-related investments such as Ginnie Maes, real estate limited partnerships, and real estate mortgage investment conduits (REMICs). These latter types of investments are attempts to give investors a chance to
  share risk with other investors and to diversify their real
  estate holdings. The success of the effort depends both on
  general market forces and the quality of management of
  the investment itself.

- Hard assets (such as gold and silver, artwork, and col-
  lectibles) are not income-producing investments. In fact,
  fees to safeguard and insure the collection can be heavy.
  The investor's intention is to buy undervalued materials,
  wait for them to appreciate, and sell them at a large profit.
  The ability to find undervalued materials calls for a great
  deal of knowledge and personal involvement, which not
  all older investors can provide. All too many buyers

purchase at the top of the market, find themselves forced to sell at the bottom, and pay heavy commissions on the sale to boot.

• Commercial annuities are a special case. Until recently, they were considered extremely conservative investments. Today, upheavals in the insurance industry make commercial annuities somewhat riskier. Commercial annuities are discussed in detail below (page 272) because of the advantages they offer older investors, including, but not limited to: tax deferral of appreciation; an income stream for the period chosen by the investor; and professional management. However, the quality of the management, and the investments chosen and retained by the annuity investment managers, are paramount in deciding whether commercial annuities belong in the older client's portfolio.

MEASURING RISK

There are many ways to estimate future risk or analyze the historical risks of an investment. The probability of losing part or all of the capital, or of a decrease in appreciation or yield rates, can be assessed by setting a percentage factor (a probability of 5% that the issuer will go bankrupt; a probability of 20% that interest rates will rise 3% or more in the next year). If it is predicted that there is a 50% chance that an investment now yielding 10% is likely to decline to a yield of 2% within a year, that investment can reasonably be considered "riskier" than an investment now yielding 6% but reliably predicted to retain its value for five years.

The historical performance of investments is often assessed by using an "index." An index allows one to see how stocks perform compared to the Dow Jones Industrial Index or the Standard & Poor's 500, for instance. "Index funds" mimic the composition of an index by investing in the same stock, so an investor in an index fund by definition cannot do worse (or better) than the index itself. However, this is not to say that the investor will necessarily be satisfied with the return, earn enough for a comfortable lifestyle, or keep up with inflation.

Financial analysts often use "beta" to measure the risk of mutual fund investments. The beta coefficient measures volatility, meaning the change in the return of an investment as compared to the change in the overall market. By way of illustration, a mutual fund with a beta of +1.00 would show exactly the same volatility as the market to which it corresponds, whereas a volatility of +1.5 shows that the fund in question is likely to increase in value 50% more than the respective market or index over a given time period. Theoretically, the higher the positive beta is, the more desirable the fund is in a bull market, because it is predicted to go up even further than the index. Conversely, that same fund would be less desirable in a bear market, where it can be expected to go down even further. A negative beta indicates an investment whose value moves in the opposite direction of the corresponding market or index.

However, a 1991 study[2] shows that measuring beta did not accurately represent the yield behavior of mutual funds in up and down markets. Writing in *Barron's*, Werner Renberg suggests that the "alpha coefficient" is a better measure of performance. Alpha compares fund performance to its risk level. Alpha is computed by first calculating the amount by which an index exceeded the return an investor could have received from a risk-free return. If T-bills went up by 5% and the index increased by 10%, investors received a risk premium of 5%. Next, the fund's beta is multiplied by the risk premium, for example, a beta of 1.2 times 5%, or 7%. Add this number to the increase in the risk-free return (5% in our example). If the fund went up 17%, as compared to 7% plus the 5% risk-free return (12%), it had an alpha of 5%. That is, it achieved an additional 5% return over and above what would have been expected from the risks taken by the fund.

Lastly, the "Sharpe ratio" looks at returns after all risks have been taken into account, by dividing the fund's excess return or risk premium (real return minus risk-free return) by the fund's "standard deviation" (variation between the fund's return and the average of all funds or the average of the index). Betas, alphas, and Sharpe ratios for funds are published in newsletters and in annual mutual fund guides put out by various organizations.

HISTORICAL RETURNS

If an understanding of history were all it took to predict the course of financial markets, historians would be the richest and most respected Americans. The lessons of the past must be learned and absorbed, but they do not tell us with certainty what will happen in the future. Historical analysis shows that over the long term, stock investments outperform income-oriented investments such as bonds. However, over the short term, stock investors who owned the entire index or a broad spectrum could be very disappointed; meanwhile, owners of individual stocks might be euphoric or depressed.

Ibbotson Associates has made a long-range analysis of the true net yield of investments. Their figures track the fate of $1 invested between 1970 and 1989. These were two eventful decades that included two market slumps (in 1974 and 1987) and an extended, overheated bull market. During this period, stocks outperformed long-term bonds and Treasury bills. Each dollar kept in the stock market grew to $8.90. After transaction costs, the $1 investor retained $7.82. Paying income taxes on the dividends and other income reduced the investment fund to $6.26; paying capital gains taxes on securities sales further reduced this figure to $5.48. But the most devastating effect came from inflation, which reduced the final outcome of the $1 investment to $1.63. In other words, in real terms, stock investors failed to double their money even after waiting twenty years.

Long-term bond investors and T-bill buyers actually lost money when all factors were considered. The return on the bonds was $5.61, reduced to $4.66 by transaction costs. After taxes, the return was $2.94 (far lower than the after-tax stock return). After inflation, the $1 investment shrunk all the way down to 87 cents. For T-bills, the gross return was $4.32; net return after the (quite modest) costs was $4.12. But after taxes, the return was a mere $2.80, and only 83 cents after inflation was taken into account.

If you seek a more expansive view, other Ibbotson studies for the period 1957-1989 show that the S&P 500 stood up to inflation far better than long-term corporate bonds, long-term government bonds, or T-bills. The S&P index returned almost 6% after inflation; the others could not even muster 2% apiece. However, if you look at common stocks by the decade, the compounded annual return (both real and nominal) was as follows: over 20% in the 1920s; almost nonexistent in the 1930s; about 8% in the 1940s (but only about 4% post-inflation); a hefty 20% (over 16% in real terms) in the 1950s; and about 7% and 5% in the 1960s. In the 1970s, the nominal compounded annual return on common stocks was close to 6%. However, the real return was negative, because inflation was so immense. In the 1980s, nominal return roared back to about 17%, and inflation was tamer but still packed a punch since real return was about 12%.

Over the 1926-1989 period, long-term corporate bonds had a negative after-inflation return between the 1940s and the 1970s. In the 1980s they did well, with a nominal return of 14% and a post-inflation return around 8%.

Research by Morgan Stanley showed that of 16 categories of investments (a broad spectrum ranging from stocks of small corporations, residential housing, farmland, and Japanese stocks to art, gold, and venture capital), eight were less valuable at the end of 1990 than at the beginning. Only five categories of investments beat inflation. The year 1990 was unusual in that many types of investments failed to conform to established patterns. Morgan Stanley figures show that between 1940 and 1990, the S&P 500 returned an average of 11.6% a year, whereas small company stocks returned 15.6%, and emerging growth stocks returned 14.1%. Residential real estate averaged 7.7% return a year, and commercial real estate returned 7.5%. T-bills averaged only 4.4%, but U.S. government bonds did a little better at 4.5%. Commercial paper beat out inflation (averaging 4.6%) by returning 5.2%. Lastly, gold performed very poorly in almost every time period.[3]

So what does history teach? It tells us that long-range investors should have a healthy common stock component in their portfolios. However, stock may play a comparatively small role in the portfolio if: (1) the client has a short-range orientation; or (2) the client is more interested in income than in growth in net worth or selling assets at a profit and reinvesting.

BALANCING RISK AND RETURN

Your job includes educating the client about the various available investments, the risks involved with each, the costs of investing (e.g., commissions, back-end charges, and/or 12b-1 charges), and the tax consequences of the various investments. Your inquiries into the client's investment background, interest in investing, objectives, and risk tolerance should give you an insight into what your client will consider an acceptable or excessively risky investment.

Clients may have unrealistic expectations with which you will have to deal. For instance, the level of risk that the client has selected may provide a rather low level of income, and yet, the client expects more current income, but does not want to add riskier investments to the portfolio. In this situation, you will have to either increase the client's comfort with the risk, or persuade him or her to liquidate some assets and use the proceeds to supplement income (or reinvest them in income vehicles).

The converse may also be true. Your client may select excessively risky vehicles that can compromise continuing retirement security. In that case, you must deliver a stern warning, and put that warning on the record. Nevertheless, if your client is competent, he or she has a right to chase rainbows and make mistakes, as long as you have given advice about the risks. When giving this advice, ensure that your client understands the full implications of a decision. Work through the implications, with numerical illustrations if possible, in order to eliminate any latent confusion or possible misunderstanding. If you think a decision is the product of confusion or senility, consult with the other members of the planning team, and discuss the senior citizen's condition with his or her family members.

Transactions are invalid if they are made by a person who lacked "contractual capacity," which is the capacity to understand the nature of a transaction and its implications. The transactions may be challenged by family members, in the course of conservatorship or guardianship proceedings, or even after the senior citizen's death in connection with a settlement of the estate. Furthermore, if you have discretionary authority over the senior citizen's portfolio, and you engage in an active pattern of transactions, you may be accused of "churning," or excessive trading to generate commissions.

Various legal devices exist to assist elderly people of diminished or absent capacities. One of the planning team's most important jobs is to assist competent people in making long-range plans in case they ever lose capacity. Also, the planning team must make sure that the financial affairs of an incapacitated person are handled properly and in the best interests of that person and his or her family. This brings us to the question of your potential role when the financial plan is being carried out by a fiduciary.

INVESTMENTS BY FIDUCIARIES

A fiduciary is anyone with responsibility for the financial or personal affairs of others. There are many situations in which fiduciaries will act for the elderly. An elderly person may create a trust, relying on the trustee to provide honest and skillful management of the trust corpus. An elderly person might also appoint an agent under a durable power of attorney. Many states permit a healthy elder to make an advance designation of someone to serve as conservator or guardian. The designation will become effective if the elder later becomes incapacitated. If no designation has been made, courts have the power to appoint conservators (who are responsible for business and money management) and limited and full guardians (with varying degrees of power over the personal affairs of the ward).

Most fiduciaries fall into one of two classes. They are either professionals, such as accountants or trust officers, or they are family members or friends. Family fiduciaries vary widely in their aptitude toward financial affairs. They also differ with respect to the amount of time they can devote to those affairs. Some may need extensive professional and/or management assistance.

Any financial plan for an elderly person should be well-organized and should include good record-keeping so that a fiduciary can easily understand the plan. This will, in turn, facilitate ease of transfers within the plan. A common financial plan for the elderly features a "stand-by" trust that is created while the elder is healthy and is unfunded or funded only to a limited extent. If and when the elder becomes incapacitated, the attorney-in-fact is authorized by a durable power of attorney (DPA) to transfer the bulk of the elder's possessions to the trust. The trust is then administered by the agent or another named trustee or trustees, for the benefit of the elder and his or her family. The transfer process is straightforward if it is known where the elder's assets can be located (and if banks and brokerages cooperate with the agent—they do not always). However, the process becomes difficult and expensive if no one is quite sure what the elder's assets are; where they are located; where the supporting documentation such as stock certificates, passbooks, and brokerage statements can be found; or even how many bank and brokerage accounts exist.

If it seems likely that management will be assumed by a fiduciary in the event the older client becomes incapacitated, surrender and transfer charges should be given special consideration when selecting investments for that client. The real cost of an investment increases (and therefore its yield decreases) if the fiduciary must incur penalties on cashing in unmatured certificates of deposit and surrendering mutual fund shares in order to assemble and administer the protected person's assets.

The essence of the fiduciary relationship is trust. A fiduciary is a person or entity who is relied on by a principal or by an appointing court. The legal system requires fiduciaries not only to be honest but to execute their duties reliably and with a high degree of care. Fiduciaries must avoid self-dealing (transactions for their own benefit) and must at all times be prudent and vigilant.

The standards by which fiduciaries act are derived from three sources: (1) directions given by a trustor in a trust instrument, or by a principal in a durable power of attorney, (2) directions given by a supervising court, if the fiduciary was appointed as conservator, and (3) state law. In cases of potential conflict between the three sources of instructions, the wise fiduciary will petition the court for an order to give his or her actions a judicial sanction. Without the court order, the fiduciary's actions may be challenged by a third party who is dissatisfied with the fiduciary's performance. If a court finds that the fiduciary acted improperly, he or she may be held personally liable for any loss which occurred as a result of a breach of fiduciary duty.

One such duty imposed upon a fiduciary is the duty to invest assets productively, yet prudently. The fiduciary must generate income while ensuring the safety of the capital. Once chosen, an investment must be monitored constantly to make sure that it continues to be appropriate. A few states impose a mandatory "legal list" of investments which are the *only* permitted investments for fiduciaries. United States government obligations and first mortgages on valuable properties are two such investments. Other states retain a "legal list" by statute, but use it as a mere guideline. A fiduciary is presumed to be acting properly if he or she invests in "legal list" investments; the fiduciary *may* be acting properly as long as he or she chooses and monitors investments with the required degree of care and skill. Another group of states has discarded the legal list entirely and merely requires fiduciaries to act prudently, with the degree of attention, skill, and care that a reasonable person would devote to his or her personal affairs.

What is a prudent investment? United States government obligations and related financial devices, such as Ginnie Maes, will usually be considered prudent investments. First mortgages on high-value saleable properties, state bonds and other obligations (as long as there is no recent history of default) also would be considered prudent. Municipal bonds are usually considered prudent investments, as long as the bond is adequately secured, such as by sufficient tax revenues. Stocks or high-rated bonds issued by solid corporations probably count as a prudent investment.

Direct investment in real estate is probably not a prudent investment, unless the property is immediately saleable and the fiduciary has the necessary expertise to manage and market the property. An unsecured loan to a person or corporation is probably imprudent. The same is true for investing in a small business, or selling property belonging to a trust or conservatorship estate in exchange for an unsecured note rather than cash or a secured obligation. A court will consider several factors when judging the prudence of a transaction, including: (1) the extent of the fiduciary's investigation of the particular investment, (2) the rating given to the investment by recognized rating agencies, (3) whether the fiduciary obtained and acted on professional advice, (4) whether the fiduciary satisfied his or her duty to keep the assets safe by adequately diversifying the mix of investments, and (5) the extent to which the fiduciary considered and accounted for inflation and tax factors.

According to 1984 figures from the Federal Deposit Insurance Corporation, corporate fiduciaries who were given investment discretion managed $276 billion in personal trust investments. Corporate common stock was the most popular investment choice, representing 48.7% of the overall amount invested, followed by U.S. obligations (12%), other notes and bonds (including state and municipal obligations) (4.4%), and cash and cash equivalents (9.6%). The remaining funds were invested in mortgages, preferred stock, real estate, and other vehicles.

Fiduciaries also have to balance the interests of various people. Trustees must administer the trust to provide adequate income to the income beneficiaries, without taking excessive risks that impair the safety of the capital that will be passed along to the remaindermen. Conservators must take care of the conservatee while also keeping in mind the needs of other family members. Furthermore, the fiduciary should consider the tax and estate planning implications of his or her choices.

Fiduciary principles evolved long before the Medicaid program was enacted, so the fiduciary is usually expected to *maximize* income as long as this can be done consistent with prudence. It is an interesting question whether the fiduciary can legitimately *minimize* income by selecting safe but low-yield investments where the motive is to preserve Medicaid eligibility. The planning team should consult state law and, if it is not illegal, give the fiduciary explicit authorization to reduce income in order to maintain that eligibility. If a conservatorship or guardianship case is before the court, the planning team should ask for a court order permitting the conservator or guardian to reduce income to Medicaid eligibility levels.

SELECTING INDIVIDUAL INVESTMENTS

Mutual Funds

A mutual fund is a company that offers investors the ability to purchase an interest in a pool of money invested in securities chosen by the mutual fund's professional management team. Most mutual funds invest in stocks, although there are also bond funds, money market funds that invest in short-term obligations, and funds that invest in both stocks and bonds.

Mutual funds are extremely popular with investors because of the convenience they offer. An investment of a few thousand dollars in a mutual fund enables the investor to share in the market performance of dozens, even hundreds of securities selected by the fund managers — a degree of diversification otherwise available only to large investors. At least theoretically, fund investors have the benefit of the investment theories of a professional staff who devote their full attention to reconfiguring the fund's portfolio to fit changing market conditions. This constant monitoring permits the investor to make a single decision to buy and hold shares in the mutual fund, or to sell the mutual fund shares based on the performance of the fund as a whole. In order to make this decision, the investor needs only to follow the performance of the fund, rather than the far more difficult task of monitoring the individual securities held by the fund.

Owning an interest in only one mutual fund permits an investor to have some degree of diversification; owning several mutual funds permits even greater diversification. Also, a convenient factor is that many funds permit shareholders to write a certain number of "drafts" of at least a minimum amount (e.g., $500) against the fund account, either to themselves or to third parties. The drafts operate like checks, so that the fund functions as a potentially high-yielding substitute for a checking account.

Each mutual fund has an investment objective. The client should select the fund or funds that fit the client's own objective. Funds and their investment objectives can be classified in many ways, but typical classifications include:

- Growth fund — a somewhat risky fund that invests in undervalued or start-up stocks, with the expectation that the value of the stocks will grow over time. An aggressive growth fund undertakes a higher degree of risk in search of even greater return. A capital appreciation fund aims at increasing the value of the investment capital, and may engage in very high risk leveraged transactions or turn over the fund holdings through frequent sales and purchases of securities.

- Income fund — a fund that chooses investments such as bonds, short-term obligations, and high-dividend stocks that produce current income which can be distributed to shareholders in the fund. Income funds differ from other funds in their risk level, because in order to produce high current income, the fund may have to invest in some securities that are at risk of default.

- Growth and income fund — a fund that seeks long term growth of investment capital while seeking current income, generally using moderate risk growth stocks, as well as preferred stocks and convertible bonds.

- Balanced fund — a fund with the objective of conserving capital by investing in both stocks and bonds, the ratio of which will vary depending on the fund manager's perception of market conditions

- Money market fund — a fund that offers convenience and liquidity by investing in short-term and very short-term obligations. Some money market funds combine corporate and government obligations. Other funds are limited to government obligations, while a third group of money market funds invest solely in tax-exempt securities which spare the shareholders a tax on the income distributed by the fund.

- United States government fund — a highly safety-oriented fund in which the investments are limited to securities issued by the U.S. Treasury and government agencies.

- United States mortgage fund — a fund heavily, if not totally invested in mortgages and other securities that are either issued or guaranteed by the government. "Ginnie Mae" funds, limited to or specializing in Government National Mortgage Association securities, are a subdivision of U.S. mortgage funds.

- International fund — a fund that invests primarily in a number of countries throughout the world, in a particular part of the world, or in a single country.

- Sector fund — a fund investing in only a particular industry or sector of the economy (e.g., precious metal mining, health care, biotechnology, or computers).

There are several steps in the mutual fund investment process for the older investor. First, a determination must be made with respect to how much of the overall portfolio will consist of mutual funds rather than individual stocks and bonds or other assets. Mutual funds are especially suitable for the small to moderate-size investment. If there is a large amount to invest, it may be worthwhile for the investor (or a professional advisor to the investor) to select individual securities for purchase and trading. Clearly, if there are several million dollars at stake, individual security purchases will probably be suitable. If there are only a few thousand involved, mutual funds will probably be the more prudent investment.

In between, the investor may prefer to have "round lots" of a few stocks. "Round lots" are groups of 100 shares, with lower brokerage commissions than on odd lots. The investor may also choose to own one or more bonds or zero-coupon bonds, in addition to owning several mutual funds with differing objectives. This strategy permits maximum diversification, while allowing the investor to participate in investment decisions by monitoring the individual securities and the mutual funds. In the process, it does not require the investor to devote his or her full time to the task of overseeing the investments made. This type of investment strategy increases the likelihood that even if one sector of the economy declines, investments in the other sector will preserve the investor's overall capital and income positions.

The next step is to choose mutual funds from within each desired group. Whatever the investor's objective, he or she is likely to find many mutual funds with similar goals. The challenge is to select the funds that will perform the best while the investor holds them. It is easy to find out how a fund has performed in the past. The financial press regularly reports mutual fund performance, and rates funds using uniform objective techniques designed to equalize performance of funds over time. (Figures published in advertisements frequently start at the fund's historical low point and end at a high point, so that fund performance is stated in the most favorable terms.) It is far more difficult to determine whether this quarter's star performer will maintain its high rating or tumble to the bottom of the charts.

Once several funds are selected in each category (based on their track record and projected future performance), the next step is to assess the funds' actual cost to the investor, based on your client's actual investment pattern. It is too simplistic to advise that investments be limited to no-load or low-load funds, because funds with a higher load can also have a higher return which, in turn, outweighs the charges and provides greater net benefits to the investor.

Funds differ greatly in the charges assessed on investors. The "front-end load" is the sales charge assessed upon purchase of the fund shares, where the loads range from none (in a true no-load fund) to 8.5%. However, a fund that is described as a no-load or low-load fund can in fact be quite expensive to the investor because of other charges, including management charges and 12b-1 charges. A 12b-1 fund assesses charges based on the cost of selling, promoting, and distributing fund shares. Funds can also have surrender charges ("back-end load"), imposed when fund shares are redeemed. Sometimes the back-end load phases out when shares have been held for a certain period of time. An active trader prefers a fund with a low back-end load because of the likelihood that fund shares will be surrendered. A buy-and-hold investor prefers a lower initial load and is willing to accept a higher back-end load because he or she is not likely to surrender the shares and incur this expense.

Customer service is also important in selecting funds. A large fund family can be advantageous, because the issuer will offer other mutual funds, and the investor may be able to exchange shares within the fund family as his or her objectives change. A large fund with high assets is more likely to be stable in bad times and to have enough liquidity to pay off all investors if a "run" occurs. The assets of a smaller or weaker fund may be frozen in this situation, leading to delays in payment. Your experience and the various mutual fund rating services will tell you which funds or fund groups have the best customer service in terms of courtesy, quality of information available to investors, speed in processing requests, and special services. For example, a fund or brokerage may offer a management service under which results of all accounts are consolidated on a single statement, and dividends can be "swept" into a high-earning account. The fund can maintain arrangements under which dividends are automatically reinvested, or under which investors make regular deposits for investment purposes.

In short, the determination of the "best" fund or funds depends on finding the fund(s) that offer the best net value (after expenses and taxes) and the best service, while matching the investor's investment and risk objectives. The process of investment selection and monitoring is a continuous one. The investor, members of the planning team, or both must continue to examine investments in light of changing conditions. For example, the tax-free money market fund that was a great buy when it yielded 7% free of tax may not look so advantageous now that it pays 3.5% and the investor is in a lower tax bracket after his or her retirement. Similarly, the sector fund that performed well two years ago may now be at the bottom of the listings. Finally, a fund's brilliant stock analyst may have moved to another company leaving the funds languishing. In these situations, it may be time for a change.

Selection of Individual Securities

Some securities are purchased with the expectation that they will provide income to the stockholder in the form of dividends. However, purchasers of stock usually have other goals in mind as well. One such objective is the creation of net worth. In this scenario, the purchaser hopes that the stock will appreciate in value, resulting in higher net worth which can be used as collateral, sold or passed on to heirs at the stockholder's death.

No clear principles have emerged that would permit reliable predictions of future stock prices. However, there are two major schools of thought. Fundamental analysis examines the intrinsic value of the corporation issuing the securities, evaluating its assets, liabilities, products, and market share. Second, technical analysis compares price movements in the stock with price movements in other stocks and the overall market, using charts to discern patterns that are believed to predict future price changes. Daily newspapers and specialized financial publications include extensive information that can be used for either fundamental or technical analysis, and brokerage houses prepare their own analyses that may be available to their customers.

Active investors must be advised of the impact of commissions on profits. Even if a pattern of in-and-out trading produces profits, the profits may be decreased by commissions and reduced to nothing once taxes have been paid. Professional advisors of the elderly must always consider the appropriateness of their recommendations in light of the client's age and portfolio size. Advisors are at risk of being accused of "churning" or recommending an excessive trading volume that is designed to benefit the advisor through fees and commissions rather than providing financial benefits for the investor.

Bonds

Because of their reputation for safety and their income orientation, bonds have always played two major roles in senior citizens' portfolios. Bonds can be held until maturity for the coupon yield or for the appreciation offered by zero-coupon bonds purchased at a deep discount. They can also be traded in the hope of earning a profit by selling the bond for more than it originally cost.

The first decision to be made with respect to bonds as part of the older person's portfolio is whether to use individual bonds or bond funds. Bonds are usually sold in large denominations (i.e., $10,000-$25,000) so that a small portfolio would be able to include only one or two bonds. To get a significant degree of diversification, a large bond investment is required. If the client can afford such a large investment, purchasing bonds directly saves some of the "load" and management fees typical of bond funds.

The next decision is whether to invest in corporate or government bonds. Corporate bonds are available in various maturities, and at various risk levels, from very safe corporate bonds to junk bonds that carry a high risk of default. Junk bonds probably should not be included in the older person's portfolio, since these clients have little time to make up for any deleterious investment choices. However, an argument can be made that not all bonds identified as below-investment-grade are in fact likely to default. Some inherently sound and well-managed companies are finding it hard to raise money and must therefore promise high rates of return despite low real risk. If these issuers can be identified, junk bonds or junk bond funds might conceivably earn a place in a large, diversified portfolio where the quest for extra income justifies more risk. Under these circumstances, a few bond losses might harm, but not destroy the financial plan.

The choice between corporate and government bonds should be preceded by a comparison of similar risky obligations and their after-tax yields. If safety is the paramount consideration, or if corporate bond yields are disappointing, then the investor can purchase U.S. obligations directly or invest in a mutual fund that is partially or entirely invested in U.S. government obligations.

Traditionally, older investors favored municipal bonds because a large variety of tax-free, perfectly safe bonds was available. The attraction was especially great for investors in states with high state and local taxes, because such obligations are typically free of taxation at all levels. The attraction lessened somewhat after 1986, because lower tax rates made tax-exempt income less compelling. The 1986 tax reforms also limited the purposes for which tax-exempt bonds can be issued, so it is necessary to ascertain whether a municipal bond's income really is tax-exempt. The Revenue Reconciliation Act of 1993 increased tax rates, and widened the spread between the highest rate of tax on capital gains (28%) and ordinary income (39.6%), but tax rates did not return to pre-1986 levels.

The risk of default has also increased, so it is important to exercise care in choosing bonds. Municipal bonds, like corporate bonds, are rated by financial information services. The various rating services have different systems for describing the risk accompanying different municipal bonds; for example, the safest bonds are triple-A rated by one particular service. Some private companies offer insurance on municipal bonds, which enhances the bonds' ratings. Some of these companies include: Municipal Bond Investors Assurance Corporation, AMBAC Indemnity Corporation, and Financial Guaranty Insurance Company. However, if there are widespread municipal bond defaults, the insurers may not be able to satisfy all of their insurance obligations.

Factors to be considered when choosing a municipal bond include: (1) the interest rate paid, (2) the safety of the bond, and (3) the source of payment. Some bonds are secured by the issuing state's or city's entire budget, as well as its ability to increase taxes. Others are paid only from the revenues of a single source, and if that source is exhausted, default is a possibility. The innovative "pre-refunded" municipal is a notably safe investment with an above-average yield. When a bond is callable, the issuer can get the bond back at a call date by paying a specified amount, thus, depriving investors of future return. The issuer generally does this if interest rates have declined and new bonds can be issued at a lower rate. However, bonds cannot be called before their call dates, no matter what has happened to interest rates in the interim. But when municipalities plan a new issue of bonds at a lower rate, they "pre-refund" the earlier issue of bonds by buying and maintaining a reserve of U.S. government obligations large enough to call the first set of bonds at the earliest call date.[4]

"Coupon" bonds pay interest in specified amounts on specified dates. A zero-coupon bond is sold at a deep discount because no interest is payable during the lifetime of the bond. Instead, the bond is redeemable for far more than its original cost. Zero-coupon bonds are useful for producing a lump sum at a defined time. For instance, a middle-aged person might buy zero-coupon bonds to produce a lump sum at retirement, suitable for buying a unit in a retirement community. One disadvantage of zero-coupon bonds is the current taxation of "phantom income" (see page 271, below, for a discussion of original issue discount). Another disadvantage is significant price volatility, which gives rise to a real risk of loss if zero-coupon bonds are sold before maturity.

Any bond trade can result in a loss. However, zero-coupon bond prices change more often and less predictably than the prices of coupon bonds. A bond's price is largely related to its yield and safety. If a bond provides more interest than other comparably safe bonds, its price will rise above face value and the bond will trade at a premium. A bond yielding less than normal interest will trade at a discount. The same is true over time. If a bond is purchased that reflects contemporary interest rates of 6.5%, an owner who wants to sell it when interest rates for comparable obligations are 10% will have to offer a deep discount to attract a buyer.

Bonds are also available in a variety of short and long terms. If the goal is to hold the bonds for income, long-term bonds are riskier (because if interest rates rise, the bond will pay a below-market rate and trade below face value). However, these bonds may also present an opportunity to lock in a high interest rate if interest rates later trend down. Shorter-term bonds require more monitoring but give the owner the chance to redeem the bonds at maturity and reinvest.

In January, 1997, the U.S. Treasury added a new tool to the older investor's tool kit: inflation-indexed 10-year bonds, known as Treasury Inflation-Protection Securities. The difference between these bonds and conventional 10-year Treasuries is that the indexed bond's rate is expressed in "real" (post-inflation) terms.

The initial return for the first issue of the inflation-indexed Treasury bonds is slightly under 3.5% (at a time when ordinary 10-year Treasuries carried interest of 6.64%). However, the principal of the inflation-indexed bond will be adjusted for inflation (or deflation) during the life of the bond. The interest rate is fixed, but the semiannual interest payments will vary as the principal amount of the bond is adjusted for any inflation or deflation that occurs between payment dates. As inflation rises, the principal of the inflation-indexed bond will increase, which will also result in higher interest payments. Deflation will have the opposite effect on a bond's principal and interest. Furthermore, at maturity, an additional payment is provided if the bond's inflation-adjusted principal amount is less than the bond's principal amount on the bond's issue date. This feature ensures the investor of the return of his or her principal amount. If the issue of 10-year inflation-indexed bonds is successful, the Treasury plans to supplement it with five-year and 30-year indexed bonds.

Is an inflation-indexed bond a good choice? Yes, if inflation averages 3% a year or more for the next 10 years. If not, the bond will prove financially less rewarding than its conventional Treasury counterpart. Even so, if an anxious older investor derives peace of mind, the lower return may prove to be a good value. Cynics point out that the government controls the indexes and might manipulate them to avoid having to raise the rate of return.

Treasuries, of course, are not tax-exempt. Owners of inflation-indexed bonds will have to pay tax on the interest they receive — and on the additional amount added to the principal to account for inflation. Bond owners will pay tax on this amount each year, even though it will not actually be received until the bond matures. One strategy, therefore, would be to purchase the bonds for IRAs or other tax-deferred plans.

No doubt the secondary market will soon provide inflation-indexed "strips," divided into interest and principal payments. The principal payments, like zero-coupon bonds, could be good choices for retirement planning because a known amount of money will become payable at the time that the investor requires an infusion of funds.

Real Estate Investments

There is at least one piece of real estate that belongs in nearly every financial plan for the elderly: a home. If the older person is or becomes a homeowner, he or she knows that eviction by a landlord is impossible. The older person also knows he or she will not be subject to increasing rent. It is true that real estate taxes may increase unpredictably, but many states provide at least some measure of tax relief for elderly homeowners. While older homeowners who have adjustable-rate mortgages are at risk of increasing mortgage rates and higher payments, they also stand to benefit from decreases in interest rates. These considerations will be largely irrelevant if the older person owns his or her home free and clear, or under a fixed-rate mortgage.

Another important argument in favor of home ownership is the favorable treatment awarded to homesteads under Medicaid law. Although Medicaid is a program for the indigent, Medicaid beneficiaries are allowed to own homes. In fact, a tenant who contemplates a Medicaid application should know that he or she is permitted by law to use the assets to buy a home (a house, cooperative apartment, or condominium unit). A homeowner has a legal right to take funds that would otherwise count for Medicaid purposes and make them exempt by "trading up" to a more expensive home, or by fixing up the home.

This would be an especially good strategy for a homeowner who is ill but prefers home care to entering a nursing home. Certain modifications can make the home suitable for a frail person, such as adding rails in the bathroom, a second bathroom on the ground floor, a wheelchair ramp, an elevator, or a staircase lift. Adding a separate entrance or a kitchenette can create a desirable living space for a home attendant, nurse, or family member caregiver. Also note that there is no Medicaid penalty for transferring ownership of the home to a child who lived in the home for a two-year period and provided care that permitted the sick parent to defer nursing home entrance.

Older investors also need a great deal of liquidity, because the need to pay for medical care can arise at any time. Even if the care will eventually be paid for by medical insurance, Medicare or Medicaid, it is frequently necessary for the patient or patient's family to make immediate cash payments and later apply for reimbursement. If the older person's major asset is an apartment building or a piece of land that might eventually be used as an industrial park, it may be impossible to find a buyer at the time of need. If a buyer is found under these circumstances, he or she may take advantage of the older person's need for fast cash and pay less than the real value of the property.

Attempts have been made to make real estate more like stocks or bonds by assembling publicly traded portfolios of property. This could be accomplished by the sale of units in real estate limited partnerships (RELPs) and real estate investment trusts (REITs). However, these investments are by no means as liquid as publicly traded stocks and bonds. There may be no buyers at all, or offers only at very low prices when an investor wants to cash out.

The REIT is defined by Sections 856-859 of the Internal Revenue Code. A REIT must have at least 100 shareholders, and be managed by one or more trustees or directors. A REIT is not a corporation and generally is not subject to corporate tax. REITS can invest directly in real estate, mortgages, or the leasing of real property. A mortgage trust is a REIT that specializes in mortgages, while an equity trust does direct investment. A hybrid trust does both.

A further problem is that disclosure deficiencies have been identified in certain RELPs, where partners were assured that the investment was prospering when in fact it lost worth or became worthless. If the value of a RELP investment has declined severely, the investor is faced with an important decision. He or she must decide whether to try to bail out (knowing that there will be a heavy loss) or to hang on, hoping that the investment will regain its initial value and not become entirely worthless. In case of severe loss, a securities lawyer should be consulted to see if the client was the victim of fraud or securities offenses, and if suing or joining an existing class action is worthwhile.

Mortgage securities backed by the U.S. government, or agencies thereof, are investments that are of interest to many senior citizens. These investments are technically known as pass-through securities, and include: Ginnie Maes, which are issued by the Government National Mortgage Association; Fannie Maes, issued by the Federal National Mortgage Association; and Freddie Macs, issued by the Federal Home Loan Mortgage Company. These investments can be purchased directly or through mutual funds, and they provide a share in both principal and interest of a pool of fixed-rate mortgages. Ginnie Maes are directly guaranteed by the U.S. government; the remaining two are implicitly but not directly guaranteed.

There is a remote risk that the mortgagors will default, which increases as the economy declines. Investors may also be disconcerted if they invest in these mortgage securities, only to find that they are kicked out of the game just when they are beginning to enjoy it. That is, payments to mortgage security investors are not just income; rather, they include payments of principal as well. But if mortgage rates drop, homeowners are likely to get a cheaper source of financing and pay off the mortgage. The investor gets a portion of the principal, and when no principal remains, the mortgage pool terminates. This is so even if the termination occurs long before the 30-year term of the mortgages expire. Investors who get unexpected prepayments have not lost their capital, but they do have to scramble for an equally productive way to reinvest. When interest rates are fairly low and falling, or many people are losing their jobs and suffering mortgage foreclosure, mortgage securities could be less attractive to the older investor.

TAX IMPLICATIONS OF INVESTMENTS

Before the 1980s, investors had to make a dramatic choice between seeking income (which could be taxed at the highest rate assessed on ordinary income) and investing for appreciation (capital gains were taxed at a much lower rate than ordinary income). Under current tax rates, high-income taxpayers have a noticeable difference between capital gains and ordinary income tax rates, but the distinction will not have much practical significance for low-and-moderate-income taxpayers.

Section 61(a)(7) of the Internal Revenue Code states that dividends must be included in gross income. The Code defines a dividend as limited to a payment made to shareholders with respect to stock ownership, out of a corporation's current or accumulated earnings and profits (E&P). If a distribution is not made from E&P, it is generally not taxed as a dividend. Instead, it is first applied to and reduces the owner's adjusted basis in the stock. When adjusted basis reaches zero, the remaining excess of adjusted basis is taxed as gain, usually as a capital gain. Under Section 316(b)(1) of the Code, amounts paid or credited to life insurance policyholders, and described as dividends, are not taxed as dividends if they have the effect of partially refunding the insurance premium. However, life insurance "dividends" are taxed as dividends if they exceed the consideration paid for the policy.

An individual (noncorporate) taxpayer who sells stocks or bonds will have a capital gain or loss. The tax impact depends on the balance between that transaction and other capital transactions. Roughly speaking, a capital asset is an investment asset, rather than inventory or depreciable property used in the taxpayer's business. A capital asset must be held for a year or more to generate long-term loss or gain. The taxpayer must examine all short-term transactions to see if there is an overall loss or gain, while doing the same for long-term transactions. Net capital gain equals net long-term gain minus net short-term loss.

If the taxpayer has nothing but short-term capital gain, the gain is taxed at the same rate as ordinary income.

Under Section 1211 of the Code, losses are deductible in any year only to the extent of gains, plus the excess of the loss over gain or $3,000 ($1,500 for married taxpayers filing separate returns), whichever is lower. If the taxpayer has additional losses, they can be carried over to following tax years.

Income from corporate bonds is fully taxable as ordinary income. Under Section 150 of the Code, interest on municipal bonds is not federally taxable unless: (1) the bond is a nonqualified bond issued for certain private activities as described in the Code; (2) the bond is an arbitrage bond, issued so the issuer can invest the proceeds in higher yielding investments; or (3) the bond fails tests of financing and guarantees set out in Section 149 of the Code. Interest paid on U.S. Savings Bonds in Series E, EE, H, or HH is fully taxable; however, certain taxpayers may be able to claim an exclusion for Series EE bond interest used to pay higher education expenses, as defined by Section 135(a) of the Code.

Older people who own tax-exempt municipal bonds must consider the impact of Section 86 of the Code. If the taxpayer's "modified adjusted gross income," plus half his Social Security benefits, exceeds $25,000 ($32,000 for a joint return), the taxpayer must include up to 85% of the Social Security benefit in gross income. "Modified adjusted gross income," for this purpose, includes tax-exempt interest.

Zero-coupon bonds do not pay current income, yet taxpayers are subject to current taxation, unless the bond is tax-exempt or has a maturity under one year. Under Section 1272(a) of the Code, the taxpayer must pay tax each year on a portion of the bond's original issue discount (OID), sometimes referred to as "phantom income." Section 1273(a) defines OID as the excess of the redemption price at maturity minus the issue price.

Because a bond has the potential to produce income and to appreciate, a market has been developing for stripped bonds and stripped coupons. A bond is stripped when the right to receive income is separated from the underlying bond obligation. This occurs when the coupons from the bond are detached and traded separately from the bond. Tax consequences of this method of investment are addressed by Section 1286 of the Code. The section generally states that the purchase of a bond after July 1, 1982 with one or more coupons stripped is treated as a purchase of a bond with OID. The purchase of the stripped coupons is similarly treated.

Many older investors choose to add residential mortgage pools to their investment portfolios. These securities, sometimes called Fannie Maes, Ginnie Maes, and Freddie Macs, after the initials of the federal agencies that package and supervise the investments, are trusts that own groups of home mortgages for resale to investors. The investors receive regular payments, (e.g., monthly payments from the "Fannie Maes" guaranteed by the Federal National Mortgage Association) consisting of part interest and part repayment of mortgage principal.

Income derived from these mortgage-backed securities is subject to the general rules of Section 61 (regarding gross income) of the Code. More detailed guidance can be found in some older Revenue Rulings: Rev. Rul. 84-10, 1984-1 CB 155 (for Fannie Maes); Rev. Rul. 74-169, 1974-1 CB 147 (for "Ginnie Maes" guaranteed by the Government National Mortgage Association); and Rev. Rul. 81-203, 1981-2 CB 137 (for "Freddie Macs" guaranteed by the Federal Home Loan Mortgage Company).

The older investor is typically a cash basis taxpayer. Therefore, he or she must report mortgage interest, prepayment penalties, assumption fees, and late payment charges received from a mortgage pool investment in the year they are received. They also may have to deduct their share of the mortgage pool fee for servicing the mortgage (i.e., monthly service charges, late payment charges assumption fees, and prepayment penalties attributable to their pool interests) in the year the payment is made.

ANNUITIES

Generally speaking, an annuity is any arrangement under which an individual receives a continuing stream of payments. Internal Revenue Code section 72 governs the tax treatment of annuities — including withdrawals from IRA accounts and payments of pensions in annuity form. However, this discussion will focus on another topic governed by Section 72: commercial annuities sold by insurance companies, brokerages, and banks. The term "annuity" will be used to refer to commercial annuities rather than all continuing payments coming within the ambit of Section 72. It will further be assumed that the person investing in the annuity will be the annuitant, rather than that one person has purchased an annuity which will make payments to another person.

The annuity is, perhaps, the classic investment choice for the safety- and income-oriented, middle-aged and older investor. (The Code imposes a penalty tax of 10% of the amount of the withdrawal in addition to the income tax on most withdrawals taken from an annuity account prior to age 59½, so young investors tend to avoid annuities unless they can afford to be very patient.) The advantages of the annuity are professional management, deferral of taxation on accumulations until withdrawals begin, and a continuing stream of income that can be tailored to a variety of financial, estate, and Medicaid planning objectives.

In the late 1990s, annuities have acquired new roles and new rationales for purchase. Thanks to the booming stock market, high returns are often available (although some investors still prefer to invest in stocks or mutual funds rather than annuities). Because of the risk that transfers for Medicaid planning purposes will be deemed criminal (see page 179), annuities can be an attractive choice because they permit the conversion of excess resources (which would make Medicaid eligibility impossible) into additional income (which can be spent down, permitting Medicaid eligibility in a "medically needy" state—see page 167).

States vary in the way they characterize annuity transactions, but most of them will accept the argument that there has been no transfer (and therefore no criminal transfer!), as long as the annuity is "actuarially sound": in other words, that the annuity payments are large enough to represent a fair exchange for the purchase price of the annuity.

The state Medicaid agency may also want special "Medicaid-friendly" provisions written into the annuity. For instance, the agency may insist on being made the death beneficiary of a single person's annuity, or may insist on being a contingent beneficiary if the Medicaid recipient's spouse is the first to die. The agency may also insist that the annuitant surrender the right to change the beneficiary. Depending on local insurance law, the state Medicaid agency's position, and the number of annuitants involved, these changes may be carried out informally — or they may require an amendment in the terms of the annuity itself, which will have to be approved by the state insurance commissioner.

A 1996 Private Letter Ruling from the IRS (PLR 9644016) addressed a long standing question about annuity investments, allowing the owner of an annuity to make a tax-free exchange under Section 1035 and replace one annuity with two annuities issued by the same insurer — as long as all that is received is the replacement annuities, not money or other consideration.

Classifying Annuities

Annuities can be categorized in various ways. One basic distinction is between the "immediate" annuity and the "deferred" annuity. In an immediate annuity, funds are transferred to an insurer (or other annuity provider, this discussion assumes that it is an insurer), and an immediate stream of payments begins. This course of action might be chosen by someone who has a lump sum to invest (e.g., insurance proceeds from the death of a spouse) and wants income right away. It might also be chosen by someone who has excess assets for Medicaid purposes, who wants to shift the assets into a stream of income that will not preclude Medicaid eligibility. (This strategy will not work in a state where Medicaid is denied to any individual with income above the Medicaid qualifying level, but in the majority of the states, a person with excess income can qualify for Medicaid by spending down the excess income on health care.)

A deferred annuity is an arrangement under which one or more payments is made to the insurer, in exchange for the insurer's promise to commence payments at a specified later date. The date is the "annuity starting date"; until that time, the annuity is in the "accumulation phase." A deferred annuity might be chosen by a middle-aged person interested in providing for a comfortable retirement — or a person who will need college tuition for kids when he or she is over 60. Immediate annuities are purchased in return for a single premium; deferred annuities can be purchased for a single premium or for an initial premium plus later deposits.

An annuity can be either *fixed* or *variable*. A fixed annuity is conceptually similar to a certificate of deposit; the insurer stipulates a rate of return (e.g., 6.75%) and a period of time (typically one or three years). The annuity will earn interest at the stated rate for the year or three years; at the end of that time, it generally earns the market rate of return, unless the annuitant elects a further guarantee period. A variable annuity is conceptually similar to an investment in a mutual fund family: the annuitant is given a number of investment choices, and return on the annuity depends on the market performance of the annuitant's choice.

In many instances, variable annuities are an excellent investment for the older client, but they are not a flexible investment: if the underlying subaccounts that fund the annuity (the mutual fund-type investment mechanisms) do not perform well, it is usually impractical to withdraw funds from the annuity because there may be tax penalties and are likely to be back-end loads imposed by the company issuing the annuity. So the only option is to switch to another subaccount within the same annuity, but the issuer is likely to limit the number of permitted switches. In any case, the issuer's other subaccounts may perform just as poorly.

Furthermore, issuers vary widely in the expenses charged against annuities; a mid-1993 survey by Morningstar Inc.'s Variable Annuity Report showed fund expenses ranging from 0.54% to 1.30%—and a three-year history of after-expense returns ranging from 1.72% to 14.59%![5] However, these differences in performance should be kept in perspective: for a person who invests $10,000 in an annuity, a 1% difference in return means a difference in income of only about $2 a week. It is certainly not worthwhile to encounter a heavy surrender charge to switch to another company's annuity, merely in order to gain a few hundred dollars a year—particularly since the second company's annuity may not perform especially well after the change.

Another important characteristic is the number of annuitants. The two major categories are the *single-life* annuity, where payments are made for a particular person's life, and the *joint and survivor* annuity, where payments are made until the second of the two annuitants has died.

Annuities also vary in their payment options. A deferred annuity can be collected in lump-sum form, but the most common annuity outcome is a series of payments. Annuitants have a wide variety of payment options:

- *Term certain* (e.g., 10 years). The insurer agrees to make payments each month for 10 years; if the annuitant dies during this time, the payments will be made to the designated beneficiary (or the annuitant's estate, if no beneficiary was designated).

- *Single life* (or "straight life"). The insurer agrees to make payments as long as the annuitant lives. This is a great deal for an annuitant who lives longer than expected — but if the annuitant dies prematurely, no further payments will be made.

- *Single life, with a refund provision.* If payments under an annuity purchased for a single premium add up to less than the single premium by the time the annuitant dies, payments to the beneficiary named by the annuitant will be continued until the entire premium has been recovered. A deferred annuity may also offer a refund provision.

- *Single life, subject to a term certain.* The insurer will make annuity payments throughout the annuitant's life. However, if the annuitant dies before the term certain (e.g., 10 years) payments will continue until the end of the period.

Similar payment options are available in joint and survivor annuities, except that two lives are involved. For instance, payment could continue after the second annuitant has died, or could cease after the second annuitant's death unless payments have been made for a term certain (e.g., 10 years).

An important decision in selecting a joint and survivor annuity is whether payments will be level (the survivor receives the same benefit that was paid while the deceased annuitant was alive) or will decline to 2/3 or 1/2 of the original level when one annuitant dies. Of course, the initial benefit under a level payout is smaller than the payout would be if a 2/3 or 1/2 option were chosen, assuming an equal amount of premiums. An argument can be made either way. Two really cannot live as cheaply as one, so a two-person household should require more income; but the effect of inflation and the loss of other income attributable to the deceased annuitant may make it worthwhile to maintain the higher benefit level.

There are many practical implications of the selection of a payment option. Life annuity payments are calculated on an actuarial basis, involving the annuitant's (or annuitants') life expectancy. The longer the life expectancy, the smaller each payment will be. The annuitant must also surrender a certain amount of income for greater security: if the insurer must take greater risk by promising to make a refund, or by promising to extend the payments even if the annuitant dies sooner, it will decrease the amount of each payment.

Two other factors should be mentioned: fees (including surrender charges) and bailout provisions. Naturally insurers charge some level of fees to compensate for the costs of marketing and administering annuities. However, the fees vary, and the size and type of fee affects the real return derived from an annuity investment. Potential charges include:

- A front-end sales charge

- A fee for administration expenses

- A back-end charge when the contract is surrendered. If this feature is present, it will typically be structured as a surrender charge set at an initial level which declines over time and eventually phases out.

A bailout provision allows annuity purchasers to surrender their fixed annuity contracts without paying the surrender charge if, at any renewal date, the current interest level being offered falls below a certain percentage. In effect, the bailout provision is an insurance provision and increases the risk undertaken by the insurer, and it should therefore decrease the current interest rate offered under the contract. If it does not, this could be a sign that the insurer is taking too many chances and the annuity might be a poor investment.

Yet another consideration is whether the annuity can be used as a vehicle for ongoing investment or whether only a single premium, with no additional investments, will be accepted. The general rule is that deferred annuities will not accept additional contributions.

Liquidity is also a significant factor. Certainly, individuals in serious need of cash can always liquidate their entire interest in an annuity and accept whatever negative tax consequences and surrender charges are imposed. However, older clients who expect to need additional cash before they begin to receive an income stream from a deferred annuity may wish to select an annuity that permits more than the conventional annual 10% "free withdrawal" or one that allows them to receive continuing payments of interest income (appreciation on the annuity) before the capital deposit itself is annuitized.[6]

An increasing trend (although for variable annuities for a term of years only) is the "right of commutation," under which the investor can get his or her money back, calculated at a rate representing the remaining contract value.[7] Planners should be aware that an increasing number of annuity issuers impose a market value adjustment (MVA) when an annuity is surrendered, to cope with changes in the underlying portfolio value.[8]

Indexed Annuities

An important annuity variation, one that has gained prevalence and popularity since the mid-1990s, is the indexed annuity. In this variation, the return that the annuitant receives is linked to a securities index, such as the Standard & Poor's 500. The amount the annuitant receives therefore fluctuates with the market index, although if the annuitant is willing to pay an additional premium, the return will be subject to a floor (e.g., a minimum guarantee that the payment will never be less than 85% of the initial monthly payment). The death benefit equals the contract's cash value as of the annuitant's death.

Indexing can be performed in various ways, depending on whether values are adjusted annually or at the end of the initial term, and whether gains in a good year can be used to offset losses in annuity value during a year of poor investment performance. It must always be remembered that no stock market rally can continue forever! Consequently, today's annuity purchasers may later recover only slightly more than their base premium. An indexed annuity can be a valuable component in a balanced investment program, but it would be imprudent for an elderly person of modest means to sink all of those means into just one indexed annuity.[9]

Annuity Market Trends

In 1994, $27.3 billion in single premium deferred annuity premiums were recorded. This amount decreased 13% to about $24 billion in 1995 (still a very significant investment sector). In 1994, variable annuity premiums totaled $30.5 billion; this sector declined in 1995 also, to about $28 billion.

In 1995, total individual net annuity premiums were close to $76 billion, and total group net annuity premiums were about $82.5 billion. (The fact that group outweighed individual premiums is attributable to the heavy use of annuities in the management of qualified corporate pension plans.)

Probably, the decline was attributable to investors' excitement about buying individual stocks and mutual funds at a time when stock prices were reaching all-time peaks. Interest in longer-range, more conservative investment vehicles was somewhat overshadowed. Yet conservative investment vehicles are often precisely what investors in their fifties, sixties, or older need and want.

A traditional analysis is that variable annuity sales parallel mutual fund sales, though the trends are reflected in annuity sales six to nine months later. This held true in 1996, when variable annuity sales for the first nine months alone were $54.7 billion; the projection for the year is more than $70 billion. The total market value of the funds invested in variable annuities during the first three quarters of 1996 was more than $320 billion. The 94 companies that sold variable annuities (as compared to only 40 insurers selling variable annuities in 1990) offered their customers a total of 3,478 sub-accounts (investment choices).[10]

Recent Results

If a 45-year-old male placed $10,000 in one of the ten top-performing single premium deferred annuities (SPDAs) on January 1, 1991, he would have an actual accumulation value of about $15,000 and a surrender value of a few hundred dollars lower by 1995. During that time period, SPDAs typically guaranteed interest rates in the 3-4% range; the actual interest rate went down from about 8.25% in 1990 to 6% in 1995.[11]

Between the mid-eighties and the mid-nineties, the monthly payout from a single premium immediate annuity (SPIA) also decreased significantly: in 1986, the average payment from a $100,000 life SPIA (with a 10-year certain feature) was $986, with a 10% interest rate. In 1996, the average payout was down to $761/month and a 6% interest rate, because even though stock prices were high, interest rates paid on investments were low in that time period. (In 1996, the average payout on a joint and 100% survivor annuity, collected since 1992, was $620 a month.)[12]

An investment of $1,000 on January 1, 1991 in a flexible premium retirement annuity, made by a 45-year-old male who made deposits each year, would be guaranteed an interest rate of about 3-4%. If he chose one of the top 10 performing annuities in this category, his accumulation value in the fifth year would be about $6,200, and the actual surrender value close to or over $6,000.[13]

Product-based planners face a new challenge in annuity sales: not just consumer preferences and market trends, but new competition because banks have been granted the power to sell annuities. In 1996, banks held about one-third of the market for annuity sales. The planner will have to be able to respond by showing genuine superiority of the products he or she sells; a complete relationship, involving personal service and a diverse range of planning ideas and products; or both.

Sample Annuities

Annuities provide a great many variations and can be tailored to client needs in many ways. Consider these samples:

ANNUITY A is a single-premium fixed deferred annuity, joint and survivor with a 10-year certain period. Payments will begin December 3, 2007 and continue until the second annuitant dies, but in any case for 10 years. There is no initial issue fee or management charge, but the annuity is subject to a surrender charge of 7% the first year, declining by 1% a year until it phases out in the eighth year. The annuitant has elected a three-year guarantee period, during which time a 7.15% rate is guaranteed. The insurer does not offer a bailout provision.

ANNUITY B is a single-premium variable straight life deferred annuity. Payments begin April 9, 2004 for the life of the annuitant, with no refund provision. There is no initial issue fee or management charge, but the surrender charge is 8%, phasing out 1% a year until the ninth year. The annuitant was given a choice of six investment vehicles, and elected the "growth with capital preservation" vehicle rather than one of the riskier high-growth choices or the more conservative government obligation vehicle. The annuitant is allowed one "switch" between vehicles each year.

ANNUITY C is a single-premium immediate single-life annuity. Payments begin within one year of the creation of the contract. Monthly payments will be made throughout the lifetime of the annuitant; however, if he or she dies before ten years have elapsed, the monthly payment will be continued to the beneficiary named by the annuitant until the ten years have elapsed. The fixed/variable distinction is not involved because there is no accumulation period.

ANNUITY D does not exclude smokers — in fact, it is available ONLY for smokers, with payouts about 10% higher than the payouts under a conventional contract. (Of course, this is due to the fact that smokers can be expected to die younger than non-smokers.) This is a single-premium product, available as either an immediate or a deferred annuity. It can be issued at ages 50-85 (immediate) or 50-75 (deferred). The minimum single premium is $5000 for the deferred, $10,000 for the immediate annuity. Interest rates are readjusted monthly and were 6% plus a 1% bonus in September, 1996. The surrender charges phase down from 7% to 1% over seven years. The deferred annuity also includes a bonus of 1% for annuitization in contract years 4-7, 3.5% in years 8-10, and 1% in later years. (The bonus is not available in the first three years.)

ANNUITY E is a flexible-premium term (10-year) deferred annuity; the return is index-linked to the S&P. The initial deposit has a guaranteed value of 90% of the initial amount plus 3% interest, or 120% of the initial premium when the 10-year term ends. Additional deposits of $1000 or more are accepted, and the policyholder can create a regular investment program adding $100 or more at a time. The annuity carries a yearly administrative fee (1% of the initial deposit). Withdrawals of up to 10% of the annuity value are permitted each year without penalty, but there is a surrender charge for complete early surrender.

The value of the annuity when the 10-year term ends equals the total return and average annual return, which is reduced by the administration fee.

At the end of the term, policyholders can annuitize (they can annuitize at any time) or withdraw part or all of the balance, or they can roll the funds over for another 10 years. Ten percent of the premium vests every year, leading to a participation rate of 100% of the premium.

ANNUITY F is an indexed annuity with a guaranteed value roughly comparable to the yield of fixed annuities. However, every month a "participation rate" is calculated. Half of the difference between the S&P 500 Index and the fixed rate is added to the value, with no limit on how much the value can increase.

This single-premium annuity is purchased for seven years (minimum purchase $5,000), with a 7% bonus in the first year. Permitted issue ages go up to 75. The interest rate is guaranteed at 3% for the life of the policy or 133% of the premium payment. After the seven years, the holder can roll over the value of the contract for another seven-year term, take a lump sum, or annuitize. If the policy is surrendered for a lump sum, there is a 10% load (calculated based on the initial premium).

ANNUITY G, another single-premium indexed annuity, is available for one, three, or five-year terms and is sold up to age 75. The investment options for the holders include a stock index, a bond index, and a fixed-rate account. When the premium is deposited (minimum $5,000 deposit), it can be divided in any way among the three. At the end of the term, the indexed value of the account is calculated. The one-year annuity's increase in value is capped at 15%; there is no limit on the potential upside for three- or five-year terms. Interest rates are set each year, subject to a guaranteed minimum of 3%. Return of premium is guaranteed for all accounts, and a return of 104.4% of premium is guaranteed for five-year accounts.

There is no penalty for withdrawing the entire premium in the first 30 days of the contract, and there is no surrender charge for withdrawing partial or full account value within 30 days after a term ends. The fixed account never carries a surrender charge, but there is a surrender charge (3% to 7%, depending on the length of the annuity's term) for the market-sensitive stock and bond indexes. The surrender charge is waived if the owner has to spend 60 days or more in a health care facility (such as a nursing home).

ANNUITY H is a variable immediate annuity ($10,000 minimum premium) indexed to the S&P 500. A minimum monthly payment is guaranteed (85% of the initial payment amount), so the product will maintain a store of value even if the stock market declines seriously. The product will be sold to persons of any age, but the issuer does not recommend the product for persons over 80, believing that they would be better served by a fixed annuity. The initial payment is made based on an assumed 4.5% annual interest rate; later payments are indexed.

The minimum payment guarantee requires a 1.25% one-time charge, and the basic sales charge is 4.5%, although it declines to 3.75% for premiums between $750,000 and $1 million. The annual fee is approximately 1.5%, divided into mortality/expense, administrative, and asset management components.

ANNUITY I is an SPDA, issued up to age 85. Interest rates are updated monthly. For the first seven years, the renewal rate will not drop lower than 1/2% below the preceding year's base rate. The renewal rate can never be more than 2% lower than the initial base rate — which is 6.2% plus a 1% bonus for the first year.

In addition to several annuitization options, holders can make annual, semi-annual, quarterly, or monthly withdrawals. Furthermore, if they want to access up to 10% of the value of the contract each year, no penalty is imposed. The surrender charge (phasing down from 7%) is waived when the annuity holder making the withdrawal is disabled or requires medical care.

Planning Strategies With Annuities

On the simplest level, it would seem that an annuity would be a good choice for a person who is expected to live longer than his or her actuarially predicted life expectancy — and a bad choice for a sick person, who will probably die sooner than the life expectancy tables would suggest. (A sick person would probably want a refund provision or a life/term certain payout even though these choices make the payment lower than a straight life annuity would provide.) However, there are subtle planning objectives that can be served with annuities.

Remember, Medicaid eligibility requires three things: not having excess resources, not having excess income (or spending down excess income, where permitted), and not having made prohibited transfers. Buying a commercial immediate annuity is not considered a transfer for Medicaid purposes, because there is no gratuitous element: the annuity buyer gets full value for the money surrendered. Furthermore, the cost of the annuity ceases to be an asset for the purchaser; he or she no longer has this money. Therefore, a person with excess assets who cannot "wait out" the penalty period may be very interested in purchasing an immediate annuity. Although people usually want to increase their income, a Medicaid applicant or beneficiary (especially one who lives in an "income cap" state) may want to simultaneously reduce income and benefit a family member. In that case, buying a joint and survivor annuity with a much younger family member (e.g., a child) as second annuitant would work out well. (Although it is conventional for joint and survivor annuities to be purchased by married couples, a non-spouse can be designated as second annuitant.) The Medicaid applicant/beneficiary removes assets from being considered "available" and impairing Medicaid eligibility. Furthermore, there is no prohibited transfer, and the beneficiary receives a small amount of income and knows that the child will continue to get income for life.

Another Medicaid planning possibility (especially for a person who will probably die soon) is to select a single-life immediate annuity with a refund provision or term certain, with the objective of passing along the refund or the remaining benefits to a beneficiary. But this must be done cautiously: If the beneficiary is a spouse and he or she is likely to apply for Medicaid, any lump-sum refund is likely to constitute excess available resources, and any continuing payment may be excess income.

California elder law specialist Mark Woolpert contributed some interesting ideas about annuity planning to the 1990 National Academy of Elder Law Attorneys conference. He suggested that the first planning step when a lump sum is received by a person about to make a Medicaid application is to fund the community spouse resource allowance (the amount of resources that can be transferred to protect the spouse who is not going into a nursing home; see Chapter 7). Some or all of the remaining excess assets can be used to buy an immediate annuity in the name of the healthy spouse. The annuity income will not be considered available to the sick spouse, because Medicaid looks at the "name on the check" to decide who owns income received by married people. Confer with the attorney in the planning team to see if this strategy will work under your state's Medicaid rules.

A deferred annuity that is still in the accumulation phase may have negative Medicaid consequences, because the value that the owner of the contract would receive in return for surrendering it is treated as an available asset.

PLANNING TIP: As discussed on page 274, the purchase of an annuity may make sense in a Medicaid plan where the couple has a lot of assets but comparatively low income. Check with a competent attorney; it may be possible to use excess assets to purchase an annuity that brings the healthy spouse's income up to the Community Spouse Income Allowance, without affecting the sick spouse's eligibility for Medicaid benefits.

Private Annuities

Another Medicaid planning possibility is for a senior citizen with excess assets to use a private immediate annuity to maximize income and shift ownership of excess assets without Medicaid penalty. Under a private annuity arrangement, ownership of assets (e.g., real estate, a stock portfolio) is changed from the senior citizen to a family member, friend, or charity in exchange for the recipient's promise to make regular payments.

Private Letter Ruling 9253031 (October 2, 1992) illustrates some important private annuity issues (although Private Letter Rulings do not have precedential effect for other taxpayers). The taxpayer's father set up a $19 million trust benefiting the 84-year-old taxpayer, who received all the trust income. The taxpayer wanted to deposit $5 million in marketable securities into the trust and to get a private annuity in return. The transaction was treated as a $1.3 million gift to the trust remainderman. That figure was calculated as follows: the relevant interest rate was 7.2%. The "table" factor for a single-life annuity for an 84-year-old was 4.5. That meant that the annuity's present value was $1.1 million, where the fund would be used up after 5.6 years of making the annuity payments. IRS tables give a factor of 3.4 for an 84-year-old person's right to receive $1 a year for life or for 5.6 years. Multiplied by the $1.1 million present value, this yields a present value of $3.7 million for the taxpayer's retained interest. The remaining $1.3 million must therefore be a gift to the remainderman.

If the regular payments are at least equal to the amounts calculated on the basis of the appropriate IRS annuity table, there has been no "transfer" for Medicaid purposes; if the regular payments are less than the annuity table figure, the transaction has both a gift and an annuity element, and the gift is a transfer for Medicaid purposes.

Private annuities are especially useful for people who are seriously ill and require extensive chronic care. They are likely to die before the life expectancy predicted by the IRS tables — which means that the family member, friend, or charity gets an especially "good deal" by getting valuable assets in return for a small number of annuity payments. They are also useful for people who are not married when they make a Medicaid plan and therefore cannot use the spousal protection provisions. But they will not work in every case. The legal fees may be too high for a small private annuity to be practical. The recipient of the property may not be able to afford the regular payments, especially if the annuitant is very old and the property is very valuable (so a large value must be allocated over the small number of payments predicted by the annuity tables). The private annuity may produce too much income for the elder, which will either preclude Medicaid eligibility or require the elder to spend down hundreds or thousands of dollars every month. The private annuity idea is worth discussing with your client, but it is a sophisticated planning device that must *never* be used without professional legal and accounting advice about income, gift, and estate tax as well as Medicaid consequences.

The IRS annuity tables (Code §7520) cannot be used if the private annuity purchaser is terminally ill (has an incurable illness or other deteriorating physical condition and at least 50 percent probability of dying within one year) — but the tables can be used if the person is merely ill, and not likely to live out a normal lifespan but also not likely to die shortly. Also, be sure to use the correct set of tables: the current tables were issued in 1989.

Annuities vs. Alternatives

There are many situations in which a client must choose between a commercial annuity and another product that would serve similar objectives. The basic tool in the decision-making process is an analysis of risk and return. What return can reasonably be predicted each year from each alternative? What will the client get to keep after taxes and expenses are paid? How will the return compare to the inflation rate? What is the investment track record of the party offering the product? What is the risk that the offeror will become bankrupt or unable to fulfill its obligations? Is there a federal or private guarantee of the offeror's obligations — and how large is the guarantee fund, and how does it compare to the demands that could be made on it if financial failures become widespread?

Under Code section 72, commercial annuities, IRAs, and qualified pension plans all share a tax advantage: taxpayers do not have to pay tax each year on the enhancement in value of their balances. This tax advantage is granted to motivate retirement planning, not to give young taxpayers a tax-free savings account. Therefore, a penalty tax is imposed on withdrawals before age 59½ unless the taxpayer fits into one of several statutory exceptions. Employers are entitled to a deduction for amounts properly contributed to qualified plans. Employees who are not covered by an employer-sponsored retirement plan may take a deduction for IRA contributions, but the deduction is quite limited and cannot exceed $2,000 per person per year ($4,000 for a married couple with one employed and one homemaker spouse) for tax years beginning after 1996. Furthermore, IRA contributions in excess of the permitted amounts are also subject to a penalty excise tax.

Amounts used to purchase commercial annuities are not tax deductible, but annuity purchasers can contribute large amounts to fund their future financial security. It is probably good strategy for those who are entitled to an IRA deduction to make the maximum contribution and claim the maximum deduction they are allowed — and also to purchase annuities if they fit into the investment plan. The limits on IRA funding make IRAs a supplement to, rather than a substitute for, a retirement investment plan for moderate- to high-income individuals.

Under ERISA, the federal law governing pensions, the normal method of paying the pension of a married retiree generally is a joint and survivor annuity. If the employee wants any other form of payout, he or she must get the written consent of the non-employee spouse. Plans are permitted but not required to offer a lump-sum payout option. Employees who select the lump-sum payout must then make investment decisions; one possibility is to purchase a commercial annuity. The question then becomes how the commercial annuity stacks up compared to the joint and survivor benefit offered by the employer (which is, in itself, an annuity). Buying an annuity gives the purchaser more choices: He or she can select a single-life or joint and survivor payment form, with timing options that affect the size of the benefit. For instance, a straight single-life annuity will pay a higher monthly benefit than a joint and survivor annuity. By choosing a commercial annuity of this type, the retiree will maximize current income but will lessen the income available to the surviving spouse. If the retiree wants a commercial joint and survivor annuity, the questions are whether the insurer offers a better deal than the employer, and what the comparative financial status is of the employer and the insurance company. (See page 226 for a discussion of new rules for the taxation of retirement income, passed in 1996.)

What about lump-sum payments of life insurance death benefits? The beneficiary can elect a "settlement option," having the insurer make payments over time — typically, monthly payments. The lump sum can also be used to purchase an annuity from the same or a different insurer. Here, the question is which choice gives a better rate of return, and which is safer. (See Chapter 2 for more discussion of settlement options.)

TAXATION OF INVESTMENT ANNUITIES

(This discussion centers on commercial annuities, although IRAs are also covered by Code section 72.)

The fundamental rule of annuity taxation is that recipients of benefits received "as an annuity" will not be taxed on the portion of each payment that merely returns their original investment; only the portion of the payment that represents interest earned on the original investment will be taxed. Until the original investment has been fully recovered, each annuity payment will be multiplied by an "exclusion ratio" to determine the taxable amount. After the recovery of the original investment, 100% of each annuity payment will constitute taxable income.

An arrangement combining annuities and life insurance (e.g., a "combination plan" bundling an immediate annuity with a 10-pay life insurance policy, with premiums paid out of income generated by the annuity) will be taxed as life insurance if the arrangement is deemed under state law to be a single contract paying a single integrated death benefit. If the arrangement does not fit the state-law definition of "life insurance," it will be taxed as two separate contracts, one taxed as life insurance, and the other under the annuity rules. (The "combination plan" given above fits the definition of life insurance.)

Annuity Starting Date

"Annuity starting date" is a legal term of art and is not necessarily the date of the first annuity payment. Instead, Code section 72(c) defines annuity starting date as the first day of the first period for which an amount is received as an annuity under the contract. The regulations expand on this definition by defining the annuity starting date as the *later* of the date the obligations under the annuity contract become fixed, or the first day of the monthly, quarterly, annual, or other payment period which ends on the date of the first payment.

If an annuity has been sold or otherwise transferred for valuable consideration, the starting date is the first day of the first period for which the transferee collects annuity payments. If it has been exchanged for another contract (see page 248, below), the starting date is the first day of the first period in which annuity payments are received under the *new* contract.

Investment in the Contract

Code section 72(c) defines "investment in the contract" as the total of consideration (e.g., premiums) paid for the contract, reduced by any amount already received under the contract but not included in the recipient's gross income (e.g., return premiums, dividends, unrepaid loans). If the annuity contains a refund feature, the Code mandates that investment in the contract must be reduced by the actuarial value (as of the annuity starting date) of the refund feature.

Investment in the contract is computed as of the annuity starting date or the date of the first payment, whichever is later, so loans, dividends, and other amounts received after the starting date or first payment will not influence the computation of investment in the contract or the exclusion ratio. If the annuity includes both investment before July 1986 and later investment (e.g., the annuity was not a single-premium annuity and was purchased before July 1986 under an arrangement permitting subsequent premium payments which were in fact made after July 1986), an election to treat these sums separately may be made.

Exclusion Ratio

The exclusion ratio is calculated by dividing investment in the contract by expected return, both calculated as of the annuity starting date. Expected return for a term annuity is the payment amount times the number of payments. Expected return for a life annuity is found by multiplying the life expectancy figure from IRS tables by one year's annuity payments. The tables set forth life expectancies for various ages, under various conditions of annuity payments (straight life, life subject to a term certain, etc.). A joint and survivor annuity has only one exclusion ratio, based on the aggregate life expectancies of both annuitants, but each annuitant applies the ratio to the payments he or she receives, either as a joint annuitant or a survivor.

Annuity investors who began receiving payments before January 1, 1987 and who live longer than their life expectancy as set forth in the government table can use the exclusion ratio on all payments, thus deriving an additional tax benefit if they are especially long-lived. For annuity investors who begin receiving benefits after 1986, the exclusion ratio applies (and, thus, a portion of each payment is not taxable) only until the investor's investment has been recovered. Payments received after this are fully taxable. If the annuitant dies before the original investment has been recovered, any beneficiary who receives payments under the annuity may exclude a portion of the payments equal to the unrecovered investment in the contract from his income.

Payments Not Received as an Annuity

As for payments not received as an annuity, for instance, cash withdrawals under an annuity contract or partial surrenders of an annuity contract, amounts that are received *before* the annuity starting date constitute taxable income for the recipient to the extent of income or interest earned on the investor's original investment in the contract. The calculation under Code section 72(e) is done by determining the cash value of the contract just before the surrender (without adjustment for surrender charges). Basically, amounts received are taxed as income first and as a return of basis second. Thus, withdrawals are taxable until the interest earned on the annuity has been completely withdrawn. Subsequent withdrawals are considered a tax-free return of basis. For this purpose, Code section 72(c) defines investment in the contract as the aggregate of premiums or other consideration already paid, minus any amount already received tax-free under the contract.

Annuity Sales and Exchanges

In the simplest case, an individual purchases an annuity and holds it until all scheduled payments have been made. However, there are circumstances under which an individual will sell an annuity (for instance, to raise cash in an emergency) or exchange annuities (perhaps if another insurer offers a better deal, or the owner is concerned about the financial soundness of the issuer of the annuity).

Code section 1035 permits a tax-free exchange of a life insurance contract for another life insurance contract, an endowment contract, or an annuity. Endowment contracts can be exchanged tax-free for endowment contracts or annuities, but annuities can be exchanged tax-free only for other annuities, not for life insurance or endowment contracts.

Regulations provide that a new exclusion ratio must be established whenever an annuity contract is transferred for valuable consideration or exchanged for another annuity contract after payments have commenced under a life income or installment option.

If an annuity contract is exchanged for another annuity contract after the old contract's annuity starting date (whether by an owner or the estate of the owner), investment in the new contract equals the actual value of consideration paid by the transferee, plus premiums and other consideration paid after the transfer by the transferee, but minus amounts received before the annuity starting date by the transferee and not included in his or her income for tax purposes.

If an annuity is sold or surrendered under circumstances that do not constitute a tax-free exchange, the former owner of the annuity contract is taxed on the excess of the consideration received over the former owner's adjusted basis in the contract that was sold or surrendered.

For this purpose, adjusted basis (tax value) equals consideration paid by the former owner before the sale, reduced (but not below zero) by any tax-free distributions already received by the taxpayer. If a taxpayer sells or surrenders a single premium annuity contract for a term certain, or that has a refund feature and receives less than his or her adjusted basis in the contract, the taxpayer reports an ordinary loss equal to the premiums paid and taxable distributions already received, minus consideration received for the sale or surrender.

Annuities in the Estate

As a basic prerequisite for qualifying for annuity treatment under the Code, an annuity contract issued after January 18, 1985 must provide for payments after the death of the annuitant before the entire interest has been distributed. If the annuitant dies before the annuity starting date, his or her entire interest must be distributed in five years or less. (However, if any portion of the annuity is payable to or for the benefit of a designated beneficiary and begins within one year of the annuitant's death, the interest may be distributed over the life of that beneficiary.) If the death occurs on or after the annuity starting date, but before the entire interest in the contract has been distributed, the insurer must continue to distribute the balance at least as rapidly as before death. For instance, if monthly payments were made, the insurer can offer a lump-sum settlement or continue the monthly payments to the beneficiary, but cannot drop back to an annual payment schedule or extend the number of payments to be made.

Also note that payments made under a commercial annuity to a surviving spouse or other beneficiary of a deceased annuitant are subject to withholding (at wage rates, if they are periodic payments, otherwise at 10%) unless the payee elects in writing not to have taxes withheld. Of course, the payee must be advised of the need to increase tax payments (and, if necessary, make estimated tax payments) if annuity payments are received and withholding is waived.

Code section 2039 provides that the gross estate of a decedent includes the value of payments made to a beneficiary under an annuity contract because the beneficiary survived the decedent. Payments includable under this provision include lump-sum or annuity payments to a survivor under a joint and survivor annuity and payments made to a beneficiary because the decedent died before the expiration of a term certain.

The decedent's estate includes the value of the annuity or other payment to be received by the beneficiary, reduced by the decedent's contributions to the purchase price of the annuity contract — not the annuity benefits received by the decedent during his or her life.

ASSET ALLOCATION PATTERNS

It is impossible to give simple formulas for asset allocation. At any given moment, clients differ in their affluence, ability to manage money, interest in managing money, personal preferences, estate plans, risk tolerance, and investment goals. Over time, market conditions, tax laws, and Medicaid laws change. Simple formulas cannot accommodate these pervasive variations and changes.

However, certain principles can be stated and certain patterns can be observed. Diversification, a basic investment principle at all ages, is particularly important for older investors. If too much of the client's money is concentrated in a single investment or even a single investment sector, economic changes could lead to serious harm that cannot be compensated for during the investor's remaining lifespan. Remember, older investors usually need all their funds to finance their lifestyle and implement their estate plans. Any loss of principal can gravely compromise these goals, so it is usually worthwhile to sacrifice a certain degree of return to maintain safety.

The exception to this generalization would be a pre-retiree or "young-old", healthy investor who has accumulated enough assets to be able to invest in both solid, safe investments and, also, "risk capital." The latter investment can be used to seek high returns or dramatic appreciation in value. This would be a good investment scheme for an investor who places a high value on creating a large estate for the surviving spouse and/or children, and who seeks appreciation.

The concept of asset allocation has become popular among investment professionals. In July 1990, for example, three experts interviewed by the New York Times discussed their model portfolios for retirees. All three models featured heavy investments in bond funds (ranging from 35-50%), with a preference for intermediate-term bond funds. They preferred the intermediate funds because short-term rates tend to be too volatile and hard to predict, while choosing a long-term bond investment could result in being subject to rates fixed far below market rates.

The asset allocation models described above also featured money market funds for safety and liquidity. Two of the models invested 25% in the money market, while the remaining model opted for 10%. The other major component of the models was the equity mutual fund. Two chose equity-income funds, while the third was comprised of growth stock funds, international funds, and 10% in an aggressive growth fund in order to give the older investor a chance to participate in dramatic market movements.[14]

In November 1990, seven members of the investment industry told the *Wall Street Journal* how they would invest a $400,000 lump-sum distribution. Again, everyone favored placing one-third to one-half of the investment in bonds or bond funds. Three of the seven plans called for a 10% nest egg in cash or cash equivalents, such as money market funds. One plan included a $55,000 investment in real estate, while another devoted 5% of the total sum to gold or gold stocks.

The rest of the plans were divided between stocks or stock funds, such as index funds, international funds, and funds seeking undervalued stocks or the stock of sound companies with temporary financial problems. Two plans called for starting with small equity investments, to be increased if market conditions became favorable.[15]

In 1992, the investment firm Bingham, Osborn & Scarborough (of San Francisco) drafted two sample senior citizen portfolios: one for a 65-year-old and one for an 80-year-old. Each portfolio was diversified, consisting of eight mutual funds of differing objectives (including an index fund to make sure that at least part of the portfolio would not trail the indexes). The difference between the two portfolios showed a shift away from non-U.S. stocks and small-firm growth stocks and toward a higher proportion of bond funds (80% versus 60%) in the "old-old" from the "young-old" portfolio.[16]

Investors should also consider the impact of greater risk tolerance on the investment of lump sums. For example, a safety-minded investor getting a 5% return on a $500,000 IRA would receive an annual income before taxes of $25,000 (5% of $500,000) or $15,000 after taxes, assuming a 40% overall tax rate. This would probably not be enough to maintain a comfortable lifestyle even taking the employer pension and Social Security benefits into account. In addition, the value of the income amount would be reduced over time as inflation increased. If a stable 10% return could be secured by accepting more risk, then the retiree could receive $50,000 of annual income before taxes or $30,000 after taxes. Of course, the investor accepting more risk must also take into account what would happen if the greater risk led to a significant loss of capital!

The elderly are often "buy and hold" investors, who insist on retaining all investments in their original form. But some financial advisors, such as San Francisco's Brouwer & Janachowski and Lansing, Michigan's Kenneth Klegon, suggest a strategy that involves planned sales of securities as a means of adding income after retirement. For instance, the older person could keep about one-third of the portfolio in a bond fund, another 10% in a money market fund (using about half the portfolio to yield current income), and divide the rest among three safe but growth-oriented mutual funds. Or, the 50% income portion could be divided between short-term and intermediate-term bond funds, with the rest dispersed among four growth funds (including an international fund), with a planned schedule of selling off a certain number of shares each year and spending the after-tax results.[17]

In mid-1993, the *New York Times* asked five financial advisors to create retirement portfolios. Each chose between five and nine funds. At the beginning of 1994, the *Times* asked them to re-assess their recommendations. They all showed a growing interest in investments outside the United States. The advisor who was most concerned with inflation-proofing shifted out of a fund that specializes in small stocks into a capital appreciation fund. Another advisor, on the contrary, increased the investment in small stocks; a third chose only "social investment" funds that insist on ecologically and otherwise socially responsible companies.[18]

In their 1990 book, *Diversify: The Investor's Guide to Asset Allocation Strategies*, Gerald W. Perritt and Alan Lavine (Longman Financial Services Publishing) give suggestions for asset "mixes" for various goals. The suggested categories include: (1) money market funds, (2) growth stock (or corresponding funds), (3) growth and income investments or funds, (4) bonds or bond funds, (5) gold or gold funds, and (6) international investment or funds. For a low risk investor, they suggest putting almost three-quarters of the investment in a money market fund, 10.5% in bonds, 9% in an international fund, and about 5% in growth-and-income investments. Small investments can be made in the remaining categories. Suggestions for medium-to-low risk investments were made and would place almost 2/3 in a money fund, 15% in international investment or funds, 10% in growth stock, and 7.5% in bonds. Again, other small investments could be made for further diversification. The authors' "income mix" portfolio for income-oriented low-risk investors includes 19% in a money fund, 28% in government securities, and 5% in international bonds. In addition to these three investments, the authors suggest investing (ranging from 5% to 19% of the total portfolio) in four mutual funds with varying objectives, such as: growth and income, safe growth, income with some growth, and payment of high dividends consistent with safety of capital. The low-risk asset allocation portfolio consisted of roughly 1/3 invested in money markets or cash equivalents, more than 1/4 in an international bond fund, 19.5% in a growth fund with an objective of long-term appreciation, and 4% to 8% in each of three growth funds, one with a secondary objective of maximizing income.

For later opinions on asset allocation, consult finance and personal finance journalism, where asset managers are frequently interviewed about their preferred allocations in light of current conditions.

In November, 1995, an article in *Smart Money* magazine suggests formulas for maintaining portfolios (for inactive, average, and active investors), with asset allocations shifting based on whether the investor is retired or if not, how many years remain until retirement. In each portfolio, the emphasis shifts from equities to income (such as bonds and money-market funds) and from riskier to less risky stocks. For example, the recommendation for an active investor five years from retirement is 30% in individual stocks chosen by the investor, 20% in lower-risk mutual funds, 10% in bond funds, and 30% in Treasury or municipal bonds, with 10% of the portfolio kept in a money market fund for liquidity.

For the same investor, the suggestion was to shift to 20% cash at retirement, and to be 50% invested in Treasury or municipal bonds, 10% in low-risk mutual funds, and only 20% in individual stock. Later in retirement, the recommendation is to shift to 20% cash, 60% Treasuries and municipal bonds, 10% low-risk funds, and only 10% in individual stocks.

Shifts are also suggested within each component of the portfolio. For instance, it is suggested that retirees have more government but fewer municipal bonds than pre-retirees, and should invest more in income-oriented mutual funds and less in growth and aggressive growth funds after retirement.

In August, 1996, the Wall Street Journal asked 14 brokerage houses about their recommendations for asset allocation (for all investors, not necessarily retirees or those with a retirement-planning orientation). The average recommendation was 11% of the portfolio in cash, 31% in bonds, and 57% in stock, although some portfolios had no cash and some had 15% in cash. One recommended keeping 63% in stock to only 25% in bonds. Some recommendations called for diversifying between U.S. and non-U.S. stocks, and some suggested including real estate in the portfolio.

At the beginning of 1997, Worth magazine surveyed four major banks (Brown Brothers, Northern Trust, Bessemer Trust, and UBS) as to their recommended portfolio allocations for investors whose objective is total return including long-term growth. Recommendations ranged from 5-10% cash. Three put a majority of the portfolio in U.S. stocks (51.7%-72%), and one invested only 35% in U.S. stocks. The other major components were domestic bonds (8%-35%) and stocks outside the United States (13%-20%).

In other words, traditional principles still prevail in 1996-97: older investors are advised to diversify, not put everything into stock (especially risky individual stocks), and to maintain some cash for liquidity while investing more of the portfolio in stock than in bonds.[19]

If the client is a cautious, low- to moderate-risk investor, your job is to choose a portfolio of conservative, safe, low-maintenance income-oriented investments. If possible, the portfolio should be maintainable over the long term, with little or no need to change investments other than rolling over certificates of deposit and similar tasks.

For investors who express a great deal of concern about inflation and who do not want to be stuck with a fixed income at a time of rising prices, inflation-indexed Treasury securities might be a good portfolio component, see page 266.

PLANNING TIP: Selection of bonds includes a consideration of whether the bonds are callable as well as their safety, return, and maturity. Make bond computations based on return to the first call date as well as yield to maturity. If a callable bond is an especially good deal for your clients, it may be called early, forcing you and the client to find additional investment opportunities.

A typical mix for an income-oriented, low-risk client could include: (1) certificates of deposit, (2) government obligations (especially tax-free municipals if income tax savings are important, however, the effect of municipal bond income on the taxability of Social Security benefits must be considered), (3) annuities, (4) equity mutual funds oriented toward income or conservative growth, (5) money market funds, and (6) blue-chip stocks, especially those that pay high dividends. When interest rates are high, older investors can get an excellent, safe return merely by investing in money market funds, certificates of deposit, or bank money market accounts. In a low interest rate environment, additional alternatives must be sought.

INVESTMENTS AND LONG TERM CARE PLANNING

Consider the case of Hypatia O'Thetical, a competent, 82 year-old widow with no children. She receives a monthly income of about $700 from Social Security, as well as a pension benefit. She also has savings of approximately $85,000. Her health is fair, and although she suffers from arthritis, she can get around. Her vision and hearing are poor, and she is under the care of both a heart and kidney specialist. Both believe her condition to be under control. Because she has no spouse or children and because her estate will be far less than $600,000, estate planning is not a major concern for her. The perfect plan might be for her to gradually use up her savings throughout her remaining lifespan, then die with nothing left over. Of course, she does not want to face an extended period after her savings are exhausted.

In terms of Medicaid planning, it is possible that she will need nursing home care or Medicaid home care. However, it is also possible that she will die within the next few years without using chronic care. Because she is unmarried, she cannot use the spousal protection provisions. And because she has no children, there are no obvious recipients of a gifting program. Perhaps she wants to benefit her nieces and nephews, friends, or a favorite charity. Let's assume that the average cost of nursing home care in her county is $3,500 a month, and the permitted asset level for single Medicaid recipients is $3,000 plus a $1,500 burial fund. She would have to transfer more than $80,000 to get down to the Medicaid level, triggering a penalty period of approximately two years. If she will need Medicaid services at all, can she wait two years to get them (risking criminal prosecution if she applies during the penalty period)? If she rents her house or apartment, perhaps it would be worthwhile to purchase a home in order to transmute the cost of the home from countable resources to an exempt homestead. If she is a homeowner, Medicaid planning might dictate reducing or paying off the mortgage or renovating the home. Her age and medical condition probably make it impossible for her to buy long term care (LTC) insurance, but it is worth investigating to see if a policy would be available and if it would be affordable.

However, purchasing an actuarially sound life annuity from a reliable insurer would meet many of her objectives. Let's assume that she invests as follows: $60,000 in an annuity; $10,000 in a safe, high-rated bond fund; $10,000 in a money market fund with check-writing privileges; and $5,000 in an interest-bearing checking account. The purchase of an annuity is not a transfer for Medicaid purposes because there is no gratuitous element. She now has additional income for daily needs from the annuity and the funds. If she needs liquidity (for instance, to pay a home health attendant), the checking account and money market fund are available. She should keep some savings rather than investing the entire amount in the annuity, because annuities do bear some risk that can be lessened through diversification, and also because she would have access to cash for special needs. If she does need to enter a nursing home, she will probably be able to get a bed faster and receive a better quality of care if she enters as a private pay patient. For these reasons, it makes sense to keep enough cash to pay for at least several months' worth of care.

Because no one is dependent on her, the fact that the annuity dies with her is not a problem. If her favorite charity offers private annuity arrangements, she might prefer this course to the purchase of a commercial annuity. In this case, she will know that if she dies before her predicted lifespan, the excess funds will benefit the charity.

Depending on her personal preferences and market conditions, she might want to put part of her savings into bank certificates of deposit, utility stocks, an equity income mutual fund, or mortgage-related investment vehicles such as Ginnie Maes.

Her nephew, Simon Sample, faces an entirely different planning horizon. Simon, 63, has taken early retirement from an executive position. He is married, has four children, and receives a $45,000 annual pension as well as earning $10,000-$20,000 a year from the crafts store where he sells the pottery he makes. His wife, Serena, is 52 years old, earns $75,000 a year as a cosmetics executive, and has no plans to retire. The Samples own a lovely $350,000 home (with a $100,000 mortgage) and have a diversified portfolio worth about half a million dollars.

Can Simon and Serena make transfers to a trust or to their children in order to qualify for Medicaid? Before the Omnibus Budget Reconciliation Act of 1993 (OBRA '93), they could count on a maximum 30-month penalty period and would probably have been able to "wait it out." But OBRA '93 makes the potential penalty period indefinite, so there is a real risk that any transfer plan will backfire unless they retain enough assets to pay privately during a very long penalty period. In addition, the Health Insurance Portability and Accountability Act of 1996 (P.L. 104-191) criminalizes some transfers. To do a transfer-based plan, they will give up control over an enormous sum of money and will probably have to compromise their lifestyle. Furthermore, if they live in an "income cap" state, excess income will bar Medicaid eligibility. They seem like perfect candidates for LTC insurance, since they are relatively young, healthy, and have extensive assets to protect. They may even be able to deduct part of the premium.

LTC insurance is probably a better alternative for them than transfer planning. However, it makes sense for them to use a durable power of attorney and/or voluntary designation of guardian or conservator and to set up a small trust now that can be fully funded by the attorney-in-fact or conservator later if Simon or Serena eventually becomes incapacitated. They can divide their assets so that each has approximately equal estates (which will also be beneficial in estate planning). They will be able to use Medicaid's spousal protection provisions and may be able to "exempt" significant assets by reducing or paying off the mortgage. Nevertheless, they still may not be able to qualify for Medicaid benefits right away, if at all. They must be prepared to pay out-of-pocket for LTC expenses that are not covered by insurance.

Simon and Serena have plenty of income. Even after Serena retires, they will probably have more than $75,000 a year in pensions and Social Security. Because Simon is somewhat older, he understands that Serena can expect a decade or two of widowhood, and he wants to provide amply for her. Thus, his plan includes sufficient life insurance, including second-to-die insurance to cope with estate taxes. On the advice of his tax accountant, he is implementing a gifting program to reduce his taxable estate through gifts to his children and grandchildren with no gift tax liability (because he uses the annual exclusion).

Both Simon and Serena are financially sophisticated and enjoy following the market. Their income is ample, so their investment goals are to increase net worth and appreciation. Therefore, their asset allocation includes: 15% zero-coupon bonds, 50% blue-chip stocks, 25% growth stocks, and 10% low-priced, risky stocks. They know that some, if not all, of these risky stocks will decline in value or even become worthless, but the amount invested in any particular stock is small. They are prepared to take the risk in the hope of greater appreciation, knowing that a loss will not seriously harm their lifestyle.

Later on, if and when either becomes incapacitated, the attorney-in-fact will be empowered under the durable power of attorney to transfer assets into the trust. The trustee will probably select a much more conservative investment strategy, by concentrating on blue chips, and possibly shifting to mutual funds so that the trustee will not have to devote time to tracking individual stocks. The trustee is likely to seek higher income to pay the cost of caring for an incapacitated person. Another possibility would be to sell many of the securities and purchase a retirement community or life-care community unit providing both housing, medical, and personal care.

Simon's 69 year-old brother, Scott, has not been as successful financially as his younger sibling. He and his wife Suzanne, 71, are retired, with pension and Social Security income totalling about

$30,000 a year. They own a mortgage-free $175,000 home and have savings and investments totalling approximately $200,000. Suzanne has had a bout with cancer, and Scott is somewhat forgetful at times. They are not particularly knowledgeable about investments and are not interested in learning at this stage of life. For them, a good plan might include a durable power of attorney and a standby trust, or perhaps an immediate creation of an irrevocable trust containing most of their assets, so that the "look back" period can pass before either makes a Medicaid application. Because of their health status, it is likely that one or both will need long-term chronic care, but the situation is not so serious that a Medicaid application in the next few months is anticipated.

If and when either enters a nursing home, he or she can use the Medicaid "spousal protection" provisions to transfer a substantial amount of resources to the other spouse and to provide a regular income for the healthy spouse living in the community. Again, they should retain enough cash for at least a few months of care as a private pay patient in a nursing home, rather than trying to find a bed as a Medicaid recipient.

The elder law attorney in the planning team should be consulted on Medicaid planning steps and in deciding whether LTC insurance is cost-effective for Scott and/or Suzanne. Their life insurance should also be examined to see if they need more life insurance coverage to protect the survivor. Estate tax planning is not a concern because it is unlikely that the estate will incur federal estate tax. The attorney and accountant in the planning team should be consulted to see if planning is required with respect to state inheritance or estate tax.

In the meantime, if the trust option is not taken immediately, Scott and Suzanne will need safe investments. They will probably want to concentrate on income because their pension and Social Security income, while well above the poverty level, is not luxurious. A reasonable choice might include: $25,000 in bank accounts and cash equivalents, such as money market funds for liquidity; $15,000 in a conservative bond fund (perhaps even a government bond fund) with a good track record; a $10,000 investment in a good zero-coupon bond, with the expectation that the higher amount yielded by the bond will be paid to the surviving spouse in the future; and $25,000 per mutual fund within a portfolio of six mutual funds, all with somewhat different objectives, including at least one growth fund to enhance the assets available to the surviving spouse after one spouse dies. The other funds could include income, balanced, and growth and income funds.

This plan provides extensive diversification, yet does not require much time or effort from Scott or Suzanne, although they might want to seek professional advice about when it is worthwhile to change investments. The plan also could easily be transferred to a trustee, attorney-in-fact, or conservator. It should provide reliable income throughout life. If it is necessary to restrict income in order to qualify for Medicaid, investments could be shifted to safe, growth-oriented mutual funds. In this scenario, even though less immediate income is produced, the value of the investment increases for the benefit of the surviving spouse or other heirs. Zero-coupon bonds could also meet this objective. Tax-exempt bonds probably would be preferable, because other zero-coupon bonds generate a tax on original issue discount even though the recipient does not get cash dividends out of which the tax could be paid.

CHAPTER FOOTNOTES

1. John Slatter, "Deceptive Dividends: High-Yield Utilities Can be Dangerous," *Barron's* August 5, 1991 p. 25.

2. Werner Renberg, "A Beta Way: Some Methods to Gauge Funds' Riskiness," *Barron's* May 27, 1991 p. 18.

3. Barbara Donnelly, "How Taxes and Costs Prey on Nest Eggs," *Wall Street Journal* September 25, 1990 p. C1; GAO/HRD-91-22, "Social Security: Analysis of a Proposal to Privatize Trust Fund Reserves," (December 1990), pp. 24-18; Andy Zipser, "Consider the Alternatives: Comparing the Performance of 16 Different Investments," *Barron's* May 20, 1991.

4. Karen Slater, "Consider the Options in Shopping for Tax-Free Bonds," *Wall Street Journal* November 14, 1990 p. C1.

5. Ellen Schultz has written several excellent articles about variable annuities for the *Wall Street Journal* see, e.g., "Variable Annuities' Returns Can Glitter, But Unwary Investors May Feel Trapped," July 10, 1992 p. C1; "Variable Annuity Buyers Warned to Check the Underlying Funds," July 13, 1993 p. C1; "Variable Annuities," January 7, 1994 p. R11, showing major growth in annual sales of variable annuities between 1986 and 1994 (estimated 1994 level: close to $50 billion in sales), and "Variable Annuities Are Proving Popular but Few Offer Top-Ranked Stock Funds," February 2, 1994 p. C1. Also see Greg Steinmetz's, "Some Appealing Annuity Deals Carry the Tricky Risks of CMOs," *Wall Street Journal* January 12, 1994 p. C1, referring to annuities funded by potentially risky collateralized mortgage obligations. For investment performance, see Robert L. Mabie's, "Five-Year History of Flexible-Premium Annuities," *Best's Review* May 1993 p. 89 (showing a decline in median interest rates from 8.35% in January 1988 to 7.50% (for renewals) in January 1992), and Roger L. Blease's, "Flexible-Premium Annuity Policy Survey," in the same issue on page 85, showing significant declines in accumulation value and monthly income between 1990 and 1993. For 1996, the average insurance company expense (fee) charged for variable annuities was 1.27%, with an upper limit of about 1.4%: Bridget O'Brian, "Variable Annuities Piggyback on the Bull," Wall Street Journal January 28, 1997 p. C1.

6. See Jim Gaines, "Quizzing Your Prospect to Find the Right Annuity," *National Underwriter* (Life/Health Edition) October 7, 1996 p. 8.

7. Ron Panko, "Annuities Sellers Shift Focus to Payout Benefits," *Best's Review* October 1996 p. 100.

8. John A. Kiczek, "Flexible Premium Retirement Annuity Histories," *Best's Review* March 1996 p. 51.

9. William Harris, "A Selling Perspective on Equity Indexed Annuities," *National Underwriter* (Life/Health Edition) November 4, 1996 p. 16.

10. Report, "Lull in Annuities Sales May Soon End," *Best's Review* November 1996 p. 59; Michael A. Farinella, "Annuity Writers Push Harder into Rivals' Turf," *Best's Review* September 1996 p. 55; Bridget O'Brian, "Variable Annuities Piggyback on the Bull," *Wall Street Journal* January 28, 1997 p. C1.

11. Report, "Lull in Annuities Sales May Soon End," *Best's Review* November 1996 p. 59.

12. John A. Kiczek, "Single Premium Immediate Annuity Payouts," *Best's Review* August 1996 p. 57.

13. John A. Kiczek, "Flexible Premium Retirement Annuity Histories," *Best's Review* March 1996 p. 51.

14. Carole Gould, "Balancing Retirement and Growth," *New York Times* July 22, 1990 p. F16.

15. Earl C. Gottschalk, Jr., "How to Invest Your Retirement Nest Egg," *Wall Street Journal* November 27, 1990 p. C1.

16. The Bingham, Osborn & Scarborough portfolio is discussed in Georgette Jasen's, "A Secure Retirement Takes Long Years of Sound Planning, Even After it Begins," *Wall Street Journal* May 29, 1992 p. C1. Also see Jonathan Clements' article, "Going Boldly Into Funds to Live Long and Prosper," on the same page.

17. The Brouwer & Janachowski and Financial Management Association allocations are found in Jonathan Clements' "Getting Growth and Income Once You Retire," *Wall Street Journal* November 12, 1992 p. C1. For arguments about permitting more risk in investments of lump sums, see Ellen E. Schultz's, "A Few Steps Can Help Simplify Retirees' Investment Decisions," *Wall Street Journal* December 21, 1993 p. C1.

18. For the five 1994 models, see Carole Gould's, "New Year Tune-up for Retirement Funds," *New York Times* January 8, 1994 p. A37.

19. Harris Collingwood, "Finding the Right Mix," *Smart Money* November 1995 p. 120; John R. Dorfman, "Despite July Jolt, Brokers Say Don't Alter Asset Mix," *Wall Street Journal* July 2, 1996 p. C1; News item, "Asset Allocation: All's Quiet," *Worth* February 1997 p. 61.

Chapter 11

SPECIAL ESTATE PLANNING NEEDS OF THE OLDER CLIENT

It's true that the actual creation of an estate plan, and drafting of documents such as wills and trusts, will be done by other members of the planning team. Primary responsibility belongs to the attorney, with help from the accountant. However, your analysis of the client's insurance needs is based on estate planning factors: how much he or she owns; who in the family needs protection or is intended to receive an inheritance; and which financial devices will yield the best tax results. It can be depressing for a client to look back on a lifetime of saving and investment, and discover that the accumulated assets are not large enough to meet the goals. It is our job, as a financial planner, to find ways to enhance net worth and use life insurance and other tools to supplement the estate. Your job as a team member is to inform the rest of the team about innovative or improved financial products and creative ways in which they can be combined to meet the client's financial needs and objectives.

The conscientious estate planner needs to find out about the client's family, friends, and favorite charities. Who is entitled to a share of the client's property if he or she dies without a will, or if the will is defective? These "distributees" have the right to challenge the client's will. The planner needs to know their names, addresses, and relationship to the client.

The basic goal of estate planning is to make sure that, after lifetime needs are met and the debts and expenses of the estate are settled, a person's property can be passed on in accordance with his or her wishes, with the smallest possible tax burden that can be arranged consistent with the law. The maximum estate/gift tax rate is 55%, and some states add their own estate or inheritance taxes, so you can see that a large estate can easily be depleted if no plans are made to protect it.

However, tax saving is not the be-all and end-all of estate planning; it can be worthwhile to incur some, or higher, taxes in order to do what the client wants, or to avoid extra trouble or expense. It doesn't make sense to spend $2,000 a year administering a trust if the only purpose of the trust is to save $1,000 in income taxes! On the other hand, the same trust (and the same $2,000 administrative cost) might be worthwhile to prevent a big estate tax bill, or to provide safe financial management for a person whose judgment is impaired by age or illness. Estate planning is the culmination of lifetime planning, and it's impossible to make a really good estate plan without the foundation of a well-designed investment and saving plan, and without good advice about steps that can be taken to save income and gift taxes.

The estate planning process begins by doing an inventory of the client's income and possessions: home, other real property, automobile, bank accounts, investment portfolio, etc., both those that already exist and those that can be expected in the future (maturing CD's or zero-coupon bonds; inheritances from others) balanced against current debts and expected future needs.

Wherever possible, the client and estate planner look for ways to limit or eliminate estate tax. Most estates are not subject to federal estate tax, either because they are too small (an estate under $600,000 is not subject to federal estate tax unless part of the "unified credit" against estate and gift taxes has been used up — which is unlikely in a smaller estate)[1] or because the marital and/or charitable deductions reduce the estate below this figure.

One common planning tactic is "estate splitting": because it is impossible to be sure which spouse will die first, a couple who have less than $1.2 million in assets can escape estate tax by dividing up their assets so that each has less than $600,000. (Generally, there's no gift tax when one spouse makes a gift to the other, although there may be income tax consequences.)

Our tax laws allow a person to leave any amount, and any percentage of the estate — up to and including 100% — to his or her U.S. citizen spouse without incurring estate tax. (More complex rules apply to foreign spouses.) That is, if a person with a $10 million estate leaves it all to the spouse, there will be no estate tax on the estate of the first spouse to die. However, making extensive use of the marital deduction is likely to lead to a "second estate" problem: that is, the spouse who inherits the big estate is likely to die with most of it intact, creating a large estate tax liability. One way to cope is for both spouses to make lifetime gifts to reduce the estate. Another way is to limit the use of the marital deduction and distribute some of the assets of the first spouse to die to the children or other heirs instead of to the spouse, so the second spouse to die will have a smaller estate.

PLANNING TIP: The "second estate" problem highlights the potential conflicts between tax planning and practical good sense. It's not a good idea to save taxes by reducing the spouse's share of the estate, if the reduced share is insufficient for the spouse's needs. The contradiction can be resolved by increasing the amount of insurance payable to the surviving spouse. As discussed on page 53, life insurance proceeds get favorable estate tax treatment. Life insurance proceeds are not included in the estate of the insured person, as long as they are payable to a named payee (not the estate of the insured person), *and* as long as the insured person did not have any incidents of ownership in the policy at death or during the three-year period before his or her death.

One common combination is the "credit shelter trust" and extensive (but not unlimited) use of the marital deduction. This combination works by setting up a trust with $600,000 (or whatever remains of the trust creator's unified credit, or whatever amount is exempt from estate taxation under then-current law) — an amount just small enough to escape estate taxation. The trust can benefit children, grandchildren, other relatives, or anyone else whom the trust creator favors. The rest of the trust creator's estate is given or left to his or her spouse, thus making use of the marital deduction. If the surviving spouse's estate is under $600,000, there'll be no "second estate" problem.

Although planners have to devote the major part of the estate plan to coping with federal tax issues, there are some states (e.g., New York) where there are significant state transfer taxes — either estate taxes (on the privilege of transmitting assets) or inheritance taxes (imposed on the privilege of receiving assets). State rules are often similar to, but not identical to, the federal rules affecting trusts and estates, so even if the planner is sure that there will be no federal estate tax, the potential impact of state taxes must also be considered.

As discussed in Chapter 7, OBRA '93 gives states much broader powers of recovery against the estates of persons who received Medicaid benefits. Plans (especially plans for the financial well-being of a surviving spouse) must be re-assessed in light of the possibility that the client will use Medicaid benefits, and that his or her estate will be reduced correspondingly.

MARITAL PLANS

Usually, the client will want to leave much (if not all) of the estate to his or her spouse. However, there are reasons why this might not be desired by the client. For example, the marriage might be on the rocks.

PLANNING TIP: People who have decided to divorce should change their wills immediately. Under the laws of most states, divorce will have the effect of revoking a legacy to "my wife" or "my husband" (or an appointment of a wife or husband as an executor or trustee) — but this doesn't happen when a couple is merely separated, not divorced. Furthermore, most states make it very difficult to disinherit a spouse; the spouse usually has a right to contest the will and demand an automatic share of the estate. Divorced ex-spouses do not have the right to an "elective share" of this kind. (A valid "antenuptial," i.e., premarital agreement, or a valid agreement entered into after marriage, can be used to limit or waive rights in the spouse's estate.)

Even in harmonious marriages, there can be good reasons for cutting down or eliminating the amount left to the spouse. For instance, the spouse may have plenty of money of his or her own, so that both spouses may think it is more worthwhile to leave money to children, grandchildren, or charities. In light of today's high divorce rate, it is common for a person who already has children to divorce, remarry, and perhaps start another family. Providing for the children of the first family may be the client's major, or an important, objective. Another possibility, if the children of the second family are still relatively young, is that it may be important to take care of their college bills and seeing that they have a good start in life.

PLANNING TIP: The Qualified Terminable Interest in Property (QTIP) or QTIP trust are very helpful in several situations, including the "second family" situation. The QTIP is a way to take advantage of the marital deduction without actually leaving money or property to the spouse outright. Under the QTIP, the spouse is given the right to the income of the property for life (as long as certain technical rules are followed) — but after he or she dies, the property or money goes to whomever was designated by the spouse who created the QTIP (for instance, his or her children) — not to the people who inherit under the QTIP recipient spouse's will.

A SECOND CHANCE: DISCLAIMERS AND OTHER POST-MORTEM PLANNING

Under the best circumstances, the team would create the best possible estate plan for the client. However, if there is no team in place, or if the estate plan that is chosen proves to have negative features, the estate and its beneficiaries may get a second chance to fix up the plan after the planning client's death. For one thing, treatment of a bequest to the spouse as a QTIP is not automatic. The executor of the estate has to file a special tax form electing this treatment. Making, or passing up, the election is a choice that depends on tax and practical factors.

There are special relief provisions in the Internal Revenue Code for owners of farms and small businesses. The executor can ask for extra time to pay estate taxes if much of the estate is illiquid because it consists largely of an interest in a closely held business. A "special use" valuation is available for certain farm and small-business real property so that the heirs are not faced with estate taxes calculated based on an exaggerated figure premised on the land being developed rather than kept for its present use.

What if the estate plan calls for an inheritance for someone who doesn't want or can't use the inheritance, or if it later turns out that a different estate plan would have been better? In this situation, disclaimers can come to the rescue. That is, the person who inherits the property can disclaim, or give it up. Instead, it will pass according to the testator's instructions for what to do with disclaimed property; or, if there were no instructions, it will pass as if the disclaimant (person making the disclaimer) had died before the testator (person making the will). There is no gift tax on the act of making a disclaimer, because the situation is treated as if the disclaimant had never received the property, rather than as if he or she got it and gave it away.

Under Section 2518 of the Internal Revenue Code, five conditions must be followed for there to be a valid disclaimer:

- The disclaimer must be made in writing.

- It must be irrevocable and unqualified.

- The disclaimant must not have accepted any benefits from the inheritance — you can't inherit something and keep it for a while to see if you like it, and then disclaim it.

- The executor must receive the disclaimer within 9 months of the date of the inheritance (or the date on which a minor heir reaches age 21).

- The inheritance must pass to someone other than the disclaimant, and without direction from the disclaimant. That is, an heir who is also a distributee is not allowed to disclaim the inheritance, then get it right back as a distributee; and the disclaimant is not allowed to say, "I disclaim this, but I give it to my cousin Marge."

PLANNING TIP: The disclaimant has to be competent — so disclaimers can't be used to get funds away from incompetent heirs and channel them to competent family members who can manage the money. Every estate plan — and especially one for an elderly person — must take into account the risk that the testator, or one or more heirs, could become incompetent.

Furthermore, the disclaimer probably *will* be treated as a transfer for Medicaid purposes, so disclaiming an inheritance will not preserve Medicaid eligibility unless the disclaimer is made before the penalty period starts.

RISK OF INCAPACITY

One way in which many estate planners fail badly is to ignore (or be unaware of) the serious financial planning challenges raised by potential incapacity and need for long-term care. Many conventional estate plans are either ineffective because much of the estate being planned for has been dissipated by health care bills, or are actually bad for the owner of the estate and his or her heirs by preventing them from becoming Medicaid-eligible. You can be very helpful to the client by constantly stressing these factors to the other team members.

The possibility of present or future incapacity has many implications for estate planning. First of all, a document (such as a will or trust) can be challenged by someone who claims that the signer did not have the capacity to understand the document and consent to it voluntarily. This could happen if one of the deceased client's children is disinherited, or receives less than expected, and claims that the parent's will should not be given legal effect because the parent signed it while incompetent, or while improperly influenced by someone who received an unfairly large inheritance.

Second, even without worrying about hostile challenges, the compassionate planner will worry about what could happen if a confused, sick, or demented older person receives large sums of money (say, a big bequest from the spouse plus significant insurance benefits). The recipient may find it difficult, or impossible, to administer the money. Some forgetful older people suffer eviction or utility cut-offs — not because they are destitute, but because they have forgotten *where* they put their checkbook, or even *what* a checkbook is. They may fall prey to get-rich-quick hustlers or "concerned" relatives who appear suddenly and fade into the background as soon as the gifts to them are made or the new will is signed.

Clearly, large sums of money should not be given to those who cannot handle such large sums, who may lose or waste the entire sum then be left without money for living expenses. One possibility is to design the estate plan so that the confused or potentially incapacitated person does not receive large lump sums. He or she could be given a QTIP providing regular income; an annuity could be purchased for him or her; a trust could be set up, perhaps providing annual income and giving the trustee discretion to invade the trust principal for the beneficiary's needs such as home repairs and medical costs. Insurance settlement options are very useful in this situation.

As usual, when the needs of the elderly are involved, there is no simple solution. Remember, a person who is incapacitated, or at risk of incapacity, is also a person who likely to need nursing home care either now or soon. For many people, that means that a Medicaid application will be made either immediately or when the funds for private payment of nursing home bills run out. But, as discussed in Chapter 7, Medicaid applications can be denied based on excessive income; excessive assets; or non-permitted transfers during the "look-back period" (which lasts a maximum of 36 or 60 months, depending on circumstances, before the application) — and criminal penalties became a possibility in 1997.

If there's plenty of time to plan ahead, excess assets are less of a problem than excess income, because the assets can be transferred. As long as the transfer occurs before the look-back period, the assets won't prevent Medicaid eligibility. (In a way, this is similar to the process of making a gift during lifetime in order to reduce the future taxable estate. Ironically, the lifetime gifts that many lawyers advise as a way of reducing the estate can also be considered transfers for Medicaid purposes — so what is good advice for one purpose may be bad advice for another.)

But consider the very common situation in which a Medicaid applicant, or someone who will soon make a Medicaid application, inherits money from a spouse or other relative, or receives insurance proceeds. Of course, the funds constitute a "resource" for Medicaid purposes. If the beneficiary gives away the inheritance or proceeds, it will be a transfer which may result in a delay in eligibility. You'd think that the simple answer would be to disclaim the inheritance, and let it go to another relative. However, some state Medicaid authorities take the position that even a disclaimer counts as a transfer.

Therefore, every estate plan must be considered carefully in terms of the effect that bequests and insurance proceeds will have on their recipients. It might make sense to cut back on bequests to potential Medicaid recipients: for instance, to leave less to the spouse, more to the children. There's another twist to worry about. A Medicaid applicant may have a duty to "elect against the will" (demand the automatic share of the deceased spouse's estate that a spouse is entitled to)! This problem can be solved, in the appropriate case, by signing a pre-marital or post-marriage agreement waiving all rights in the other spouse's estate.

The most conventional — but also the most drastic, and probably the least desirable — solution to the financial problems caused by incapacity is to go to court and have a conservator or guardian appointed.[2] Then the conservator or guardian can manage the money. This is a drastic solution, because it is expensive, and because a person who is an "adjudicated incompetent" loses any powers and civil rights (such as the right to make a contract, and perhaps even the right to vote). Furthermore, the process of getting a conservator or guardian appointed is time-consuming, which is a problem because it is usually started during an emergency when time is of the essence.

In short, it is much more practical — and does much more to preserve the dignity of the elderly — to plan ahead and create alternatives for financial management so that conservatorship or guardianship will not be needed. Trusts are useful in the lifetime/estate plan for tax reasons; they are also useful as a way of providing professional management and supervision of the property of people who are financially unsophisticated, uninterested in taking care of business matters, confused, potentially incapacitated, or incapacitated. Depending on the terms of the trust, trusts can provide regular income; income only when necessary; regular distributions of capital; or distributions of trust principal at the beneficiary's request, or whenever the trustee thinks it is necessary. Under a "spendthrift trust," the beneficiary is not allowed to demand payment of the principal, and the principal is insulated against the claims of the beneficiary's creditors. (A person cannot set up a spendthrift trust for himself so as to defeat his creditors.) The trust can also handle routine matters such as making mortgage and real estate tax payments.

DURABLE POWERS OF ATTORNEY IN THE ESTATE PLAN

An important tool — and a fundamental part of the combined lifetime and estate plan for the elderly — is the "durable power of attorney" (DPA). Any competent adult can sign a DPA. The DPA designates another person as an "attorney in fact"[3], or agent, who can act for the principal, either in all matters or only in specific matters as set out in the DPA. The power of attorney is called "durable" because, unlike the traditional version of the power of attorney, it remains effective even after the principal who created the power becomes incompetent.

Giving somebody a power of attorney is a big decision. Durable powers of attorney are generally drafted to give the agent broad powers. This degree of discretion carries a risk of abuse, such as the agent's wrongful appropriation of the principal's property for the agent's own benefit. So the chosen person must be trustworthy; must have objectives that are similar to those of the principal (because honest disagreement can cause many problems); and must be willing and available for service for at least as long as the principal's lifespan. This last factor means that it is not necessarily a good idea to name a spouse as attorney-in-fact. Choosing a child is often a better idea — although this can create bad feeling on the part of the other children (who weren't chosen), or even on the part of the child serving as agent who is saddled with a major and continuing responsibility.

Because the attorney-in-fact is so powerful, many people resist granting a DPA, which they see as a loss of their own autonomy and ability to manage their own affairs. That's why the "springing power of attorney" evolved. A springing power of attorney doesn't become effective as soon as it is created — instead, it "springs" into action *only* when the principal becomes incapacitated. Of course, it is important to think carefully about how "incapacity" will be defined, just as it is important to allocate and define the attorney-in-fact's powers carefully.

An important step in drafting a DPA is to consult your state's law. Most of these statutes set out a list of powers which are automatically available to attorneys-in-fact, or which are given to the attorney-in-fact unless the principal says otherwise. Also, some states mandate the use of the official state form; others suggest a form, but allow other forms to be used.

A risky decision (risky because of the potential for abuse, as well as potential court disapproval), but one which is helpful in some situations, is to allow the attorney-in-fact to make gifts and transfers to save taxes and for Medicaid purposes. Spell out the extent to which the attorney-in-fact can make gifts to himself and his family. This could be benign and helpful, if the attorney-in-fact is a family member or friend who would eventually inherit from the principal anyway — or, it could be a "license to steal" for a principal who depletes a helpless person's estate for his own benefit.

If the purpose of the gift is to remove property from the taxable estate, the IRS and the courts will examine the text of the durable power of attorney to see if the agent was explicitly given the power to make gifts. If the document is not clear, state law will be examined to see if agents are presumed to have this power. See *Estate of Ridenour*, 36 F.3d 332 (4th Cir. 1994), *Townsend v. U.S.*, 889 F.Supp. 369 (D.Neb. 1995), *Estate of Goldman*, T.C. Memo 1996-29. Also see TAM 9601002: when the decedent's daughter, acting as attorney-in-fact, withdrew funds from a revocable trust created by her father, the withdrawn amounts were included in his taxable estate—because the trust agreement did not include a gifting power. The DPA allowed the attorney-in-fact to make annual exclusion gifts, but did not refer specifically to the revocable trust.

Although state law may come to the rescue, it is better to spell out the exact scope of the agent's power in the text of the durable power of attorney itself.

In addition to powers of attorney that deal with property, many states allow "health care powers of attorney," under which the designated agent can make health care decisions (such as whether an operation should be performed; whether life support should be used or withdrawn). Health care powers of attorney vary from state to state, so check with the attorney in your planning team about when and by whom these powers should be used.

ESTATE PLANNING FOR THE FAMILY BUSINESS

One of the toughest planning tasks is to come up with a plan for passing on the family business. Many otherwise sound businesses fail because:

- The business founder won't let go of the reins. Sooner or later, the children or other potential heirs quit in disgust.

- The business founder stays on too long, and begins to make bad decisions.

- No provisions are made to train a successor, so nobody is available inside the family to take over from the founder. Instead, the business is sold to (or hostilely acquired by) an outside company.

- Various people within the family or the company think of themselves as the obvious successor, and devote more of their time to infighting than to managing the company efficiently and profitably.

- The business founder, in an effort to be fair, drafts a gift or estate plan that gives each of several children, grand-children, nieces, and nephews an equal percentage of stock in the company. The upshot is that no one ends up with enough stock to earn a meaningful dividend income. Even worse, the company often faces deadlock as squab-bling shareholders constantly form new alliances in order to control the board of directors (and, thus, control corpo-rate policy).

- The opposite situation can be just as bad: one branch of the family ends up controlling the board and hogging all the salaried positions. Sure, members of the other branch(es) of the family own stock in the company, but the controlling branch makes sure that dividends are slim or nonexistent, leaving more money for their own salaries and pension benefits. If the shut-out family members try to sell their stock, they may be stymied by transfer restrictions that keep them from selling to willing buyers; or, there may be no interested buyer except the corpora-tion or other family members.

In short, part of running a successful business is making a moderate, workable plan for succession. Understandably, business founders like to flatter themselves that they're completely indispensable and irreplaceable — and often damage the business by failing to train well-informed successors and failing to prevent (or even encouraging) political infighting.

Another consideration is the fact that family businesses often skimp on qualified retirement plans. The anti-discrimination rules tend to make it expensive for a company to award generous pensions to its top executives, because at least some pension benefits are required to "trickle down" to the rank and file employees. To cut costs, cash-strapped businesses may pay passable salaries but little or no retirement benefits. The business founder has even less incentive to retire if retirement means an immediate and huge drop in income!

FREEZING THE VALUATION OF THE BUSINESS

The founder of a successful business is likely to die owning a taxable estate. Estate tax can be eliminated or reduced in various ways, such as using the marital deduction and making personal or charitable gifts. Nevertheless, these measures may be unsuitable in a particular estate plan, or may not be sufficient to completely eliminate the estate tax liability.

Tax planners developed an ingenious measure called the "estate freeze" or "preferred stock freeze" technique. The business founder who was planning to step down would arrange for the business to be recapitalized. The founder would receive dividend-paying preferred stock, and would make a gift of common stock to children or other business successors. (The gift would probably be subject to gift tax, but the value assigned to the common stock was usually very low. If the retiring founder wanted additional retirement income, generous dividends could be declared on the preferred stock. Alternatively, a founder with sufficient retirement income might influence the corporation to avoid declaring dividends on the preferred stock, so that the corporation could accumulate more cash and perhaps invest the cash in a manner that would enhance the value of the common stock owned by the younger generation.) As the business grew and prospered, the appreciation in value would mostly benefit the younger-generation owners of common stock. The gift of common stock would be removed from the owner's estate (because it was an outright gift) — and so would the appreciation in value of the common stock; the value of the preferred stock would be treated as if it were "frozen" at the value of the time of the gift.

Congress has enacted various statutory provisions, and IRS has proposed several sets of Regulations, to control the use of estate freezes as a tax avoidance device.

The current set of valuation rules, effective for most transfers made after October, 1990, are found in Chapter 14 of the Internal Revenue Code and its regulations. The basic theme of Chapter 14 is to impose a significant gift tax cost at the time of the transfer. Advice from a tax lawyer or accountant as to whether the practical and estate tax benefits of the transaction outweigh the gift tax cost is essential before your clients make gifts of stock in their corporations, or before they enter into intrafamily remainder-purchase transactions.

This book concentrates on life during the retirement years, not the earlier stages of life, so little discussion has been given to life insurance planning within the small business corporation. A few words are in order here about estate planning consequences of such plans. Even if the corporation, rather than the business founder, has the incidents of ownership in the policy, the corporation's possession and exercise of incidents of ownership (e.g., transferring the policy as a gift, or for less than adequate compensation) may be attributed to the controlling shareholder — thus forcing inclusion of life insurance proceeds in the controlling stockholder's estate. This may be true even if the transfer by the corporation occurred within three years of the stockholder's death — and even if he or she was no longer a stockholder at the time of death. See Revenue Ruling 90-21, 1990-1 CB 172, and Private Letter Ruling 8806004. Even the transfer of the stock can be treated as a transfer of the underlying insurance policy. Once again, this is a matter for individual tax advice.

Also see Technical Advice memorandum (TAM) 9127007 issued by the IRS National Office. The Memorandum explains the consequences of a situation in which the decedent owned 50% of the stock in a corporation. He had signed a buy-sell agreement that permitted him to repurchase from the corporation the insurance policy on his life owned by the corporation. The corporation assigned the policy to an irrevocable trust owned by the decedent. The assignment occurred less than three years prior to his death. The TAM mandated inclusion of the policy proceeds in the decedent's estate, based on several arguments. In the IRS view, either the decedent exercised his right to buy the policy from the corporation (so he had incidents of ownership), or the policy was a distribution to him from the corporation with respect to his stock.

ESTATE ADMINISTRATION

The estate plan should also deal with the processing, administration, and disposition of the estate. A valid will should appoint an executor — someone to get the will "probated" (getting the necessary court approval) and distribute the estate in accordance with the terms of the will. It is possible to have more than one executor at a time (perhaps a family member and a banker, lawyer, or financial advisor), and it is important to name a "successor executor" to serve if the original executor is unable or unwilling to serve.

The executor has to "marshal the assets" of the estate — find out what the testator (person who made the will) owned, where it is, and collect all debts owed to the estate. (If there will be estate or transfer taxes, it is helpful for the will to specify how the tax will be divided among the various bequests; whether the bequests will be "net," which means that the entire amount is paid to the heir free of tax; and whether the estate tax should come out of the residue.) The executor must also discover and pay the testator's debts, and pay any estate or transfer taxes that are owed. Then the remaining assets are available for distribution.

Settling an estate can be a lengthy process, and in the meantime, the testator's family may need money even if eventually they'll receive an ample inheritance. One of the most valuable traits of life insurance is its ability to provide "estate liquidity" — money to meet the survivors' needs (including paying estate taxes, if any are due) until the estate is "wound up." It also makes sense for each spouse to maintain a separate bank account, with enough cash for a month or two of normal living expenses — even if most of their money is kept in a joint bank account.

DRAFTING THE WILL TO PROMOTE EFFICIENT ADMINISTRATION

There are many ways to draft a will, even a simple will. The goal is to dispose of the entire estate — but not to dispose of anything that cannot pass by will (such as joint property); not to dispose of any property that is no longer in the will (such as artwork that was sold years before the testator's death, or a car that was totalled in a wreck); and not to dispose of more than 100% of the estate.

A specific bequest leaves a particular sum of money ("I hereby bequeath the sum of $5,000 to my most helpful and efficient secretary, Lillian Montclair, if she survives me") or a particular item to someone ("I leave my silver tea set to my cousin Angela Bricker of Salena, Kansas"). If the item is not part of the estate at the testator's death, and the testator does not make an alternative provision ("or the sum of $1,500, if the tea set does not form part of my estate at the time of my death"), the intended beneficiary is out of luck.

A formula bequest gives someone a percentage of the overall estate, or of the residue (the amount remaining after specific bequests). Common sense must be used, and the estate planner must make some projections of possible future events. The estate may be worth much more — or much less — when the testator dies than when the will is drafted. Five percent of the estate may be either a generous inheritance or little or nothing. If the formula bequest is intended to support a spouse or family member, care must be taken to make sure that the resources, and the income they yield, will be suitable for the purpose. If not, additional insurance on the life of the testator may be needed to fill in the gap.

Good will drafting also includes "gifts over" (over to someone else) if the original beneficiary "predeceases" (dies before) the testator. When a major bequest is involved, the most sensible course of action is to redraft the whole will; but gifts over must still be provided. All too many people *never* make a will; and all too many people make one will, and don't bother to have it reviewed periodically and re-drafted to deal with changes in family structure, the testator's wishes, the size of the estate, and changes in the law (especially tax law).

Many wills contain a "pour-over" provision. Some of the assets of the estate (or the "residue" left over after other dispositions are made) are transferred — poured over — into a trust. On the other hand, a trust can be written so that the assets in the trust at the time of a particular person's death can be transferred to that person's estate, and distributed according to his or her will. (Of course, some provision must always be made for the residue — even if a pour-over is not suitable.)

Traditionally, a technical distinction was drawn between "bequests" of personal property and "devises" of real property, so that it would be correct to say "I bequeath and devise my entire estate to my beloved wife," covering both real and personal property, but awkward to say "I bequeath and devise my 1989 Honda Civic," because a car is personal property. The Uniform Probate Code, which has influenced the inheritance laws of many states, allows the term "devise" to be used for either real or personal property.

Real estate can be left outright; left to more than one person as either joint tenants or tenants in common; or put into a trust (including a QTIP trust). Furthermore, a person can be left a "term of years" or a "life estate": the right to occupy (but not sell) the property for the specified number of years, or until his or her death. When the limited estate ends, the property passes to the heir designated by the original testator.

Especially careful planning is needed if the testator owns real estate in states other than the state where he or she was domiciled. A separate, or ancillary, administration may be required in the other state or states. A local executor may have to be appointed. The problem can sometimes be avoided through joint ownership of the property, or transferring ownership of the property to a trust. There is also a possibility that estate or inheritance taxes will be imposed on the property both in the state where it is located and the state of the testator's domicile.

TAX CONSIDERATIONS IN ESTATE PLANNING

Even for the vast majority of estates, which have no estate tax liability, there are significant income tax questions to be settled. One of the executor's major responsibilities is making sure that the appropriate income tax returns are filed for the decedent. Furthermore, the estate itself is a taxpayer, for the time between the decedent's death and the time the estate is wound up — because estates earn investment income.

A person's tax year ends when he or she dies. However, the surviving spouse of a married decedent is allowed to file a final joint return with the deceased spouse for the year of the death (unless he or she remarries before the end of the tax year, in which case he or he can file jointly with the new spouse but not with the deceased spouse).

PRACTICE TIP: Virtually all individuals are "calendar year" taxpayers, whose tax year runs from January 1 to December 31, with the income tax return due the following April 15. Most people wait until the last minute (or beyond) to file their tax returns. Therefore, if a person dies in the first three and a half months of the year, the executor should check to see whether the tax return for the previous year was filed — and to get it filed, if the decedent did not handle it.

PRACTICE TIP: A single, divorced, or widowed decedent might not have to file an income tax return during life (e.g., if income was too small to require a return). However, the executor or administrator (administrators are court-appointed when there's no executor named) must file IRS Form 1310 (which must be attached to a tax return) if the decedent was entitled to a tax *refund*. (This is not necessary for married decedents filing joint returns — the joint return includes the refund claim — or for personal representatives filing a Form 1040, 1040A, or 1040EZ for a decedent.)

The executor must also find out if there is any income in respect of a decedent (IRD) — generally, income that the decedent had a legal right to, but was not reportable before his or her death for accounting reasons. This is true of income accrued but not received before death by a cash basis taxpayer, or of certain income earned by a partner before death. IRD is reported as income either by the estate or by the beneficiary who receives it. Generally speaking, if the IRD can be distributed directly to a surviving spouse, the tax burden will be less than if it is taxed to the estate.

PRACTICE TIP: An executor is not allowed to make a deductible IRA contribution to the IRA of the decedent for the year of his or her death. However, the surviving spouse is generally permitted to deposit and deduct up to $2,000 in a spousal IRA for the year of the decedent's death. A distribution can be made to the spouse so that the spouse can make a deductible IRA contribution.

The medical expenses of a person's last illness can be treated several ways for tax purposes. If the surviving spouse pays the expenses, he or she can get a medical expense deduction, subject to the usual rules (i.e., only expenses that are not reimbursed by insurance or otherwise are deductible; only expenses over 7.5% of Adjusted Gross Income are deductible; the deduction is available in the tax year the expenses were paid).

Another possibility is for the estate, rather than the spouse, to pay the bills. Expenses paid within one year of the decedent's death can be charged to the last income tax return, the estate tax return, or split between the two returns — but the expenses falling below the 7.5% AGI limitation can't be deducted on the estate tax return. If the estate is too small for estate tax to be due, naturally the expenses will go on the income tax return instead. Note that the surviving spouse can still get a medical expense deduction if payment of last illness expenses is spread out over more than one year — which is a real possibility if the illness generated many unreimbursed bills.

SUBSTITUTES FOR A WILL: JOINT OWNERSHIP

Joint bank accounts are a good example of "will substitutes": types of property that are distributed based on legal rules other than those for a will. Joint property is initially owned by more than one person. When the first owner dies, the property passes automatically to the other owner or owners. This is much faster than waiting for probate of a will! In one sense, joint property is simple, a "poor man's will" for those who are impatient with fancy legal devices. But the legal, tax, and Medicaid consequences of joint property are complex (you can imagine the hassles that develop when a couple plans to divorce), and careful legal advice is necessary to decide which assets should be held in separate name, which should be jointly held.

Federal estate taxation of joint property is governed by Code Section 2040. States may use different rules for calculating estate and inheritance taxes on joint property. It is also important to distinguish between property owned jointly (with ownership passing automatically to the surviving joint tenant(s) when one joint tenant dies) and property owned as tenants in common (where each tenant in common owns a separate share of the property, and can pass this share by will, not necessarily to the other tenants in common).

For estates of decedents who die after 1981 and interests created after 1976, and for property 100% owned by a married couple who are joint tenants with right of survivorship or who own the property as tenants by the entireties (a special form of marital property permitted by some states), only *half* the value of the property is included in the estate of the first spouse to die. This is true no matter which spouse paid for the property.

If the joint tenants are not a married couple, or a married couple share joint ownership with someone else, or the interest was created prior to 1976, estate taxation depends on how the joint tenants (for instance, a parent and child; a couple who live together but are not married; a brother and sister; Mr. and Mr. Smith and Mrs. Smith's sister) acquired the property.

For property that was acquired by purchase, a deceased joint tenant's estate includes a percentage of the fair market value of the entire property, measured on the date of death. If the deceased joint tenant paid the full cost of the property, or if there are no records to prove the source of the funds, the entire fair market value is included in the decedent's estate. However, if the survivor can prove what his share of the purchase price was (and that the decedent didn't give him the money to contribute to the purchase price), that portion of the value will be excluded from the estate of the decedent. For instance, if the property cost $200,000, was worth $300,000 at the time of the decedent's death, and the decedent paid 25% of the purchase price, $75,000 — 25% of the fair market value — will be included in the decedent's gross estate for federal estate tax purposes.

On the other hand, if the property was inherited or given as a gift, and there are no other legal rules to the contrary (e.g., state inheritance laws), the decedent's gross estate includes the value of the property divided by the number of joint tenants. Under this rule, if two brothers and a sister inherit a parcel of land as joint tenants with right of survivorship, the estate of the first to die will include one-third the value of the property. (If the surviving siblings continue to own the property as joint tenants, and do not add further joint tenants, the estate of the second to die will include one-half the value, because there are two joint tenants at the time.)

SUBSTITUTES FOR A WILL: REVOCABLE TRUSTS

Revocable trusts are another will substitute. Revocable trusts also allow property to be passed quickly, without waiting for probate (and without paying the legal fees and court costs involved in probating a will). Wills and probate records are also public documents, and therefore they are unattractive to people who want to keep their financial affairs confidential. Revocable trusts provide a lot of flexibility, but they don't provide significant tax advantages; again, the planning team must think hard about legal, Medicaid, and tax consequences before recommending a revocable trust.

THE COMPLETE ESTATE PLAN

To sum up, even a simple estate plan can contain many elements, such as joint accounts, other bank accounts, property held jointly, separate property, a DPA, a will, life insurance, pension benefits and death benefits provided by an employer, and one or more trusts. A good estate plan must meet many criteria:

- It must satisfy the client's wishes (as long as they can be accommodated legally).

- It must be easy and economical to administer.

- It must take income, gift, and estate taxes (of both testator and beneficiaries) into account.

- It must look at Medicaid considerations (again, for both the maker of gifts and the recipient of gifts).

- It must provide liquidity.

- It must have enough flexibility to deal with changes in the law and in practical factors.

- It must deal with the risk that both the maker of the plan and the recipients of income and assets may become incapacitated; gifts and legacies to children must take their legal disabilities into account (e. g., by placing the legacy in trust, or making a gift under the state's Gifts to Minors or Transfers to Minors statute).

- It must take inflation and market factors into account — giving someone the income from a stock portfolio, or the rent on a property, can be either generous or useless, depending on how well the stocks are doing and on whether or not a tenant can be found.

- It must cope with contingencies — beneficiaries dying before the testator; property not being in the estate; the estate growing or shrinking; the executor(s) being unavailable or unwilling to serve; tax laws penalizing segments of the existing plan, or making more generous planning options available.

- It must provide the most comfortable provision that is available for the surviving spouse, children, and other objects of the testator's bounty.

TRUSTS IN LIFETIME AND ESTATE PLANNING

Trusts are a powerful yet flexible instrument for achieving many objectives. However, careful planning is necessary, because trusts have many implications, in terms of administrative costs and difficulties, income, gift, and estate taxation, Medicaid, and issues of fiduciary conduct. Trusts can be analyzed in many ways: for instance, how they are created; how long they last; who receives the income; if part of a trust's capital can be distributed before the trust ends. These choices also have legal and tax consequences.

A trust is an arrangement for management and distribution of property. In the simplest trust, someone who owns money or other property places the property into trust by signing a trust document and transferring the property to a trustee. The original owner of the property is known as the trust creator, settlor, or grantor. The trust document contains instructions about how the trustee should manage the property, and what should be done with the trust's income each year. The people who are to receive the trust income are known as income beneficiaries.

If the trust distributes all its net income each year (after expenses and any taxes), it's called a simple trust; if the trust document allows some or all of the income to be accumulated and plowed back into the trust, it's a complex trust. The accounting computations required to prepare a complex trust's tax returns are extremely sophisticated.

PRACTICE TIP: It is definitely a good idea for a trustee to get professional assistance in completing the trust's tax forms — this is absolutely essential for a complex trust. Legal and/or accounting advice is a necessary part of deciding whether or not to accumulate income. Don't forget, the trust itself is a taxpayer, and the trustee is responsible for filing the necessary tax returns and making the payment.

The trust document also specifies the duration of the trust. (Most trusts are not allowed to continue forever. The Rule Against Perpetuities, a legal doctrine, pretty much limits the trust's term to two or three generations, plus enough time for the grantor's grandchildren or great-grandchildren to reach the age of majority.) When the trust term expires, the trustee must distribute whatever remains in the trust (the original trust corpus or principal, plus income that was earned but not distributed). The trust will contain instructions about distributions to the remaindermen (people chosen to receive distributions from a terminating trust).

Trusts vary greatly in the powers given to the trustee. Sometimes the trustee must simply carry out the detailed program set up in the trust (invest this way, distribute this much to these people on such-and-such a date, give out the remaining property to these remainder-men on such-and-such a date). Other trusts, however, give the trustee a tremendous amount of discretion. If it is a so-called "spray" trust, the trust document names a class of potential income beneficiaries (for instance, the grantor plus the grantor's spouse, children, and grand-children), and the trustee then decides which of these people needs to receive trust income, and how much each should be given.

One of the most important decisions in setting up a trust is whether any trust beneficiaries should be given the right to demand part of the trust principal in case of financial need. A distribution of principal generally reduces the trust's ability to generate income. It is also true that principal that is distributed to one beneficiary is not available to be distributed to the remainderman when the trust ends. Therefore, the trust creator must balance the interests of various people.

Another important question is whether the trustee has discretion to make a distribution of principal to any beneficiary if the trustee thinks the beneficiary needs it (for example, to cope with a sudden financial emergency). Giving the trustee this power greatly adds to flexibility; but it has important consequences on the balance of power within the family (the remaindermen may not be too happy if the amount they expect to receive is reduced!) and also has consequences on the Medicaid eligibility of trust beneficiaries.

Usually, the goal of the trust is to achieve as much current income as possible consistent with proper conduct by the trustee. (Trustees are not allowed to take wild risks.) But there may be circumstances in which it is worthwhile to cut back on trust income: to save taxes, or because a beneficiary's Medicaid plan is impaired by getting more income. It may be worthwhile to draft the trust to make it clear that the trustee can invest in long-range growth investments that yield little or no current income.

CLASSIFICATIONS OF TRUSTS

An inter vivos trust is one set up and operating during the grantor's lifetime. A testamentary trust is one that forms part of the grantor's will, and goes into operation when he or she dies. There can also be an inter vivos trust designed to end when the grantor dies, with all the remaining trust property being transferred into his or her estate and distributed as the will provides — or a will provision calling for part of the estate to be placed into a trust that already exists.

A revocable trust is one that gives the grantor the power to amend the trust terms, or even take back the property. Revocable trusts are sometimes used as a way to avoid probate.

An irrevocable trust is one which the grantor cannot amend or revoke; he or she has given up all control over the trust assets. Why sacrifice so much flexibility, and put property entirely outside one's reach? Because property placed in a properly-drafted irrevocable trust is excluded from the grantor's federally taxable estate.

In simple terms, a person's gross estate includes the property that he owned at the time of death. An important exception is property left to the surviving spouse; whether property is given to a spouse, inherited by a spouse, or placed in a trust benefiting only the spouse, more liberal tax rules will be applied than if the property were transferred to a non-spouse.

Property can be removed from the estate by giving it away. An outright gift will remove property from the estate; so will certain transfers into trusts. But to remove the property, the transferor must make the transfer during life (rather than including trust provisions in his will). Furthermore, the transferor can't change his mind; the transfer must be irrevocable. Control must be surrendered totally. The transferor cannot retain a life estate, the ability to change the terms of the trust, or the power to direct who will get the property. (Under Code Section 2042, life insurance proceeds will also be included in the estate if incidents of ownership were transferred within three years of the decedent's death.)

The tradeoff facing a person contemplating creating a trust is that transfer into the irrevocable trust is considered a gift for tax purposes. Either gift tax must be paid at once, or part of the unified credit against gift and estate tax must be used up, with the result that the eventual estate tax may be higher. Of course, this is not a problem if estate planning techniques can be used to eliminate the obligation to pay estate tax.

If the irrevocable inter vivos trust includes property that has appreciated or can appreciate in value, there is an additional planning benefit. The trust creator doesn't have to pay tax on the appreciation during lifetime, and his estate doesn't have to pay tax on the appreciation because the entire property, appreciation and all, has been removed from the taxable estate. The irrevocable trust will also be excluded from the probate estate, and fees for probating an estate are usually calculated based on the size of the probate estate; a smaller probate estate means lower probate fees.

For a wealthy family, saving estate taxes can be worth a certain sacrifice of control. But the surrender of control must be total, or nearly so; retaining more than token rights to receive benefits from the trust or to control trust administration will result in inclusion of the trust property in the grantor's estate.

Tax law contains a wealth of complexities. Under Technical Advice Memorandum (TAM) 9122005, IRS took the position that a supposedly irrevocable trust should be included in a decedent's estate because the decedent was not only the trust grantor but also a co-trustee who had the power to use principal from the trust to discharge his support obligations to his wife. Under this analysis, the mere power to do so called for inclusion of the trust in the decedent's estate, whether or not he actually used the trust to support his wife. The trust was not insulated from inclusion in the estate merely because the trust language required the trustees to consider the spouse's other means of support before using trust principal for her needs. The elder care planning team should keep this in mind when drafting trusts, because it is common under state laws for spouses to have a legal obligation to provide "necessaries," including medical care, to each other. The right to invade could trigger inclusion in the estate of the spouse who established the irrevocable trust precisely to *remove* assets from his estate.

To sum up, then, a trust is a way to provide management of trust assets, and distribution of trust income and principal according to the wishes of the grantor (which may be very complex). The trust document *must* name a trustee or trustees and should name at least one successor trustee to serve in case an originally named trustee refuses to serve, or is or becomes unable to serve. Most state laws specify the powers that trustees have automatically; it may be worthwhile to give them additional powers, and describe these powers in the trust document. The document must name income beneficiaries and remaindermen. It is possible, though not necessary, to allow beneficiaries the right to demand a certain amount of principal; trustees can also be given the power to distribute principal.

Finally, when the trust term expires, the remaining funds are distributed to the remaindermen. It's also possible to set up a trust calling for staged distributions. If the grantor doesn't trust his children's ability to manage money, each can be given a certain amount of principal at age 20, with more arriving at age 30 and age 40, with the trust terminating when the youngest reaches 40.

WHY CREATE A TRUST?

There are many reasons for setting up a trust:

(1) Saving income taxes. Trust income is taxed to either the grantor, the trust, or the trust beneficiary. Income is taxed to the grantor (a grantor trust) if:

- Trust income and/or principal can be used to meet the grantor's legal obligations — such as obligations to support spouse and children.

- Trust income can be used to pay premiums on insurance policies on the life of the grantor or spouse.

- The grantor has significant influence over the way the trust property is distributed.

As one can see, this is a pretty comprehensive list, and a drafter has to work hard to keep a trust from being a grantor trust!

Otherwise, income is generally taxed to the trust if accumulated, or taxed to the beneficiary if distributed. However, there is little to be gained by "income-shifting" (using a trust to shift income from a high-bracket family member to a trust or low-bracket family member. There used to be many tax brackets, with a wide range between the top and bottom brackets. Today, there are few brackets, with a much narrower range. It's still possible for the very wealthy to achieve some income tax savings by using trusts, but it requires top professional advice. For most middle class and upper middle class people, trusts will not achieve income tax savings (although they may provide other extremely valuable benefits).

Under the Revenue Reconciliation Act of 1993, trusts, like individuals, are taxed in the 15%, 28%, 31%, 36%, or 39.6%

bracket. The difference is that the brackets for trusts (and estates) "kick in" at a much lower level than for individuals. The maximum trust bracket of 39.6% applies to all trust income over $7,500; only the first $1,500 of trust income qualifies for the lowest, 15% bracket, with income from $1,500-$3,500 taxed at 28%, income from $3,500-$5,500 taxed at 31%, and income from $5,500 to $7,500 taxed at 36%. (All brackets are subject to inflation adjustments.) In many instances, income taxed to a trust will generate more income tax than if it had been payable to an individual (especially a retiree whose tax rates as well as income declined after retirement).

(2) Dealing with the needs of minors. If an outright gift or bequest is made to a minor child or grandchild, there are legal restraints on the recipient's use of the property. In order to sell the property, or engage in many other transactions, a guardian must be appointed. If, instead, the property is placed in trust, the trustee can manage the property until the recipient reaches the age of majority. If the grantor doesn't think that a young family member has good sense when it comes to money, then the younger-generation beneficiary can be given trust income only, or distribution of principal can be delayed. The trustee can then have a supervisory financial role, agreeing to a principal payment to go to graduate school, turning down a request for money to buy a sports car. The principal of a "spendthrift trust" can't be reached by the creditors of the trust's beneficiaries.

> PLANNING TIP: A person can set up a spendthrift trust to protect trust assets against someone else's creditors — but not his own. A person can't transfer his money into trust, then tell his creditors to go fly a kite because it is a spendthrift trust.

> PLANNING TIP: What if the clients want to give or leave something to minor children or grandchildren, but not enough to justify the trouble and expense of creating and managing a trust? Check state law — there is probably a law setting up a simple mechanism for Gifts or Transfers to Minors, allowing the parents or other responsible adults or institutions to manage the gift or bequest for the benefit of the young recipient.

> • Coping with incapacity due to aging. An older person who doesn't want to manage money can turn the task over to a trustee, who will take care of paying bills and make sure

that income is available for a comfortable lifestyle. An older person who fears becoming unable to manage money can set up a trust which, combined with a durable power of attorney (see page 313) can serve as a much better, more dignified, more efficient, and more economical alternative to conservatorship or guardianship. However, Medicaid considerations must be paramount when designing a trust of this type.

- Carrying out complex plans in a flexible manner. It is perfectly possible for a trust to name twelve different beneficiaries (or even "classes" of beneficiaries, such as "all of my son Robert's children born before my death") and create a complex system of rules under which each can or must receive income and/or principal. The trustee can be given discretion to decide who needs money, how often, and how much, and whether the trust should concentrate on giving out income now or growing to provide a large sum to the remaindermen.

- "QTIPs." As discussed on page 308, it is possible to get an estate tax marital deduction for provisions made for the surviving spouse without actually giving the spouse the money or assets outright. This is done by giving the spouse a "Qualified Terminable Interest in Property (QTIP)." One motive for using a QTIP is to give a surviving spouse the protection of lifetime income, while making sure that the trust corpus goes to the grantor's children (this is a common strategy if the grantor has remarried and the children are hostile to the second spouse). Another motive is to provide income for the needs of a spouse who is unused to, or incapable of, administering a large sum of money. The assets in question can be placed into a trust, with the surviving spouse as income beneficiary.

- Saving estate tax. In order to get the trust assets out of the taxable estate, the trust must be irrevocable; the grantor must not possess a significant "beneficial interest" in the property (although some minor powers may be retained). Furthermore, if the grantor surrendered certain rights and powers over the property in trust less than three years before death, (e.g., if the grantor kept a "life estate" in trust property, but gave it up less than three years before death), the trust property is "thrown back" into the taxable estate.

PLANNING TIP: One of the factors that determines whether trust corpus is included in the grantor's estate is whether the grantor has incidents of ownership in a life insurance policy held in the trust.

Therefore, one of the factors in deciding to adopt an irrevocable trust is whether there is likely to be a taxable estate. Anyone likely to have a taxable estate needs professional tax advice before making a transfer to an irrevocable trust, and needs occasional review of the trust and the whole estate plan in light of current tax law.

TRUSTS AND GIFT TAX

The creation of a trust is an event with theoretical gift tax implications. In most instances, the implications remain theoretical. Gifts to the spouse are generally free of gift tax, regardless of the size, timing, or motive of the gift. Furthermore, a gift of up to $10,000 per donee per year (or up to $20,000 per donee per year, if the giver's spouse agrees to join in the gift) is usually free of gift tax.

There are two important characteristics of gifts that qualify for this annual exclusion. First, the gift must be irrevocable: the giver cannot have the right to take it back. Second, the gift must be a gift of a present interest, not a gift that takes effect in the future.

One of the questions the lawyer and the accountant in the planning team must address is whether a proposed trust structure would give rise to present-interest gifts (qualifying for the $10,000 or $20,000 annual exclusion) or future-interest gifts (generating gift tax liability). In general, complex trusts that are allowed to accumulate income are not considered present-interest trusts, so the advantages of accumulating income must be balanced against gift tax liability.

Tax law permits the use of certain specific trust provisions to ensure that the trust will be a present-interest trust. For example, if the trust is for the benefit of a minor, and the provisions of Code Section 2503(c) are followed, directing the trustee to use trust principal and income for the minor's benefit, a present rather than future interest gift will be involved and the annual exclusion will be available. Another possibility is the "Crummey Trust" taking advantage of a 1968 tax case. A Crummey Trust gives the beneficiary the right to demand a specified amount of money from the trust each year; the ability to make the demand, even if it is never exercised, makes the transfer of property into the trust a present-interest gift rather than a future-interest gift. Crummey Trusts have other tax implications, which must be explored by the planner.

Very few people ever have to pay gift tax, because they are allowed to give up to $10,000 per year per donee (or $20,000 a year per donee if the spouse agrees to join in the gift). However, to qualify for the annual exclusion, the gift has to be an outright gift, with an irrevocable transfer of ownership. Furthermore, it must be a gift of a present interest — a gift that takes effect now, not in the future. Therefore, certain trusts (including complex trusts that are allowed to accumulate their income) do not qualify for the $10,000 or $20,000 exclusion, and gift tax may result. This is another matter to be discussed with the lawyer and accountant in the planning team.

GRANTOR AS TRUSTEE

For income tax purposes, trusts will be disregarded, and the grantor will be treated as the owner of the trust and will be obliged to pay income tax on the trust's income, if the grantor retains excessive powers. The "grantor trust" rules are found in Code Sections 671-678. If the grantor is the only trustee, the trust will generally be a grantor trust. If the grantor is not a trustee, or if the grantor serves as co-trustee with another party or parties, whether or not the trust is a grantor trust depends on the balance of power among the trustees.

Under these rules, a trustee or other person is nonadverse to the grantor if the party has no beneficial interest in the trust; has only an insubstantial interest in the trust; or if the party's interest in the trust is not affected whether or not the power is exercised. An adverse party is one who has a substantial beneficial interest in the trust which *is* adversely affected by the exercise or nonexercise of the power. For instance, a remainderman is adverse to a grantor who is an income beneficiary with the power to demand invasion of principal, because the invasion decreases the size of the remainder that will eventually be paid to the remainderman.

Most of the trusts used in elder care planning are grantor trusts, because these trusts are usually designed to provide income to senior citizens while insulating the trust corpus from treatment as an available asset for Medicaid purposes. This is true because Code

Section 677 makes a trust a grantor trust if the grantor or a person who is not adverse to the grantor has the power to distribute income to the grantor or the grantor's spouse. If it is very important to save income taxes, and the trust is in a much lower bracket than the grantor, it may be possible to handle the problem by giving an adverse party (e.g., a child who is a trust remainderman) control over the income. This is not always acceptable to the older client. The client may prefer paying income taxes to the chance that the child will cut off the parent's income!

Under Section 677, income is also taxed to the grantor if it can be held or accumulated for future distribution to the grantor or spouse, or if it may be used to pay premiums on insurance on the life of the grantor or spouse. Actual use of trust income to support the grantor's dependents (but not a mere power to do so) makes the income taxable to the grantor.

Section 677 makes an exception if the consent or approval of an adverse party is required for discretionary distributions of trust income to the grantor or spouse. However, the adverse party must have real powers. In *Dubois*, TCM 1986-160, trust income was taxed to the grantor even though the trust instrument required consent from an adverse party-trustee, because the adverse party was a trustee in name only and all the decisions about trust administration were made by the grantor.

The grantor trust rules create a complex system of rules, exceptions, and exceptions to exceptions. A full exploration is beyond the scope of this work. However, certain general rules should be noted here. Under Section 676, a revocable trust is necessarily a grantor trust if the power to revoke or amend the trust can be exercised by the grantor or a nonadverse party, or both. Under Section 673, if more than 5% of the value of the trust corpus can revert to the grantor, the trust is a grantor trust (e.g., if the trust instrument provides that half the trust corpus should be paid back to the grantor after the trust has been in existence for five years). Code Section 675 severely limits the powers which the grantor can exercise as trustee in administering the trust without the trust becoming a grantor trust.

The grantor/trustee's ability to invade principal for *any* beneficiary can also result in inclusion of the trust corpus in the grantor's estate, on the grounds that he retained a degree of control incompatible with an irrevocable transfer. There is an exception for a power subject to an "external standard." The external standard gives trustees the power to invade the principal and distribute it to a beneficiary, subject to an external or ascertainable standard, such as the "maintenance of the beneficiary in reasonable health and comfort" or "payment of the beneficiary's medical and educational expenses."

The planner faces many thorny dilemmas. An irrevocable trust paying income to the grantor and spouse, but with no discretion on the part of the trustee to invade principal, will provide professional management of assets which can be very useful in case of incompetency of the grantor and/or spouse. However, the trust will be a grantor trust for income tax purposes. Flexibility to invade principal is often useful, but can lead to inclusion of the trust in the grantor's estate unless an "ascertainable standard" is used. Unfortunately, these latter types of power have negative Medicaid consequences.

TRUSTS AND MEDICAID

There are many difficult questions to be answered about the interaction between trusts and Medicaid. As discussed in Chapter 7, eligibility for Medicaid depends on three factors, principally the applicant's income; assets; and transfers made during the penalty period.

Since 1988, the rule has been that, when spouses get income from a trust, the income is deemed "available" for Medicaid purposes based on the terms of the trust. For instance, if William and Eunice Barber get income from a trust, William has applied for Medicaid, and the trust provides $100 monthly income to William and $200 to Eunice, William's available income includes $100 from the trust, but not Eunice's $200. However, the $200 could be taken into account in determining whether Eunice has a duty to support William. If the trust says "$300 a month to William and Eunice Barber," then half the income is treated as available to each spouse. However, if William is in a nursing home, he has the right to prove that more than half of the money should be allocated to Eunice (thus reducing his own available income, and making it more likely that he will be eligible for Medicaid or able to spend down his excess income to the eligibility level). If there are other beneficiaries besides William and Eunice, income is deemed available to William and Eunice based on their share of the income paid to all the beneficiaries.

Putting money into a trust is a transfer for Medicaid purposes. OBRA '93 changed the way the look-back period is calculated for trusts. If the trust is irrevocable, and the terms of the trust keep the grantor from getting either principal or income from the trust, the look-back period is 60 months. Thus, if the trust is set up more than five years before the Medicaid application, it will not affect Medicaid eligibility, but very few people can plan that far in advance. If the trust is irrevocable, but the grantor can get principal and/or income, the look-back period is 36 months.

That is, if the trust was created less than three years before the application, the amount transferred into the trust (plus all other non-exempt transfers) will be divided by the average cost of nursing home care in the relevant geographic area. The result will determine the length of time the grantor will be ineligible for Medicaid nursing home benefits (and certain Medicaid home care benefits). If the trust is revocable, it will be treated as if all the funds in the trust belonged to the grantor. The theory is that he or she can just cancel the trust and get the money back, so the money is still his or hers for Medicaid purposes.

Perhaps the most difficult problem is whether a trust is an "available asset." Before 1985, a common (and successful) Medicaid planning tactic was to transfer assets to an irrevocable trust, usually a "spray" trust which could (but didn't have to) provide income for the grantor and spouse. The grantor would not have the right to demand principal. The grantor simply took the position that the trust was not "available."

However, as discussed on page 172, the Comprehensive Omnibus Reconciliation Act of 1985 (COBRA) amended the Social Security Act (which contains the federal Medicaid law) to define an inter vivos trust set up by an individual to benefit him and/or his spouse as a "Medicaid qualifying trust." If a trust is a Medicaid qualifying trust, the maximum amount that the trustee *could* distribute (not the maximum amount that the beneficiary has a right to *demand*) constitutes an available asset — even if the trustee never does distribute anything to the Medicaid applicant.

PLANNING TIP: A trust set up by a child for a parent, or by a parent for a disabled child, is not a Medicaid-qualifying trust, and is not subject to these rules.

OBRA '93 changed this rule, too. The Medicaid Qualifying Trust rules stay in effect for trusts set up *before* OBRA '93 was enacted. But for later trusts, the most important factor is not whether or not the trustee has discretion. What counts is whether the Medicaid applicant or recipient has any rights, under the trust, to get income or principal from the trust.

For instance, "income" trusts — trusts that pay part or all of their income to the grantor — are popular. So are trusts that permit the trustee to invade the principal if the grantor needs extra money for medical expenses, or general living expenses. On the other hand, some trusts are set up as a way for the grantor to give away money (to a charity; to a child or spouse), and do not give the grantor any access at all to principal or income. Trusts of this type might be used by a wealthy person who wants to remove assets from his or her estate so there will be less — or no — estate tax at his or her death.

Under OBRA '93, if the grantor *can* get any principal or income from the trust, whatever he or she does receive will be considered available income or available assets for Medicaid purposes. Any principal or income that goes to another person (say, a spouse or child) will be considered a transfer made by the Medicaid applicant or recipient. The look-back period for this type of trust is 36 months.

If the grantor *cannot* get anything from the trust, the whole amount put into the trust will be considered a transfer for Medicaid purposes. The look-back period for this type of trust is 60 months — longer than for any other kind of transfer.

Planners must take another factor into consideration. Under the OBRA '93 rules, a trust may not prevent the grantor from qualifying for Medicaid or receiving Medicaid benefits. However, when the grantor dies, the trust may be subject to claims from the state Medicaid agency, which may have a right to be paid back whatever is spent on the grantor's medical bills. The Medicaid agency is entitled to be reimbursed before the trust can be distributed in accordance with the grantor's wishes. In many cases, little or nothing will be left over after reimbursement.

Another problem is that many trusts were actually drafted for estate planning purposes, without thinking about Medicaid. If the trust contains a "five or five power," the person who has the power is unlikely to qualify for Medicaid. Medicaid applicants have a legal duty to collect all the income and assets they're entitled to, so they have to demand the 5% or $5,000 before making a Medicaid application — and collecting the funds is likely to make them ineligible for Medicaid.

If the trust contains an "external standard," such as the support or health of the beneficiary, there are subtle legal problems whenever the beneficiary makes a Medicaid application. Depending on state law, and the position the courts take, the beneficiary may be forced to try to get the trustee to provide funds. After all, a person who is in a nursing home, or about to go in, certainly needs "support" and has significant "medical expenses" — so an argument can be made that the trustee has a *duty* to invade the principal for these purposes.

But can the state Medicaid authority order the trustee to do so? (An argument can also be made that the grantor would want the beneficiary to get Medicaid benefits instead of using up the trust assets — especially if there are other beneficiaries, or other remaindermen, involved.) Can the beneficiary force an unwilling trustee to invade principal — or keep a willing trustee from invading principal and giving the beneficiary money that will block a Medicaid application? These are difficult questions that courts have answered in various ways, based on technical criteria that are too lengthy to go into here. The only thing the planning team can do is keep informed about your state's Medicaid rules and the latest court decisions.

PLANNING TIP: One approach that may work is for the trust to state explicitly that it is a "luxury trust" intended to supplement, not replace, public benefits, and that the trustee cannot invade principal to pay any bill that would otherwise be paid by public funds. But this approach works much better in trusts set up by parents for their disabled children. When people set up trusts for their own elder-law planning, they are likely to fall afoul of the "Medicaid qualifying trust" rules, or the rules that forbid creation of a spendthrift trust to protect against one's own creditors.

OBRA '93 made it clear that luxury trusts (sometimes known as Supplemental Needs Trusts, or Special Needs Trusts) set up be parents, grandparents, or courts for disabled persons over 65 will not fall afoul of the harsh rules otherwise applied to trusts under OBRA '93 — on condition that the corpus of the trust revert to the state after the disabled person's death.

When this book went to press in April, 1997, it was not clear how the Health Insurance Portability and Accountability Act of 1996 (P.L. 104-191) transfer ban (see page 179) would apply to trusts. It seems likely that creating an irrevocable trust that cannot provide benefits to the grantor will be subject to a 60-month look-back period for Health Insurance Portability and Accountability Act of 1996 purposes also. In other words, it might be a criminal act to transfer funds into an irrevocable trust within 60 months before a Medicaid application — unless the transfer is exempt for another reason (it is made for the sole benefit of the Medicaid applicant's spouse, for instance).

Clearly, the creation of a trust, especially an irrevocable trust, requires intense scrutiny by an attorney who is not only aware of tax rules but understands the latest application of the 1996 legislation.

LIFE INSURANCE TRUSTS

Life insurance is a feature of most elder care plans; trusts are a feature of any such plans. The combination of the two — in a life insurance trust — can secure potent management and tax advantages (especially estate tax savings) that are not available when the two planning tools are used separately. New Jersey financial planner Steven B. Enright told the New York Times that nearly all of his clients (especially those with assets over $1 million) have life insurance trusts; "It's almost a dunk shot when you're planning for high net-worth individuals."[4]

The life insurance trust is usually set up as an irrevocable trust — that is, once your client sets up the trust, he or she cannot have a change of heart and end the trust and recapture the trust assets.

PLANNING TIP: That means that, if the insured person divorces, he or she cannot change the trust. The way to cope with that risk is to make the beneficiary (or one of the beneficiaries) "my husband/wife at the time of my death," with provisions for an alternate beneficiary if the insured person is widowed or divorced when he or she dies.

Depending on client wishes, various methods can be used to set up and fund a life insurance trust. In an unfunded life insurance trust, policies are merely deposited with the trustee. The insured continues to make premium payments (unless a paid-up policy is used for this purpose). Sometimes revocable trusts are used as depositaries for unfunded life insurance trusts.

In an investment trust (also known as a partially funded trust), the grantor makes periodic deposits of cash or securities into the trust. The trustee uses whatever portion of the deposit that is necessary to maintain the insurance premiums. If anything is left over, it is placed in a second trust which remains in effect until the grantor dies; then the second trust is distributed in accordance with its trust instrument.

A fully funded trust contains both the insurance policy or policies and a quantity of income-producing assets (e.g., bonds; dividend-paying stocks) sufficient for the trustee to use the income to pay the insurance premiums.

Life insurance trusts are usually funded. Note that, under Code Section 677(a)(3), life insurance trusts are grantor trusts, so the grantor is taxed on trust income, even if the trust is irrevocable or unfunded; even if the trustee has discretion to use trust income to pay premiums, but is not obliged to do so; even if the grantor has no right to make a further change of beneficiary; and even if the policy is payable to the trustee.

The general rule for estate taxation is that insurance proceeds are includable in the insured's estate for tax purposes, if (1) proceeds are payable to the insured's estate, or (2) the insured retained "incidents of ownership" in the policy. Incidents of ownership include the right to surrender or assign the policy; take a policy loan; use the policy as collateral for a loan; or change the beneficiary or the way proceeds are paid out.[5]

But an irrevocable life insurance trust is not subject to either of these problems (as long as it is set up more than three years before death; see below). The proceeds are payable to a trust, not the insured person's estate; and there are no incidents of ownership in the policy (as long as the trust is properly drafted) because the trust is irrevocable. (This discussion assures that the insured person will also be the grantor of the life insurance trust; if this is not the case for a client, the situation should be discussed with the lawyer on the planning team.)

PRACTICE TIP: A good provision to include is an obligation on the insured person's part to give "reasonable cooperation" to the insurer — for instance, by taking insurance physicals. Otherwise, it might be argued that the insured person can stop cooperating and therefore force the insurer to cancel the policy.

Life insurance trusts are especially effective for long-range planning. This is because Code Section 2035(d)(2) says that, if incidents of ownership were transferred more than three years before the death of the insured person, the policy proceeds are not includable in the estate. That means that, if the insured person sets up a life insurance trust at age 70, and contributes life insurance policies to the trust, then dies at age 72, the proceeds will still be included in his or her estate. But if he or she lives past age 73, the proceeds will not be (unless the trust falls afoul of another tax rule).

Another possibility is for the trust, not the insured person, to buy the policy (a trust has an insurable interest in the insured person's life) — but if the insured person contributes cash to the trust for the purchase, the same three-year problem arises — unless the insured person never had any incidents of ownership in the policy[6].

PLANNING TIP: Of course, you can't tell whether your clients will survive the creation of the trust by three years. So, to make it clear that the purchase of the policy was the trustee's independent decision (that is, the trustee was not a mere agent of the insured person) make sure that the insured person stays far away from the insurance purchase! The trustee should buy the policy; when the insured person contributes to the trust, the contributions should *not* match the premium amounts; the trustee should pay the premiums (instead of endorsing over the insured person's check).

The major advantage of the life insurance trust is that, if the appropriate tax rules are followed, the proceeds of the insurance policies will escape estate tax because they will neither be included in the estate of the insured person, nor in the estate of his or her spouse. To keep the proceeds out of the spouse's estate, the rules of Code Section 2036 must be followed. That is, the insured person's spouse should not contribute a policy which he or she owns to the life insurance trust, nor should the spouse contribute a policy which the trustee can use to meet the spouse's support obligations.

In Private Letter Ruling 8819001, the IRS took the position that, where a policy was transferred to a life insurance trust more than three years before the decedent's death, the trust's exchanging the policy for another policy during the three-year period will not cause the proceeds to be included in the decedent's estate — even if he or she signed the application for the new policy. This result is reached because the policy could have been issued without the signature, and he or she held no incidents of ownership during the three-year period.

The tax and estate planning rules to follow in setting up a life insurance trust include:

- Limiting the powers of the insured person over the trust. The more powers he or she has, the more likely that he or she will be treated as having incidents of ownership in the insurance policies, thus making the trust's assets part of the insured person's taxable estate. Also, the grantor trust rules must be consulted to determine whether the insured should serve as trustee and, if so, what limitations should be placed on his powers. The trustee(s) must be independent, not controlled by the insured person.

  The insured person also should not be given the right to remove or replace trustees arbitrarily, because this will be treated as control over the trust (with negative estate tax consequences). The negative consequences will not be imposed if the insured person is allowed to remove the trustee for good cause — for instance, breach of fiduciary duties.

- Many life insurance trusts call for annual additions to the trust (this is necessary to pay premiums, unless paid-up policies are placed in the trust or the initial level of funding is high). Under the Internal Revenue Code, the annual contributions may be subject to gift tax. An exception is if the trust falls under Code Section 2503 ("present-interest trusts"). One way to make sure that a life insurance trust is a present interest trust is to draft the trust to include a "Crummey power."[7] That is, the trust beneficiaries (typically family members of the insured person) can be given the right to withdraw some money from the trust.

- If the combined lifetime and estate plan calls for a QTIP, the life insurance trust can be used to provide a lifetime interest for the surviving spouse. Furthermore, if there is any risk that the insurance trust will be included in the insured person's estate, the QTIP can save estate tax because the amounts going to the surviving spouse as a qualified terminable interest qualify for the marital deduction and thus are deductible from the insured person's estate.

The disadvantage of life insurance trusts is that, as irrevocable trusts, they are not very flexible. Therefore, they must be only one part of a comprehensive plan, not the total plan. One way to gain a little flexibility is for the planning team to draft the trust so that the trustees are allowed to lend money to the estate of the insured person (or insured person's spouse) at a reasonable rate, or to buy unwanted property from the estate (again, the payment must be reasonable — neither a giveaway nor an exorbitant price for assets of small value). That way, the estate will have cash for immediate needs, which may include paying estate taxes.

The life insurance trust, of course, can make regular payments to beneficiaries to meet *their* financial needs; income can also be accumulated in the trust. Beneficiaries have the right to get all the income from the trust. However, they don't have to take it; they can let it build up — which might be the choice of the insured person's spouse who wants to leave more money for the children. The New York Times article cited above gives the example of a $1 million policy left intact for 30 years, with an annual 6% growth rate; the final outcome would be a fund of close to $6 million.

Life insurance trusts also usually give beneficiaries the right to demand a certain amount of the trust principal if they need a lump sum — for instance, to travel; for an operation; for home repairs; or for a child's college tuition. A common "withdrawal" provision is the "five or five power": the right to demand up to 5% of the trust assets, or $5,000 a year from the trustees. The trustees must automatically pay out the amount demanded by the holder of a "five or five power."

The trust can also be written to allow withdrawals of principal at the discretion of the trustee(s), but such a provision renders the maximum amount that could be withdrawn "available" for Medicaid purposes.

CHARITABLE GIVING AND TRUSTS

The charitable trust is another special-purpose trust that fits well into the financial and estate plans of some elderly clients (especially the wealthy). A charitable trust gives the grantor an opportunity for "doing well by doing good": helping himself (from the estate planning viewpoint, and perhaps saving some income tax) while also benefiting a charity. Charitable trusts are especially attractive to wealthy individuals who are single, widowed, or divorced (and therefore cannot take advantage of the marital deduction) and either have no children or have made adequate provision for their children in other ways.

Although the use of a trust offers certain advantages, not all charitable transfers are made in trust form. An individual can make an outright charitable gift, thus removing the assets from the estate and qualifying for an income tax deduction. If the gift is very large, part of it may be non-deductible; clients planning major charitable gifts should get legal advice first. Advice is crucial if a gift of appreciated property — which is not worth more than the potential giver paid for it — or depreciated property is contemplated.

Plenty of tax traps lurk in gifts of property whose value has changed. This problem doesn't arise when money, rather than property such as real estate or art objects, is contributed.

PLANNING TIP: A wealthy person may want to make a big charitable contribution during his or her lifetime, yet hesitate because it seems unfair to deprive spouse or family members of part of their inheritance. A possible solution is to make the gift during lifetime; take the permissible charitable deduction against income tax — and use the amount that would otherwise have gone to pay income taxes, to buy insurance on the life of the giver, benefiting the family members who lost out because of the lifetime charitable gift.

Lifetime charitable gifts have a major drawback: the giver loses all access to the funds or other donated property. The charitable trust makes it possible to retain certain benefits of the assets during the giver's lifetime (or to make certain benefits available to family members or other beneficiaries) and still help the charity.

There are two basic categories of charitable trusts: the "charitable remainder trust" (which, in turn, is divided into the annuity trust and the unitrust) and the "charitable lead trust." The Internal Revenue Code also gives favorable treatment to donations to a charitable "pooled income fund."

Under a charitable remainder trust, the giver transfers a large sum of money (or other types of property) to the trust. The trust then makes payments to a designated beneficiary who is not a charity — typically, the giver, or the giver's spouse, child, grandchild, etc. If it is an annuity trust, a fixed amount is paid at least annually either for the person's lifetime or for a certain number of years. The maximum duration of a charitable remainder trust for a term of years is 20 years. When the annuity period ends, the charity gets the remainder (whatever is left in the trust). The Code's rules require that, each year, the non-charitable beneficiary must get at least 5% of the trust's initial value.

If it is a unitrust, the non-charitable beneficiary gets whatever percentage of the trust assets is specified in the trust document. To qualify for tax advantages, the percentage must be at least 5% of the trust's value for that year — unlike annuity trusts, unitrusts have to be revalued each year. The trust can be drafted to vary the amount of payment to a certain extent. Another difference between the two types of charitable remainder trust is that it is OK to make later contributions to a unitrust — but once a charitable annuity trust is set up, that is it. No further additions to trust corpus are allowed[8].

PLANNING TIP: Appreciated property can be contributed to a charitable remainder trust without the giver being taxed on the appreciation in value. This is true even if the trust sells the property. However, there is a tax penalty if the trust is drafted to *require* the trustee to sell the appreciated property and buy tax-exempt securities. There are also tax disadvantages to funding a charitable remainder trust with property that is encumbered by a mortgage.

In effect, in a charitable remainder trust, the giver or his or her family member gets "first crack" at the trust, receiving its income until the trust terminates. A charitable lead trust works the other way: the designated charity gets the income for the term of the trust, then the remainder of the trust goes to person designated by the giver. This might be a good technique for benefiting a child or grandchild who is still too young to manage money responsibly. The charity gets the income; when the remainderman grows up, he or she gets a capital sum.

POOLED INCOME FUNDS

Setting up a trust usually involves legal fees. It may be necessary to pay a fee each year to the trustee for management services. All in all, it probably is not worth setting up a trust with less than $150,000 because the initial fees for setting up and funding the trust, and the continuing fees for maintaining it, are uneconomical in light of the few thousand dollars of income the trust will produce each year. What happens when people have a charitable intention, and a financial/ estate plan that would benefit by charitable trust — but they don't have $150,000 to spare?

One possibility is investment in a pooled income fund. A pooled income fund is similar to a mutual fund created by a charity. It allows many small "investors" to get the advantages of a charitable trust at a lower cost. A donation to a pooled income fund permits the giver, or another beneficiary designated by the giver, to get a life interest in the income earned by the pooled income fund. When the beneficiary dies, the charity gets the remainder of the amount contributed by the giver. If the Internal Revenue Code tests are met, the donated amounts are excluded from the giver's estate, and he or she may be entitled to an income tax deduction.

Under OBRA '93, disabled persons over 65 can use trusts similar to pooled income funds, administered by charities, to ameliorate some of the harsh consequences of the new Medicaid trust rules.

PLANNING TIP: Many large charities have "planned giving" divisions that will be happy to educate the planning team about the latest IRS rules, and about the trusts and pooled income funds maintained by the charity. They're a good (though not totally objective!) source of information about incorporating deferred charitable gifts into a plan.

CHAPTER FOOTNOTES

1. Originally, gift tax and estate tax were completely separate. As a result, some people abused lifetime giving as a way to reduce their taxable estates. To combat this, Congress changed the tax structure to create a single, unified gift and estate tax system. Whenever an individual makes a taxable gift that is not otherwise exempt (for instance, gifts of present interests of up to $10,000 per year per donee, or $20,000 per year per donee if two spouses join in a gift) he or she must either pay gift tax or use up part of the unified credit, thus reducing the amount of credit that is available to reduce estate taxes.

2. State laws differ, but generally probate courts have the power to appoint a conservator to take care of the property of a person who is no longer able to manage financial transactions effectively. A guardian, who has broader powers, can be appointed to take care of a person who is too impaired to care for him- or herself. Guardianship terminates many of a person's civil rights.

3. Lawyers are called "attorneys at law," to distinguish them from agents, who are "attorneys in fact."

4. "The Life Insurance Trust," *New York Times* August 12, 1990. p. F17.

5. Code Section 2042. For a good introduction to life insurance trusts, see Ronald D. Aucutt and Catherine Veihmeyer Hughes, "Irrevocable Life Insurance Trusts Still Have Planning Possibilities After TAMRA," *Journal of Taxation* October 1989 p. 258.

6. See *Estate of Headrick*, 90-2 USTC ¶60,049 (6th Cir. 1990); *Estate of Leder*, 90-1 USTC ¶60,001 (10th Cir. 1989); *Estate of Perry*, 91-1 USTC ¶60,064 (5th Cir. 1991) similarly holds that the decedent had no incidents of ownership in the policy at his death. Later proceedings in the same case, *Perry Estate*, 91-1 USTC ¶60,073 (5th Cir. 1991) forced IRS to pay the family's attorneys' fees for the appeal, because IRS was unjustified in pursuing the appeal in light of the recent case law explicating incidents of ownership issues.

    Also see TAM 9128008, in which the decedent assigned a life insurance policy on his own life, but retained the right to repurchase the policy by repaying the assignee for premium payments made plus 10% interest. The TAM includes the policy in the decedent's estate on the grounds that he possessed incidents of ownership. IRS' alternative theory was that part of the proceeds (equal to the proportion of total premiums paid by the decedent) should be included in the estate as a transfer within three years of death.

7. This is the type of power to demand payments from the trust permitted by the important tax case of *Crummey v. Comm'r*, 397 F.2d 82 (9th Cir. 1968).

8. See Jan M. Rosen, "Aiding Charities and One's Family," *New York Times* August 25, 1990, which points out that sample trust documents approved by the IRS can be found in Revenue Procedures 90-30 through 90-33, 1990-1 CB 534-552; Andree Brooks, "Making a Gift That Pays for Life," *New York Times* February 12, 1994 p. A36, showing the results of placing $100,000 worth of municipal bonds into a charitable remainder unitrust: a one-time income tax deduction of $28,000; removal of the $100,000 from the estate; and annual income of 7% of the current value of the trust corpus (i.e., income can increase or decline, based on investment factors).

Chapter 12

THE COORDINATED PLAN

Let's take a look at four hypothetical situations, each fairly typical of a situation that might impel a person or couple to consult a planning team. The team must look at a number of factors, but the predominant factors will change from case to case. For some people, the greatest need is for advice about insurance; for others, it is investment advice. The affluent need extensive advice to save current income taxes and reduce the estate tax burden. For some clients, a Medicaid application is a real possibility in the near future; for others, a Medicaid application is remote or so unlikely that little attention need be paid to the prospect.

There is never a single right answer to a financial planning question, and frequently team members will disagree about the best way to proceed. Wherever this is possible within legal boundaries, your job as a team is to carry out the wishes of the clients. Your advice will help them sort out prudent from imprudent choices; but, in the end, they must make the decision based on their personal values.

THE GILBERTS: ACTIVE PRE-RETIREES

Your clients are Thomas and Alice Gilbert. He's 63; she's 59. Both of them are still working, healthy, and with a history of vigorous exercise and good health habits. They want to make sure that, when they retire, they will be able to afford the active lifestyle they enjoy (travel, fishing, hiking, gardening).

Thomas is an engineer, earning $65,000 a year. Alice works for local government in a senior administrative post, earning $46,000 a year. Thomas is already eligible for early retirement (at a pension of $30,000 a year); if he remains at work, his pension will increase (up to a maximum of $40,000 for retirement at or after age 70). Alice will be eligible for retirement at age 63, with a pension of $22,000. Neither

Thomas nor Alice's retirement plan includes an option of a lump-sum distribution.

A $10,000 mortgage remains on their townhouse condominium, which is now worth $217,000, although Thomas and Alice are worried about declines in the real estate market.

They have not tended to save much of their income. Thomas is interested in investments, but has had mixed success. Their portfolio is now worth about $100,000. They are very worried about downturns in the stock market, or even another Depression.

Thomas has $50,000 in group insurance and a $75,000 whole-life policy payable to Alice. Alice has $30,000 in group insurance and no individual life insurance.

Thomas and Alice have two children (Jeffrey, 35, and Coral, 31) and five grandchildren (Jeffrey's children, Nina, 5, and Stuart, 2, and Coral's children, Edward, 8, and the 6-year-old twins Craig and Alicia). Coral and her husband are more financially successful than Jeffrey and his wife, which might suggest that Thomas and Alice should leave more to Jeffrey...but as a counterbalance, they want to provide for all their grandchildren, and Coral has more children.

Planning Objectives

Thomas and Alice want to have an active retirement, and there is every reason to believe that they can succeed in this objective. Although they have not been devoted or particularly successful financial planners, their careers have yielded pensions that should provide a comfortable life-style. They have taken care of themselves, so they can expect to be vigorous for years to come. However, the planner must make them aware of the risks of sudden death and incapacity.

Thomas could retire now, but Alice is not eligible yet, and would be very unwilling to sacrifice the retirement security that is a major incentive to civil service careers. (Of course, she could leave employment, and have a smaller payment of her vested pension payable at retirement age, but she prefers to retire with the full pension.) Therefore, the choice is whether Thomas should retire first or wait until Alice's eligibility date. That is a personal choice (how does he feel about his job? Would he regret the loss of status and contacts with fellow-workers?) as well as a financial choice. Their pre-retirement incomes are higher than their pensions, so each year they defer retirement could be a chance to practice saving and investment to create a larger investment portfolio.

Health Insurance Factors

Health insurance is an important factor in early retirement. If Thomas retires now, he will not be eligible for Medicare. Alice won't be eligible for Medicare for another six years. The planner must check each employer's policy of providing retiree health benefits, and how likely these benefits are to continue until age 65. (If Thomas is covered under Alice's health plan, and if she will remain employed until he reaches age 65, this problem is less serious.) The cost of continuation coverage must be compared to the cost of buying individual health insurance or group coverage (such as coverage issued by a religious or professional organization). A Medigap policy won't help: it supplements Medicare benefits once those become payable, but does not pay the cost of care of those too young for Medicare.

Thomas and Alice could be excellent candidates for LTC insurance. For reasons discussed below, they are unlikely to qualify for Medicaid. Now they are in good health, and likely to stay that way for a long time...but there is no predicting who will be struck by early Alzheimer's Disease, or injured in a car crash, or stricken with cancer. Because they are comparatively young, an LTC policy would be cheaper than if they waited until an older issue age. They might be able to purchase LTC insurance for a premium that is close to the potentially tax-deductible amount (see page 102) — although they will probably get little if any real tax relief, because they will get a medical deduction only to the extent that this and other eligible medical expenses exceed 7.5% of their fairly substantial Adjusted Gross Income.

If they are concerned about cost, "partial self-insurance" could be the answer: a less-expensive LTC policy with a longer waiting period or a smaller daily benefit, leaving part of the responsibility with the couple but lessening the risk of a catastrophic bill.

Treatment of the House

Both of Thomas and Alice's children are homeowners, so there is less pressure to keep the family home in the family. Thomas and Alice might be appropriate residents for a specialized retirement community. The best of these communities provide attractive, low-maintenance housing (perhaps with housekeeper service and restaurant facilities) combined with sports and recreation facilities and congenial company of other healthy retirees. If Thomas and Alice think they would enjoy this life-style (some people greatly prefer living in a mixed-age community), it is worthwhile to check out local retirement communities, and retirement communities in areas with pleasant climates.

Could they sell their home, satisfy the mortgage, buy into a retirement community, and still have money left over? Or would the retirement community unit cost more than the home sale proceeds, causing them to dip into savings or apply for a mortgage? (They probably could get a mortgage, because of their high pension income, despite their comparatively limited life-spans.) If the new unit is more expensive than the old home, then home-sale profits can be "rolled over;" if it is less expensive, the Section 121 exclusion is available to shield part or all of the profits.

As of February 1997, the issue of making the Section 121 exclusion even more generous attracted broad bipartisan support, so by the time you read this, the planning options may be even wider.

If the retirement community is set up so that residents acquire an equity interest, then they still have a home which can be devised, and they still have a homestead for Medicaid purposes. However, if it is set up so that residents have only a right to live in the unit for their joint lives, but no equity interest, these considerations will not apply.

If Thomas and Alice decide that retirement community living is not for them, or there are no suitable, affordable facilities anywhere they want to move, they can stay put in the old home, or buy another house or condominium unit. It is often a good idea to devote some time, energy, and money to fixing up the home to make it trouble-free and perhaps making some capital improvements that make the home more suitable for the elderly. Although they are in good health now, later on they may need a chair lift for the stairs or changes in the kitchen and bathroom to promote wheelchair accessibility. If they do choose to move, they should think about future medical needs as well as tax considerations.

They should also take a look at their mortgage. If it was written when interest rates were much higher, they can do better by using some savings to pay off the mortgage — because they probably pay a higher interest rate than they can earn on their investments. On the other hand, if it is below current rates, and if their investment success is greater than the mortgage rate, keeping the mortgage could be a good move — taking Medicaid considerations into account.

Medicaid Planning

Their future Medicaid eligibility depends on the state in which they live. Make sure to check with the attorney in your planning team about current state rules. Their major asset is a house, which is likely to be an exempt homestead (unless they move to a retirement community with a non-equity structure). For Medicaid purposes, paying off the mortgage would probably be a wise move, because it converts cash that would be an "available resource" (blocking Medicaid eligibility) into an exempt asset (the homestead).

The Gilberts also have additional assets (investments). Because they are comparatively young and healthy, they might be able to make Medicaid-oriented transfers without hitting the 36-month look-back period. For instance, they could give some of their investments to their children or grandchildren, or sell part of the portfolio and make a gift of the cash. (Which is a better choice? That's a tax question for the lawyer or accountant in the planning team.)

After the Health Insurance Portability and Accountability Act of 1996's effective date of January 1, 1997, all Medicaid-oriented transfers must be scrutinized carefully for potential criminal liability. Given the Gilberts' comparatively young ages and good health, perhaps they can make transfers now and assume that they will not even want to make an application at any time in the next 36 months. Most elder law attorneys would advise them either to abandon any possibility of Medicaid planning, or to restrict their transfers and retain funds that can be used to pay privately for care (and defer the Medicaid application so that there will be no penalty period).

It might be worthwhile to transfer ownership of the home (to prevent recoupment if Medicaid benefits are eventually received). Some homestead transfers are exempt under the Health Insurance Portability and Accountability Act of 1996, but the Gilberts do not have a minor, blind, or disabled child, or a brother or sister who has an equity interest in the home and has lived there for one year. As of now, they do not have a "caregiver child" (one who has resided with them and provided supportive care for two years) because they don't need a caregiver's assistance. If, in the future, they do need assistance, the availability of Jeffrey or Coral as a caregiver child should be assessed.

However, apart from resource issues, they have a substantial amount of income. Not all states allow "income spend-down" (using the excess income to pay medical bills, then applying for Medicaid). Furthermore, no one is allowed to assign or transfer future pension benefits — and most of their post-retirement income will come from pensions.

That's why LTC insurance can be an important part of their plan. However, if they don't want LTC insurance, or can't get an affordable policy, they could concentrate on alternatives, such as health insurance with benefits for preventive care. If they need help in the home, they could hire a part-time housekeeper or health aide. They can simply assume the risk of heavy nursing home bills if and when one of them does require chronic care. It's a big risk, though, and could lead to depletion of their savings.

Investment Considerations

Thomas and Alice haven't saved all that much, and they have some investments but not a huge portfolio. They must realize that, although they will have a much higher income than most retirees, their income will drop substantially after they both retire (which could motivate one or both to keep working after normal retirement age). Either they can change their lifestyle now, and save and invest more so the gap will be less, or they must be prepared for a bump!

Thomas and Alice are both competent, and likely to remain so for at least several years. They will probably be interested in retaining significant control over their investments. (In fact, investing will probably be an important source of activity and psychological satisfaction for them after they retire and leave the business world.) However, the planner can give them advice about asset allocation and specific investments — if they're willing to listen!

Their $100,000 portfolio can probably be increased to about $150,000 if they continue working for 2-5 more years and increase their rate of saving and investment. Of course, diversification and prudence are important. They could adopt several sensible strategies:

- They have enough income for basic needs, so they can see the portfolio more as a source of capital formation and appreciation than as a source of income. They might therefore buy some growth stocks (especially with creating an estate for the children and grandchildren in mind) and some zero-coupon bonds, balancing these investments with low-risk CDs and treasury securities. If they feel a high degree of concern about inflation, they might like the new inflation-adjusted treasury products. They might like stocks such as utility stocks that are traditionally safe and provide a high level of dividend income. Depending on their degree of interest in active investing and on cost factors (such as loads and brokerage commissions), they might prefer growth funds to individual growth stocks, or just the opposite. If they want to trade in individual stocks, they might consider their Social Security checks "mad money" to be invested in three or four stocks a year, with pension income paying the costs of everyday living.

- They might, however, prefer to invest for income, because they want to replace some of the income lost by retiring. Under this strategy, they'd concentrate on bonds, perhaps municipal bonds (although they are likely to encounter a tax on some Social Security benefits if they have both high income and high tax preferences) or bond funds. They might also consider money market funds and CDs, with an a mixture of equity investments to provide diversification. They might be willing to put part of their investment into a junk-bond fund, to get even higher income — if they are willing to deal with the risk.

- If they want to invest to make sure that the survivor will be well-provided for, and if creating an inheritance for their children is a major factor, they might consider specializing in zero-coupon bonds and real estate investment. Real estate investment takes a great deal of management — which might be an enjoyable task for Thomas and Alice; or, if they don't want to handle the day-to-day management tasks, they could hire a professional real estate manager or invest in REITs rather than property. They must, of course, be advised of the risk if they sell zero-coupon bonds before maturity, and the significant risks involved in the real estate market (especially the risk of being unable to find a buyer if cash is needed).

Incapacity Issues

Thomas and Alice are now healthy and vigorous, and can be expected to remain that way for a while. Although planning for incapacity is not an emergency need, it can not be neglected. Some time in the future, one or both might become mentally or physically ill, restricting their ability to manage funds. Because they have plenty of time to plan ahead, it seems very unlikely that conservatorship or guardianship will be needed.

Instead, Thomas and Alice should make a plan for future incapacity. Each should sign a durable power of attorney (DPA). Because Alice is somewhat younger, she might be a suitable attorney-in-fact for Thomas — but if he chooses her, he must be sure to name an alternate in case she dies or becomes incapacitated before he becomes incapacitated. Age factors make him an unsuitable choice for her attorney-in-fact. The couple's children could be good choices; so could other relatives or professional advisors.

Because both Thomas and Alice are likely to cherish their autonomy, it is probably a good idea to make the power of attorney a "springing" one which becomes effective *only* after the signer becomes incapacitated. It is important to draft the DPA carefully, to extend the right powers to the attorney-in-fact (for instance, to do tax and Medicaid planning), and to define incapacity in a way that preserves the dignity of Thomas and Alice but gives them help when help is needed.

Many states allow healthy people to sign a document indicating their choice of guardian or conservator if one ever becomes necessary. That way, the court hearing the case becomes aware of the wishes of the subject of the proceeding, and nearly always honors them. Check with the lawyer on the planning team to see if your state allows this, and what the proper form is for making the designation.

It may also be a good idea to create a trust for each spouse that is unfunded or has a small amount of funds in it. If and when Thomas or Alice becomes incapacitated, the attorney-in-fact can transfer enough assets to the trust to meet day-to-day expenses. The planning team should consider whether the bulk of each spouse's (or the couple's) resources should be transferred to such a trust, so that the trustee can take over the task of money management. Consideration should also be given as to whether either spouse should be given the power to *demand* that some of the trust's principal be paid to him or her, and whether the trustee should have discretion to apply principal, either in general or for specified reasons of health and welfare. The choice that is made will have significant income and estate tax and Medicaid consequences.

It may seem remote now given that both spouses are healthy, but consideration should also be given to having a "living will" specifying each spouse's feelings about respirators, artificial feeding, and other life-support devices. Depending on state law and practice, it can also be worthwhile to designate someone (such as the spouse or a child) as a health care proxy who can make decisions if the principal is unconscious or otherwise incapacitated. Make sure that the two documents conform — otherwise, there is a risk that a doctor or hospital will refuse to comply with the documents, claiming that there is a risk of malpractice liability because of the conflict.

Estate Planning Issues

It seems unlikely that either spouse will have an estate large enough to incur estate tax. Therefore, decisions can be made without reference to saving estate taxes. As discussed above, it may be worthwhile to create a trust for use in asset management after incapacity. Because the couple have a relatively high income, but do not have very high assets, it is less likely that creating an irrevocable trust to remove assets from the estate will be a worthwhile tactic. If there is a compelling reason to avoid probate, creation of a revocable living trust may be worthwhile. It may also be a good idea to start a giving program to children and grandchildren. It is unlikely that enough money will be involved to make it practical to set up a trust for the grandchildren. Instead, it is easier and cheaper to use the gift-to-minor statutes.

Naturally, each spouse should have a will. It is likely that Thomas will die first, so the focus of his will should be to provide adequately for Alice. Because of her own income, and if they are living in a mortgage-free home or retirement community at the time of Thomas' death, perhaps Alice will not need a large bequest from Thomas. If this is so, then Thomas' will can include bequests to children, grandchildren, and charities. However, if, after examining their life expectancies and making projections about inflation, it is determined that Alice will have limited resources, then most or all of his estate should go to her, with her will benefiting the family and charities.

The estate plan should also take into account the fact that Alice might die first. Thomas' needs should be taken into consideration in that situation.

When one spouse dies, the best plan is for the surviving spouse to make a new will, based on a new estate plan. However, as a safety measure, each spouse's will should include "gifts over" and contingency provisions dealing with the situation of the other spouse dying first with no changes being made in the will.

It is especially important for the will of the second spouse to die to make reasonable provisions for disposition of the family home and its contents. Long-simmering family feuds have erupted over items such as silver, china and furniture of moderate or even trivial monetary value. Consideration should be given to what each family member expects ("Grandma promised me I could have that porcelain after she passed away"; "You don't need it because you live all alone in that tiny apartment, but I have to entertain and keep up a position in the community"), and the financial provisions provided to each beneficiary under the will. If one child or grandchild gets most of the heirlooms as well as the largest bequest, bad feeling among the other family members is very likely. (Of course, the testator won't be around to listen to the arguments!) This could in fact be the fairest or best plan, but the potential for resentment should be kept in mind.

Insurance Considerations

The couple have very little life insurance. Financial planners would differ on how important it is to correct this deficiency. If Alice dies first, Thomas' financial situation will probably not be hurt much. Although her pension is useful in paying the bills, he has his own pension, investment income, and can liquidate some of the investments if necessary. (If they agreed to take her pension in single-life form, in order to increase current income during her lifetime, the pension will die with her; many plans provide that the survivor annuity is only 50% of the pension that was paid when both spouses were alive.) However, if Thomas dies first, Alice may find herself short of funds, particularly if his pension was paid in single-life form and she is restricted to her own pension, her Social Security, and her share of Thomas' estate.

Furthermore, either spouse may need expensive medical or custodial care. If they choose to buy LTC insurance, and the insurance covers much of the expense, this is less of a problem. If they go without this coverage, and medical and nursing home bills are high, the estate will be greatly depleted. With this in mind, it is probably worthwhile for them to beef up their insurance coverage (especially coverage on Thomas' life).

Although they are not young, they are healthy, so at least a reasonable amount of coverage should be available at affordable rates.

The choice between term and whole-life depends on whether they are likely to want policy loans, and how investment-oriented insurance coverages compare to the investment results. Because their income is above-average, but their assets are not, it is almost certainly a better idea to continue making regular premium payments out of income rather than seeking a single-premium policy. However, because income might decline or expenses increase, it is worthwhile to purchase a policy that can be converted to paid-up insurance rather than lapsing if premium payments are missed.

PLANNING TIP: The attorney-in-fact must be advised of all insurance coverage and premium obligations, to prevent policies from lapsing simply because the policyholder is too forgetful or impaired to make the payment, and the fiduciary is unaware of the need to do so.

A large policy might "tilt" one or both spouse's estates into the taxable category, so it is important to handle the beneficiary designation properly. Clearly, each spouse has an insurable interest in the other's life, and can purchase a policy and make premium payments out of his or her own income. Another option is for the couple's children to buy and pay for the policy, initially benefiting the surviving spouse and contingently benefiting themselves or their own children. Unless there is a good legal, tax, or accounting reason to do so, though, avoid making the policy payable to an estate, and avoid all incidents of ownership in the insured spouse.

GORDON AND AMY RAWLINGS: PLANNING A LARGER ESTATE

Gordon Rawlings is 73 and retired; Amy, 56, is his second wife. Gordon and his first wife, Maria, had two children, Mariette, 48, and Gordon Jr., 45. Maria died of cancer last year. Maria had divorced Gordon after discovering that Gordon and Amy were having an extramarital affair. Maria's death compounded the hostile feelings that Mariette and Gordon Jr. have toward Amy, Gordon, and Amy's daughter, Kylie, 15. Gordon loves all his children and is sorry for the family disharmony.

Gordon retired from the vice-presidency of a major business corporation in 1994. He took his $637,000 pension account in lump-sum form. Amy is self-employed on a part-time basis as a landscape designer, earning $10,000-$20,000 a year. She has a Keogh plan for the business now worth $49,500, but this money cannot be touched for at least 3½ more years without triggering a tax penalty (unless one of the exceptions applies).

Gordon and Amy live in a mortgage-free home currently worth $328,000. In addition to this home, they have a summer cottage and some beachfront land worth about $100,000, and an interest in a real estate limited partnership now worth about $75,000. Gordon is worried that its value will decline, but he is also aware that limited partnership investments are not very liquid. The houses are jointly owned, and the limited partnership is in Gordon's name.

They also have stock holdings worth $227,800 and a bond portfolio worth about $85,000, most of them in Gordon's name. Amy is the owner of two policies on Gordon's life: she is the beneficiary of a $500,000 policy, and Kylie is the beneficiary of a $250,000 policy (which will be paid to Amy as Kylie's guardian if Gordon dies while Kylie is still a minor). There is no insurance on Amy's life.

Although they are now in good health, both Gordon and Amy have recently experienced potentially serious health problems. Gordon had a mild heart attack in 1995, from which he made a good recovery. In 1996, Amy was treated for skin cancer. Although her doctors believe that the cancer was arrested, it could recur.

Overview

Gordon and Amy need a complete plan that unites estate planning with lifetime planning. The plan must take into account the fact that they have very extensive assets, which must be prudently managed now and in future generations.

Although this is not certain, it is very likely that Amy (because she is much younger than Gordon) will survive him, very possibly for two decades or more. Furthermore, although she does have some income and can expect some benefits from the Keogh plan, she is essentially financially dependent on Gordon.

There is also a meaningful possibility that Gordon will die while Kylie is still a minor, or a college or graduate student who has not established herself economically, so provisions must be made for her. Furthermore, Gordon would like to make provisions for his "first family." Because of the hostility, it is unlikely that Mariette or Gordon, Jr. would be a suitable executor, trustee, or health care proxy in any situation that might benefit "that woman" or her child.

Estate Planning Issues

It is evident that, if Gordon dies first (the most likely scenario), his estate will be potentially taxable. However, with good planning, it seems likely that the liability can be diminished or eliminated.

The simple "all to my wife" scenario is not very suitable for a large estate — especially one in which there is a minor child and a "first family" to be considered. However, adequate provision must be made for Amy. Under state law, she will probably be entitled to "take against the will" if she is given less than a certain percentage of the estate (typically 1/3 to 1/2 in a situation in which there is a child of the marriage). If Gordon wants to avoid this, and Amy is willing, a postnuptial agreement can eliminate the interest in the estate or prevent the surviving spouse from contesting a legacy that is smaller than the statutory percentage. (In the second-marriage situation, many couples enter into a prenuptial agreement waiving the right of election.)

A strategy to consider is to establish several trusts. Irrevocable trusts benefiting the children and/or grandchildren can, if properly drafted, remove assets from Gordon's estate. (They will also remove the money from his control, and make it unavailable for his personal use, but it seems likely that he has enough resources to spare some for this purpose.) A QTIP trust — giving Amy life income but preventing her from disposing of trust principal, which will go to Mariette and Gordon Jr. on Amy's death, is another option that can be very helpful in this situation.

If the trusts involved would be too small to be administered economically, another alternative is a "giving program" under which Gordon can give up to $10,000 a year per donee free of gift tax (and without reducing his unified credit against estate and gift tax) to any number of donees. He can increase the gift to $20,000 a year per donee with Amy's consent — but it is unlikely that she will consent if the donees are the hostile Mariette and Gordon, Jr. and their families! A provision that benefits both wealthy grandparents and their tuition-paying and orthodontia-buying children is the fact that no gift tax is imposed on gifts made directly to a medical or educational institution to pay someone else's medical or educational expenses. However, if Gordon gives the money directly to Mariette or Gordon Jr., and they use the money to pay tuition or medical bills, the usual gift tax rules apply.

Furthermore, lifetime charitable gifts, or charitable bequests, can be helpful in avoiding estate tax. The "planned giving" directors at Gordon's favorite charities will be happy to advise; so will his "personal banker," tax attorney, and the managers of his Alma Mater's endowment fund. A charitable remainder trust or unitrust, yielding income to Gordon and Amy, might be a worthwhile tactic.

"Estate splitting" — interspousal gifts from Gordon to Amy, designed to give each an estate below $600,000 and thus not taxable — may be helpful here. Legal, accounting, and tax advice is necessary to see which assets should be held jointly, which in an individual name. Remember, joint property cannot be disposed of by will — it passes directly to the surviving joint tenant or joint tenants.

Gordon's estate will be rather large (as will Amy's, if she survives him and does not significantly deplete her inheritance), so steps should be taken to simplify administration (e.g., by maintaining adequate records; by frequent conferences with the designated executor(s) and trustee(s) to keep them informed about changes in the family finances) and to ensure liquidity during the time each estate is being settled. That can be done by making sure each spouse has a personal account sufficient to meet several months' expenses, or with life insurance.

Tax Problems

As wealthy individuals, Amy and Gordon will need professional advice to minimize the tax burden. In order to cut current taxes, it might be worthwhile to make current charitable gifts (to get an income tax deduction); invest in tax-exempt securities (this may trigger taxation of some Social Security benefits, but this is a relatively trivial factor in their financial plan), and accelerate deductions. An important planning objective is minimizing the Alternative Minimum Tax that will be added to their conventional income tax; the AMT is designed to tax income of the wealthy that would otherwise escape taxation because of tax preferences. Ever since the 1986 tax reforms (which reduced the number of tax brackets as well as tax rates), tax planning has gotten much tougher. It might be possible to score some tax savings by setting up a trust in such a way that trust income is taxed to the trust, not to Gordon and/or Amy — but this is a tricky matter, requiring the utmost professional skill.

Investment Choices

At this stage in their lives, Gordon and Amy's investment choices must reflect attention to tax and estate planning considerations as well as a desire for high profit or safety (the tradeoff between "eating well" and "sleeping well"). A strategy that might work could be to invest a major portion of the portfolio into growth stocks, which yield little income now (thus reducing current tax burdens) but enhance net worth and provide a legacy for Amy's widowhood, Kylie's future, and to pass on to the "first family" and Gordon's grandchildren.

Gordon and Amy can afford to purchase individual stocks and bonds rather than mutual funds, and still get adequate diversification. Their portfolio is large enough to require constant "hands on" management. If he is interested in doing so, Gordon can continue to have major management responsibility (at least for the next few years), but it could be a good time to transfer major management responsibility either to Amy or to a professional manager. If Amy is not sophisticated in financial management, this is a good time for her to learn; she can expect to be a wealthy widow, and will need to manage her funds well and/or know how to find the best professional assistance.

Investment goals must dovetail with their preferred lifestyle and estate planning goals. If they want to maintain their pre-retirement lifestyle, they may spend more than current income — which, in turn, will mean either a shift toward income-oriented investments (and higher income tax unless appropriate tax-exempt investments can be found), or depleting Gordon's estate. (Depleting the estate is not necessarily a bad thing, if it avoids estate tax, and as long as Amy and Kylie are adequately provided for and the inheritance expectations of Gordon Jr. and Mariette are not too severely disappointed.)

Insurance Issues

Once again, the various plans must dovetail. If Gordon's will heavily favors the "first family," and if he dies in the next few years, Amy may not be comfortable with the lifestyle she can get by investing the $500,000 life insurance proceeds (or by having the proceeds paid out under a settlement option). In that case, Amy might consider purchasing additional insurance on Gordon's life if the cost of the insurance does not outweigh the potential benefits to be derived from it. However, if Amy is a, or the, major beneficiary of Gordon's will, or if his estate plan includes a large QTIP trust giving Amy significant income for her life, the life insurance is probably already adequate. The lawyer in the planning team should review and discuss the advisability of including a life insurance trust in the plan — and, of course, because there is a possibility of estate taxes, all ownership and beneficiary arrangements must be reviewed.

The policy benefiting Kylie is probably large enough, because her mother will have adequate assets (over and above this and other insurance) to take care of Kylie until she reaches economic independence. Because Amy's economic contribution to the family is fairly minor, it is probably not necessary to have insurance on her life. However, if it seems likely that there will be a "second estate" problem, a second-to-die life insurance policy is an option well worth considering.

If Gordon does not have Medigap insurance, he should consider whether the cost of an available policy would lead to savings (he is likely to encounter more acute-care costs, and more Medicare deductibles and copayments, to take care of his heart condition) — or whether, given his income and age, it is more economical to "self-insure." Amy is not yet Medicare-eligible, so a Medigap policy is not an option for her. As a self-employed person, she definitely needs health insurance; your job includes finding an attractively priced policy for her.

LTC insurance for both spouses must be considered carefully. Insurance for Gordon would be hard to find and very expensive (though certainly not beyond their capacity to pay) — the question is whether the expected benefits from the insurance outweigh the risk of prolonged institutionalization. A compromise strategy might work: using LTC insurance as a "stop-loss," buying a smaller policy with a shorter term of benefits and a longer waiting period, so that Gordon partially self-insures, but will be able to collect benefits if he undergoes prolonged institutionalization.

LTC insurance for Amy would be much less expensive (because she is much younger, and the level premium assessed for most LTC policies depends on entry age). Furthermore, she is available to provide a great deal of personal care that will make it less likely that Gordon will need a nursing home. If he dies and she survives him, she will not be able to look to him for personal care! In fact, unless she remarries, she is likely to live alone (a major factor in spurring institutionalization). Even if she remarries, she is likely to choose another man older than she is — and more likely to need than to give personal care.

Because of the Rawlings' high income, it is very unlikely that they will get a tax deduction for the LTC insurance purchase. For them, the real value is preservation of the value of the estate, although it's also important and worthwhile to have cash available to pay for care when necessary.

Medicaid And Incapacity Issues

Although it is not entirely impossible that a Medicaid plan could be made for Gordon or Amy, it is unlikely that such a plan could be put into operation without causing major deterioration in their lifestyle. The transfers to be made would be large enough to trigger a very long penalty period — raising the question of whether Gordon (if he is institutionalized at all) will need nursing home care within that time. If the question is making a plan for Amy after Gordon's death, she will not be entitled to use Medicaid's spousal protection provisions (unless she remarries), making Medicaid eligibility less likely. The attorney in the planning team should definitely consider steps that could be taken under a Medicaid plan — but is likely to determine that neither Gordon nor Amy is likely to receive Medicaid benefits.

If the Rawlings do make a Medicaid plan, unless the transfers they make are interspousal (probably Gordon to Amy, because he is the wealthier spouse and more likely to need care soon) or otherwise exempt, they have to worry about criminal liability under the Health Insurance Portability and Accountability Act of 1996. Because they have significant assets, the long penalty period would make it quite plausible that an application might be made during the penalty period — the scenario which is criminalized by the 1996 legislation. It's not clear how prosecutors will treat Medicaid transfer cases, but it's easy to imagine the local prosecutor selecting the Rawlings as an example of loophole-seeking "greedy geezers" who could be prosecuted to great public relations effect.

The next step is to find alternatives: probably LTC insurance for Amy (though, for Gordon, cost and availability makes this a less likely source of funds). They might find a luxury life-care community, which includes some degree of nursing home care, a good choice (though Amy might not be comfortable in an environment where most of the neighbors are much older than she is). They can probably afford the entry and continuing fees without depleting all their resources, and thus would be able to carry out their normal estate plans, perhaps in modified form.

They also have enough funds to retain a geriatric care manager (GCM) to inform them about private-sector services available to the elderly. As Gordon's care needs increase, they might be met by hiring one or more home attendants and having private nurses come to the house (if Gordon isn't well enough to be driven to the doctors' offices for attention). If they already have part-time domestic workers, this might be a good time to shift to a live-in housekeeper who could be trained to assume some care tasks in the future. If the real estate market improves, Gordon and Amy might consider selling the real estate liquid partnership and the beach house, and investing the after-tax proceeds in a highly liquid form, creating an informal "care fund" that could be drawn down to pay home attendants and nurses. GCMs have many success stories of older people who can remain happily in the community, at less cost than if they were forced into nursing homes, because an appropriate service package can be created.

However, this plan will not be effective if either spouse suffers a catastrophic illness such as Alzheimer's Disease requiring round-the-clock care that can best be delivered in an institution. In this situation, unless insurance is available, the cost of nursing home care will severely reduce the couple's savings (or Amy's inheritance, if she is institutionalized during widowhood). This is the gamble that everyone takes in a system in which affordable long-term care cannot be guaranteed.

The plan must also cope with the risk of incapacity. If nearly all of the assets are fully managed by professionals, the risk is lessened. However, if Gordon and Amy have the hands-on responsibility, plans must be made for the situation in which they cannot make prudent decisions. Management trusts are useful in this situation; so is the durable power of attorney (DPA). It could be very tricky selecting an attorney-in-fact; because of the family conflict, a professional such as an attorney or accountant might be a suitable candidate (but might also misappropriate assets if not properly monitored). The professional's greater objectivity is a two-edged sword. He or she would not be embroiled in emotional conflicts — but also would not take manage-ment of family funds as seriously, and might not achieve results as good as someone who took a more personal interest.

If their home state permits, it would be very worthwhile for both spouses to name an appropriate person as guardian or conservator in case of need. The most vicious contested conservatorship and guardianship cases (and the ones that generate the biggest fees, which act as a drag on the family's funds) are those in which there are substantial assets at stake, combined with severe conflict within the family.

LINDA BRYANT AND EMILY PARKINS: "WHAT CAN WE DO ABOUT MOM?"

Your client is 46-year-old Linda Bryant, who brings her 74-year-old mother, Emily Parkins, to your office. Ms. Bryant is the one who contacted you, and who will be paying your fees (if you are a fee-based planner) and the fees of other members of the planning team.

Ms. Bryant is worried about her mother, who lives alone in a small apartment. Mrs. Parkins, a widow, is in moderate health. Her heart condition is being monitored by a cardiologist; her internist takes care of her high blood pressure; her ophthalmologist wants to wait a little before operating on her cataracts. Mrs. Parkins walks somewhat stiffly, and is a little afraid of going outside (especially during the winter) because she broke an ankle and a wrist in a bad fall on the ice two years ago. Mrs. Parkins is helped by neighbors, who sometimes bring her groceries, and by Ms. Bryant, who visits her twice a week but finds the visits emotionally stressful and difficult to fit in to her own career and family responsibilities.

Mrs. Parkins exhibits some confusion and forgetfulness. It is unclear whether this is due to loneliness and depression (her husband's death three years ago was a severe blow), drug interactions, cerebral arteriosclerosis related to her high blood pressure, or the early stages of Alzheimer's Disease.

Mrs. Parkins' husband did not have an extensive estate, but she did inherit cash and securities worth about $100,000 and a $100,000 insurance policy. In the two years since her husband's death, Mrs. Parkins has spent about $35,000 of this sum on living expenses and health care not covered by Medicare. Mrs. Parkins says she doesn't understand "things like that"— her late husband took care of family financial transactions — so she keeps the balance in bank CDs, rolling them over each time they come due. She receives about $12,000 a year in income from this source.

She receives Social Security benefits of $615 per month (slightly more than her $600 rent) and a pension payment from her late husband's employer of $200 a month. Occasionally, Ms. Bryant and her brother, Gary Parkins, who lives almost 1,000 miles away, help out by paying bills or giving Mrs. Parkins gifts of money. Ms. Bryant is very worried about what will happen to her mother, and asks you and the other team members to draft a plan that will provide the necessary supportive care for Mrs. Parkins.

Ethical Alert

This situation highlights one of the most serious ethical problems in elder care: "Who is the client?" After all, your ethical obligations as a planner (and the obligations of other members of the care team) go to the client. It is your job to get the best deal you can for the client, within the bounds of the law and good faith. The client is the one who pays you for your work. For instance, if your plan involves Mrs. Parkins making transfers with the intent of qualifying for Medicaid, the question is who should receive the transfers. If Ms. Bryant is your client, then she will seem like the most appropriate transferee — yet, in a more objective sense, other family members might have a greater need of the transferred funds, or might have been more helpful to Mrs. Parkins in the past, or might be her favorites.

Theoretically, we have an adversary system, in which justice emerges after a vigorous contest involving advocates for all sides. Yet, when the elderly are involved, this model doesn't work perfectly. In one sense, the entire family is your client. Unless the family is very wealthy, the family's financial resources will be severely depleted if a separate care team has to be assembled to represent the interests of each family member. It takes a long time (with lawyers and accountants often being paid by the hour) to work out a solution by negotiation among adversaries. In real terms, there must usually be a single planning team, but the team must temper the usual adversarial model with some concern for fairness and the interests of other parties. It is a difficult balance.

Furthermore, there are temptations involved in either fee-based or product-based planning. No doubt you can resist the obvious temptation to pad your bills, or to recommend an inferior product because it produces a higher commission for you. Yet there are subtler temptations that affect your objectivity if you don't keep close watch. Is that more elaborate plan really adopted to help your client, or because it involves more hours of your time? Are your recommendations really objective, or has your opinion been influenced by personal financial factors?

Care-Oriented Plan

The first two hypotheticals involved situations that were primarily financial in nature, with a secondary need for acute and custodial medical care. This situation is primarily care-oriented: the question is *how* to get Mrs. Parkins the care she needs, and only secondarily how to plan her investments for her estate.

In a situation like Mrs. Parkins', the benefits of including a good geriatric care manager (GCM) in the care team are obvious. The GCM can assess Mrs. Parkins' needs, and find out what kind of medical care she needs (probably her needs are already appropriately addressed by the specialists she consults), if she needs help getting to the doctors' offices (many local programs provide transportation for the elderly and disabled), and especially what services she needs to remain in the community (*if* she wants to stay home instead of entering a nursing home). Furthermore, once a care plan is developed, the GCM can implement the plan, and make sure that it continues to work and is changed as Mrs. Parkins' needs change — providing important reassurance for Ms. Bryant and her far-away brother.

The GCM and attorney should work together to see if Mrs. Parkins can get home care benefits under Medicare Part A, a program that can provide services such as skilled nursing, assessment and monitoring of an older person's condition (e.g., checking to see that there are no side effects from drug interactions), and homemakers and home health aides to perform chores such as shopping, house cleaning, and assisting Mrs. Parkins with walking, dressing, eating, and bathing. She may fit the definition of "home-bound," and certainly needs skilled care to monitor her condition and keep it from deteriorating. If these benefits are initially denied, but the attorney believes that Mrs. Parkins qualifies, it may be necessary to contest the denial at a hearing.

The GCM and attorney should also be familiar with programs run by state and local government, and by philanthropic organizations. Frequently, these programs include extensive services embracing home health care; custodial care at home; day health centers that treat the medical needs of the aging; adult day care that provides social contacts for isolated elderly people; and homemaker and chore service. Some of these programs are free. For others, a fee is assessed on a sliding scale based on income.

It is also worthwhile for the GCM to recommend a good geriatric psychiatrist or psychologist to assess Mrs. Parkins' mental conditions. If her problem is psychological in nature, therapy could help. Maybe changing her drug dosage would make her feel better. If the problem is loneliness and isolation, programs such as adult day care and para-transit (to transport those with mobility difficulties) would be useful.

Mrs. Parkins' assets, although not unlimited, probably provide a source of funds for private care to supplement the public programs. This determination must be made based on a consideration of her income and other expenses, and after considering various investment scenarios (see below).

Incapacity Issues

In this case, future incapacity is a real threat, and one which must be addressed immediately. If any documents must be signed (such as wills, transfer instruments), it is important to have them signed while Mrs. Parkins has the capacity to do so. It may even be worthwhile to videotape planning sessions so that, in case of challenge, it can be shown that Mrs. Parkins received adequate information, which she was capable of understanding, and that she was not unduly pressured to take financial steps.

The planning team must use care and patience to deal with someone who may be somewhat impaired mentally. It may be necessary to give detailed explanations of commonplace matters, or to repeat explanations several times or on several occasions. Consultation with Mrs. Parkins' doctors may be helpful in finding out the time when she is most alert; if she is suffering from drug interactions, she may be more alert if her drug dosage is changed.

It is important that Mrs. Parkins designate an attorney-in-fact to take care of practical matters if she becomes incapacitated. Ms. Bryant would seem like the natural choice, but the planning team must exercise all of its diplomatic skills to find out if the obvious choice is appropriate. Sometimes a seemingly caring child is actually attempting to exercise personal or financial domination over the parent. Furthermore, sometimes the parent prefers another child, or another relative or friend or clergymember, even over a child who is sincerely devoted to the parent's best interests.

Convenience joint accounts — under which someone like Ms. Bryant is named as a joint tenant who has the right to make withdrawals from the account — can be very useful in this situation. If Ms. Bryant becomes a convenience joint tenant, she can pay her mother's bills from the account. However, there is obvious potential for abuse in this device, and it should not be taken until the tax and Medicaid consequences have been assessed.

The combination of a trust and the durable power of attorney is useful in many situations of incapacity or potential incapacity. In this instance, however, it does not seem likely that Mrs. Parkins' assets are large enough to make a trust worthwhile.

Although a full-scale individual trust is probably not a good idea (because of the difficulty and expense of setting it up and administering it), two trust-like alternatives might work. The first is a charitable annuity, under which Mrs. Parkins purchases an annuity from a charity she wishes to benefit. She receives income (for a term of years or for life), and the charity's professional managers take care of the financial decisions. However, the funds placed into the annuity will not be available for Ms. Bryant to inherit.

The second is a "pooled fund" trust operated by a charity on behalf of a group of disabled people, who receive income and perhaps services from the trust. The money placed into the pooled fund is not considered available for Medicaid purposes — but the tradeoff is that after the fund participant's death, first the charity gets reimbursed for its fees, and next the state Medicaid agency gets reimbursed for whatever benefits it provided to the fund participant. Therefore, it is very unlikely that any part of the fund will remain to be inherited by the fund participant's family.

Medicaid Issues

The team's attorney and GCM should be familiar with local Medicaid policy, and the extent and quality of Medicaid home care services. States vary widely in this regard; but some states provide very extensive health and social services to Medicaid recipients living in the community. (One interesting service that Medicaid programs are beginning to offer is "monitoring" a regular telephone call, or alarm device, given to Medicaid recipients to see if they are all right. This service provides great reassurance to the elderly and their families.)

In some states, such as New York, Medicaid home care (in contrast to Medicaid benefits for a nursing-home stay) can be provided without regard to transfers that were made during the penalty period before the Medicaid application. (After OBRA '93, some states may exercise the option to impose transfer penalties on home care, even if they did not do so before OBRA '93.) If this is true in Mrs. Parkins' state, and if she is not disqualified on the grounds of excess income, Mrs. Parkins could transfer her excess assets to her children or other desired beneficiaries, then apply for and get home care under Medicaid. However, this strategy can backfire badly if Mrs. Parkins' condition deteriorates and she needs nursing home care before the penalty period expires. She will then be disqualified for Medicaid because of the transfer, yet will not have the money, because it has been transferred, unless the transferees can be persuaded to give it back so she can spend it for medical needs.

Mrs. Parkins is a widow, so she cannot make use of Medicaid's provisions for asset transfers or an income allowance to the spouse who is not a nursing home patient.

Mrs. Parkins, her family, and the planning team will have to make some difficult decisions. How does Mrs. Parkins feel about nursing homes? How good are the local facilities? Are there good Medicaid-certified facilities? Is it likely that she will die of an acute condition at home or in the hospital, rather than entering a nursing home for chronic care? Can her needs be met in the community, and, if so, for how long? Given her age and life expectancy, it may be unlikely that Mrs. Parkins can make transfers and survive the penalty period.

Mrs. Parkins is not a homeowner. If she, her family, and the planning team want to maximize her Medicaid eligibility, she could use most of her assets to purchase a house, co-op apartment, or condominium unit (as long as she can manage the costs of ownership, such as real estate taxes, maintenance charges, and fuel bills. The homestead will be exempt during her lifetime, but will be subject to recoupment if it is her property when she dies while receiving Medicaid benefits. This isn't a problem as long as Mrs. Parkins and her family don't mind. However, if she is interested in leaving an estate, other steps must be taken. (There are potential ethical problems to grapple with, if Ms. Bryant expects to inherit the homestead, or have it transferred to her, as recompense for her role in caring for her mother — and if Mrs. Parkins has other plans.)

Mrs. Parkins can purchase the homestead and transfer its ownership immediately, hoping that she will remain in the community until the penalty period expires. Or, if Ms. Bryant actually lives with her and provides care for two years, Mrs. Parkins can transfer the homestead to Ms. Bryant as a "caregiver child." Needless to say, this may not fit into Ms. Bryant's plans!

It may also be a good idea for Mrs. Parkins to move into Ms. Bryant's home, or even to move a thousand miles away and live with her son Gary; but not every situation in which an elderly parent lives with a child is a harmonious one. Furthermore, if Ms. Bryant and her brother and her sister-in-law are all employed full time, it will still be necessary to have some degree of care provided for Mrs. Parkins while the family she lives with is at work.

Depending on the size of Mrs. Parkins' so-called "small apartment," it might be possible for her to get a "roommate," for instance a college student or nursing student. The roommate could pay a small rent, providing extra income that could be useful in practical terms (but negative in Medicaid terms). Although the roommate would not be qualified to provide medical care, he or she could handle chores such as shopping and meal preparation — and provide important reassurance that Mrs. Parkins would not be left alone and unable to get help if she suffered a health crisis. The Gray Panthers run "home sharing" programs; so do check with some state and local agencies for the aging.

Insurance Issues

Mrs. Parkins has been encountering extensive medical costs over and above Medicare payments. The planning team should investigate the availability of Medigap insurance for Mrs. Parkins. Because such coverage is likely to be expensive, its usefulness should be assessed in light of changes in Medicare reimbursement for doctors (which will reduce their fees and severely limit "balance billing"), thus limiting the amount that older persons will have to pay. However, older persons will still be responsible for deductibles and coinsurance, plus the costs of hospitalization over and above what Medicare covers.

Mrs. Parkins may be an excellent candidate for LTC insurance. Clearly, there is a meaningful risk that she will be institutionalized, and a real risk that she will be Medicaid-ineligible for much or all of her remaining lifespan. The question is whether coverage can be obtained without unduly depleting her income and remaining resources. Your job is to keep abreast of LTC offerings and find the best one for Mrs. Parkins.

Depending on Mrs. Parkins' feelings about leaving an estate (discussed below), and depending on the cost of coverage, it may be worthwhile for Mrs. Parkins to purchase a life insurance policy benefiting one or both of her children and/or her grandchildren. Because she is likely to die within three years of the purchase, even if she transfers the policy it is likely to end up in her estate — but there is very little chance that she will have a taxable estate, so this is not a significant worry.

Investment Issues

Mrs. Parkins has behaved in an extremely passive way, placing the bulk of her assets in CDs and automatically reinvesting the CDs as they come due. Nevertheless, she has not made a bad choice that requires immediate redress — only a mediocre choice that can be improved upon. In the late 1990s, CDs are yielding very low interest rates, but the principal is secure, and an elderly person with limited assets may rationally decide to accept less income in order to eliminate the risk of losing part of her or his capital.

The threshold question is whether Mrs. Parkins wants to make transfers to qualify for an eventual Medicaid application. If so, then she will be left with virtually no non-exempt assets. The decision is a very risky one, leaving her both at risk of destitution if she never makes the Medicaid application, and at risk of Medicaid disqualification or even prosecution if she makes the Medicaid application during the penalty period. The risk is much lower for married couples because they are entitled to spousal protection measures, but Mrs. Parkins is a widow.

If the decision is made that Mrs. Parkins probably will not make a Medicaid application, then the question is how best to invest a sum of approximately $165,000 ($100,000 inheritance plus $100,000 insurance proceeds, of which about $35,000 has already been spent). Although this is a significant sum, it isn't enough to justify elaborate planning mechanisms.

Probably, the best choice is a program that safely provides Mrs. Parkins with more income during life, without tying up her capital unduly. (She may need funds at any time for medical or other needs.) Her preferences must be consulted: is it important for her to leave an estate, or is she content to deplete her assets over her remaining lifetime? If she chooses the second course, it is important to make sure that she doesn't deplete her assets too long before she dies, leaving a "gap" period devoid of resources.

One possibility is purchase of an annuity. A well-chosen annuity will provide income for life, or for a chosen period. In Mrs. Parkins' case, a life annuity would probably be better than a term annuity, because the goal is ensuring her lifetime income. However, if she is very interested in leaving an estate for her children, a term annuity with a refund feature will provide a bequest if she dies before her predictable lifespan. (Of course, she won't be able to buy an annuity with a term longer than her predictable lifespan.)

Although CDs are safe investments, and suitable for cautious elderly investors, they have the disadvantage of comparative illiquidity. That is, if money is needed quickly, the CD can only be tapped by paying an interest penalty. It would probably be better for Mrs. Parkins to invest in a money-market fund with a check-writing feature. That way, she has a safe, income-oriented investment that can easily be tapped. (Her attorney-in-fact should be given the power to write checks on the account.) Mrs. Parkins is in a low tax bracket, so the choice between a taxable and tax-exempt fund will probably favor a higher-yielding taxable fund.

In order to provide diversification, some stocks (such as high-dividend) utility stocks, or an income or growth-and-income mutual fund, could be purchased. Certainly, Mrs. Parkins is not an appropriate speculator in high-flying growth stocks!

Especially if the local real estate market is down, purchase of a home or condominium or co-op unit can be a good investment, on the assumption that Mrs. Parkins will have a home for the rest of her life, and an asset that can be left to her intended beneficiaries, with the possibility of appreciation if the market turns up again. (There is also the risk that housing prices will continue to decline, and that carrying costs and repair costs will increase to crippling levels.)

Estate Planning Decisions

Mrs. Parkins will probably use most of her funds for her own needs during the balance of her lifetime, leaving a small or even nonexistent estate. There is very little likelihood that she will have a federally taxable estate, so steps need not be taken to reduce or eliminate the federal tax.

Older people differ in their feelings about leaving an estate. For some, this is a high priority, one which will justify significant hardships during life. Others are indifferent to the prospect, and don't mind if they exhaust their funds during lifetime. It can be hard to find out which category a particularly older person belongs — especially if a "helpful" son or daughter, who expects a sizable inheritance, is sitting a few feet away! Therefore, it is important to have at least some discussions with Mrs. Parkins alone, without the presence of Ms. Bryant.

If Mrs. Parkins does not make inheritance a priority, the plan should concentrate on giving her safe income during her lifetime. However, if she does want to leave an estate, then consider purchase of an insurance policy on her life; adding equities to her investment portfolio; and favoring a term rather than a life annuity. Purchase of a home also tends to create an estate, unless Mrs. Parkins receives Medicaid benefits and the home is subject to recoupment.

Even if Mrs. Parkins is not particularly interested in creating an estate, she should have a will to govern the disposition of personal items and whatever assets remain. Once again, Ms. Bryant is the natural choice for executor — though the team should explore to see if there is a reason to choose a different, non-obvious executor (e.g., if Ms. Bryant is financially exploiting her mother; or, on the contrary, if she is worn out by devoted care of her mother and unwilling to take on additional tasks after her mother's death).

Mrs. Parkins' feelings about life support should be discussed, and it may be a good idea to express them in a written living will and to designate a proxy decision-maker. Remember, not everyone wants "the plug to be pulled," and it is just as important to get the preference for maximum treatment on the record as to stipulate a preference for termination of treatment. Several issues are involved:

- Feelings about respirators and similar machinery.

- Feelings about the provision of nutrition and hydration through tube feeding.

- Feelings about use of cardio-pulmonary resuscitation (CPR) in case of a cardiac or respiratory arrest.

- What constitutes adequate evidence under state law of a person's wishes?

- The powers that state law gives to other people to make decisions for a person who is now incompetent to make decisions for himself.

In practical terms, a patient's attending physician has a great deal of power in these situations. Therefore, it is important to choose an attending physician who agrees with your views, and will carry them out. If there is a choice about where someone will be hospitalized, or which nursing home a person will enter, the facility's policy about these matters is a very important factor in the choice. It is much easier to choose a health care provider who shares your views, and will carry them out, than to force an unwilling doctor or hospital to follow your directions.

JOE AND ANGELA MILLER: MEDICAL EMERGENCY

Angela Miller called her lawyer when her husband, Joe, 71, was hospitalized. (Angela is 68.) The lawyer, recognizing that the problems were outside his area of knowledge, referred her to an elder law attorney, who assembled a care team including you. The hospitalization settled the question of what had been causing the puzzling symptoms that troubled Joe for years. He has been diagnosed as suffering from multiple sclerosis, as well as a kidney infection.

He will be in the hospital for a few more days, until his condition stabilizes. The question now is, what to do? How can his predictably increasing medical needs be met? What about Angela's medical needs (she has arthritis and suffers from failing hearing and high blood pressure) and her financial needs?

The Discharge Plan

Under federal law, all Medicare beneficiaries (including Joe) are entitled to "discharge planning" before they are discharged from a hospital. The discharge planner must devise a written plan suitable for meeting the patient's medical needs. Involvement of the geriatric care manager (GCM) in the process is very useful.

One possibility is for Joe to enter a skilled nursing home for a short recuperative stay after hospitalization. He probably qualifies for Medicare Part A nursing home benefits (as long as he was hospitalized for at least three days, and enters the nursing home within 30 days of discharge) because he will need recuperation, monitoring to see if his kidney infection has stabilized, and information about how to cope with multiple sclerosis. Medicare will cover the entire cost of the first 20 days of an SNF stay; there is a coinsurance requirement for days 21-100, and no coverage after the 100th day.

Multiple sclerosis is a disease of "exacerbation and remission," which means that he will have good days and bad days. However, a predictable decline in his condition is virtually inevitable, and it is likely that he will eventually need a cane to walk, then a walker, then a wheelchair. Angela is not strong enough to move him from bed to wheelchair, or to bathe him once he loses the ability to do this himself. That means that the long-range care plan must cope with the need for home care and/or nursing home care.

Financial Matters

Joe still works part-time in the hardware store his family has owned for generations. He doesn't really get a salary; the family agrees that he can reach into the cash register occasionally when he needs money. He began collecting Social Security benefits at age 66, when he stopped working full-time and drawing a salary. The lawyer in the planning team must immediately assess the situation to see if he has been collecting Social Security benefits improperly — if he is really "retired" as the Social Security system defines it. If not, he may have to repay improper benefits, or repay benefits that should have been reduced because he worked after retirement and before age 70. If the benefits were proper, the fact that he is working now will not reduce his benefits because he is over 70.

Joe wants to keep working as long as this is physically possible. The lawyer will probably want some arrangement to regularize the financial situation. It may be possible for the family to give him a lump sum to buy out his interest in the business if and when he can no longer work. This lump sum, in turn, could be transferred to Angela, either preventively or incident to Joe's entering a nursing home, as a spousal protection measure.

Angela is a retired teacher, and has her teacher's pension and Social Security. The mortgage on their two-story home is paid. Because of the Medicaid spousal-protection provisions (see below), she will probably not suffer crushing financial loss if Joe must be institutionalized. Both of them would see this as a personal tragedy, however, so the focus of the plan must be on maximizing the use of home care.

Getting The Care

Right now, Joe's physical condition is not too bad, but plans must be made for future deterioration. He and Angela cope with normal housekeeping, shopping, cooking, and so forth, but heavy chores are beyond them. The GCM can advise them about whether the local agency for the aging has a "chore program" that provides periodic help of this kind to senior citizens. Some programs even have a "credit bank," in which healthy senior citizens help out those in worse shape, receiving credits which can be "cashed in" as the volunteer workers need help themselves. Joe and/or Angela might be able to accumulate some credits in such a program. Philanthropic agencies often have programs to provide intermittent assistance to senior citizens, either free or on a fee based on what they can afford.

Later on, as Joe grows weaker, he will need someone to help him dress, bathe, use his wheelchair, etcetera. At least at first, it may be possible to handle this informally. A "home sharing" program may produce a perfect match: for instance, a kind-hearted college athlete who needs rent-free accommodations and a quiet place to study, and who sees assisting Joe as a novel form of weight training! Eventually, however, it is likely that home health aides, and skilled nursing at home, will be required.

Depending on their children's living situations, one or more of them might be available to provide some degree of care. As discussed in Chapter 7, the home can be transferred to a child who lived in the home for two years and provided care that delayed institutionalization. Even after the Health Insurance Portability and Accountability Act of 1996, the transfer will not affect Medicaid eligibility, and will keep a Medicaid lien from being imposed.

Medicaid Considerations

Until and unless Joe becomes "homebound," he will not qualify for Medicare home care benefits. That leaves private payment and Medicaid as options for the home care he will need. The Millers may be able to pay for a limited amount of care privately, but it is clear that, as Joe's condition deteriorates, a Medicaid application will be required.

The Millers want Joe to stay at home. The first question (which the GCM will be able to answer) is how good a Medicaid home care program the state offers. If it is a good program, his needs can probably be met at home; if it is poor or very limited, a difficult choice must be made between getting less care, but staying at home, and going into a nursing home.

The next question is whether the Medicaid home care program, if adequate, is subject to Medicaid transfer and recoupment rules. "Waivered" care is always subject to the same rules as nursing home care. OBRA '93 expands states' options to impose restrictions on non-waivered Medicaid home care.

The Millers' assets are limited (their house, plus savings accounts and U.S. Savings Bonds worth about $20,000), so the transfer problem is not a severe one. He will probably be able to transfer all excess assets to Angela under the state's spousal protection provisions (discussed in Chapter 7). However, if the state places a low limit on the amount that can be transferred to a spouse, the Millers have other planning options.

First of all, they can use some of their savings to fix up the house so that it is suitable for a person with mobility limitations (widen the kitchen and bathroom doorways, add a wheelchair ramp in front and a lift on the stairs). This will reduce the amount of assets, but will make it possible for Joe to stay at home longer. (It is not a transfer, because there is no "give-away" element.)

The lawyer in the planning team must grapple with another Medicaid issue: whether Joe's interest in the family hardware store business is an "asset," and if so, whether it is "available" to him. It makes sense to settle this before the Medicaid application is made, perhaps by having the family members enter into a contract setting out their various rights and obligations to the business, and paying Joe to buy out his interest.

Insurance Options

As part of the planning process, Joe and Angela must explore insurance options. It will be difficult for a 71-year-old with a diagnosed health problem to find LTC insurance including meaningful home care benefits, but it may be possible at a price that can be tolerated in light of the dual effect of deferring institutionalization (and the Medicaid application) and reducing excess assets. Angela is younger and healthier, and thus LTC insurance is likely to be more available and affordable. Her needs must not be forgotten: she is neither young nor perfectly healthy, and is at risk of needing institutionalization (especially after Joe's death). They should also consider Medigap insurance. In one sense, they are good prospects (because it is hard for them to afford Medicare cost-sharing and balance-billing); in another sense, they may be poor prospects, in that the insurance premium could be more than they can afford in light of the risk.

If Joe has a life insurance policy, it may be possible to purchase a "living benefits" rider (see Chapter 2) that will permit Joe and Angela to access part of the insurance proceeds during Joe's life to pay medical costs. (The living benefit rider may also be available without cost; in fact, some life policies automatically include the rider at no additional cost, so you should investigate the availability of living benefits under Joe's existing coverage.) Note that, for Medicaid purposes, only $1,500 in cash value is an exempt resource. If a Medicaid applicant has a policy with greater cash value, the excess will be an asset, and will affect eligibility.

The Health Insurance Portability and Accountability Act of 1996 has resolved some tax questions about accelerated death benefits and viatical settlements. If Joe does receive a lump sum accelerated death benefit at a time when he is chronically ill, and uses it for health care, the lump sum will not be taxed.

If he gets accelerated benefits in periodic form, up to $175/day or the actual cost of care (whichever is greater) can be received tax-free — again, with the limitation that the funds must be used to pay for care, not for other purposes. (If Joe receives the funds at a time when he has been diagnosed as terminally ill, the purpose limitation will not apply — the money will be tax-free no matter how it is used.)

So, from a strict tax perspective, acceleration of the death benefit would be a sensible method of funding care. However, the original motivation for purchasing the insurance — probably Angela's needs — must be considered. If the original motive is still in force, the death benefits should not be accelerated except in an emergency, when other funds for care are lacking.

Estate Planning Issues

Clearly, neither Joe nor Angela will have a taxable estate, since either will die owning only a joint interest in the house, plus a share of whatever savings remain after medical and other expenses of living have been paid. However, each one should have a simple will. Probably the best plan is "all to my spouse," because the surviving spouse is likely to need additional income. Joe does not have any formal pension (and may have to pay back some Social Security benefits already received, which is normally done by deductions from future checks). Angela has her teacher's pension and Social Security benefits, so she will probably be able to survive (even if not luxuriously) after Joe's death — particularly if he makes a spousal protection transfer of his share of their savings, plus any lump sum he receives from the family business.

Why bother to have a will at all? Each state has its own "law of intestacy" that governs the distribution of the estate of people who die without leaving a will. Usually, for a married person with children, the surviving spouse gets less than the entire estate (typically 1/2 to 1/3). This "intestate share" (mentioned above as a protective device for the surviving spouse, who generally has a right to demand this much if left a smaller amount) may not be enough for the surviving spouse's financial security. If it is not, the other spouse will want to leave more, or the entire estate, to the survivor.

Although both spouses are fully mentally competent now, incapacity must be planned for — certainly with a durable power of attorney (DPA); maybe with a conservatorship/guardianship designation. (There probably is not enough money involved to make a trust worthwhile.) Given their ages and physical condition, it is probably not a good idea for either to name the spouse as attorney-in-fact; a child, younger friend, clergy member, or congregant (if they are religious) is likely to be a better choice.

Joe's physical condition makes the question of living wills and other "right to die" matters especially crucial. Note that state living will provisions are triggered by a person being a "qualified patient," which usually refers to people who are terminally ill (with a very short life expectancy) or permanently unconscious, not just those with a chronic disease that impairs the quality of life. Under the 1990 budget bill, Medicare and Medicaid recipients (including those who get home care) are entitled to information about living wills and other "self determination" matters from the health care provider, and their medical records must include a statement of their wishes.

Investment Questions

When older people have a small stake saved up, they can not afford to lose it, or even risk earning much less than they are earning now.

The best course of action for the Millers might be to do absolutely nothing! Savings accounts and savings bonds aren't glamorous, go-go investments, and when interest rates are high (as they were in the early 1980's, for example), they pay much less than other safe investments. However, today interest rates are down, and good safe investments are hard to find. It probably makes sense (unless the lawyer in the planning team states that there are adverse Medicaid consequences) for the accounts and bonds to be held jointly by the spouses. Another possibility is an account in one spouse's name "payable on death" to a chosen beneficiary (such as a grandchild) — a simple will substitute.

Savings accounts and U.S. Savings Bonds aren't the only choices for small savers. A worthwhile alternative might be a money market fund with check-writing privileges: a safe, liquid investment. Whether it pays to switch investments depends on the difference in the rate of return. If the money market fund pays only 1% more than the savings accounts and bonds, it may not be worth the trouble.

The late 1990s are a time when the stock market is booming and interest rates paid to net lenders are quite low. There are many stock or stock and bond mutual funds that have achieved excellent records without engaging in high-risk transactions. Perhaps the Millers should put a part of their savings into a no-load or low-load mutual fund that offers check-writing privileges and that includes capital preservation in its objectives.

Perhaps it might be worthwhile to shift some of their savings to mutual funds to increase return (or to a growth-oriented mutual fund to increase the assets available to them in later life, or to the surviving spouse) — but only if the return accurately reflects the excess risk.

SUMMARY

These four "cases" are a quick, "issue-spotting" look at four typical situations that confront planning teams. If the same fact situations were presented to ten different planning teams, it is likely that ten different plans would result! There are few right or wrong answers; instead, the client's own needs and wishes must be explored and predictions must be made about the client's likely financial and physical health in the future. The plan must be shaped by these projections, steering around the "shoals" of Medicaid and tax rules, and balancing risk against true long-term return after all transaction costs and taxes are taken into account.

INDEX

Use the handy postage-paid card below to order additional copies of *Financial Planning For The Older Client*, 3rd Edition, or to order the Continuing Education Course.

Or call: **1-800-543-0874** or Fax order card to 1-800-874-1916

Single copy	$25.95
5 copies, ea.	23.95
10 copies, ea.	22.95
25 copies, ea.	21.65
50 copies, ea.	20.30
100 copies, ea.	19.60
250 copies, ea.	18.85
500 copies, ea.	17.80
1,000 copies, ea.	16.90

Prices effective through 12/31/99

SHIPPING & HANDLING (Additional)

Order Total	Shipping & Handling
$ 0.00 - $19.99	$5.00
20.00 - 39.99	6.00
40.00 - 59.99	7.00
60.00 - 79.99	9.00
80.00 - 109.00	10.00
110.00 - 149.99	12.00
150.00 - 199.99	13.00
200.00 - 249.99	15.50

Any order of 10 or more items or over $250 will be billed by actual weight, plus a handling fee.

SALES TAX (Additional)

State sales tax is required for residents of the following states; CA, DC, FL, GA, IL, NJ, NY, OH, PA.

2-BG

NATIONAL UNDERWRITER®

The National Underwriter Co.
Customer Service Dept. #2-BG
505 Gest Street
Cincinnati, OH 45203-1716

Financial Planning For The Older Client, 3rd Edition, and the accompanying Continuing Education Course offered by The American College are $120 and have been approved in most states for Continuing Education credit (and for PACE credits for CLU's and ChFC's). Call 1-800-543-0874 for more information.

PLEASE SEND:

_____ Copies of *Financial Planning For The Older Client*, 3rd Edition (#297) @ $25.95 each (plus shipping & handling and any applicable sales tax).

_____ Copies of *Financial Planning For The Older Client*, 3rd Edition, Continuing Education Course (#289) @ $120.00 (includes book and shipping & handling charge).

❑ Check enclosed*   ❑ Bill me   ❑ Visa/MC/AmEx (circle one)

Card # _____ Exp. Date _____

Signature _____

Name _____ Title _____

Company _____

Address _____

City _____ State _____ Zip+4 _____

Business Phone (_____) _____ Fax (_____) _____

*Make checks payable to The National Underwriter Company. Please include the appropriate shipping and handling charges and any applicable sales tax.

2-BG

NATIONAL UNDERWRITER®

The National Underwriter Co.
Customer Service Dept. #2-BG
505 Gest Street
Cincinnati, OH 45203-1716

Financial Planning For The Older Client, 3rd Edition, and the accompanying Continuing Education Course offered by The American College are $120 and have been approved in most states for Continuing Education credit (and for PACE credits for CLU's and ChFC's). Call 1-800-543-0874 for more information.

PLEASE SEND:

_____ Copies of *Financial Planning For The Older Client*, 3rd Edition (#297) @ $25.95 each (plus shipping & handling and any applicable sales tax).

_____ Copies of *Financial Planning For The Older Client*, 3rd Edition, Continuing Education Course (#289) @ $120.00 (includes book and shipping & handling charge).

❑ Check enclosed*   ❑ Bill me   ❑ Visa/MC/AmEx (circle one)

Card # _____ Exp. Date _____

Signature _____

Name _____ Title _____

Company _____

Address _____

City _____ State _____ Zip+4 _____

Business Phone (_____) _____ Fax (_____) _____

*Make checks payable to The National Underwriter Company. Please include the appropriate shipping and handling charges and any applicable sales tax.

BUSINESS REPLY MAIL

FIRST CLASS MAIL   PERMIT NO. 68   CINCINNATI, OH

POSTAGE WILL BE PAID BY ADDRESSEE

The National Underwriter Co.
Customer Service Dept. #2-BG
505 Gest Street
Cincinnati, OH 45203-9928

BUSINESS REPLY MAIL

FIRST CLASS MAIL   PERMIT NO. 68   CINCINNATI, OH

POSTAGE WILL BE PAID BY ADDRESSEE

The National Underwriter Co.
Customer Service Dept. #2-BG
505 Gest Street
Cincinnati, OH 45203-9928